Electronic Commerce

Principles and Practice

Electronic Commerce

Principles and Practice

Hossein Bidgoli

School of Business and Public Administration
California State University
Bakersfield, California

ACADEMIC PRESS

A Harcourt Science and Technology Company

San Diego   San Francisco   New York   Boston   London   Sydney   Tokyo   Toronto

Academic Press
A Harcourt Science and Technology Company
525 B Street, Suite 1900, San Diego, California 92101-4495, USA
http://www.academicpress.com

Academic Press
Harcourt Place, 32 Jamestown Road, London NW1 7BY, UK
http://www.academicpress.com

Library of Congress Catalog Card Number: 2001089146

International Standard Book Number: 0-12-095977-1

PRINTED IN THE UNITED STATES OF AMERICA
01 02 03 04 05 06 EB 9 8 7 6 5 4 3 2 1

To so many fine memories of my brother,
Mohsen,
for his uncompromising belief in the power of education

Contents in Brief

Part IV
Appendix and Glossary

Contents

Part I
Electronic Commerce Basics

Chapter 1

Getting Started with Electronic Commerce

Chapter 2
Electronic Commerce Fundamentals

Chapter 3
Electronic Commerce in Action

Chapter 4
Intranets and Extranets

Chapter 5

Electronic Data Interchange

Part II
Electronic Commerce Supporting Activities

Chapter 6

Electronic Payment Systems

Chapter 7
Marketing and Advertising on the Web

Part III
Implementation and Management Issues in Electronic Commerce

Chapter 8

Technologies and Applications to Support Electronic Commerce

Chapter 9

Infrastructure for Electronic Commerce

Chapter 10

Personal, Social, Organizational, Legal, Tax, and International Issues

Chapter 11

Security Issues and Measures: Protecting Electronic
Commerce Resources

Chapter 12

Building a Successful Electronic Commerce Site: A Life Cycle Approach

Part IV
Appendix and Glossary

Appendix A
Basic Web Literacy and Instructions for Creating Web Pages

Preface

Electronic commerce (e-commerce) improves the efficiency and effectiveness of businesses, governments, and not-for-profit agencies. The ability to conduct business all over the world 7 days a week and 24 hours a day is a major advantage of being online. In many cases e-commerce technologies lower the cost of production and distribution of goods and services. However, going online does not guarantee success if a sound business model is not followed and if the limitations and strengths of this evolving technology are not carefully analyzed. In the past few years, thee-commerce world has experienced many successes and failures. At the same time, the number of goods and services sold online has increased daily. Puree-businesses, such as eBay, and traditional businesses, such as Dell Computer, have demonstrated significant savings and increased revenues by using the Web. This book is filled with many successful applications of this growing technology.

To build an e-business or establish a Web presence, several key issues must be analyzed, including the various e-commerce models and the key technologies and applications, and this book does just that. This book should interest students majoring in business, economics, information systems, and computer science, as well as managers and executives in many service industries, such as marketing, real estate, banking, and health care. Managers and administrators in government and public organizations will also find this book a practical guide for designing and managing e-commerce applications.

The text is divided into four parts, which include 12 chapters, a comprehensive appendix, and a glossary. Part I (Chapters 1–5) starts with a general discussion of the past, present, and future of the Internet, providing a detailed overview of e-commerce, its various categories, advantages, disadvantages, and successful case examples. Web auctions and several segments of the service industries that use e-commerce are explored. Part I also explains intranets, extranets, and electronic data interchange as three of the important infrastructure technologies that support e-commerce.

Part II (Chapters 6–7) explores activities that are crucial to the success of e-commerce. It starts with a detailed discussion of electronic payment systems, their different categories, advantages and disadvantages, and electronic transaction security issues. Also explained are marketing, promotions, and advertising on the Web, comparing and contrasting Web marketing with traditional marketing and presenting guidelines for effective Web marketing and advertising.

Part III (Chapters 8–12) discusses tools, techniques, applications, and issues that are crucial to the successful design, implementation, and management of e-commerce. Chapter 8 explains various network technologies that constitute the backbone of an e-commerce site. Chapter 9 focuses on additional infrastructure for e-commerce, presenting a detailed discussion of Transmission Control Protocol/Internet Protocol (TCP/IP) and other hardware and software for e-commerce design and management. Chapter 10 looks at the personal, social, legal, organizational, tax, and international issues of e-commerce. Chapter 11 examines e-commerce security issues and measures. Chapter 12 introduces several alternatives for a successful e-commerce implementation, accompanied by a discussion of advantages, disadvantages, and suitability of each alternative and the management issues.

Part IV includes a comprehensive appendix and a detailed glossary. The appendix includes a step-by-step process for designing an operational Web page, introduces popular tools and techniques for developing Web Pages, and reviews popular Web programming tools and techniques. The glossary is a quick reference for most of the key terms and vocabulary of e-commerce.

This text presents several unique features to prepare future executives for effective utilization of these growing technologies.

1. Each chapter starts with two information boxes (some chapters include more than two). These information boxes serve as minicases and discuss the practical applications of e-commerce in general and the application of a specific topic discussed in a given chapter. These presentations also highlight the importance and versatility of a particular e-commerce technology.

2. The text presents a comprehensive discussion of personal, social, organizational, international, ethical, legal, and tax issues of e-commerce (Chapter 10). These important topics help the reader to understand and appreciate both the positive and negative impacts of e-commerce.

3. Chapter 1 discusses in detail the information superhighway as the foundation for e-commerce. This chapter introduces e-commerce terminology to beginners and reviews important topics for more advanced readers.

4. Chapter 3 discusses Web auctions and the applications of e-commerce in several sectors of the service industries. This presentation provides a real-world view of e-commerce and its versatility.

5. Chapter 4 discusses intranets and extranets as two of the most popular infrastructures and applications of the Internet and e-commerce. Several real-life examples of companies that successfully use these technologies are featured.

6. Chapter 5 comprehensively covers electronic data interchange (EDI) and introduces supply-chain management as two important technologies and applications of business-to-business e-commerce.

7. Chapters 8 and 9 provide thorough coverage of the software and hardware technologies and platforms for successful e-commerce implementation. After studying these two chapters, the reader will have a clear understanding of the behind-the-scene technologies of e-commerce.

8. Chapter 11 is devoted entirely to e-commerce security issues and measures. This chapter provides valuable information regarding security threats and measures, including a thorough examination of firewalls and biometrics and their effectiveness in the e-commerce environment. This chapter also discusses the denial-of-access phenomena and offers some possible solutions.

9. The text presents numerous e-commerce applications in functional areas of business. Using this approach puts the discussion in perspective, and the reader will more easily understand my presentation.

10. Each chapter begins with learning objectives that list the measurable goals to be achieved after each chapter is studied. A brief introduction lists topics covered. Each chapter summary at the end distills the essence of the chapter.

11. Every chapter ends with an industry connection that introduces a leading company with significant e-commerce expertise accompanied by selected products and services offered by this company. Descriptions of these companies (in most cases) are strategically located in chapters where similar products or services are discussed. This adds a more real-world view to the text. Students can log onto the web sites of these companies and learn more about their offerings and their e-commerce experiences.

12. Each chapter concludes with 25 to 30 review questions that reinforce the topic covered.

13. Each chapter lists key terms and includes a comprehensive reference list. I also introduce 15 to 25 projects that can be used as class assignments or for further investigation of a particular topic. Most of these projects encourage the student to log onto numerous e-commerce sites and explore new products, services, and different e-commerce strategies. In some cases these web sites provide access to software demos and product descriptions. These materials provide a hands-on environment for the text.

14. There is a vast array of software products on the market. Several of these products can enhance and facilitate e-commerce design and utilization. Throughout the book, where appropriate, I introduce these products. This information should facilitate the actual e-commerce design and management.

15. A comprehensive appendix teaches readers how to design basic web pages. This appendix also provides basic Web and e-commerce literacy from a hands-on perspective.

16. A comprehensive glossary at the end of the book lists the majority of buzzwords and acronyms used in the e-commerce field. This should provide a condensed and easy-to-access reference for the readers of this book.

17. For academic use, I have prepared an instructor's manual that includes a test bank, lecture outlines, Power Point slides, and class discussion materials. These materials will be available as both hard copy and in electronic format.

About the Author

HOSSEIN BIDGOLI, Ph.D., is professor of management information systems at California State University, Bakersfield. Dr. Bidgoli helped set up the first personal computer lab in the United States. He is the author of 43 textbooks, 27 manuals, and over 4 dozen technical articles and papers on various aspects of computer applications, e-commerce, and information systems published and presented throughout the world. Currently he serves as the editor-in-chief of the *Encyclopedia of Information Systems* to be published by Academic Press. Dr. Bidgoli's background includes experience as a systems analyst and information systems and e-commerce consultant, and he was the director of the Microcomputer Center at Portland State University.

Dr. Bidgoli is a two-time winner of Meritorious Performance and Professional Promise Award for 1985–1986 and 1988–1989, School of Business and Public Administration, California State University, Bakersfield, and the recipient of 1999 El Paso Energy Teaching Excellence Award. These awards were based on outstanding performance in teaching, research, and school and community service. He was selected as the 2001/02 Outstanding Professor at California State University, Bakersfield, an award for excellence in teaching and research activities. Dr. Bidgoli has designed a three-part certificate program in e-commerce (beginning, intermediate, and advanced) that has been successfully implemented in California. In addition, he has initiated over 30 executive seminars in computers and information systems, which have been successfully implemented in Oregon and California.

Acknowledgments

Several colleagues reviewed different versions of the manuscript and made constructive suggestions. Without their assistance the text could not have assumed its present shape, and I greatly appreciate their help and comments. I am grateful to students in my undergraduate and graduate classes who provided feedback. Also, executives who attended my seminars in e-commerce provided insights regarding the practicality of the materials. They helped me fine-tune the manuscript during its various stages. My friend and colleague Andrew Prestage read Chapter 2 of the book and provided comments for improvement. My old friend Assad Karimi deserves special recognition for providing moral support throughout the years.

A group of professionals from Academic Press assisted me in various stages in completing this text. First and foremost, Dr. J. Scott Bentley, senior editor, assisted me in various stages of the development process and in fine-tuning the project. His timely editorial process and his finding qualified reviewers kept the project ahead of schedule. It has been a pleasure working with Scott for the past 6 years. Bonnie Baranoff and Mara Conner, product marketing managers, provided superb marketing assistance, and Eileen Favorite, production editor, shepherded the book to completion. I appreciate their help.

Last, but not least, I want to thank my wonderful wife, Nooshin, and my two lovely children, Mohsen and Morvareed, for being so patient during this venture. They provided a pleasant environment that expedited the completion of this project. Thanks, family, we did one more book together. My dears, Morvareed and Mohsen, please keep bringing those excellent report cards. They encourage Daddy to work harder. Also, my sisters, Azam and Akram, provided moral support throughout my life. I am grateful for all their support.

Part I

Electronic Commerce Basics

Chapter 1

Getting Started with Electronic Commerce

Learning Objectives

After studying this chapter you should be able to do the following:

- Review electronic commerce (e-commerce) and its major components.
- Understand the role of the Internet as the backbone of the information superhighway and e-commerce.
- Review the history of the Internet.
- Define popular Internet tools and navigational techniques.
- Discuss the Internet services that support e-commerce.
- Explore economic and future issues of the information superhighway.
- Discuss Internet 2 as a new development in the Internet and e-commerce environments.

INFORMATION BOX 1-1

The Internet and E-Commerce Applications: A Short List

Advertising
Distance learning
Electronic conferencing
Electronic mail (e-mail)
Electronic posting
Health-care management
Home shopping
Interactive games
Inventory management
Marketing
Newsgroups and discussions
News on demand
Online banking
Online employment
Online software distribution
Online training

Politics (voting, participating in political forums and chat groups, keeping in touch with the White House, Senate, and the Congress, using the Web for political fundraising).

Remote login
Sale of products and services
Software distribution
Telecommuting
Transferring files with file transfer protocol (FTP)
Video on demand
Videophones

Virtual classrooms bring the world into your home anywhere in the world with Internet connection by tapping into expertise throughout the world.

Online demo of products and services throughout the world
Virtual reality games

Microsoft web site Sidewalk offers a broad menu of local arts and entertainment listings, restaurant reviews and tourism guides.

Software programs like CHESS (Comprehensive Health Enhancement Support System), developed by the University of Wisconsin, allow patients with a home computer and modems to access a number of medical libraries at the best medical schools.

Many businesses use the Web for request for proposal (RFP), request for quotes (RFQ), and request for information (RFI).

INFORMATION BOX 1-2

Facts about the Internet and E-Commerce

In 2000, Microsoft, Excite, IBM, Netscape, and Ziff-Davis were the top five advertisers on the Web. Yahoo, Netscape, Infoseek, CNET, and Lycos received the highest amount of advertising dollars.

According to the U.S. Department of Commerce, between December 1998 and August 2000, the share of American households with Internet access jumped from 26.2% to 41.5%. In 2000, more than half of U.S. homes have PCs.

According to eMarketer, the average amount of money that consumers spend online annually will grow from $705 in 2000 to $1130 by 2003.

According to A. T. Kearney (2000), poor web site design is forcing customers to abandon many online transactions. Other reasons for abandoning online purchases are too much information required, the customer did not want to enter credit card details, web site malfunction, the customer could not find a product, could not specify product, had to make a phone call, and the customer did not like the returns policy.

According to Visa International, Germany, the United Kingdom, and France will account for more than 80% of the business-to-business (B2B) purchase volume in 2003. The European B2B market is estimated to increase to $176 billion by 2003, up from $7.15 billion in 1998.

According to the Internet Industry Almanac (as of October 2000), the United States has an overwhelming lead in Internet users, with almost 40% of the total 280 million Internet users; however, the United States is only ranked fourth in Internet users per capita. Canada is the per capita leader, as nearly 43% of all Canadians are regular Internet users.

According to Internet Software Consortium, the number of Internet hosts increased from 43,230,000 in January 1999 to 93,047,785 in July 2000.

INFORMATION BOX 1-3

E-Commerce Initiatives at Nestlé

Nestlé, one of Europe's largest Internet-ready companies plans to invest $1.8 billion within the next 3 years in order to become one of the world's web-smart elite. Nestlé plans on utilizing the Web to take orders, buy raw materials, sell products, cut inventories, and to better market its products and services worldwide. Nestlé sells a variety of products, from infant formula to cat food, and is preparing to become the most web-savvy company around. Nestlé's chief executive, Peter Brabeck-Letmathe, believes in this transformation and calls the process "an e-revolution." In 1999, its first year of e-commerce initiative as well as other restructuring efforts, Nestlé's profits rose to $1.7 billion in the first half of 2000. Starting July 2000, grocery stores as well as mom-and-pop stores have been able to purchase Nestlé's products online by logging onto its web site. This simple process could eliminate over 100,000 phoned or faxed customer orders received annually and could cut customer expenses from $2.35 to .21¢ per order. The web site also allows merchants to track their orders or to change their orders with a click of the mouse!

Nestlé also links electronically with its partners and could adjust production to match demand. If demand increases, Nestlé's production line will increase as well. The digital Nestlé has also cut out high-cost suppliers, and reduced its cost by 20%. Nestlé plans to eliminate more than 20% of its TV and print ads and go directly to online advertising.

SOURCE: William Echikson (December 11, 2000). "Nestle: An Elephant Dances." *Business Week,* pp. EB 44–47.

1-1 INTRODUCTION

This chapter briefly defines electronic commerce (e-commerce), its major applications and technologies, and highlights the road map of the book. I review the basics of the Internet as the backbone of the information superhighway and e-commerce. After providing a brief history of the Internet, I review Internet access options, navigational tools, and the Internet services that support e-commerce. The chapter includes economic and development issues of the information superhighway and concludes with a discussion of the Internet's future issues, Internet 2, and highlights Netscape Corporation as the industry connection.

1-2 WHAT IS ELECTRONIC COMMERCE? A ROAD MAP FOR THE BOOK

To better understand e-commerce one should distinguish between e-commerce and electronic business (e-business). E-commerce means electronic buying and selling on the Internet. E-business is any electronic transaction (e.g., information exchange), which subsumes e-commerce. E-business encompasses all the activities that a firm performs for selling and buying services and products using computers and communications technologies. E-business includes a host of related activities, such as online shopping, sales force automation, supply chain management, electronic payment systems, and order management.

E-commerce sites are either pure e-businesses, such as Amazon.com, or they have an e-commerce presence, such as Wal-Mart Stores. Some e-commerce sites sell products, such as CDs and computers. Some e-commerce sites sell services, such as computer training and consulting. Any company could have an e-commerce presence, but it is not necessarily an e-business.

To design and implement a successful e-commerce program, a number of theories, applications, and technologies must be carefully analyzed and understood. This is how this book addresses these theories, applications, and technologies:

Chapter 1 reviews the fundamentals of the Internet and information superhighway and introduces the Internet tools and techniques that support e-commerce.

Chapter 2 defines value-chain analysis and e-commerce business models and then reviews e-commerce in detail and highlights advantages and disadvantages, introducing various categories of e-commerce, including mobile and voice-based e-commerce.

Chapter 3 defines online auctions as successful applications of e-commerce and reviews the role of e-commerce in selected segments of service industries.

Chapter 4 defines intranets and extranets as two important infrastructures for e-commerce implementation, reviews the process of developing these systems, and introduces several applications of these technologies.

Chapter 5 discusses electronic data interchange (EDI) as one of the oldest e-commerce infrastructures and applications and reviews the process of introducing EDI in an organization.

Chapter 6 provides a detailed discussion of electronic payment systems and their roles in a successful e-commerce program.

Chapter 7 explores marketing and advertising on the Web, introduces various tools and technologies used for Web marketing, and provides guidelines for an effective marketing and advertising program.

Chapter 8 defines some of the infrastructures for a successful e-commerce implementation, including local, wide, and metropolitan area networks, wireless networks, and client–server model.

Chapter 9 reviews additional infrastructures for e-commerce, including Transmission Control Protocol/Internet Protocol (TCP/IP), server platforms, server operations, and criteria for choosing a web server.

Chapter 10 discusses organizational, legal, social, personal, tax, and international issues of e-commerce design and implementation.

Chapter 11 explores diverse e-commerce security issues and measures and offers guidelines for a comprehensive security system.

Chapter 12 introduces four approaches for building an e-commerce site, including online auctions, Internet shopping malls, web hosting services, and building the site from scratch.

Appendix A reviews basics of hypertext markup language (HTML) and offers guidelines for building simple web pages and reviews important web programming tools and techniques.

These materials should collectively provide a solid foundation for designing, implementing, and managing a successful e-commerce program. Let's go to work and study it!

1-3 THE INFORMATION SUPERHIGHWAY AND THE WORLD WIDE WEB

The backbone of the information superhighway and e-commerce is the Internet. The Internet is a collection of millions of computers and network systems of all sizes. One can simply refer to the Internet as the "network of networks." The information superhighway is also known as the Internet. No one actually owns or runs the Internet. Each network is locally administered and funded, in some cases, by volunteers. It is estimated that more than 200 countries are directly or indirectly connected to the Internet. This number increases daily and makes global e-commerce a reality.

The Internet started in 1969 as a U.S. Defense Department Advanced Research Projects Agency project called ARPANET. It served from 1969 through 1990 as the basis for early networking research and as a central backbone network during development of the Internet. Since the Internet's inception in 1987, the network has grown rapidly. Table 1-1 provides a review of the major events in the Internet's development [2,3,4,7].

ARPANET evolved into the National Science Foundation Network (NSFNET) in 1987. NSFNET is considered the initial Internet backbone. The term *Internet* was derived from the term *internetworking,* which signified the networking of networks. NSFNET initially connected four supercomputers located at San

Table 1-1

Major Events in the Development of the Internet

Date	Event
September 1, 1969	ARPANET is born.
1971	Ray Tomlinson of BBN invents an e-mail program to send messages across a distributed network.
January 1, 1983	Transition from Network Control Protocol (NCP) to TCP/IP[a]
1987	The National Science Foundation creates a backbone to the National Research and Education Network. It is called NSFNET[b] and signifies the birth of the Internet.
	E-mail link established between Germany and China uses CSNET protocols, with the first message from China sent on September 20.
1988	Development of World Wide Web at the Conseil Européen pour la Récherche Nucléaire (CERN)
November 2, 1988	Worm virus attacks over 6000 computers connected to the Internet, including the U.S. Department of Defense.
February 11, 1991	Bush administration approves Senator Al Gore's idea to develop a high-speed national computer, and the term *information superhighway* first appears.
January 1992	High Performance Computing Act signed into law.
October 15, 1992	The number of Internet hosts surpasses 1 million.
November 1993	Pacific Bell publicizes plan to spend $16 billion on the information superhighway.
January 1994	MCI announces a 6-year plan to spend $20 billion on an international information communications network.
October 13, 1994	The first beta version of Netscape Navigator is made available on the Web.
October 1994	White House home page is established on the Internet, with the following address: <http://www.whitehouse.gov>
April 1995	Netscape becomes the most popular graphical navigator for surfing the Web.
August 1995	Microsoft releases the first version of Internet Explorer.
April 1996	Yahoo!, the most popular directory, goes public.
June 1998	A U.S. appellate court rules that Microsoft can integrate its browser with its operating system, allowing the company to integrate almost any application into the Microsoft operating system.
February 2000	Denial of access (the newest hacker threat) shuts down several popular e-commerce sites, including Yahoo!, Ameritrade, and Amazon.com for several hours.
2005	According to Jupiter Communications (an Internet research company) business-to-business e-commerce online will approach $6.3 trillion (estimates).

[a]Transmission Control Protocol/Internet Protocol, the standard and software that divide data into packets and forward the packets to the IP protocol layer in the TCP/IP stack, will be discussed in Chapter 9.
[b]NSFNET, National Science Foundation Network.

Diego, Cornell, Pittsburgh, and Illinois to form the backbone. Other universities and government labs were subsequently added to the network. These backbones linked all existing networks in a three-level structure:

- Backbones
- Regional networks
- Local area networks (LANs)

Backbones provide connectivity to other international backbones. The network access points (NAPs) are a key component of the Internet backbones. A NAP is a public network exchange facility where Internet service providers (ISPs) can connect with one another. The connection within NAPs determines how traffic is routed over the Web, and they are also the focus of Internet congestion. LANs provide the standard user interface for computers to access the Internet. Phone lines (twisted pair), coaxial cables, microwaves, satellites, and other communications media are used to connect LANs to the regional networks. TCP/IP is the common language of the Internet that allows the network systems to understand each other. Protocols are conventions and rules that govern a data communications system. They cover error detection, message length, speed of transmission, and so forth. Protocols provide compatibility among different manufacturers' devices.

The NSF and state governments have subsidized regional networks. NSFNET's acceptable use policy initially restricted the Internet to research and educational institutions; commercial use was not allowed. Due to increasing demand, additional backbones were allowed to connect to NSFNET and commercial applications began. Initial NSFNET throughput (the amount of information that could go through) was 45 Mbps (million bits per second). The throughput in 2001 is more than 600 Mbps. TCP/IP divides network traffic into individually addressed packets that are routed over different paths.

The World Wide Web (WWW or the Web) changed the Internet by introducing a true graphical environment. Proposed in 1989 by Tim Berners-Lee at CERN, WWW is an Internet service that organizes information using hypermedia. Each document can include embedded reference to audio, images, full-motion video, or other documents. The WWW consists of a large portion of the Internet that contains hypermedia documents. Hypermedia is an extension of hypertext. Hypertext allows a user to follow a desired path by clicking on highlighted text to follow a particular thread or topic. This involves accessing files, applications, and computers in a nonsequential fashion. Hypermedia allow for combinations of text, images, sounds, and full-motion video in the same document and allows information retrieval with the click of a button. Hypertext is an approach to data management in which data are stored in a network of nodes connected by links. The nodes are designed to be accessed through an interactive browsing system. A hypertext document includes document links and supporting indexes for a particular topic. A hypertext document may include data, voice, and images. This type of document is called hypermedia. In hypertext documents the physical and logical layouts are usually different. This is not the case in a paper document. In a paper document the author of the paper establishes the order and readers are forced to follow the predetermined path.

A hypertext system provides users with nonsequential paths to access information. This means that information does not have to be accessed sequentially as in a book. A hypertext system allows the user to make any request that the author or designer of the hypertext provides through links. These links choices are similar to lists of indexes and can lead the reader on a "custom path."

Any computer that stores hypermedia documents and makes them available to other computers on the Web is called a server or a web server. The computers that request these documents are called clients. A client can be a PC at home or a node in a LAN at a university or an organization. The most exciting feature about the Internet and the WWW is that these hypermedia documents can be stored anywhere in the world. A user can as easily jump from a site in the United States as to a site in Paris, France, all in a few milliseconds. I will discuss client–server computing in detail in Chapter 8.

1-4 INTERNET-ACCESS OPTIONS: WHICH ONE IS RIGHT FOR YOU?

Four popular types of Internet access options are currently available:

- Terminal or shell accounts
- Dial-up protocol service
- Direct connections
- Online services

Terminal or shell accounts and **dial-up protocol service** are the two primary Internet-access options for PCs. Terminal accounts require modem and communications software to dial a host computer connected to the Internet. With this access method, a PC serves as a dumb terminal; it sends and receives information with no processing power of its own. Since many of these host computers are UNIX-based, this option can be complicated because of the commands required when navigating the Web. Another drawback is that users are restricted to host computer options that may be limited. However, this is the least expensive access option. Terminal accounts generally are text-based and not graphical, but the user can download images to a PC and view them outside the host connection.

Dial-up protocol service gives a user full access to the Web. A computer can be connected to the Web via a telephone line utilizing a high-speed modem. In addition, TCP/IP software is installed on the PC to provide an interface. There are two types of dial-up protocols: serial line Internet protocol (SLIP) or point-to-point protocol (PPP). With SLIP connections, packets (a unit of data) travel faster; however, reliability is lower because packets are not evaluated as they are sent. The PPP option, on the other hand, is a newer protocol that monitors packet traffic to ensure the accuracy of packets received. The PPP option may be a slower method of transmission, but it is more reliable.

There are more than 200 U.S. commercial access providers on the market in 2001, and the number is increasing. Price and reliability of service should be considered before selecting a provider. Local providers can eliminate the cost of long-distance phone calls. Fixed rates for unlimited connect time can also pay off. Access may be limited if users frequently receive busy signals when attempting to connect to the Web. Therefore, the quality of service should be examined before choosing one of these options. User support is also sometimes essential for navigating the complex paths of the Web. Also, an increasing number of ISPs in the United States offer free Internet connection. These ISPs in return offer advertisement on the recipient monitors.

Direct connections are the most expensive access option. Accordingly, this option is normally limited to large networks that have UNIX-operating systems. Both SLIP and PPP accounts and direct connections require that TCP/IP software be installed on each computer in the network.

Online services such as America Online, Earthlink, Prodigy, Geni, Delphi, and CompuServe also offer Internet access. Initially, their services were quite minimal and limited to e-mail, newsgroups, and basic file transfer options. However, they now offer a number of value-added services, such as stock trades, news, maps, weather conditions, and much more.

Fast-speed communications using cable modems and digital subscriber lines (DSL) are available in many parts of the United States. DSL, a copper-based technology, is a common carrier service and is promoted as one of the high-speed access capabilities to remote LANs and the Internet, providing speeds of up to 51 Mbps. DSL provides both traditional voice transmission and high-speed full-duplex digital data transmission. There are several types of DSL services available, although it has distance limitations. **Cable modems** provide fast Internet access and enable the user to receive information over cable TV lines. Cable modems provide in-bound throughput of up to 27 Mbps, with about 2.5 Mbps of bandwidth for outbound throughput. This bandwidth far exceeds that of the commonly used modems, with speeds of 28.8 or 56 Kbps. These kinds of connections improve the efficiency and effectiveness of e-commerce applications.

1-5 DOMAIN NAME SYSTEMS

Before a user can begin to navigate the Web and use it for personal use or e-commerce, an understanding of domain name systems (DNS) (also called domain name servers) is essential. Domain names are unique identifiers of computer or network addresses on the Web. The following are examples of domain names:

- Netscape.com
- Microsoft.com
- Un.org
- Whitehouse.gov

They come in two forms: English-like names and numeric or Internet Protocol (IP) addresses. The Internet Corporation for Assigned Names and Numbers (ICANN) is a nonprofit corporation that assigns and keeps track of these addresses. This was previously performed under U.S. Government contract by the Internet Assigned Numbers Authority (IANA) and other entities.

IP addresses are less convenient because numbers are harder to remember. The English-like names are electronically converted to IP addresses for routing (transferring information from one network to the other network). Domain names are used in universal resource locators (URLs) to identify particular web pages. For example, in the URL http://www.csub.edu/~hbidgoli, the domain name is csub.edu. Every domain name has a suffix that indicates which top-level domain (TLD) it belongs to. In the above example, the suffix is edu, for educational institutions. Combinations of the letters of the alphabet as well as the numbers 0 through 9 can be used in domain names. The hyphen is the only other character utilized; spaces are not allowed.

The TLD is the field on the far most right. It denotes the type of organization or country the address specifies. TLDs are divided into organizational (generic) and geographic (country code) domains (see Tables 1-2 through 1-4).

This system makes it easy to identify the type or location of the organization by looking at the last section of the domain name. Organization, which is the

Table 1-2

Organizational Domains (Generic Top-Level Domains)

.com	Commercial organizations (e.g., Microsoft)
.edu	Education and academic organizations (e.g., California State University)
.int	International organizations (e.g., United Nations)
.mil	U.S. military organizations (e.g., U.S. Army)
.gov	U.S. government organizations (e.g., Internal Revenue Service)
.net	Backbone, regional, and commercial networks (e.g., The National Science Foundation's Internet Network Information Center)
.org	Other organizations such as research and nonprofit (e.g., The Internet Town Hall)

Table 1-3

Some of the Proposed New Domain Names

.arts	for entities emphasizing cultural and entertainment activities
.biz	for businesses
.firm	for businesses or firms
.inc	corporations
.info	for entities providing information services
.law	for the legal profession
.nom	for individuals or family names
.news	for news-related sites
.rec	for entities emphasizing recreation and entertainment activities
.shop	for businesses offering goods and commodities
.store	for electronic storefronts
.web	for entities emphasizing activities related to the World Wide Web
.xxx	for adult content

Table 1-4

Sample Geographic Domains: Country Code Top-Level Domains

.au	Australia
.br	Brazil
.ca	Canada
.fr	France
.de	Germany
.hk	Hong Kong
.il	Israel
.jp	Japan
.kr	Korea (Republic)
.ru	Russia
.es	Spain
.uk	United Kingdom
.us	United States
.va	Vatican City State
.zw	Zimbabwe

second field from the right, simply refers to the name of the organization. A name for a small company is as easy as a company name. The two left-most fields of the domain name refer to the computer. This is relevant for large organizations with several levels of subdomains. A relatively complete Internet address is the address of a document in the Virtual Tourist web site as follows:

http://www.vtourist.com/vt/usa.htm

A brief explanation from left to right follows:

http   (hypertext transfer protocol). Means of access. This is how the majority of web documents are transferred.

www.vtourist.com   This is the address of a web site. It is uniquely defined and differentiated from any other web sites. WWW (discussed earlier) is an Internet service that organizes information using hypermedia

Vt   This is a path or directory. A server may be divided into a series of directories for a better organization.

usa.htm   This is the document itself. The htm extension indicates that this is an html document. The authoring language used to create documents on the Web, html defines the structure and layout of a web document by using a variety of tags and attributes. (I will further discuss html in Appendix A). All hypermedia documents are written in html format. Servers that do not support long extensions display htm, while other servers display html.

1-6 NAVIGATIONAL TOOLS, SEARCH ENGINES, AND DIRECTORIES: AN OVERVIEW

Navigational tools allow the user to surf the Web, and search engines provide access to various resources available on the Web, such as library searches for writing a term paper or making a reservation for an airline ticket. Directories use indexes of information based on keywords in the document. As will be discussed later in the chapter, Yahoo! is the most popular directory on the Web.

The original command language of the Internet was based on computer commands and was difficult for most users to learn. Character-based languages were used for tasks such as downloading files or sending e-mail. These languages are UNIX-based, meaning the user was required to know the specific syntax of many commands. Everything was communicated in plain text, and graphics, sound, animation, and voice data were not available. The introduction of graphical browsers such as Netscape Navigator changed all this. Microsoft Internet Explorer and Netscape Navigator are the best known graphical browsers available for navigating the Web. Each of these browsers combine powerful graphics, audio, and visual capabilities. Each web server has a home page that publishes information about the location. Using character-based browsers such as Lynx, a user will find this information in text form, while graphical browsers such as Microsoft Internet Explorer support images and sound clips as well.

1-6-1 NAVIGATIONAL TOOLS

Microsoft Internet Explorer and Netscape Navigator are among the popular navigational tools. The following paragraphs provide a brief description of each navigational tool.

1-6-1-1 Microsoft Internet Explorer

Microsoft Internet Explorer is the most popular graphical browser in the Internet world. With strong marketing support from Microsoft and improvement in the features, Internet Explorer has become the leader in the browser market. Figure 1-1 illustrates the initial screen of Microsoft Internet Explorer.

Figure 1-1   Initial Microsoft Internet Explorer screen.

1-6-1-2 Netscape Navigator

Netscape Navigator is another graphical browser available for all major platforms. Netscape is similar to Internet Explorer and provides a true graphical environment that allows the user to surf the Web using a mouse and the point-and-click technique. Similar to other Windows applications, Netscape Navigator features a standard menu bar and toolbar buttons for frequently used commands. Figure 1-2 illustrates the Netscape Navigator initial screen.

1-6-2 SEARCH ENGINES AND DIRECTORIES

There are several search engines and directories in use. Yahoo! is the most popular directory, and Excite, Infoseek, and Google are three of the popular search engines. These programs allow a user to scan the Web and find information for a term paper, an exotic antique for a personal collection, or anything in between. The following paragraphs briefly describe these search engines.

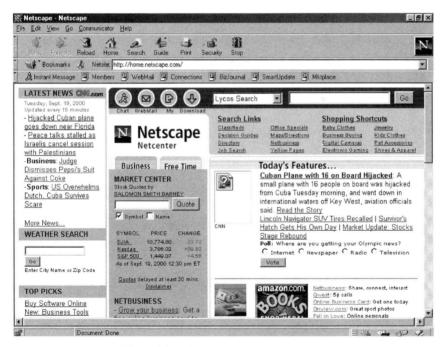

Figure 1-2   Initial Netscape Navigator screen.

1-6-2-1 Yahoo!

Jerry Yang and Dave Filo founded Yahoo! in April 1994. Yahoo! is one of the best known directories on the Web. A directory is a search service that classifies web sites into hierarchical subject-based structure. For example, Yahoo! includes categories such as art, business, and entertainment. These categories are organized by topic. The user can go to a category and then navigate for specific information. Yahoo! also includes an internal search engine that can expedite the search process. Yahoo! soon expanded to offer other services and became a portal on the Web. Portals are discussed in greater detail in section 1-7. Some of the services offered by Yahoo! include Yahoo! Travel, Yahoo! Classifieds, Yahoo! Pager, Yahoo! Autos, and many more. Figure 1-3 is a Yahoo! screen.

1-6-2-2 Excite

Founded in June 1994, Excite, Inc.'s basic mission is to provide a gateway to the Web and organize, aggregate, and deliver information to meet users' needs. The Excite Network, including the Excite and WebCrawler brands, contains a

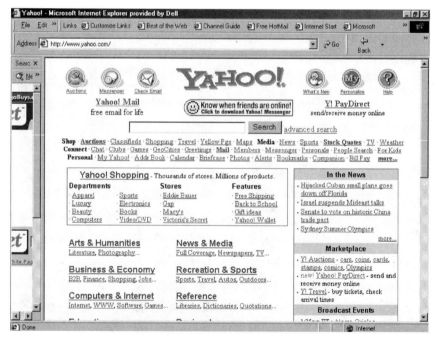

Figure 1-3 Initial Yahoo! screen.

suite of specialized information services that combine proprietary search technology, editorial web reviews, aggregated content from third parties, and bulletin boards. The Excite Network serves as a central place where consumers can gather and interact during each web experience. Excite PAL is an instant paging service. By entering the names and e-mail addresses of friends, family, and colleagues into Excite PAL, you can find them online. Figure 1-4 illustrates an Excite screen.

1-6-2-3 Altavista

Founded in 1995, AltaVista is a majority-owned company of CMGI, Inc. Figure 1-5 illustrates an AltaVista screen. The following are some of the services offered by this company:

AltaVista Search is a comprehensive search service.

AltaVista Live has real-time programming for news, entertainment, financial data, weather, and so forth.

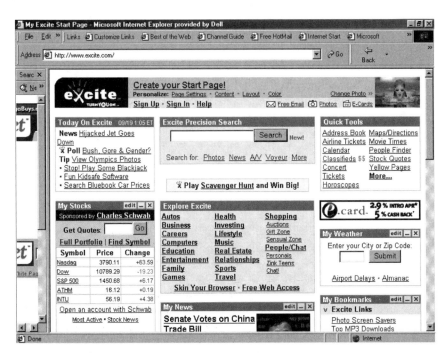

Figure 1-4   Initial Excite screen.

Figure 1-5   Initial AltaVista screen.

AltaVista Shopping.com provides information on shopping with millions of products, users' reviews, and comparative shopping by products and value.

AltaVista Local Portal Services Through partnerships with several news organizations, users can quickly find information that is specific to who they are, where they live, and what they need to accomplish on the Web or in their hometown.

1-6-2-4 Google

Larry Page and Sergey Brin, two Stanford Ph.D. candidates, founded Google in 1998. Google helps its users find information with high levels of ease, accuracy, and relevancy. The company delivers services to individuals and corporations through its own public site, www.google.com, and through co-branding its web search services. In the initial Google screen, enter the desired search item(s), for example "e-commerce," and then press the enter key or click on **Google Search.** In a few seconds the items that closely match your search items are displayed. By clicking the preferences to the right you can choose a language other than English; however, the default language is English. Figure 1-6 shows the initial screen of the Google search engine. Figure 1-7 shows a comparison of dif-

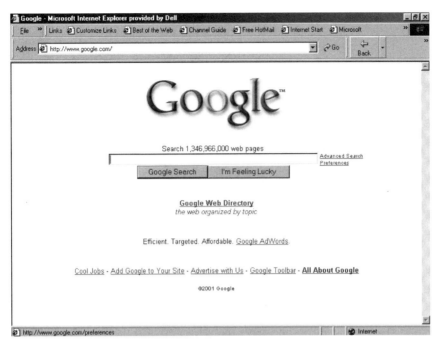

Figure 1-6 Google screen.

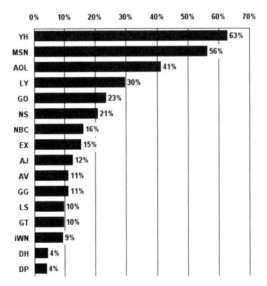

Figure 1-7 Media Matrix's ratings for February 2001, including audience reach, which is roughly the percentage of web surfers estimated to have visited each search engine during the month. Because a web surfer may visit more than one service, the combined totals exceed 100%. YH, Yahoo; MSN, Microsoft News; AOL, America Online; LY, Lycos; GO, Go.com; NS, Netscape; NBC, NBCi; EX, Excite; AJ, Ask Jeeves; AV, AltaVista; GG, Google; LS, LookSmart; GT, GoTo; iWN, iWon; DH, Direct Hit; DP, Dogpile. For links, see the *Major Search Engines* and *Major Metacrawlers* pages.

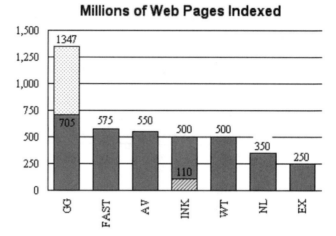

Figure 1-8   The charts show the size of each search engine's index. The larger the index, the more likely the search engine will be a comprehensive record of the web. This is especially useful for those looking for obscure material. Sizes are as reported by each search engine as of April 6, 2001. KEY: GG, Google; FAST, FAST; AV, AltaVista; INK, Inktomi; WT, WebTop.com; NL, Northern Light; EX, Excite. See the *Major Search Engines* page for links to these services. Source: <http://searchenginewatch.com/reports/sizes.html>.

ferent search engines. Figure 1-8 shows the largest search engines based on the estimated indexed pages.

1-7 WEB PORTALS: EMERGING APPLICATIONS

A portal or gateway for the WWW is a new application that serves as an information search organizer. Portals provide single-point integration and navigation through the system. Portals create an information community that can be customized for an individual or a corporation. Portals serve as a major starting site for individuals connecting to the Web. Netscape, America Online, Yahoo!, Lycos, CNet, AltaVista, Excite, Microsoft, Snap, Go.com (www.go.com), and CNBC are examples of popular portals. Portals are an example of software "mass customization," and many of the early search engines are now portals. Excite is among the first of many portals that offer users the ability to create personalized sites for specific needs and interests. Many of the ISPs offer portals to their users. For example, when you connect to America Online (AOL), you connect to the AOL portal that includes a number of private web sites. Some of the services offered by portal sites include a listing of web sites, news, stock quotes,

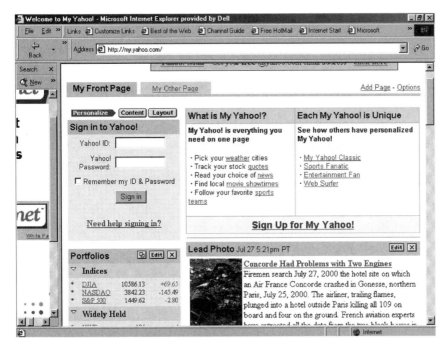

Figure 1-9   Yahoo! custom portal page.

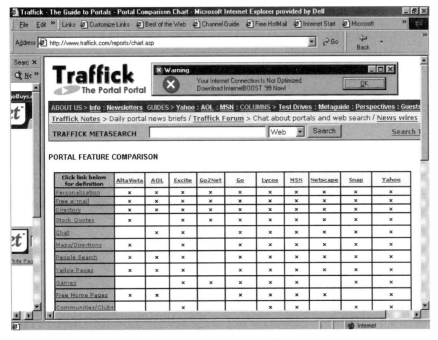

Figure 1-10   Portals Comparisons <http://www.traffick.com/reports/chart.asp>.

e-mail, real-time chat options, online trading sites, weather, search options, telephone, and map information. Corporate portals can automate identification and
distribution of relevant information, and they can go beyond simple search and
retrieval capabilities in order to provide content sensitivity. Increasingly, wireless
and voice portals are being introduced to the market. These options further promote the popularity of Internet portals. The screen shown in Figure 1-9 from Yahoo! allows a user to create and customize his or her own portal. The table in
Figure 1-10 compares features in different portals. For detailed specifications,
visit the Traffick web site and click on the links for each feature.

1-8 INTERNET SERVICES THAT SUPPORT E-COMMERCE

This section provides a quick review of some of the most popular services
available on the Internet that enhance a successful e-commerce program. These
are electronic mail (e-mail), news- and discussion groups, Internet relay chat
(IRC), instant messenger, and Internet phone.

1-8-1 ELECTRONIC MAIL

E-mail is one of the most popular services available on the Web. Using e-mail,
one creates a letter electronically and sends it over the communications media.
New products and services can be announced to customers using e-mail. Confirmations can be sent using e-mail, and also many business communications can
be effectively performed using e-mail. When sending an e-mail, the message
usually stays in the recipient computer until he or she reads it. In many e-mail
systems, the receiver is able to store the e-mail message in an electronic folder
for future reference. E-mail is fast and will get to the recipient's computer in a
matter of seconds or minutes. All that is needed to send an e-mail message is the
e-mail address of a recipient on the Web. A single e-mail message can be sent to
a group of people at the same time. One can usually apply all the word-
processing tasks, such as spell checking and grammar correction, before sending
the e-mail message. You can usually attach document files to an e-mail message,
and you can ask for delivery notification. Using e-mail, you can usually establish various folders with different contents and send a particular e-mail to
a specific group. Using e-mail enables you to establish an effective message-
distribution system for advertising products and services. Figure 1-11 illustrates the initial screen of Microsoft Outlook Express as a typical e-mail software application.

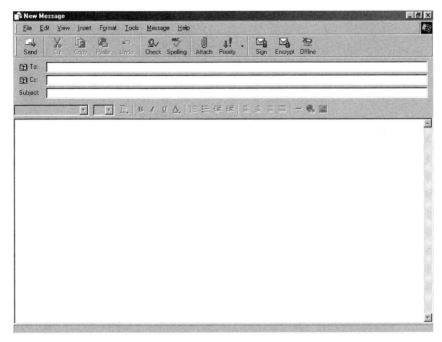

Figure 1-11 The initial screen of Microsoft Outlook Express.

1-8-2 NEWSGROUPS AND DISCUSSIONS

The Internet brings together people with diverse backgrounds and interests. Discussion groups that share opinions and ideas facilitate this. Every person in a discussion group can post messages or articles that can be accessed and read by others in the group. Newsgroups can be established for any topic or hobby and they allow people to get together for fun and entertainment or for business purposes. For example, you may join a newsgroup that is interested in ancient civilization. Or you may join a newsgroup that can help you to write and debug a computer program in a specific programming language. Newsgroups can serve as an effective advertising medium in e-commerce environment. I will further discuss news- and discussion groups in Chapter 7.

1-8-3 INTERNET RELAY CHAT

IRC enables one to interactively communicate in a written form with other users from all over the world. It is similar to a coffee shop where people sit around a table and chat. The two major differences between this electronic coffee shop and a real coffee shop are that there is no coffee and you do not see the people that you are chatting with. However, one is able to participate in many different discussions with people with similar interests anywhere in the world.

To start the electronic conversation, start the IRC program on your PC and then choose a channel in which to participate. Everyone in that particular channel will see all the messages you send, and you will see all the messages they send to you. You can choose to respond or not to respond to a message or a series of messages. You can also become involved in more than one conversation by joining multiple channels. Switching back and forth does this. If you are reluctant to give your real name, you can remain anonymous in IRC by using a nickname that is not being used by anybody else during the course of that conversation. The nickname of all the participants will be displayed on the right side of the screen. Therefore you know all the people with whom you are conversing. The IRC can be used for a serious discussion, brainstorming, and exchange of ideas, or it can be used for fun, for finding new friends, and for getting to know people with the same interest. Microsoft NetMeeting is another example with IRC capabilities and more.

Microsoft NetMeeting allows the user to conduct video conference calls, send text messages, collaborate on shared documents, and draw on an electronic whiteboard over the Internet or an intranet.

1-8-4 INSTANT MESSENGER

Instant messenger is a communications service that enables a user to create a private chat room with another user. There are several instant messenger platforms on the market. AOL has a commanding lead in this space. Different instant messengers offer different capabilities. They typically alert a user whenever somebody on his or her private list is online, then a user may initiate a chat session with that particular individual. According to AOL, its instant messenger (AIM) allows the user to do the following:

- Share Instant Images and sound files with friends and family
- Stay up-to-the-minute with Instant Stock, Buddy, and E-mail Alerts
- Converse PC-to-PC with AIM Talk
- Track financial success with Stock Ticker Enhancements
- Find out which features the user buddy's software can support with capabilities
- Access the user's complete and combined Buddy List from any computer
- Play online games against the user AIM buddies

1-8-5 INTERNET PHONE

Internet telephony is the use of the Internet rather than the traditional telephone company infrastructure and rate structure to exchange spoken or other telephone information. Because access to the Internet is available at local phone connection rates, an international or other long-distance call will be much less expensive than through the traditional calling arrangement. This could be a major cost savings for an e-commerce site for offering hotline services, help desk, and so forth.

Internet Phone by VocalTec was released in February 1995. It provided telephone-like communication over the Internet. Long-distance costs were traded for an Internet access fee. An internet phone kit complete with a speakerphone, handset, and PC sound card is commercially available now. Internet phone quality is similar to a CB radio, in that users experience one or two-second delays, and only one person can speak at a time [8].

Currently, Internet phone is available as through Netscape Communicator and Microsoft Internet Explorer browser's application suites. The software still needs to be the same to use it between two PCs, but there are gateways that allow you to call from your PC to a regular telephone. If the user is already accessing the Internet for a fee or for a flat fee using a local call, there is no marginal cost for Internet phone compared to time-based long-distance charges. If a PC has a standard sound card with speakers and a microphone, then the user can use Internet phone, and there is no need to have the same hardware at the receiving end. Other Internet calling choices include the following:

- Aplio Phone
- IDT Net2Phone Direct
- InnoMedia InfoTalk
- Dialpad.com

Telephone capabilities can now be added to a PC by adding a telephony board, available for under $300, which combines the functions of modem, soundboard, speakerphone, and voice mail system. A telephony board is often integrated into new machines targeted for small business and home office users. The quality of Internet phone has not yet been brought to a level where it is comparable with traditional telephones. When the appropriate infrastructure (bandwidth and speed) is in place to support high quality, Internet telephony is likely to become a widespread and cost-effective solution both for individuals and businesses. Three new services are now or will soon be available on the Web:

1. The ability to make a normal voice phone call (whether or not the person called is immediately available; that is, the phone will ring at the location of the person called). In most of the technologies currently

available, a "phone meeting" must be arranged in advance, and then both parties log on to the Web at the same time to conduct the conversation.

2. The ability to send fax transmissions at very low cost (at local call prices) through a gateway point on the Internet in major cities.

3. The ability to leave voice mail at a called number.

1-9 ECONOMIC ISSUES ON THE WEB

The lack of bandwidth or network capacity may soon become an issue with increasing number of users, high-volume e-commerce activities, and large files such as multimedia applications. New multimedia capabilities such as transmitting live video will consume extensive Internet resources. At this rate, it would not take many users to perform activities to exceed the information-carrying capacity of the Web. Even with the new very high-performance Backbone Network Service (vBNS) with capacities of up to 600 Mbps, more bandwidth will be needed.

With the growing popularity of bandwidth-demanding applications, such as the WWW, that incorporate text, graphic, audio, and visual capabilities, we may frequently see slow or no response, usually at the peak times. Some video or sound will lose quality as the network nears capacity. Estimates are that the bandwidth capacity of the Internet needs to increase by a factor of thousands to accommodate these applications and that the new vBNS will fall short of that figure [5].

Current Internet pricing usually involves a fixed rate for unlimited throughput. With no pricing controls, users can exploit the maximum capacity. Unlike the highway system where a single driver can only put one automobile on the road at a time, the Internet allows a single user to send a widely varying amount of traffic, ranging from a small e-mail message to hundreds of bandwidth-demanding applications.

One proposal is to route Internet traffic based on type: e-mail, file transfer, real-time voice and video broadcasts, and so forth. E-mail and file transfer can tolerate delays but require accuracy. Real-time voice broadcasts generate more throughputs but can tolerate distortion. Real-time video tolerates neither distortion nor delay. The key to successful implementation of such a proposal would be correct identification of traffic by users. However, they may be motivated to label all traffic as real-time video to obtain the highest quality of service [6].

Usage-based pricing may be the answer; however, even this approach offers significant problems. Compare the accounting for a single phone call. One entry is required. A comparable one-minute Internet message may consist of 4000 or more individual packets. The resulting accounting entries are overwhelming. Each month, NSFNET alone handles 60 billion packets [9]. Another impediment is the inability to identify the source of the traffic at any level lower than the originating host computer. This is analogous to the telephone system where phone numbers rather than callers are tracked.

Current Internet routing is based on the first-in first-out principle (FIFO). However, increasing privatization may force implementation of allocation and pricing mechanisms. Matching prices to costs on the Internet would involve changes in three areas:

- Cost of connection
- Cost of additional capacity
- The social cost of congestion

Direct cost of usage is not considered because of the associated burdensome accounting previously mentioned. Connection charges can easily be assigned; however, incremental capacity is not so easily charged. A peak demand-pricing scheme similar to electrical usage would work except for the fact that there are no off-peak hours (except within each country) with the global nature of the Internet. Congestion costs are measured in terms of delays or packet losses experienced by other users. The prioritization of packets based on bids may be a solution. As an incentive, packets are not priced at the user's bid but rather at the bid equivalent to the lowest priority packet accepted for throughput. Users inflating the priority of their packets will pay inflated prices accordingly. With the open-access capabilities of the Internet, should the sender or the receiver be billed? Unsolicited file transfers and other requests may dearly cost those institutions that provide free services if they are charged as senders of information [6].

The pricing of Internet services poses a significant challenge. The growing demand for services that exceeds volunteer network-available resources may force the issue. Due to the decentralized nature of the Internet, the creation of billing accounts is impractical because information may be obtained from thousands of different computers. It would be too burdensome to establish a user account at each computer site. Pricing by replication will not work with information commodity. The value is not in the transport but in the information being transported. Software is a good example. Once it has been developed, the replication costs are minimal. Therefore, what will prevent someone from electronically obtaining software and redistributing it in an unauthorized manner? These and other issues will have to be resolved in the months and years ahead [6].

1-10 RECENT DEVELOPMENTS

Increasingly, the Internet and Internet access will change and become like a phone system with easy connection and use. The arrival of mobile commerce (m-commerce) and voice commerce (v-commerce) are a clear indication of this trend. We will discuss these new developments in Chapters 2 and 8. In addition to the traditional methods, the Internet can already be accessed using wireless devices, television sets, voice portals, and telephone connections. Internet services will be obtained from both cable and telephone providers, and the separate networks will have exchange agreements. In addition, long-distance voice and data communications will be consolidated with video and images into one medium. The "convergence" of voice, video, and data will be complete, and e-commerce activities will be conducted over this new medium in addition to traditional media. New devices and gadgets will be available that will simplify Internet access. These devices will be used as an alternative to PCs and workstations for users that want to only have Internet access. The telephone of the future will be an advanced form of the present-day PC. The common phone call will be enhanced by possibly offering callers the option of sharing videos and computer data as they speak. However, convergence requires vast infrastructure upgrades. Ultimate success, however, will depend on the desirability of applications to consumers. In addition to Internet 2, which will be discussed in the next section, the following are other initiatives that may play a role in the further development of the Internet, particularly in offering expanded bandwidth for those applications that are demanding a very high-bandwidth environment:

- Mbone
- Giganet
- NII (National Information Infrastructure)

MBone, or multicast backbone, is videoconferencing routing software for the Internet. Mbone, a volunteer effort, is an outgrowth of the first two Internet Engineering Task Force (IETF) "audiocast" experiments in which live audio and video were multicast from the IETF meeting site to destinations around the world. The goal is to construct a semipermanent IP multicast test bed to carry the IETF transmissions and to support continued experimentation between meetings. **Giganet** is derived from the Gigabit Testbed Initiative that is currently testing billion-bit-per-second transmissions at five U.S. computer sites. The **NII** is the Clinton administration's vision of making the highway accessible to all citizens [1]. Information Box 1-4 discusses some of the projects underway to expand the information-carrying capacity of the Internet.

INFORMATION BOX 1-4

The Internet in action: Several projects are underway to expand the Internet bandwidth capacity.

Bandwidth (information-carrying capacity) is the most important factor for global success of e-commerce and for the delivery of multimedia information around the world. To expand the bandwidth capacity of the Internet, several projects are concurrently underway. The Next-Generation Internet initiative (NGI), sponsored by the White House, consists of five components: (1) The Collaborative Advanced Interagency Research Network (CAIRN). This consists of a network of Ascend gigarouters (now a part of Lucent Technologies) that allow researchers to experiment with new technologies and new Internet protocols. (2) The National Transparent Optical Network Consortium (NTONC) is planning to build a prototype network in California to test the performance of optical communication devices. NTONC foresees a network that may eventually carry up to 100 Terabits (10^{12}) of data per second, which is several orders of magnitude higher than anything currently under use. (3) The Multiwavelength Optical Networking (MONET) network connects Washington, D.C., with New Jersey. Similar to the network that is planned by NTONC, MONET will be an experimental multiwavelength optical network. (4) The Advanced Technology Demonstration Network (ATDNet), an OC-48 (optical fiber) network, operates at 2.4 gigabits per second (Gbps). It was created to allow federal agencies to test Asynchronous Transfer Mode (ATM) and Synchronous Optical Network (SONET) technologies. (5) The Multidimensional Applications Gigabit Internetworking Consortium (MAGIC) is a group working on an ATM internetwork that connects several U.S. Department of Defense computers, experimenting with IP multicast (a videoconferencing routing software for the Internet), ATM, and connecting of ATM with non-ATM LANs.

SOURCE: Ferriss, Paul. (1998). "Imagine a World Free of a PC OS." *Computing Canada*. May 25, Vol. 24, No. 20, p. 13.

1-11 THE INTERNET 2

A recent development in the Internet world is the Internet 2 (I2). The I2 is a collaborative effort by over 120 major universities in the United States and several corporations including AT&T, IBM, Microsoft, and Cisco Systems to develop advanced Internet technology and applications essential to the research and education missions of higher education. Started in 1987, the I2 project has been envisioned as a decentralized network where participating universities in the same geographic region will form an alliance to create and found a local connection point-of-presence called **Gigapop** (point-of-presence). Gigapops are regional network aggregations being formed by I2 participants to connect a variety of high-performance networks. Gigapops provide scalable high-speed connectivity points. Physically, a Gigapop is a secure and environmentally conditioned location that houses a collection of communications equipment and supporting hardware. A Gigapop's key function is the exchange of I2 traffic with specified bandwidth. One of the major objectives of the I2 project is to demonstrate new applications that can significantly enhance researchers' ability to collaborate and conduct scientific experiments.

The I2 relies on the NSF and MCI's vBNS high-performance connection program. Started in April 1995, vBNS was designed as a high-bandwidth network for research applications. It is a nationwide network that operates at a speed of

622 Mbps using MCI's advanced switching and fiber-optic transmission technologies. Some of the applications of I2 include the following:

1. **LearningWare** Internet 2, through the proposed Instructional Management System (IMS), provides a unique platform for the delivery of a distributed instructional environment. This will enable students to learn in an anytime, anywhere environment. At the same time this technology will provide instructors with easy access to a broad range of instructional materials.

2. **Digital libraries** By using a high bandwidth, I2 will allow the transfer of multimedia information including text, audio, and live video. I2 will also provide real-time assistance and expert consultation via multimedia conferencing. This technology offers opportunities to enrich and extend the current state of the art in information access and retrieval systems.

3. **Tele-immersion** A tele-immersion system allows individuals at various locations to share a single virtual environment. Multimedia and virtual reality have significant applications in educational, scientific, manufacturing, and collaborative decision making. This technology will further improve the quality and quantity of these growing applications.

4. **Virtual laboratories** This is an environment designed specifically for scientific and engineering applications. This virtual laboratory enables a group of researchers connected to the I2 to work together on joint projects. This may include large-scale simulations, access to global databases, large-scale modeling, and so forth.

1-12 INDUSTRY CONNECTION: NETSCAPE CORPORATION

Netscape Corporation
501 E. Middlefield Road
Mountain View, California, 94043
Telephone: (650) 254-1900
Fax: (650) 528-4165
Web site address: <http://www.netscape.com>

Netscape Corporation was founded by Dr. James Clark (founder of Silicon Graphics) and Marc Andreessen (founder of Mosaic software) in April 1994. Netscape stocks went public in August 1995, only 16 months after its founding. In November 1998, AOL, the largest ISP in the world, bought Netscape. Netscape Navigator's early lead in the graphical web browser market established it as the leader in browser applications, a position that was soon challenged by Microsoft's Internet Explorer. Netscape software enables corporate users to link to the Internet as well as to create internal intranets, which help them to improve communications. Netscape offers a full line of clients, servers, development tools, and commercial e-commerce applications. The following are some of the products and services offered by Netscape Corporation:

Netscape Navigator This graphical browser is used to navigate the Internet, intranets, and extranets.

Netscape Communicator is an integrated set of client software for e-mail, groupware, web page editing, calendaring, and web browsing. Internet phone, chat, whiteboarding, voice mail, and newsgroup capabilities are some of the other features offered. Together with Netscape SuiteSpot servers, Netscape Communicator advances the features and capabilities of the Internet and corporate intranets.

Netscape Server Products The Netscape server family allows companies and individuals to set up and maintain servers for publishing and sharing information and for conducting commercial operations on corporate intranets and the Internet. The Netscape Server Application Programming Interface (NSAPI) allows servers to be extended or integrated with commercial or custom applications, such as user or transaction databases or full-text search engines. I will discuss NSAPI in more detail in Chapter 9.

Netscape SuiteSpot is an integrated suite of server software products that enables organizations to communicate, access, and share information on an intranet, extranet, or the Internet.

Netscape FastTrack Server is an entry-level web server designed to allow corporate employees, developers, small businesses, or other users to create and manage web sites on the Internet or an intranet. Netscape FastTrack Server supports Java and JavaScript programming languages for creating and managing dynamic and live content.

Netscape Commerce Applications The Netscape CommerceXpert family consists of several products, including ECXpert, DeveloperXpert, SellerXpert, BuyerXpert, PublishingXpert, and MerchantXpert. These software products are built on the underlying web server software and create services for buying, selling, merchandising, and delivering content over the Internet. They are based on the same open protocols and scalable security architectures that are used for communication over the Internet. CommerceXpert allows enterprises to automate their procurement process as well as market, sell, and deliver personalized content and services directly to customers over the Internet. This platform can be effectively used for B2B e-commerce (discussed in Chapter 2).

Netscape Enterprise Server is high-performance, scalable web server software for deploying large-scale web sites. I will further discuss this product in Chapter 9.[1]

---

[1]This information was gathered from the company web site and other promotional materials. For detailed information and any update, contact the company.

1-13 SUMMARY

This chapter provided an overview of the Internet as the foundation of the information superhighway and e-commerce. E-commerce was briefly defined and the book summarized. The chapter provided a brief history of the Internet, reviewed various access options, domain name systems, navigational tools, directories, and search engines. Popular Internet services that support e-commerce were briefly mentioned as well as the economic issues of the Internet. The chapter concluded with an outlook for the future development of the Internet, a discussion of Internet 2, and highlighted Netscape Corporation as the industry connection.

1-14 REVIEW QUESTIONS

1. How did the Internet start? What is ARPANET? Who sponsored ARPANET? Discuss. What is the WWW?
2. What is e-commerce? What is e-business? What are some of the differences between the two? Discuss.
3. What are some of the technologies and applications that support e-commerce? What is the road map of this book?
4. What are some of the popular Internet access options? What are the differences between these various options?
5. What are domain name systems? How are educational institutions identified? The military? The U.S. government?
6. What are some examples of navigational tools? What is Netscape? Why has Internet Explorer gained so much popularity? What has been the trend in designing navigational tools?
7. What are some of the popular Internet services that support e-commerce? What is e-mail? What is instant messenger?
8. Compare and contrast e-mail with regular mail. What are some advantages of e-mail over regular mail? What are some of the applications of e-mail in e-commerce? Discuss.
9. What are news- and discussion groups? What are their applications in e-commerce?
10. What are some of the economic issues of the Internet?
11. How are we going to resolve the bandwidth issue of the Internet in the near future? Discuss.
12. What are some of the future development trends in the Internet environment? Discuss.
13. Many universities are offering online courses. What are some of the advantages and disadvantages of these kinds of instructions?

14. What is I2? What are some of the objectives of the I2? Discuss.
15. What are web portals? Why have they become so popular? What is their role in the e-commerce environment?
16. What are some of the services offered by web portals? Who are some of the major players of web portals?
17. What are some of the limitations of Internet phone?
18. What are some of the applications of Internet phone in the e-commerce environment? Discuss.

1-15 PROJECTS AND HANDS-ON EXERCISES

1. Log onto the web site of the Netscape Corporation at the following URL:

   <http://www.netscape.com>

   What are some of the software products offered by this company? Why has Netscape Navigator lost its leadership in the browser market to Microsoft Internet Explorer? What are some of the differences between these two browsers? What are some of their similarities? Discuss. What other products and services offered by Netscape Corporation can be used in the e-commerce environment? Discuss. AOL purchased Netscape Corporation. What is the significance of this merger in the e-commerce world? Discuss.

2. Log into the following web site:

   <http://www.igoldrush.com>

   This web site includes valuable information regarding country domain names throughout the world. It also lists all the countries that are either directly or indirectly connected to the Web. According to the information presented in this site, how many countries are connected to the Web? What else is available in this site?

3. The World Wide Web Consortium (W3C) is a significant organization in the Internet world that develops interoperable technologies (specifications, guidelines, software, and tools) to lead the Web to its full potential as a forum for information, commerce, and communication. It also provides comprehensive information on the Web history. Log on to the following site, review the materials presented here and at other related sites, and prepare a two-page report on http and html. How are these two protocols used in the e-commerce world? Discuss.

   <http://www.w3.org/pub/WWW>

4. The following web sites are among the most popular sites in the Internet world. Log onto each site and research the latest information on e-commerce. Based on your findings, prepare a two-page report on e-commerce. What are the latest developments in e-commerce? What is m-commerce (hint: consult Chapter 2)? Why is m-commerce gaining popularity? What is v-commerce?

> ESPnet   <http://espnet.sportszone.com>
> Infoseek <http://www.infoseek.com>
> Lycos   <http://www.lycos.com>
> Netscape <http://www.netscape.com>
> Yahoo!   <http://www.yahoo.com>

5. Using e-mail software with which you are familiar, create a distribution list that contains five e-mail addresses. Send a message to these five individuals announcing a new product for ABC Company. You can always send an e-mail to the author at

> <hbidgoli@csubak.edu>

Send me e-mail about the new information you have learned so far.

6. There are over 200 ISPs on the market. How do you evaluate a service provider for personal use and for business use? What criteria constitute a good provider? List seven criteria that you consider important for such a selection. Why are some ISPs free? What do they get in return for their free service from their customers? What is the quality of service offered by these ISPs? (Hint: http://netzero.com is an example.)

7. Using Google and other search engines, search the Web and prepare a two-page report on e-commerce applications in Wal-Mart Stores. How is Wal-Mart gaining competitive advantage by using e-commerce? In which business area has e-commerce been the most successful? Discuss.

8. The following site provides the best price for electronics and computers. Log onto the site and find out the price of the latest PC on the market. Compare this price with the offering price of a computer store. Do you see any savings? How much is the difference between these two prices?

> <http://www.pricewatch.com>

9. The following site offers valuable information for promoting an e-commerce site. Log onto the site and by examining different links, write down 10 tips and tricks that will keep potential customers coming back to an e-commerce site.

> <http://www.promotionbase.com>

10. Expedia.com provides all sorts of travel and entertainment services. Log onto the site and find out about the offerings under the Traveler Tools. By clicking on Airport Information, find out relevant information on Los Angeles International Airport. What is the function of the Currency Converter? What is the function of e-cards? Using this site, how do you book a flight from Los Angeles to New York? How do you find the weather conditions in Chicago?

<http://www.expedia.com/Default.asp?MSID=44CE3DF1FD7B4E37A DB5B674AF4F0F15>

11. The following site provides information on software support for recruitment:

<http://www.sourcer.com>

Log onto the site and find out about the following functions used in a human resource department:

- Résumé scanning
- Résumé text search
- Correspondence tracking
- Skill matching

How beneficial are these services in a large organization? What type of organization will benefit the most from such services? Discuss.

12. The following site provides all sorts of financing information, including mortgage calculations.

<http://www.homeowners.com/index2.html>

Log onto the site and find out the latest interest rate on a 30-year and a 15-year loan. Using the calculator, calculate the monthly payment on a $100,000 loan, 30 years, and an 8.25% interest rate. What is the monthly payment on the same loan in a 15-year contract? What is the monthly payment on the same loan at 6% interest rate?

13. The following site is a music store with some free sample download. Log onto the site and do the following:

<www.musicblvd.com>

- Which songs are included among the top 100?
- What can you download from this site?
- What is available under the Custom CDs option?

14. Playhere provides all sorts of free products and services. Log onto the site and answer the following questions:

<www.playhere.com>

- What is available under Screen Savers? Under Wallpapers? Under Stereograms?
- Under Post Office? Under Live Cameras?

15. Chevron Corporation's web site for children is an innovative site.

<http://www.chevroncars.com>

Log onto the site and click on the **about this site** option and read the specifications on the site. At the bottom of the screen click on **Free Stuff** option. What is available here? In your opinion what is so unique about this site? Discuss.

16. The following site provides Internet services such as chat rooms:

<http://www.talkcity.com>

Log onto the site and answer the following questions: What types of chat rooms are available through this site? Which chat group has the highest number of members? Which chat group is the least popular?

17. The following site provides comprehensive information on search engines, directories, and other search techniques and tools:

<http://doc.altavista.com/adv_search/ast_toc.html>

Log onto the site and answer the following questions: When do you use the phrase NEAR in a search? What are automatic and manual phrases? How do you search by date? What are the differences between directories and search engines? Discuss.

18. The following site provides comprehensive art collections by famous artists:

<http://art.com>

Log onto the site and answer the following questions: Who are some of the top artists listed in this site? What are some of the options under My Gallery?

19. The following site is an online dictionary:

<http://www.yourdictionary.com>

Log onto the site and find out how many languages are supported by this online dictionary. Does it offer any multilingual dictionaries? How do you find a synonym for a word using this dictionary?

20. Log onto the following web site:

<http://webshots.com>

It provides several hundred screen savers and other artwork for free.

How does a site such as this generate revenue? Who will use a site like this? What are some of its offerings?

21. Log into the web site of Virtual Tourist at the following URL:

<http://www.vtourist.com/vt>

By clicking on North America, view the map of North America. What are some of the countries listed on this map? What are some of the countries listed under Asia? By pressing the back and forward buttons, switch between different pages.

1-16 KEY TERMS

ARPANET, 6
Domain name systems, 10–13
Economic issues, 26–27
Electronic business (e-business), 5
Electronic commerce (e-commerce), 5
Electronic mail (e-mail), 22–23
Information superhighway, 6–9
Instant messenger, 24

Internet, 6–9
Internet 2, 29–30
Internet access options, 9–10
Internet phone, 25–26
Internet relay chat (IRC), 23–24
Navigational tools, 13–15
Newsgroups and discussions, 23
Web portal, 20, 22

REFERENCES

[1] Begley, Sharon, and Adam Rogers (February 27, 1995). "MBones and Giganets," *Newsweek,* p. 58.
[2] Bidgoli, Hossein (2000). *Handbook of Business Data Communications: A Managerial Perspective.* Academic Press, Inc., San Diego, California.
[3] Boisvert, Lisa (Winter 2000). "Web-based Learning: The Anytime Anywhere Classroom," *Information Systems management,* pp. 34–35.
[4] Comer, Douglas E. (2000). *The Internet Book: Everything You Need to Know about Computer Networking and How the Internet Works.* Prentice Hall, Upper Saddle River, NJ.
[5] Hudgins-Bonafield, Christine (March 1, 1995). "How Will the Internet Grow?" *Network Computing,* pp. 80–90.
[6] Mackie-Mason, Jeffery K., and Hal Varian (Summer, 1994). "Economic FAQs About the Internet," *Journal of Economic Perspective,* Vol. 8, No. 3, pp. 75–96.
[7] Perry, James T., and Gary P. Schneider (2000). *The Internet,* (2nd ed.). Course Technology, Cambridge, MA.
[8] Wilder, Clinton (February 27, 1995), "Pulling in the Net." *Information Week,* p. 96.
[9] Wilder, Clinton (January 23, 1995), "Online Security Push." *Information Week,* p. 24.

Chapter 2

Electronic Commerce Fundamentals

Learning Objectives

After studying this chapter you should be able to do the following:

- Explain value chain and the role of electronic commerce (e-commerce) in the value-chain process.
- Discuss important e-commerce business models.
- Define e-commerce and compare and contrast it with traditional commerce.
- Explain the major categories of e-commerce.
- Discuss the advantages and disadvantages of e-commerce.
- Elaborate on the business-to-consumer e-commerce cycle.
- Review major business-to-business models, including seller-controlled marketplace, buyer-controlled marketplace, third-party-controlled marketplace, and trading partner agreements.
- Elaborate on mobile commerce and voice commerce as two growing categories of e-commerce.

INFORMATION BOX 2-1

Facts and Figures about E-Commerce

According to Forrester Research, more than 40 million U.S. households will shop online by 2003, producing $108 billion in revenues.

According to Yankee Group, 56% of small businesses online in 2000 regard the Internet as "essential" to their success.

IBM does business with over 12,000 suppliers over the Web. It uses the Web for sending purchase orders, receiving invoices, and paying suppliers. IBM uses Internet and web technologies as its transaction-processing network.

IBM now is doing business with nearly 95% of its suppliers over the Internet.

According to Jupiter, an Internet research company, business-to business (B2B) online trade will rise to $6.3 trillion by 2005.

In 1998 there were only 400 B2B e-marketplaces. This number passed 1000 in 2000.

Consumers will benefit more from B2B and business-to-consumer (B2C) e-commerce by being able to purchase products and services at a lower cost and in a timelier manner.

E-commerce may put small businesses on the same footing as large corporations.

E-commerce will continue to reduce cycle times and inventories in all types of organizations.

E-store, e-catalog, e-order entry, and e-payment will become commonly used web applications.

Mobile and wireless networks will play a major role in e-commerce utilization.

More and more proprietary electronic data interchange (EDI) applications will be replaced by web-based EDI.

Using the Web to generate requests for quotations (RFQ), requests for information (RFI), and requests for proposals (RFP) will become common business applications of the Web.

There will be more integration between all categories of e-commerce, enterprise resource planning, and supply-chain management.

INFORMATION BOX 2-2

Dell Computer: E-Commerce in Action

Dell Computer sells computers, hardware, and software products directly to its customers. Dell is one of the most successful personal computer (PC) manufacturers in the world. Its business model is based on direct selling, just-in-time (JIT) inventory system, mass customization, and heavy use of the Web. Compared to its competitors, Dell enjoys lower manufacturing cost, high delivery speed, and customized products and services. Dell customers are individuals as well as business customers. Using e-commerce and JIT inventory models, Dell Computer has become the leader in build-to-order (BTO) systems. In 1996, Dell started selling computers through its web site. In 2000, it sold more than $50 million in products each day over the Web.

The Dell e-commerce model offers value, quality, mass customization, and selection to its customers. Dell targets keeping inventory no more than 8–11 days at its manufacturing facilities. This is in contrast to the industry standard of 80 days. Dell uses the Web to create a community around its supply chain. Dell has created customized web pages for its high-volume suppliers. These suppliers can log onto a secure and personalized site and view demand forecasts and other sensitive information. This information enables them to better manage their production schedules. For many of its customers, Dell also has created Premier Pages containing approved configurations, prenegotiated prices, and new work flow capabilities.

Gigabuy.com, a part of Dell's e-commerce operations, sells a comprehensive list of hardware and software manufactured by Dell and other computer manufacturers. Dell's storefront enables customers to configure their desired computer and then order these systems over the Web.

SOURCE: <http://www.Dell.com>

2-1 INTRODUCTION

This chapter first defines value-chain analysis, explains the e-commerce role in the value-chain process, and reviews popular e-commerce business models used by successful e-businesses. It then defines e-commerce and e-business and reviews the major components of e-commerce. E-commerce is compared to traditional commerce and the major categories of e-commerce are discussed, including business-to-consumer (B2C), business-to-business (B2B), consumer-to-consumer (C2C), organizational (intrabusiness), consumer-to-business (C2B), and nonbusiness and government. The chapter explores the advantages and disadvantages of e-commerce and the major activities involved in a C2B e-commerce life cycle. Discussion includes various B2B e-commerce models, including seller-controlled marketplace, buyer-controlled marketplace, third-party-controlled marketplace, and trading partner agreements. The chapter concludes with an overview of wireless and voice-based e-commerce as the most promising growth areas in the e-commerce environment and highlights Amazon.com as the industry connection.

2-2 VALUE CHAIN AND E-COMMERCE

One way to look at e-commerce and its role in the business world is through value-chain analysis. Michael Porter introduced the value-chain concept in 1985 [9]. It consists of a series of activities designed to satisfy a business need by adding value (or cost) in each phase of the process. A typical business organization (or a division within a business organization) designs, produces, markets, delivers, and supports its product(s) or service(s). Each of these activities adds cost and value to the product or service that is eventually delivered to the customer. For example, in a furniture-manufacturing firm, the firm buys raw materials (wood) from a logging company and then converts these raw materials (wood) into finished product (chair); chairs are shipped to retailers, distributors, or customers. The firm markets and services these products (chairs). In addition to these primary activities that result in a final product or service, Porter also includes supporting activities in this process. These supporting activities include the following:

- Obtaining various inputs for each primary activity
- Developing technology to keep the business competitive
- Managing human resources
- Managing company infrastructure

In the above example, the value chain may continue after delivering chairs to the furniture store. The store, by offering other products and services and mixing and matching this product with other products, may add additional value to the chair. Also, value-chain analysis may highlight the opportunity for the furniture manufacturer to manufacture chairs directly. This means it may enter in the logging business directly or through partnership with others. In any industry, an enterprise is located in a value chain when it buys goods and services from suppliers, adds value, and sells them to customers.

E-commerce, its applications, and its supporting technologies, as will be discussed throughout this book, provide the business platform for realizing Porter's visions. The Internet can increase the speed and accuracy of communications between suppliers, distributors, and customers. Moreover, the Internet's low cost means that companies of any size will be able to take advantage of value-chain integration. E-commerce may enhance value chain by identifying new opportunities for cost reduction. The following are some examples:

- Reducing cost: Using e-mail to notify customers versus using regular mail
- Revenue improvement or generation: Selling to remote customers using the company web site. These sales would not have been materialized otherwise, or selling digital products such as songs or computer software or distributing software through the Web.
- Product or service improvement: offering online customer service or new sales channel identification.

Many companies have taken advantage of the Web and e-commerce to reduce cost, improve revenue, and increase customer service. For example, Microsoft Direct is a web site that provides online order-management and customer-assistance services to shoppers acquiring Microsoft products. It operates using online storefronts that hand shoppers over to Microsoft Direct as soon as they have selected the products they want to order. Dell Computer generates a large portion of its revenue through the Web by eliminating the middleman. Cisco Systems sells much of its networking hardware and software over the Web, improving revenue and reducing cost. United Parcel Service (UPS) and Federal Express use the Internet to track packages that result in enhanced customer service. I will present many other applications in the rest of this book regarding the application and role of e-commerce in value-chain process.

2-3 E-COMMERCE BUSINESS MODELS

Similar to traditional businesses, the ultimate goal of an e-business is to generate revenue and make a profit. It is true that the Internet has improved productivity for almost all the organizations that are using it. However, the bottom line is that productivity must be converted to profitability. The fall of many "dot-com" companies in 2000 and 2001 is a clear indication of this phenomenon. The survivors are clearly those businesses with a sound business model of how they plan to make a profit and sustain a business for future growth.

To achieve profitability as the ultimate goal, different e-businesses or e-commerce sites position themselves in different parts of the value-chain model discussed in the last section. To generate revenue, an e-business either sells products or services or shortens the link between the suppliers and consumers. Many B2B models try to eliminate the middleman by using the Web to deliver products and services directly to their customers. By doing this they may be able to offer cheaper products and better customer service to their customers. The end result would be a differentiation between them and their competitors, increased market share, and increased customer loyalty.

Products sold by e-businesses could be either traditional products, such as books and apparel, or digital products, such as songs, computer software, or electronic books. E-commerce models are either an extension or revision of traditional business models, such as advertising and auction models, or a new type of business model that is suitable for the Web implementation, such as informediary, selling information collected over the Web about individuals and businesses to other businesses. The most popular e-commerce models are the following [1]:

- Merchant
- Brokerage
- Advertising
- Mixed
- Informediary
- Subscription

The **merchant model** is basically the transferring of an old retail model to the e-commerce world by using the Internet. There are different types of merchant models. The most common type of merchant model is similar to a traditional business model that sells goods and services over the Web. Amazon.com (featured at the end of this chapter) is a good example of this type. An e-business similar to Amazon.com utilizes the services and technologies offered by the Web to sell products and services directly to the consumers. By offering good customer service and reasonable prices, these companies establish a brand on the Web. The merchant model is also used by many traditional businesses to sell goods and services over the Internet. Dell, Cisco Systems, and Compaq are popular examples. These companies eliminate the middleman by generating a portion of their total sale over the Web and by accessing difficult-to-reach customers.

Using the **brokerage model,** the e-business brings the sellers and buyers together on the Web and collects a commission on the transactions. The best example of this type is an online auction site such as eBay, which can generate additional revenue by selling banner advertisement on their sites. Other examples of the brokerage model are online stockbrokers, such as NDB.com, eTrade.com, and Schwab.com, which generate revenue through commissions from both buyers and sellers of securities.

The **advertising model** is an extension of traditional advertising media, such as radio and television. Search engines and directories such as AltaVista and Yahoo! provide contents (similar to radio and TV) and allow the users to access this content for free. By creating significant traffic, these e-businesses are able to charge advertisers for putting banner ads or leasing spots on their sites.

The **mixed model** generates revenue both from advertising and subscriptions. Internet service providers (ISPs) such as America On-line (AOL) Time Warner generate revenue from advertising and their customers' subscription fees for Internet access.

E-businesses that use the **informediary model** collect information on consumers and businesses and then sell this information to interested parties for marketing purposes. For example, Netzero.com provides free Internet access; in return it collects information related to the buying habits and surfing behavior of customers. This information is later sold to advertisers for direct marketing. eMachines.com offers free PCs to its customers for the same purpose. E-businesses such as bizrate.com collect information related to the performance of other sites and sell this information to advertisers.

Using a **subscription model,** an e-business might sell digital products to its customers. *The Wall Street Journal* and *Consumer Reports* are two examples. Sreeet.com is another example of this model that sells business news and analysis based on subscription.

2-4 DEFINING E-COMMERCE

As briefly introduced in Chapter 1, e-business encompasses all activities that a firm performs for selling and buying products and services using computers and communications technologies. In broad terms, e-business includes a host of related activities, such as online shopping, sales force automation, supply-chain management, electronic payment systems, Web advertising, and order management. E-commerce is buying and selling goods and services over the Internet. Based on this definition, e-commerce is part of e-business. However, in many cases the two are used interchangeably.

E-business, a major contributor to the popularity of global information systems, is a system that includes not only those transactions that center on buying and selling goods and services to generate revenue, but also those transactions that support revenue generation. These activities include generating demand for goods and services, offering sales support and customer service, or facilitating communications between business partners.

E-commerce builds on traditional commerce by adding the flexibility offered by computer networks and the availability of the Internet. By generating and delivering timely and relevant information through computer networks, e-commerce creates new opportunities for conducting commercial activities online, and thus it fosters easier cooperation between different groups: branches of a multinational company sharing information for a major marketing campaign; companies working together to design and build new products or offer new services; or businesses sharing information to improve customer relations.

Table 2-1 lists some of the major beneficiaries of e-commerce. A close examination of these businesses and entities reveals the potential for e-commerce to generate revenue and reduce costs. For example, banks (as will be further discussed in Chapter 3) use the Web for diverse business practices and customer service. The entertainment industry utilizes the Web extensively for offering diverse products and services (discussed further in Chapter 3).

Different branches of governments using e-commerce applications have experienced major cost savings. For example, the U.S. federal government uses electronic data interchange (EDI) for requests for quotes (RFQs), quotes, award notices, purchase orders, and invoices. (I will further discuss the applications of e-commerce in the entities listed in Table 2-1 in Chapters 3, 5, and 7).

Table 2-2 lists business uses of the Internet. As you will learn throughout this book, these services and capabilities are a core part of a successful e-commerce program. They are either parts of a value chain or are included as supporting activities discussed earlier in the chapter.

Table 2-3 lists some popular products and services that can be purchased online. Close examination of these products and services reveals their suitability

Table 2-1
Major Beneficiaries of E-Commerce

Banks

Entertainment

Government

Insurance

Marketing

Online publishing

Retailers

Training

Travel industries

Universities

Table 2-2

Business Uses of the Internet

Buying and selling products and services

Collaborating with others

Communicating within organizations

Gathering information

Gathering information on competitors

Providing customer service

Providing software update and patches

Providing vendor support

Publishing and disseminating information

for e-commerce transactions. Several successful e-businesses have established their business models around selling these products and services.

Table 2-4 lists companies using e-commerce, highlighting the products and services that are most suitable for web transactions. Table 2-5 lists the top 10 countries with the highest sales volume in e-commerce operations. The table is a guide for the investigation and implementation of e-commerce on the international scene. As this table shows, e-commerce is estimated to generate approximately $3.2 trillion in revenue in the United States in 2004.

Table 2-6 lists the top online retail sites based on sales volume in 2000. Again this table highlights those e-businesses that have been able to generate the highest sales in 2000. A close investigation of the business model used by these companies may serve as a guide for others.

Table 2-3

Popular Products and Services Purchased Online

Airline tickets and travel

Apparel and footwear

Banking services

Books and music

Computer hardware, software, and other electronics

Flowers and gifts

Stock brokerage services

Table 2-4

Examples of Companies Using E-Commerce

Amazon.com (as will be introduced at the end of the chapter) provides access to several million books electronically. It also sells music CDs, electronics, software, toys, video games, prescription drugs, and much more.

Drugstore.com, and CVS.com refill and sell new drugs and vitamins and other health and beauty products online.

American Express successfully uses e-commerce for credit card transactions.

Apple Computer sells computers online (apple.com).

Auto-by-Tel sells cars over the Web.

Charles Schwab, National Discount Brokers, and E-Trade have successfully used e-commerce for online security transactions.

Cisco Systems sells data communications components over the Web.

Dell Computer and Gateway sell computers through their web sites and allow customers to configure their systems on the Web and then purchase them.

Epicurious sells exotic foods over the Web.

Peapod sells groceries over the Web.

Proctor & Gamble and IBM conduct order placements electronically.

Virtual Vineyards sells expensive wines from small vineyards over the Web.

Table 2-5

Top 10 E-Commerce Countries[a]

	Total sales (%)	E-commerce sales (in $ billions)	
Country	2004	2000	2004
1. United States	13.3	488.7	3,189.0
2. Japan	8.4	31.9	880.3
3. Germany	6.5	20.6	386.5
4. United Kingdom	7.1	17.2	288.8
5. Australia	16.4	5.6	207.6
6. France	5.0	9.9	206.4
7. South Korea	16.4	5.6	205.7
8. Taiwan	16.4	4.1	175.8
9. Canada	9.2	17.4	160.3
10. Italy	4.3	7.2	142.4

[a]Source: Forester Research and INFOWORLD, May 15, 2000, p. 20.

Table 2-6

**Top Online Retail Sites Based on Sales
Volume in 2000**[a]

Amazon.com

Ticketmaster.com

Buy.com

CDnow.com

Sears.com

Barnesandnoble.com

JCPenny.com

Real.com

Pets.com

[a]Source: *INFOWORLD,* September 25, 2000, p. 22.

2-5 E-COMMERCE VERSUS TRADITIONAL COMMERCE

Although the goals and objectives of both e-commerce and traditional commerce are the same—selling products and services to generate profits—they do it quite differently. In e-commerce, the Web and telecommunications technologies play a major role. In e-commerce there may be no physical store, and in most cases the buyer and seller do not see each other. Table 2-7 compares and

Table 2-7

E-Commerce versus Traditional Commerce

Activity	Traditional commerce	E-commerce
Product information	Magazines, flyers	Web sites
		Online catalogs
Business communications	Regular mail, phone	E-mail
Check product availability	Phone, fax, letter	E-mail, web sites, and extranets[a]
Order generation	Printed forms	E-mail, web sites
Product acknowledgments	Phone, fax	E-mail, web sites, and EDI[b]
Invoice generation	Printed forms	Web sites

[a]Extranets are the connection of two or more intranets. Intranets are internal networks that use web technologies. (They both will be discussed in Chapter 4.)
[b]Electronic data interchange (discussed in Chapter 5).

contrasts traditional commerce and e-commerce. However, it is important to notice that currently many companies operate with a mix of traditional and e-commerce. Just about all medium and large organizations have some kind of e-commerce presence. The Gap, Toys-R-Us, Wal-Mart Stores, and Sears are a few examples.

2-6 MAJOR CATEGORIES OF E-COMMERCE

The several categories of e-commerce in use today are classified based on the nature of the transactions, including business-to-consumer (B2C), business-to-business (B2B), consumer-to-consumer (C2C), consumer-to-business (C2B), and nonbusiness and government, and organizational (intrabusiness). In the following paragraphs we define these categories.

2-6-1 BUSINESS-TO-CONSUMER

In B2C e-commerce, businesses sell directly to consumers. Amazon.com, barnesandnoble.com, and Onsale.com are three good examples of this category. As discussed at the end of the chapter, Amazon.com and its business partners sell a diverse group of products and services to their customers, including books, videos, DVDs, prescription drugs, online auctions, and much more. In addition to pure B2C e-commerce players such as Amazon.com, other traditional businesses have entered the virtual marketplace by establishing comprehensive web sites and virtual storefronts. Wal-Mart Stores, the Gap, and Staples are examples of companies that are very active in B2C e-commerce. In these cases, e-commerce supplements the traditional commerce by offering products and services through electronic channels. Some experts believe that, in the long term, these types of businesses should be more successful than pure e-commerce businesses. Some of the advantages of these e-commerce sites and companies include availability of physical space (customers can physically visit the store), availability of returns (customers can return a purchased item to the physical store), and availability of customer service in these physical stores. Figure 2-1 illustrates a B2C configuration.

2-6-2 BUSINESS-TO-BUSINESS

B2B involves electronic transactions among and between businesses. This technology has been around for many years through EDI (discussed in Chapter 5) and electronic funds transfer (EFT) (discussed in Chapter 6). In recent years

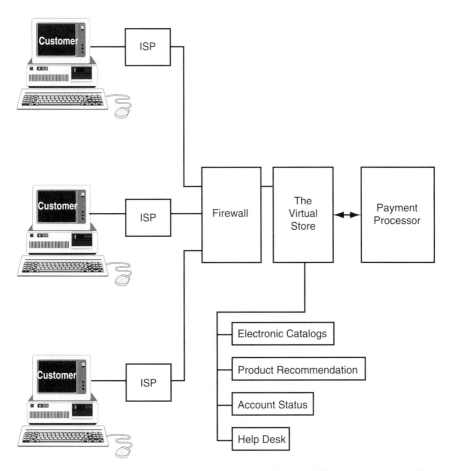

Figure 2-1 A business-to-consumer (B2C) e-commerce configuration. ISP, Internet service provider.

the Internet has significantly increased B2B transactions and has made B2B the fastest growing segment within the e-commerce environment. As discussed in Chapter 4, in recent years extranets have been effectively used for B2B operations. The reliance of all businesses upon other companies for supplies, utilities, and services has enhanced the popularity of B2B e-commerce. An example of B2B is an auto exchange formed by Ford, Daimler Chrysler, and General Motors called covisint (http://www.covisint.com). This system offers services in areas of procurement, supply-chain management, and collaborative product development. Partners achieve build-to-order capability through connectivity among the key lines of business and throughout an individual company's supply chain.

Companies using systems such as covisint report millions of dollars in savings by increasing the speed, reducing errors, and eliminating many manual activities. Wal-Mart Stores are another major player in B2B e-commerce. Wal-Mart's major suppliers (e.g., Proctor & Gamble, Johnson and Johnson, and others) sell to Wal-Mart Stores electronically; all the paperwork is handled electronically. These suppliers can access online the inventory status in each store and replenish needed products in a timely manner. Figure 2-2 illustrates a generic B2B configuration. As this figures shows, in a B2B environment, purchase orders, invoices, inventory status, shipping logistics, and business contracts handled directly through the network result in increased speed, reduced errors, and cost savings.

2-6-3 Consumer-to-Consumer

The C2C category involves business transactions among individuals using the Internet and web technologies. Using C2C, consumers sell directly to other consumers. For example, through classified ads or by advertising, individuals sell services or products on the Web or through auction sites such as ubid.com. eBay.com is a good example of a C2C e-commerce company. Using this web site, consumers are able to sell a wide variety of products to each other. Figure 2-3 illustrates a generic C2C e-commerce configuration that offers catalogs, auctions, and escrow services. Consumers are also able to advertise their products and services in organizational intranets (discussed later in the chapter) and sell them to other employees.

2-6-4 Consumer-to-Business

Consumer-to-business (C2B) e-commerce involves individuals selling to businesses. This may include a service or product that a consumer is willing to sell. In other cases an individual may seek sellers of a product and service. Companies such as priceline.com, travelbid.com, and mobshop.com for travel arrangements are examples of C2B. Individuals offer certain prices for specific products and services. Figure 2-4 illustrates a generic C2B e-commerce configuration.

2-6-5 Nonbusiness and Government

The e-commerce applications in government and many nonbusiness organizations are on the rise. Several government agencies in the United States have

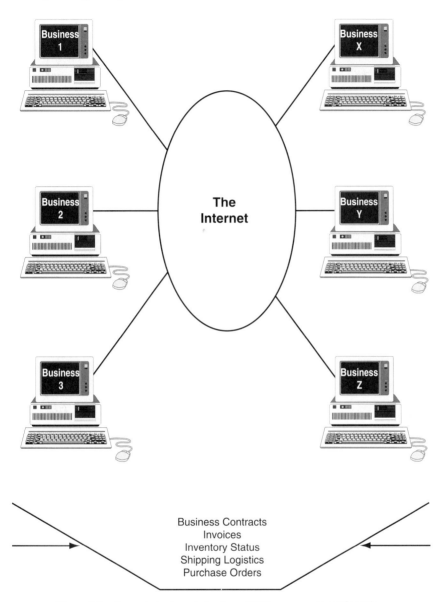

Figure 2-2   A generic business-to-business (B2B) e-commerce configuration.

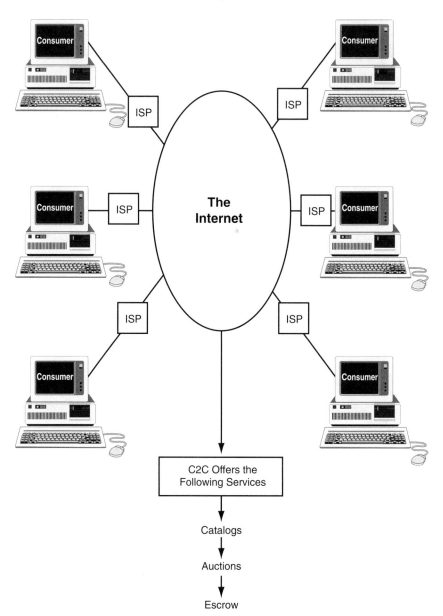

Figure 2-3   A generic consumer-to-consumer (C2C) e-commerce configuration. ISP, Internet service provider.

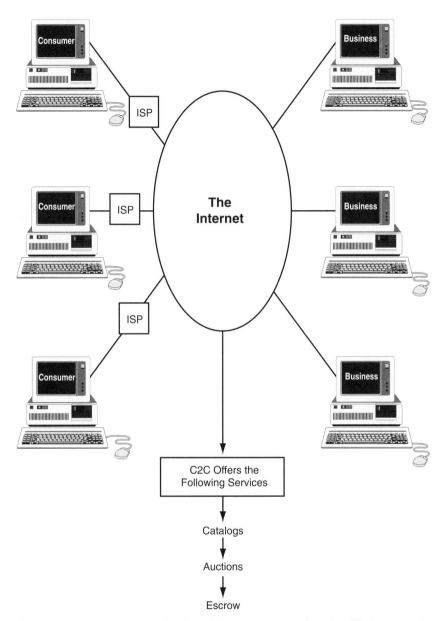

Figure 2-4 A generic consumer-to-business (C2B) e-commerce configuration. ISP, Internet service provider.

been using e-commerce applications for several years, including the Department of Defense, Internal Revenue Service, and the Department of Treasury. Universities are using e-commerce applications extensively for delivering their educational products and services on a global scale. Not-for-profit, political, and social organizations also use e-commerce applications for various activities, such as fundraising and political forums. These organizations also use e-commerce for purchasing (to reduce cost and improve speed) and for customer service.

2-6-6 ORGANIZATIONAL (INTRABUSINESS)

Organizational or intrabusiness e-commerce involves all the e-commerce-related activities that take place within the organization. The organization intranets provide the right platform for these activities. (I will discuss intranets in detail in Chapter 4). These activities may include exchange of goods, services, or information among the employees of an organization. This may include selling organization products and services to the employees, conducting training programs, offering human resources services, and much more. Although they are not direct selling and buying, some of these activities provide support for a successful e-commerce program in human resources management, finance, and marketing.

2-7 ADVANTAGES AND DISADVANTAGES OF E-COMMERCE

Similar to traditional businesses, e-commerce presents many advantages and disadvantages. As you will see throughout this book, if the e-commerce is established based on the correct business model, the advantages of e-commerce significantly outweigh its disadvantages. Table 2-8 highlights some of the advantages of e-commerce [5].

In the e-commerce world, doing business around the globe 7 days a week, 24 hours a day is a reality. Customers in any part of the world with an Internet connection can log onto the e-commerce site and order a product or service. Holidays, weekends, after hours, and differences in time zones do not pose any problem.

Using various tools such as cookies, e-mail, and the company web site, the e-commerce site is able to gain additional knowledge about potential customers (discussed further in Chapter 7). This knowledge could be effectively used to better market products and services. For example, the e-business would know the customer preferences, shopping habits, gender, age group, and so forth.

Table 2-8

Selected Possible Advantages of E-Commerce

Doing business around the globe 7 days a week, 24 hours a day

Gaining additional knowledge about potential customers

Improved customer involvement

Improved customer service

Improved relationships with suppliers

Improved relationships with the financial community

Increased flexibility and ease of shopping

Increased number of customers

Increased return on capital and investment, since no inventory is needed

Personalized service

Product and service customization

In the e-commerce environment, customer involvement could be significantly improved. For example, the customer can provide an online review of a book that he or she has recently purchased from the e-commerce site. Or the customer may participate in various open forums, chat groups, and discussions.

An e-commerce site, by using tools such as an online help desk, company web sites, and e-mail is able to improve customer service. Many of the customers' questions and concerns are answered using these tools with minimum cost. Printing forms online, downloading software patches, and reviewing frequently asked questions (FAQs) are other examples of customer service.

As will be discussed later in this chapter and in Chapters 4 and 5, a B2B e-commerce site can improve its relationships with suppliers. E-commerce technologies enable these businesses to exchange relevant information on a timely basis with minimum cost. Using B2B e-commerce assists businesses in managing a comprehensive inventory management system. An e-commerce site can improve its relationships with the financial community through the timely transfer of business transactions and a better understanding of the business partner's financial status.

Increased flexibility and ease of shopping is a significant advantage of e-commerce. The customer does not need to leave his or her home or office and commute to purchase an item. The customer does not need to look for parking in a shopping mall during holidays, nor risk losing the supervision of his or her small children (for even a short period) or elderly relatives. Shopping tasks can be done from the privacy of the home with a few clicks of mouse!

An e-business or a traditional business with an e-commerce presence could increase its potential customers. Customers from remote locations and those outside of the business's geographical boundaries can purchase products and services from the e-commerce site.

In many cases an e-commerce site should be able to increase return on capital and investment since no inventory is needed. An effective e-commerce program is able to operate with no inventory or with minimum inventory. In some cases an e-commerce site serves as middleman, taking orders from customers, routing orders to suppliers, and making a profit. In other cases an e-commerce site is able to maintain minimal inventory and fill customers' orders through a JIT inventory system. By having no or minimal inventory, the e-commerce site could avoid devaluation in inventory due to the release of a new product, change in fashion, season, and so forth.

In many cases an e-commerce site by using various web technologies is able to offer personalized service to its customers and at the same time customize a product or service to suit a particular customer (see Chapter 7). By collecting relevant information on different customers, a particular product or service could be tailor-made to customer taste and preference. In some cases, the customer may pick and choose, as in sites that allow the customer to create his or her own CD, travel plan, PC, automobile, and so forth.

Many of the disadvantages of e-commerce are related to technology and business practices. These disadvantages should be resolved in the near future. Table 2-9 lists some of the disadvantages of e-commerce. In the following paragraphs I provide a brief description of these disadvantages.

Possible capacity and bandwidth problems could be a serious problem (see Information Box 1-4 in Chapter 1); however, several projects are underway to resolve this issue in the near future.

Security issues are major concern for many consumers. Security issues and measures are expected to improve in coming years, through the use of media other than credit cards on the Web, such as e-Wallet, e-cash, and other payment

Table 2-9

Some Disadvantages of E-Commerce

Possible capacity and bandwidth problems

Security issues

Accessibility (not everybody is connected to the Web yet)

Acceptance (not everybody accepts this technology)

A lack of understanding of business strategy and goals

systems (discussed further in Chapter 6), acceptance of digital signatures, more widespread application and acceptance of encryption technology, and greater awareness and understanding of customers' concerns.

The accessibility of customers issue will certainly become more manageable, as the number of Internet users increases daily. Also, the reduction in cost of PCs, handheld, and other Internet appliances should further increase Internet applications and result in further accessibility of e-commerce.

Similar to other technologies, acceptance of e-commerce by the majority of people will take time. However, the growth of the Internet and of online shopping points to further acceptance of e-commerce applications in the near future. When the technology is fully accepted, a company's e-business strategies and goals will also become better understood.

2-8 A BUSINESS-TO-CONSUMER E-COMMERCE CYCLE

As Figure 2-5 shows, there are five major activities involved in conducting B2C e-commerce:

1. **Information sharing.** A B2C e-commerce model may use some or all of the following applications and technologies to share information with customers:

- Company web site
- Online catalogs
- E-mail
- Online advertisements
- Multiparty conferencing
- Bulletin board systems
- Message board systems
- Newsgroups and discussion groups

2. **Ordering.** A customer may use electronic forms (similar to paper forms, available on the company's web site) or e-mail to order a product from a B2C site. A mouse click sends the necessary information relating to the requested item(s) to the B2C site. Figure 2-6 is a screen from the Amazon.com electronic order form.

3. **Payment.** The customer has a variety of options for paying for the goods or services. Credit cards, electronic checks, and digital cash are among the popular options (discussed in detail in Chapter 6).

4. **Fulfillment.** The fulfillment function could be very complex depending upon the delivery of physical products (books, videos, CDs) or digital products (software, music, electronic documents). It also depends on whether the

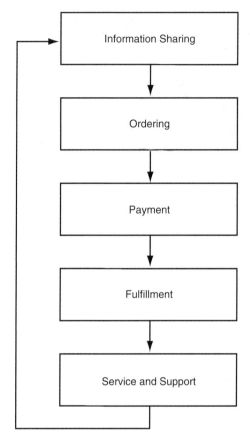

Figure 2-5   Major activities for business-to-consumer e-commerce.

e-business handles its own fulfillment operations or outsources this function to third parties. In any case, fulfillment is responsible for physically delivering the product or service from the merchant to the customer. In case of physical products, the filled order can be sent to the customer using regular mail, FedEx, or UPS. The customer usually has the option to choose from these various delivery systems. Naturally for faster delivery, the customer has to pay additional money. In case of digital products, the e-business uses digital certificates to assure security, integrity, and confidentiality of the product. It may also include delivery address verification and digital warehousing. Digital warehousing stores digital products on a computer until they are delivered. Several third-party companies handle the fulfillment functions for an e-business with moderate costs.

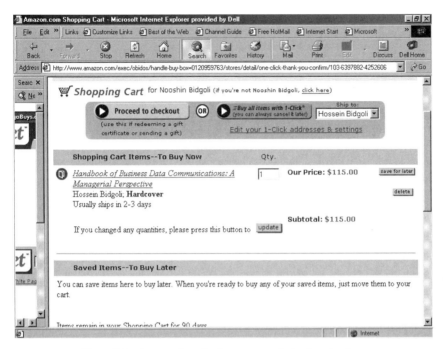

Figure 2-6 A screen from the Amazon.com electronic order form.

5. **Service and support.** Service and support are even more important in e-commerce than traditional businesses because e-commerce companies lack a traditional physical presence and need other ways to maintain current customers. It is much cheaper to maintain current customers than to attract new customers. For this reason, e-businesses should do whatever that they can in order to provide timely, high-quality service and support to their customers. The following are some examples of technologies and applications used for providing service and support:

- E-mail confirmation
- Periodic news flash
- Online surveys
- Help desk
- Guaranteed secure transactions
- Guaranteed online auctions

E-mail confirmation, periodic news flash, and online surveys may also be used as marketing tools. E-mail confirmation assures the customer that a particular order has been processed and that the customer should receive the product or service by a certain date. In most cases, the e-mail confirmation provides the customer with a confirmation number that the customer can use to trace the product or service.

Periodic news flash is used to provide customers with the latest information on the company or on a particular product or offering. Although online surveys are mostly used as a marketing tool, their results can assist the e-commerce site to provide better services and support to its customers based on what has been collected in the survey.

Help desks in the e-commerce environment are used for the same purpose as in traditional businesses. They provide answers to common problems or provide advice for using products or services.

Guaranteed secure transactions and guaranteed online auctions assure customers that the e-commerce site covers all the security and privacy issues. These services are extremely important because, as mentioned earlier, many customers still do not feel comfortable conducting online business.

The B2B e-commerce model uses a similar cycle, as shown in Figure 2-5; however, businesses use the following four additional technologies extensively:

- Intranets (see Chapter 4)
- Extranets (see Chapter 4)
- EDI (see Chapter 5)
- EFT (see Chapter 6)

2-9 BUSINESS-TO-BUSINESS E-COMMERCE: A SECOND LOOK

B2B is the fastest growing segment of e-commerce applications. B2B e-commerce creates dynamic interaction among the business partners; this represents a fundamental shift in how business will be conducted in the 21st century.

According to Jupiter, B2B online trade will rise to $6.3 trillion by 2005. B2B e-commerce reduces cycle time, inventory, and prices and enables business partners to share relevant, accurate, and timely information. The end result is improved supply-chain management among business partners [3,7]. Table 2-10 summarizes the advantages of B2B e-commerce. The following paragraph provides brief descriptions of these advantages.

A B2B e-commerce lowers production cost by eliminating many labor-intensive tasks. More timely information is achieved by the creation of a direct online connection in the supply chain. Accuracy is improved because fewer manual steps are involved. Cycle time improves because flow of information and products between business partners is made simpler. In other words, raw materials are received faster and information related to customer demands is more

Table 2-10

**Advantages of Business-to-Business
E-Commerce**

Lower production cost

More timely information

Increased accuracy

Improved cycle time

Increased communications

Improved inventory management

quickly transferred. Naturally this close communication between the business partners improves overall communication, which results in improved inventory management and control.

2-10 MAJOR MODELS OF BUSINESS-TO-BUSINESS E-COMMERCE

The three major B2B e-commerce models are determined by who controls the marketplace: seller, buyer, or intermediary (third party). As a result, the following three marketplaces have been created:

- Seller-controlled marketplace
- Buyer-controlled marketplace
- Third-party exchanges marketplace

A relatively new model, called trading partner agreements, facilitates contracts and negotiations among business partners and is gaining popularity. Each model has specific characteristics and is suitable for a specific business. The following paragraphs provide a description and examples of each.

2-10-1 SELLER-CONTROLLED MARKETPLACE

The most popular type of B2B model for both consumers and businesses is the seller-controlled marketplace. As Figure 2-7 shows, businesses and consumers use the seller's product catalog to order products and services online. In this model the sellers who cater to fragmented markets such as chemicals, electronics, and auto components come together to create a common trading place for the buyers. While the sellers aggregate their market power, it simplifies the buyers search for alternative sources.

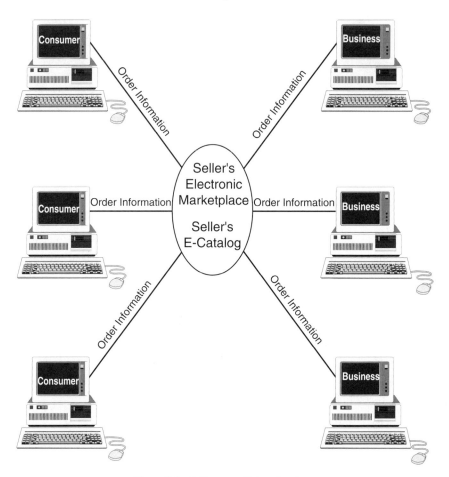

Figure 2-7   Seller-controlled marketplace.

One popular application of this model is e-procurement, which is radically changing the buying process by allowing employees throughout the organization to order and receive supplies and services from their desktop with just a few mouse clicks. E-procurement significantly streamlines the traditional procurement process by using the Internet and web technologies. This results in major cost savings and improves the timeliness of procurement processes and the strategic alliances between suppliers and participating organizations. It also offers all of the benefits and advantages outlined in Table 2-10.

Using e-procurement, the business logistics and processes reside on the side of the purchasing company (the receiving partner). The procurement application often has workflow procedures for the purchasing-approval process, allows connection to only company approved e-catalogs, and provides the employee with prenegotiated pricing. The main objective of e-procurement is to prevent buying from suppliers other than the preapproved list of sellers, which many companies will have for their normal procurement activities, and also to eliminate processing costs of purchases. Not following this process can be costly to the receiving company because it may result in paying higher prices for needed supplies [10].

By using ongoing purchases, e-procurement may qualify customers for volume discounts or special offers. E-procurement software may make it possible to automate some buying and selling, resulting in reduced costs and improved processing speeds. The participating companies expect to be able to control inventories more effectively, reduce purchasing-agent overhead, and improve manufacturing cycles. E-procurement is expected to be integrated into standard business systems with the trend toward computerized supply-chain management (discussed in Chapter 5). Using e-procurement, buyers will have local catalogs with negotiated prices and local approvals. Information Box 2-3 describes e-procurement applications at Schlumberger. Table 2-11 lists some of the major suppliers of e-commerce and B2B solutions. For the specific features of these solutions, contact the company.

INFORMATION BOX 2-3

E-Procurement at Schlumberger

E-procurement for order processing has paid off significantly at Schlumberger. The e-procurement application from Commerce One has reduced the cost of each order from $50 to $150 in wages for the time spent to fill out paperwork, route purchase orders for approval, get executive approval, and other administrative tasks to $10 to $20 for each order.

In order to control spending on office supplies and repair equipment, Schlumberger has employed e-procurement systems by releasing control of purchasing from a central station out to its employees. This system enables Schlumbergers' employees to contact hundreds of preapproved suppliers from their desktop. Employees are able to customize catalogs from preferred vendors to facilitate the ordering process. This new web-based e-procurement system replaced Schlumberger's proprietary EDI system. This new system has created a user-friendly interface, resulted in cost savings, and has increased flexibility by enabling Schlumberger to conduct business with a much more diverse group of suppliers. The Internet, by providing an inexpensive connection and an open platform, has significantly improved the availability and affordability of EDI. In most cases, Internet-based EDI is faster and considerably less expensive than traditional systems.

SOURCE: Ovans, A. (May–June, 2000). "E-procurement at Schlumberger." *Harvard Business Review*, pp. 21–22.

Table 2-11

**Major Vendors for Business-to-Business
E-Commerce Implementation**

Ariba

Aspect Development

Baan

BEA Systems

Broadvision

Commerce One

Heatheon/Webmd

I2 Technologies, Inc.

Internet Capital Group

Oracle

PeopleSoft

SAP

VerticalNet

Vignette

2-10-2 BUYER-CONTROLLED MARKETPLACE

Large corporations (e.g., General Electric or Boeing) with significant buying power or a consortium of several large companies use this model. In this case a buyer or a group of buyers opens an electronic marketplace and invites sellers to bid on the announced products or RFQs (request for quotation). The consortium among Daimler Chrysler, Ford, and General Motors (to which Toyota recently joined) is a good example of this model. Using this model the buyers are looking to efficiently manage the procurement process, lower administrative cost, and exercise uniform pricing [4].

Companies are making investments in a buyer-controlled marketplace with the goal of establishing new sales channels that increase market presence and lower the cost of each sale. By participating in a buyer-controlled marketplace a seller could do the following:

- Conduct presales marketing
- Conduct sales transactions
- Automate the order management process
- Conduct postsales analysis

- Automate the fulfillment process
- Improve understanding of buying behaviors
- Provide an alternate sales channel
- Reduce order placement and delivery cycle time

Figure 2-8 illustrates a buyer-controlled marketplace configuration. As this figure shows, the suppliers can bid on products or RFQs announced by the buyer or a group of buyers.

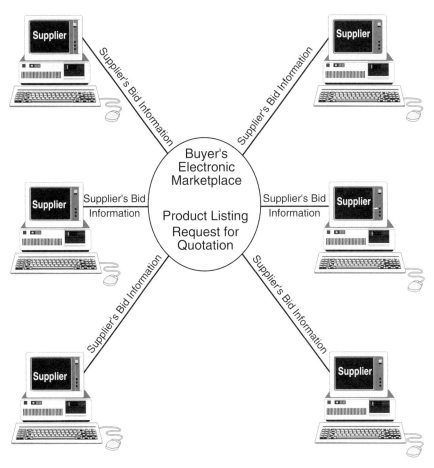

Figure 2-8 Buyer-controlled marketplace.

2-10-3 THIRD-PARTY-CONTROLLED MARKETPLACE

A third-party-controlled marketplace model is not controlled by sellers or buyers, but rather by a third party. The marketplace generates revenue from the fees generated by matching buyers and sellers. These marketplaces are usually active either in a vertical or horizontal market. A **vertical market** concentrates on a specific industry or market. The following are some examples of this type:

- Altra Energy (energy)
- Cattle Offering Worldwide (beef and dairy)
- Neoforma (hospital product supplies)
- PaperExchange.com (supplies for publishers)
- PlasticsNet.com (raw materials and equipment)
- SciQuest.com (laboratory products)
- VerticalNet.com (Provide end-to-end e-commerce solutions that are targeted at distinct business segments through three strategic business units: VerticalNet Markets, VerticalNet Exchanges, and VerticalNet Solutions.)

A **horizontal market** concentrates on a specific function or business process. They provide the same function or automate the same business process across different industries. The following are some examples of this type:

- IMark.com (capital equipment)
- Employee.com (employee benefits administration)
- Adauction.com (media buying)
- Youtilities.com (corporate energy management and analysis)
- BidCom.com (risk and project management services)

A third-party-controlled marketplace model offers suppliers a direct channel of communication to buyers through online storefronts. The interactive procedures within the marketplace contain features like product catalogs, request for information (RFI), rebates and promotions, broker contacts, and product sample requests.

Figure 2-9 illustrates a third-party-controlled marketplace configuration. As this figure shows, this is a virtual market with many buyers and many sellers that come together to conduct electronic transactions.

2-10-4 TRADING PARTNER AGREEMENTS: AN EMERGING APPLICATION

The main objectives of the **trading partner agreements** B2B e-commerce model are to automate the processes for negotiating and enforcing contracts be-

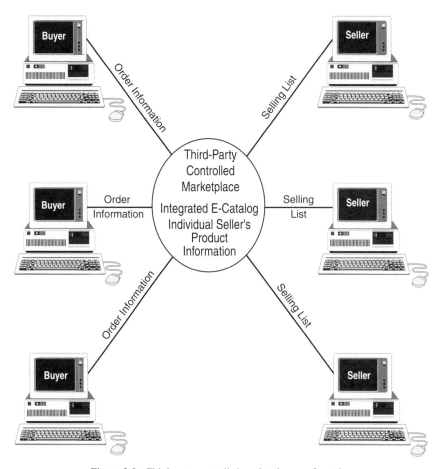

Figure 2-9   Third-party controlled marketplace configuration.

tween participating businesses. This model is expected to become more common as extensible markup language (XML) and the e-business XML initiative (ebXML) become more accepted. This worldwide project is attempting to standardize the exchange of e-business data via XML, including electronic contracts and trading partner agreements. Using this model enables customers to submit electronic documents that previously required hard-copy signatures via the Internet. An act passed by the U.S. Congress (in October 2000) gives digital signatures the same legal validity as handwritten signatures. By electronically "clicking" on the "button" entitled "I Accept," the sender inherently agrees to all of the terms and conditions outlined in the agreement. Using this model,

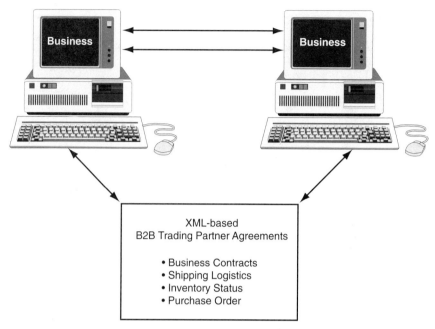

Figure 2-10   Trading partners agreements configuration. XML, extensible markup language; B2B, business-to-business.

business partners can send and receive bids, contracts, and other information required in the offering and purchase of products and services.

The agreement ensures that bids, signatures, and other documents related
to transactions are genuine when received electronically over the Internet.
The agreement is a substitute for all the hard-copy forms, ensuring that all
obligations created are legally binding for all trading partners. It binds the
parties to all the previously agreed upon requirements of the documents and
regulations.

XML, a subset of the standard generalized markup language (SGML), is a recent and flexible technology for creating common information formats that share
both the format of the information on the e-commerce infrastructure. XML describes the content in terms of what information is being described and transmitted. For example, a <BCONTRACT> could indicate that the information
transmitted was a business contract. In this case, an XML file is processed purely
as information by a program, stored with similar information on another web
site, or, similar to an HTML document, displayed using a browser. Using this
XML-based model, contracts are transmitted electronically, and many processes
between trading partners are performed electronically, including inventory sta-

tus, shipping logistics, purchase orders, reservation systems, and electronic payments.

The main advantage of XML over hypertext markup language (HTML) is that it can assign data type definitions to all the data included in a page. This allows the Internet browser to select only the data requested in any given search, leading to ease of data transfer and readability because only the suitable data are transferred. This may be particularly useful in m-commerce (mobile commerce); XML loads only needed data to the browser, resulting in more efficient and effective searches. This would significantly lower traffic on the Internet and speed up delay times during peak hours. At present, the technology for trading partner agreements is mostly based on EDI technology, either Web-based or proprietary. As will be discussed in Chapter 5, more and more proprietary EDI applications are being replaced with Web-based EDI. This will enhance ease of use, lower cost, and increase the availability of this technology for smaller and medium-sized corporations. Figure 2-10 illustrates a trading partner agreements configuration.

2-11 WIRELESS AND VOICE-BASED E-COMMERCE

Wireless e-commerce based on the wireless application protocol (WAP) has been around for several years. European countries have been using wireless devices for various e-commerce applications for many years. Many telecommunications companies including Nokia have been offering Web-ready cellular phones. Microsoft is offering a wireless version of its Internet Explorer called Mobile Explorer. Motorola, Nokia, and Ericsson are in partnership with Phone.com to offer wireless browsers. Phone.com has a full product line that allows complete information services to be developed and deployed for wireless devices. Major e-commerce companies are developing the simple, text-based interfaces required by today's screen-limited digital phones. Already, Amazon.com has made it possible to purchase various products using these wireless devices. Online brokerage firms such as Charles Schwab offer stock trading using wireless devices. Delta Air lines is testing a system to offer all flight information through wireless devices. (I will further discuss wireless e-commerce in Chapter 8). The next step in this revolution is voice-based e-commerce [6].

Just imagine picking up a phone and accessing a web site and ordering a product. This application already exists. At the core of these new services are voice recognition and text-to-speech technologies that have improved significantly during the past decade. Customers will be able to speak the name of the web site or service they want to access, and the system will recognize the command and respond with spoken words. By using voice commands, consumers would be able to search a database by product name and locate the merchant with the most competitive prices. At present, voice-based e-commerce will be suitable for applications such as the following [2]:

- Placing a stock trade
- Receiving sports scores
- Reserving tickets for local movies
- Buying a book
- Finding directions to a new restaurant

One method to conduct voice-based e-commerce is to use digital wallets (e-wallets) online (discussed in detail in Chapter 6). In addition to financial information these wallets include other related information, such as the customer's address, billing information, driver's license, and so forth. This information can be conveniently transferred online. Digital wallets are created through the customers' PCs and used for voice-based e-commerce transactions. Security features for voice-based e-commerce are expected to include the following:

- Call recognition, so that calls have to be placed from specific mobile devices

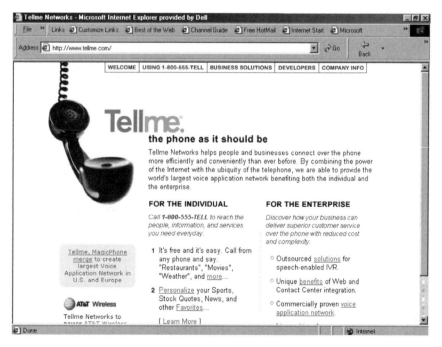

Figure 2-11   The initial screen of Tellme.com.

- Voice recognition, so that authorizations have to match a specific voice
- Shipping to a set address that cannot be changed by voice

There are already several voice portals on the market. The following are among the popular ones:

- BeVocal.com
- InternetSpeech.com
- Talk2.com.
- Tellme.com

Figure 2-11 shows the initial screen of Tellme.com voice portal. You may want to log onto this site and find out the latest on voice-based e-commerce.

2-12 INDUSTRY CONNECTION: AMAZON.COM CORPORATION

> Amazon.com Corporation
> 1200 12th Avenue South, Suite 1200
> Seattle, Washington 98144-2734
> Phone: 206-266-1000
> Fax: 206-266-2910
> Web site address: <http://www.amazon.com>

Amazon.com is one of the leaders in B2C e-commerce. Amazon.com opened its virtual stores in July 1995 with a mission to use the Internet to transform book buying into the fastest and easiest shopping experience possible. Amazon.com offers numerous products and services including books, CDs, videos, DVDs, toys, games, electronics, free electronic greeting cards, online auctions, and much more. In addition to an extensive catalog of products, Amazon.com offers a wide variety of other shopping services and partnership opportunities.

Amazon.com's business model is based on the merchant model discussed earlier in the chapter. By creating customer accounts, using shopping carts, and using the 1-click technology, Amazon.com makes the shopping experience fast and convenient. E-mail is used for order confirmation and customer notification when new products that suit a particular customer become available. Allowing customers to post their own book reviews, creates an open forum between the storefront and its customers. Using Amazon.com a prospective shopper can do the following:

- Search for books, music, and many other products and services
- Browse virtual aisles in hundreds of product categories from audio books, jazz, and video documentaries to coins and stamps available for auction.

- Get instant personalized recommendations based on the shopper's prior purchases as soon as the shopper logs on.
- Sign up for the Amazon.com e-mail subscription service to receive the latest reviews of new titles in categories that interest the customer.
- Browse Amazon.co.uk (for British books in print) and Amazon.de (for German books in print)

Amazon.com offers a safe and secure shopping experience by guaranteeing its shopping and auction services. It also offers 24-hour-a-day, 7-days-a-week help desk services to assist shoppers who experience difficulties. The Amazon.com family of web sites includes the following:

- The Internet Movie Database (www.imdb.com), the Web's comprehensive source of information on more than 150,000 movies and entertainment programs and 500,000 cast and crew members dating from 1992 to the present
- Live-event auctions (amazon.livebid.com), a provider of live-event auctions on the Web
- Web-based address book (www.planetall.com), a calendar and reminder service

Amazon.com partners include the following

- An online retail and information source for health, beauty, personal care, and pharmacy products, at www.drugstore.com
- An online sporting-goods company that offers new equipment in a wide range of categories, at www.gear.com
- An integrated Internet grocery-shopping and home-delivery service, with operations in Seattle, Washington; Portland, Oregon; Orange County, Los Angeles County, and San Diego, California; and Dallas, at www.homegrocer.com
- A comprehensive pet-supply company on the Web and a valuable source of free information for pet owners, at PETsMART.com (formerly www.pets.com)
- An online retailer of luxury products offering new and classic watches, fragrances, leather accessories, sunglasses, and writing instruments, at www.ashford.com
- A comprehensive site to find everything for the home, including furniture, bedding, lighting, linens, accessories, free professional advice, interactive design tools, and more, at www.living.com
- A leading online retailer of handcrafted products from around the world, at www.eziba.com[1]

---

[1]This information was gathered from the company web site and other promotional materials. For detailed information and any update, contact the company.

2-13 SUMMARY

This chapter defined value-chain analysis, explained the e-commerce role in the value-chain process, and reviewed popular e-commerce business models used by successful e-businesses. The chapter provided a detailed definition of e-commerce and e-business and reviewed the major components of e-commerce. E-commerce was compared to traditional commerce and the major categories of e-commerce were defined, including business-to-consumer (B2C), business-to-business (B2B), consumer-to-consumer (C2C), organizational (intrabusiness), consumer-to-business (C2B), and nonbusiness and government. The chapter explored the advantages and disadvantages of e-commerce and then explained major activities involved in a C2B e-commerce life cycle. Various business-to-business e-commerce models were described, including seller-controlled marketplace, buyer-controlled marketplace, third-party-controlled marketplace, and trading partner agreements. The chapter concluded with an overview of wireless and voice-based e-commerce as the most promising growth areas in the e-commerce environment and highlighted Amazon.com as the industry connection.

2-14 REVIEW QUESTIONS

1. What is value-chain analysis? What is the role of e-commerce in the value-chain process? Discuss.
2. What are some of the popular e-commerce business models? Why did so many "dotcom" companies go out of business in 2000 and 2001? Discuss.
3. What is e-commerce? Who are some of the pioneers in e-commerce developments? Discuss.
4. What is e-business?
5. What is the role of e-commerce in global information systems? Discuss.
6. Which businesses are the major beneficiaries of e-commerce? Which industries are among the first e-commerce users? Discuss. Why were these industries the earliest to adopt e-commerce?
7. What are some of the business uses of the Web? Discuss.
8. What are some of the products and services that can be purchased online?
9. Which companies are successfully using e-commerce?
10. Discuss the similarities and dissimilarities of e-commerce and traditional commerce.
11. How are orders generated in traditional commerce? How are they generated in e-commerce? Compare and contrast these two processes.

12. What are six major categories of e-commerce? Which category is the fastest growing? Discuss.
13. What are some of the differences between B2B and B2C e-commerce? Discuss.
14. What are some of the advantages of e-commerce? What are some of the disadvantages? Discuss.
15. How might some of the disadvantages and shortcomings of e-commerce be eliminated in the near future? Discuss.
16. What are some of the top B2C web sites? What do these popular sites do?
17. How does an e-business share information with its customers? What are some of the technologies and applications used for this process? Discuss.
18. What are some of the activities for conducting a B2B e-commerce?
19. What technologies and applications are used in B2B e-commerce? What are the roles of intranets and extranets? Discuss.
20. What are some of the advantages of B2B e-commerce? Discuss.
21. What are some of the major industries using B2B e-commerce? Do you see any similarities among these different industries? Discuss.
22. What are some of the advantages of e-procurement?
23. What are some of the popular B2B models? Discuss.
24. What has been achieved by e-procurement at Schlumberger? Discuss.
25. What are some examples of major platforms and software products for B2B e-commerce implementation?
26. Wireless and voice-based e-commerce are gaining in popularity. What are some of the unique features of these Web portals? What are some of their limitations? Discuss.

2-15 PROJECTS AND HANDS-ON EXERCISES

1. Log onto the web site of the Amazon.com Corporation at the following URL:

<http://www.amazon.com>

What products and services are offered by this company? Find a couple of e-commerce books sold by Amazon.com. Try to order a book or a CD from this site. This would be a great exercise and will show you the e-commerce cycle discussed in the chapter.
2. Log onto the following sites one-by-one and examine the materials presented on e-commerce.

InfoWorld	<www.infoworld.com>
Internet Week	<www.techweb.cmp.com>
Internet World (formerly Web Week)	<www.internetworld.com>
ComputerWorld E-commerce	<www.computerworld.com>
E-commerce.gov	<www.ecommerce.gov>
Computer Reseller News	<www.crn.com>
The New York Times	<www.nytimes.com>
GPO Access	<www.access.gpo.gov>

Prepare a three-page report regarding e-commerce operations and different categories of e-commerce discussed in the chapter. What are the latest on e-commerce presented on these sites?

3. Forrester Research provides information on information technologies and e-commerce. Log onto this site and find out the latest statistics on e-commerce:

<www.forrester.com>

According to this site, what are the best-selling items on the Web? What is the latest on B2B e-commerce? Discuss.

4. MasterCard allows you to apply for a credit card online. Log onto the following site and go through the first few screens in order to see how this process works. Also examine other services and products offered by this company.

<www.mastercard.com>

5. Wells Fargo provides all sorts of banking, e-commerce, and B2B services. Log onto the following site and click on Personal Finance:

<http://www.wellsfargo.com>

What services are offered under this category? Under Small Business? Under Commerce Services? What other banking and brokerage services are offered through this site?

6. Covisint B2B, an auto exchange formed by Ford, Daimler Chrysler, and General Motors, is a popular example of a B2B site. Log onto this site and click on "about covisint" to learn more about this B2B site. Then click on Procurement Tour, Catalog Services Demo, Seller Auctions Demo, and Buyer Auctions Demo one by one in order to understand how a B2B site operates.

<http://www.covisint.com>

7. Log onto FedEx (U.S. operations, www.fedex.com) and find information on e-commerce projects and services.

8. Log onto www.iprint.com and create your own business card.

9. Log onto www.ford.com and configure a car.

10. The following site from IBM provides comprehensive information on e-commerce. Log onto the site and review the e-commerce materials. By searching through the IBM site, examine other IBM e-commerce participations.

    <http://www.as400.ibm.com/developer/ebiz/documents/ecommerce.html#1>

11. The following site (Purchasing Online) includes valuable information on B2B e-commerce. It also includes comprehensive information on e-procurement:

    <http://www.manufacturing.net/magazine/purchasing/archives/2000/pur0323.00/032isupp.htm>

    By reviewing the materials presented in this site and other sources, prepare a two-page report on e-procurement. How is this technology saving money for its users? How does e-procurement improve efficiency? What are four main advantages of e-procurements over traditional procurements? Discuss.

12. The following sites include valuable information on trading partner agreements:

    <http://www.bcbsil.com/provider/ec/Etpains1.html>
    <http://www.wapa.gov/cso/procurmt/tpa.htm>

    By consulting these sites and other sources, prepare a two-page report on this B2B e-commerce model. What types of industries will benefit the most from this type of B2B model? What are some of the advantages of this model? What are some of its disadvantages? Discuss.

13. The following site (winmag.com) includes a listing of some of the best business sites:

    <http://www.winmag.com/101/standard/cov0048a.htm>

    Log onto the site and examine five of these sites. How might a small business benefit from this information? What are the differences between these online sites and their off-line counterparts? Discuss.

2-16 KEY TERMS

REFERENCES

1. Afuah, Allan, and Christopher L. Tucci (2000). *Internet Business Models and Strategies.* McGraw-Hill-Irwin, Boston, Massachusetts.
2. Anonymous (March 28, 2000). "Voice-Based E-Commerce Looms Large." *E-Commerce Times.* <http://www.ecommercetimes.com/news/articles2000/000328-1.shtml>
3. Banham, Russ (July 2000). The B-to-B. *Journal of Accountancy,* pp. 26–30.
4. Blankenhorn, D. (May 1, 1997). "GE's e-commerce network opens up to other marketers. *Net-Marketing.* http://www.tpnregister.com/tpnr/nw_ra.htm
5. Fickel, L. (June 1, 1999). "Online Auctions: Bid Business." *CIO Web Business Magazine.* http://www.cio.com/archive/webbusiness/060199_auct_content.html
6. Greenberg, Paul A. (December 22, 1999). "Get Ready for Wireless E-Commerce." *E-Commerce Times.*
7. Kobielus, James G. (2001). *BizTalk: Implementing Business-to-Business E-commerce.* Prentice Hall, Upper Saddle River, NJ.
8. Ovans, A. (May-June, 2000). "E-procurement at Schlumberger." *Harvard Business Review,* pp. 21–22.
9. Porter, Michael E. (1985). *Competitive Advantage: Creating and Sustaining Superior Performance.* Free Press, New York.
10. Purchasing online. Available: http://www.manufacturing.net/magazine/purchasing/archives/2000/pur0323.00/032isupp.htm

Chapter 3

Electronic Commerce in Action

Learning Objectives

After studying this chapter you should be able to do the following:

- Define online auctions.
- Explain the advantages and disadvantages of online auctions.
- Elaborate on the various types and categories of online auctions.
- Understand basic auction terminology.
- Identify key players in online auctions.
- Discuss important issues for managing an online auction site.
- Review the role of e-commerce in several important service industries, including tourism, publishing, higher education, real estate, banking, health care, and software distribution.

INFORMATION BOX 3-1

E-Commerce in the Spotlight

More and more companies are using business-to-business (B2B) auctions. Schlumberger, Inc., uses reverse auctions on the Web for product sourcing. Using reverse auctions, there is one buyer and many sellers (a many-to-one relation). Schlumberger's goal is to integrate Commerce One Auction Services with the company's SAP and other enterprise resource-planning systems.

The U.S. state and federal governments also use auctions for different purposes. For example, in January 2001, the State of California used online auctions to receive bids for electricity and gas supplies.

Many companies increasingly use Web portals or marketplaces, online auctions, and electronic bid and quote systems to reach their customers and suppliers.

Jim Zuffoletti, director of marketing for FreeMarkets, Inc., which conducts "controlled" reverse auctions for large buying organizations, says, "E-auctions can be valuable tools where buyers either do not have access to global market information or they wish to standardize their buys." For example, he says, "Individual suppliers will often negotiate different terms and conditions for contracts. Third-party market makers can equalize those terms."[a]

Zeus Tours and Yacht Cruises use the Web for press releases and e-mail for on-line bookings and communications.

Online employment agencies provide information about many available jobs worldwide and allow résumé posting and various online searches.

The Great Voice Company <http://greatvoice.com> helps people learn how to use their voices in interviews.

Several sites, including <www.resume-link.com> and <www.jobweb.com> assist in résumé writing and then post them on the Web.

[a]SOURCE: <http://www.evyaapaar.com/verticals/hospitality/knowledge/knowledgecenters20.asp> (Date of access: April 12, 2001).

INFORMATION BOX 3-2

Online Auctions Save Millions for Quaker Oats and SmithKline Beecham

Since 1997, Quaker Oats has saved $8.5 million by purchasing products and services via reverse online auctions, according to Carl Curry, vice president of integrated purchasing and logistics. SmithKline Beecham, a pharmaceutical and consumer health-care company, recently announced $3 million in savings through online auctions. Using reverse auctions, many sellers or suppliers bid prices down to win contracts. Both companies chose to conduct auctions at FreeMarkets, Inc. (freemarkets.com). Another popular web site where buyers can hold reverse auctions is BidtheWorld.com <http://www.bidtheworld.com>.

To conduct a reverse auction on the FreeMarkets web site, one first chooses which contracts will be offered for bid. A supplier evaluation process then begins, where the buying company decides which suppliers will be offered a chance to bid for the contract. At that point, FreeMarkets also searches its own list for qualified suppliers. The next step, Curry says, is to write the request for quotation (RFQ) and send it out via e-mail to all qualified suppliers, along with information as to when the bidding will take place.

After that, the buying company uses its Web browser to click onto the web site and watch the bidding. "The auctions generally take place in about 20 to 30 minutes," Curry says. "Then we determine who won the bid and award the contract from there."

SmithKline Beecham began using FreeMarkets in 1999 and since then has bid out more than $38.2 million worth of goods and services. Company management says this number represents a 10% decrease as compared to prices they used to pay.

FreeMarkets says it has facilitated more than $575 million worth of bids for indirect goods and services, saving an average of 13% for its global 1000 clients. The company says that, to date, 21 clients have used the electronic marketplace to source indirect material in more than 46 different product and service categories.

SOURCE: Purchasing Online: March 23, 2000. <http://www.manufacturing.net/magazine/purchasing/archives/2000/pur0323.00/032isupp.htm>

3-1 INTRODUCTION

This chapter first provides an overview of online auctions, their advantages and disadvantages, and explores several factors for their popularity. Commonly used auction terminology are introduced and different types of auctions reviewed, including consumer, B2B, English, Dutch, sealed-bid, double, and Vickrey second-price auctions. Major industry leaders in the auction world are introduced and important considerations for online auction site management discussed. The second part of the chapter covers the role of e-commerce in several service industries, including tourism, publishing, real estate, higher education, online employment, banking, brokerage firms, health care, and politics. The materials presented in this chapter clearly highlight the versatility of e-commerce and its phenomenal growth.

3-2 ONLINE AUCTIONS: AN OVERVIEW

Auctions help to determine the price of goods and services for which there is no predetermined price. An online auction is a straightforward yet revolutionary business concept. It brings traditional auctions to the Web by providing services to a geographically dispersed customer base and thus increases significantly the number of goods and services auctioned. Based on the brokerage business model (discussed in Chapter 2), auctions bring the buyers and sellers together in a virtual marketplace. Most of the revenue is generated by collecting commissions from the seller, buyer, or both. Auctions bring together buyers and sellers with similar interests who are geographically dispersed. Usually consumers participate in auctions for two specific reasons:

1. To buy an item for personal use, such as buying a piece of jewelry
2. To buy an item for resale, such as antiques

Individuals who have expertise in certain areas can find attractive deals using online auctions for resale purposes. Online auction companies allow users to include a description (in some cases also photos) of a product or service and a bid price to be auctioned for a limited time on their virtual auction sites. No inventories, delivery services, or money transactions (except for the posting fee) are involved in this service. For these reasons, this business model offers enormous profits for leading auctioneers. eBay, Inc. (the industry connection for this chapter) is a good example of a successful auction site.

Online auctions are the fastest growing segment of e-commerce. The popularity of online auctions is due to the following factors:

- The auctioneer collects fees from both sellers and buyers.
- The auctioneer sells advertisement on the site.
- Just about anything and everything (as long as it is legal) can be auctioned.
- The "virtual" audience spans the entire planet, providing an unprecedented customer base.

Online auctions are particularly cost effective for selling excessive inventories, memorabilia, or exotic automobiles. Corporations use B2B auctions to get rid of excessive inventories. The following are three of the most popular auction sites on the Web:

- ebay.com
- ubid.com
- priceline.com

3-3 BASIC AUCTION TERMINOLOGY

To better understand the discussion on online auctions, one should be familiar with the following list of common terminology:

Bidding. The act of placing a bid on an item that is being auctioned.

Bid cancellation. The cancellation of a bid by a seller or a buyer. Sellers may cancel the bid of any customer with whom they would be uncomfortable completing a transaction.

Bid increment. The predetermined amount by which a bid will be raised, based on the current high bid. This amount depends on the price of the product or service being auctioned.

Bid retraction. A cancellation of the bid by the bidder. Participants should exercise this option only in unusual circumstances because in many U.S. states by placing a bid, one is in a binding contract with the seller.

Minimum bid. The lowest amount that can be entered as a bid for a specific auction. This amount is established by the seller and posted on the auction page.

Proxy bidding. Placing a maximum bid, which is held in confidence by the online auction site. Depending on the auction site, the system will use only as much of the maximum bid as is necessary to maintain the bidder's high-bid position.

Relisting. Relisting is when an item has not sold and the seller wishes to list it again. This feature allows the seller to relist the item without reentering the original information. This process may vary in different auction sites.

Close date. Depending on a specific auction site, listings close at the hour specified by the seller. These dates are not automatically extended by last-minute bids, so it is possible for the listing to close between the time when the customer clicks "Bid Now" and the customer finally submits his or her bid. Closed items may continue to appear in listings for a few additional minutes, but the customer will not be allowed to bid on them.

Bid history. The list of bidders and activities for the item, including the customer, the bidder ID, bid amount, quantity won, bid date, as well as the status of each bidder, winning or losing. This page is updated on a real-time basis.

3-4 TYPES OF AUCTIONS

Online auctions have been established based on several business models. Some charge a fee to sellers, some to buyers, some to both. Some don't even charge a fee; they generate revenue by selling advertisement on their sites, taking a percentage of the transaction, or by charging commercial organizations a monthly fee. For the most part, they are based on the brokerage model (discussed in Chapter 2).

William Vickrey [8] established the basic classification of auctions based on the order in which prices are quoted and the manner in which bids are tendered. Auctions are also categorized by the dynamics of their offerings. There are two main categories of auctions: **consumer auctions** and **B2B auctions.** The major auction types under these categories are the following (see Figure 3-1):

- English
- Dutch
- Sealed-bid
- Double
- Vickrey

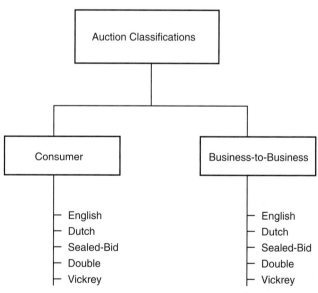

Figure 3-1   Auction classifications.

3-4-1 CONSUMER AUCTIONS

Online consumer auctions offer buyers the opportunity to purchase products or services that are not easily available at a fair price. Sellers benefit by offering very specific products and services to a broad target market that normally would be extremely narrow. A quick visit to an online auction site such as eBay confirms the above statement. Figure 3-2 shows the initial screen of eBay.

Online consumer auctions compared with traditional auctions present several drawbacks for consumers. Because most consumer auction sites are not directly involved in the actual transactions, satisfaction is not guaranteed by any of the parties. Most of the complaints are related to miscommunication and failure to meet buyers' expectations. Also, in some cases cheating may take place. For example, the seller may bid on his or her own product or service to increase the price. Other drawbacks are directly related to the nature of online shopping. To help meet the customer's expectations, auction sites encourage sellers to post quality photos and detailed descriptions of their products and services. This increases the perceived quality of the service and the tangibility of the product.

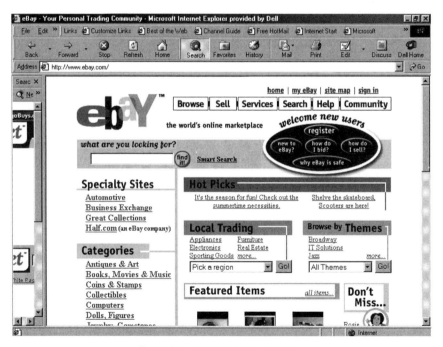

Figure 3-2   The initial screen of eBay.

To increase the reliability and satisfaction of online auctions, eBay created a rating system in which after each transaction, buyers can submit ratings of sellers and vice versa, providing an online history of business transaction satisfaction. eBay does not allow customers who have a feedback ratio of 1:3 negative over positive to do any transactions on its site. Additionally, sites such as eBay, Amazon, and Yahoo! have started offering a refund policy as a significant measure to attract uncertain potential customers. Also, as is introduced in the industry connection, auction sites such as eBay offer additional services, such as free insurance, escrow accounts, authentication, investigations and dispute resolution, reserve pricing (bids are not disclosed until after the auction ends), private auction (bidders' identities and winning bid amount are never disclosed), and proxy bid (the bidder specifies the maximum amount he or she is willing to pay and the system automatically bids for the customer against other participants until it reaches the maximum bid specified).

3-4-2 BUSINESS-TO-BUSINESS AUCTIONS

As opposed to consumers, corporations use B2B auctions. One of the major applications of B2B auctions is to get rid of excess inventory. This type of auction eliminates the need for liquidations brokers. Additionally, this type of auction optimizes the supply-chain process of very specialized or fragmented industries, such as chemicals.

A very creative B2B model is the one used by FreeMarkets.com (http://freemarkets.com). This company conducts online auctions for industrial parts, raw materials, commodities, and services. In these auctions, suppliers compete in real time for the purchase orders of large buying organizations by lowering their prices until the auction is closed. It also coordinates private online auctions where businesses solicit bids from potential suppliers, avoiding the lengthy process of sending information proposal packages to every participant. Figure 3-3 shows the initial screen of FreeMarkets.com.

As Figure 3-1 illustrates, both the consumer and business auctions can use English, Dutch, sealed-bid, double, or Vickrey auctions. A description of each type follows.

3-4-3 ENGLISH AUCTIONS

In English auctions (also called ascending price, open-outcry, or open auctions), the bidder openly offers a price and the maximum bid wins. In this type of auction, usually there is a minimum bid. If nobody offers a price larger than the minimum bid, the item is usually pulled out and not sold. If multiple quan-

Figure 3-3   The initial screen of FreeMarkets.com.

tities are offered, it is called a **Yankee** auction. The highest bidder gets all the items requested, and the remaining items are sold at successively lower prices. The major drawback to the bidder of the English auction is the spontaneous and emotional nature of the bidding process. It has been shown that a bidder may pay above and beyond his or her allotted budget for the product or service.

As an example of a Yankee auction, consider the following. Suppose there was a listing for 50 items. You bid $200/unit for 25 items. Another bidder then bids $200/unit for 50 items. Since the second bidder has bid on a larger quantity at the same price, that bidder would win.

3-4-4 DUTCH AUCTIONS

In a Dutch auction (also called descending-price auction), usually more than one item is up for bid at a time. The winning bidder pays the same price for all the items, which is the lowest winning bid on the items. In contrast with the English auction, the Dutch auction starts at a specific price and goes down.

Example #1: Single item requested: If 40 bids were made for 20 items, each bidder is bidding for one item, and the 20th highest bid was $65, all 20 high bidders will pay $65—even if the highest bidder bid was $95.

Example #2: Multiple items requested: A single seller puts 12 identical items up for sale in a Dutch auction. At the close of the auction, there are multiple bids from four different bidders. Bidder one has bid $20 on each of the six items; bidder two has bid $14 on three items; bidder three has bid $10 each on three items; and bidder four has bid $8 on two items. In this case, bidder one would receive all six for $10 each, and bidder two and three would receive three for $10, while bidder four's bid would be unsuccessful. In essence, high bids secure a "right to buy" among the winning bidders.

3-4-5 SEALED-BID AUCTIONS

Using sealed-bid auctions the bidder submits only one bid, and the bid is kept secret from the other bidders. The bidder with the highest bid wins and pays his or her bid. Because only one bid is allowed for each bidder, the preparation of the bid is important. The advantage of this approach is that it is free from the threat of collusion, as no one knows what anyone else is doing, and emotional bidding will not take place here.

3-4-6 DOUBLE AUCTIONS

Using double auctions both sellers and buyers submit bids, which are then ranked from highest to lowest to generate demand-and-supply profiles. From the profiles, the maximum quantity exchanged can be determined by matching selling offers (starting with the lowest price and moving up) with demand bids (starting with the highest price and moving down). This format allows buyers to make offers and sellers to accept those offers at any particular moment.

3-4-7 VICKREY SECOND-PRICE AUCTIONS

The second-price auction or the Vickrey auction is named after William Vickrey, winner of the 1996 Nobel Prize in Economic Sciences. Similar to sealed-bid auctions, the bids are sealed, and each bidder is unaware of other bids. The item is awarded to the highest bidder at a price equal to the second-highest bid (or highest losing bid). In other words, a winner pays less than the highest bid. If, for example, bidder X bids $20, bidder Y bids $30, and bidder Z offers $40, bidder Z would win; however, he or she would only pay the price of the second-highest bid, namely $30.

3-5 KEY PLAYERS IN ONLINE AUCTIONS

eBay, Inc. (introduced at the end of the chapter) is the industry leader of online consumer auctions, specializing in consumer auctions. It has more than 6 million registered customers. One source of revenue for eBay is a fee collected from sellers. Although some competitors offer their services for free, eBay's CEO claims that its fee strategy keeps quality products on their site. However, in response to competitors' pressure, eBay changed its policy to a final-value fee in which sellers only pay if they sell their items. Other key players in online auctions include the following:

- Amazon Auctions
- Auction World <http://www.a-world.com>
- Bid.com
- Egghead.com (formerly onsale.com)
- Priceline.com
- Ubid.com
- Yahoo! Auctions

Some online auction sites target niche markets, such as GolfClubExchange.com, CNET Auctions (trades mostly electronics and computer hardware and software), and GunBroker.com. Because the market is starting to become very competitive with these types of companies, newcomers are reaching specialty markets such as toys, real estate, art, firearms, and computers. Auction pioneers are expanding geographically and focusing in regional areas to better serve local demands. For example, eBay recently opened eBay L.A., eBay Australia, eBay Canada, eBay Germany, eBay Japan, and eBay United Kingdom.

As a result of increased competition and the need to increase their markets, online auction companies are creating partnerships and merging with conventional auction houses. For example, eBay recently acquired Butterfields, the third largest U.S. auction house (www.ebaygreatcollections.com). In addition, companies such as Microsoft are creating business partnerships with companies with a strong online presence, such as Excite@Home, to enter the online auction business.

3-6 ONLINE AUCTION SITE MANAGEMENT

Undoubtedly online actions could be a very lucrative business, particularly for those companies with a strong brand name recognition such as eBay. However, some key issues must be regularly monitored to assure the continued success of this fast-growing e-commerce. Similar to any other businesses, online auction sites should offer quality customer service. It is generally believed that keeping current customers is a lot cheaper than attracting new ones. Also, because competition is on the rise, competitive pricing and service differentiation play important roles for continued success.

As will be introduced in Chapter 12, the majority of e-commerce suites or B2B platforms provide auction-building facilities. Suites or platforms are combinations of hardware and software that collectively provide many of the tools and features needed for creating an e-commerce presence, such as templates, authoring tools, hosting services, auctions, shopping carts, and so forth. Oracle, Ariba, and Commerce One are some examples of these platforms. The key challenges for online auction sites are the delivery of timely, high-quality service and maintaining site security and customer privacy.

What the site offers should be carefully analyzed. Whether to offer products such as alcohol, weapons, pornography, and tobacco could raise liability issues and negative publicity. Timeliness is essential. Sites that offer the best service in the fastest time are the winners. Early in 2000, eBay operations were halted for several hours for lack of bandwidth. In February 2000, several major sites were forced to suspend operations for a few hours due to the denial of access created by computer hackers. These important issues must be carefully analyzed. (I will explain social and legal issues in Chapter 10 and security issues and measures in Chapter 11).

3-7 E-COMMERCE IN SERVICE INDUSTRIES: AN OVERVIEW

In addition to online auctions described earlier, several service industries have significantly benefited from e-commerce and its supporting technologies. E-commerce has enabled these businesses to offer their services and products to a broad range of customers with more competitive prices and convenience. The Web offers numerous tools and advantages to these businesses to sell their products and services all over the world. However, the fall of many e-commerce sites (dotcom companies) in 2000 and 2001 is a clear indication that the winners are those who have a sound business model. In addition to using rigorous marketing and advertising tools (discussed in Chapter 7), e-commerce sites should also consider the following factors in order to bring customers to their site and encourage these customers to come back for repeat shopping:

• Use of communities
• Rich content
• Price discrimination
• Bundling
• Building economies of scale

In the rest of the chapter I review the major beneficiaries of e-commerce. In addition to industries introduced in the next few pages, it should be noted that many retailers are also taking advantage of this new sales channel and are complementing their traditional businesses with an e-commerce presence. Toys-R-Us, the Gap, Wal-Mart Stores, Sears, and K-mart are a few successful examples. Also, B2B continues to grow, and many businesses report significant savings by doing transactions among business partners online.

3-7-1 TOURISM AND TRAVEL

Tourism and travel industries have significantly benefited from various e-commerce applications. The Tropical Island Vacation <http://www.tropicalislandvacation.com> (Figure 3-4) home page directs prospective vacationers to an appropriate online brochure after responding to a few brief questions about the type of vacation they would like to take. Customers simply point and click on appealing photographs or phrases to explore further. Zeus Tours <http://zeustours.com> has been very effective at offering unique and exciting tours, cruises,

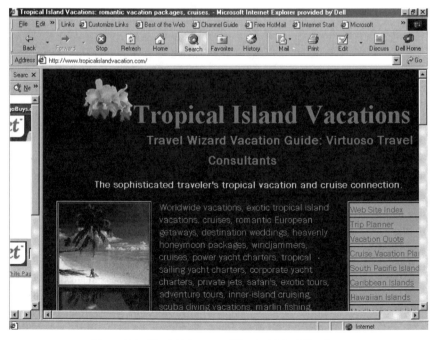

Figure 3-4   The initial screen of Tropical Island Vacations.

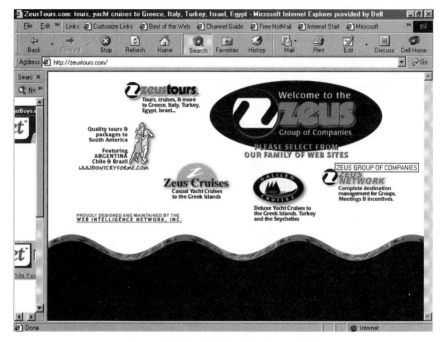

Figure 3-5   The initial screen of Zeus Tours.

and other travel packages online (see Figure 3-5). Many web sites allow customers to reserve tickets for planes, trains, buses, cruises, hotels, and resorts. Sites such as biztravel.com <http://biztravel.com> allow business customers to plan a trip, book a vacation, gather information on many cities, gather weather information, and much more.

3-7-2 Publishing

Many major textbook publishers in the United States have home pages. A student or a professor can read the major features of forthcoming books or books in print before ordering them. Some publishers include a sample chapter from specific books on the Web. Some book publishers even include several complete books that you can read online for free for 90 days. Harcourt, a major textbook publisher, allows online customers to purchase portions rather than the entire book. Figure 3-6 shows the initial screen of Academic Press, the publisher of this text. As you see in this screen, a prospective buyer can search the online catalog

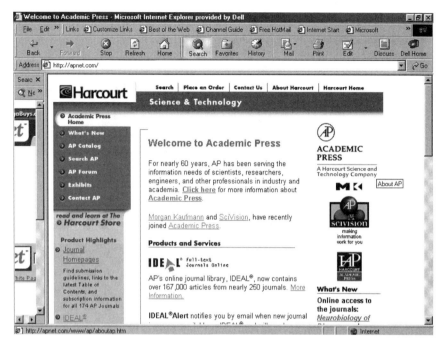

Figure 3-6   The initial screen of Academic Press.

based on the author's name, the title of the book, and so forth. When the desired book is found, it can be ordered online.

The forthcoming *Encyclopedia of Information Systems* project (for which I serve as editor-in-chief) <http://www.apnet.com/infosys> uses the Web to stay in touch with authors, editors, progress reports, and editorial guidelines. The encyclopedia offers A–Z coverage of key information systems topics.

3-7-3 HIGHER EDUCATION

Major universities also have home pages. One can tour the university and read about different departments and programs, faculty, and academic resources. Many universities throughout the world are creating virtual divisions that offer entire degree programs on the Web. Many professional certificate programs are also offered through the Web. These programs and courses provide opportunity and convenience for individuals in remote areas and individuals who cannot attend regular classes. They also provide a source of revenue for many colleges

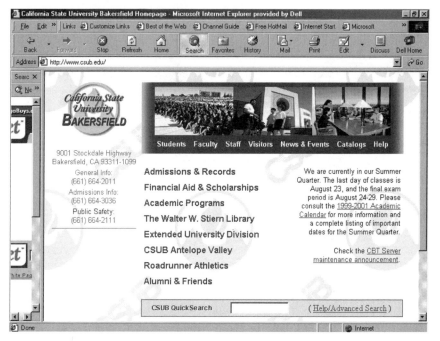

Figure 3-7   The initial screen of California State University, Bakersfield.

and universities facing enrollment decline. They also allow renowned experts to teach a course to a broad geographic audience. Figure 3-7 is the initial screen of California State University, Bakersfield, where I teach.

3-7-4 REAL ESTATE

Numerous real estate web sites provide millions of up-to-date listings of existing and new homes for sale throughout the world. These sites are devoted entirely to buying and selling real estate. The buyer or seller can review neighborhoods, schools, and local real estate prices. These sites allow the customer to find a realtor or a brokerage firm and learn many home-buying tips. Some of these sites offer or will soon offer virtual tours. These virtual tours enable a buyer to view a prospective property from a distance. This is achieved by using virtual reality technologies. For example, eHome (www.ehome.com) (Figure 3-8) provides step-by-step online purchasing and selling instructions. Figure 3-9 shows

Figure 3-8 The initial screen of eHome.com.

Figure 3-9 Yahoo! real estate site.

the initial screen of Yahoo! Real Estate. Some of the services offered by this real estate site are listed below:

- Appraisal services
- Buying
- Neighborhood profiles
- School profiles
- Financing
- Home-improvement advice
- Obtaining credit reports
- Posting a free listing
- Renting services
- Selling advice and much more

Table 3-1 lists other major real estate sites.

3-7-5 EMPLOYMENT

Employment service providers have established a Web presence. Table 3-2 lists some of the popular sites to find or recruit for a job, especially if it involves information technology. Figure 3-10 shows the initial screen of Monster.com. Most companies provide classified ads and job search information, but they differ in the software tools that they offer. Career Connections allows companies to hold online job fairs by leasing its Internet site. Online shelf life is longer than with newspaper ads. When you run an ad in the newspaper, you receive the bulk of your responses in the first two or three days after it appears. When you put something online, you get responses for three or four weeks.

Table 3-1
Online Real Estate E-Commerce Examples

Prudential California (prudential.com) provides wireless listing services and property data for agents.

ERA (era.com) is an Internet-based application with listing information for agents.

Century 21 (century21.com) is an electronic system for tracking agent referrals worldwide.

Re/Max (remax.com) is a contact management tool for agents that interface with Palm Pilot.

Homestore.com lists more than 1.3 million properties throughout the United States.

Mortgage Expo (mortgageexpo.com) lists more than 800 home lenders throughout the United States.

Table 3-2

Some of the Popular Sites to Find or Recruit for a Job

Career Connections

Career Mosaic

Careerbuilder.com

E-Span

Hotjobs.com

Monster Board

Monster.com

Online Career Center

Webhire

Headhunter <http://www.headhunter.net>

Dice <http://www.dice.com>

Guru <http://www.guru.com>

Figure 3-10   Monster.com initial screen.

Home pages for recruiting should contain company information, including objectives and culture, employee benefits, and job opportunities. Basic home pages can be developed with moderate cost. Many companies develop home pages for just about any type of business. Readily available tools enable a user with minimal computer skills to design basic home pages. With proper training these tools can also be used for designing sophisticated home pages. Examples of these tools include the following:

- Macromedia Dreamweaver
- Microsoft FrontPage
- Netscape Composer

Packages (discussed further in Chapter 12) such as the following also provide step-by-step instructions for creating sophisticated Web pages and e-commerce sites:

- Bigstep.com (Bigstep.com Corp.)
- FreeMerchant <http://freemerchant.com>, a division of Network Commerce Inc.)
- Ecargo.com <http://ecargo.com>

3-7-6 BANKING AND BROKERAGE FIRMS

Online banking is here. Many U.S. and Canadian banks and credit unions offer online banking services. Figure 3-11 shows the initial screen of Wells Fargo, a leader in online banking. Although online banking has not been fully accepted by customers, many banking-related resources are being utilized. For example, many banks use e-mail to communicate with their corporate customers. E-mail is a less expensive alternative to a telephone call, especially for long distances. Financial reports for banks can be easily distributed via e-mail to mutual-fund investors or customers.

The banking industry's ultimate goal is to carry out many of their transactions through the Web. Consumer reluctance has kept this business from exploding. It is generally believed that a secure nationwide electronic banking system is almost in place. Soon people will use their PCs and the Web to do all types of banking activities.

As will be discussed in Chapter 6, digital signatures are a key technology for the banking and brokerage industry, as they provide an electronic means of guaranteeing the authenticity of the sending party and assurance that encrypted documents have not been changed during transmission. The current trends in mergers and acquisitions and frequent downsizing within the financial industry strongly support Internet banking. Table 3-3 lists some of the services available by using the Web for banking activities [4].

Figure 3-11 The initial screen of Wells Fargo Bank.

Brokerage firms such as Charles Schwab, National Discount Brokers, and Merrill Lynch offer stock and other security transactions online, including quotations for stocks, bonds, and other securities. To encourage more customers to use these services, they offer discounts. Figure 3-12 shows the initial screen for National Discount Brokers, a highly successful online brokerage firm. Fidelity Investments has established a home page to provide mutual fund information, interactive financial planning modules, and other financial services.

3-7-7 Software Distribution

Several major software vendors offer online software on the Web. Customers can view listings of available software and order and designate an installation time. Microsoft and several other software companies already offer free software via the Web. Routine downloading of the Netscape Navigator and Microsoft Internet Explorer browser applications are two good examples. Both are relatively small programs (12 to 22 MB). In contrast is the Microsoft Office Suite, which would take significantly longer to download through an online application service provider. Given today's communications throughput and bandwidth

Table 3-3

**Some of the Services Available Using the Web
for Banking Activities**

Customer service by e-mail, 24 hours a day, 7 days a week

Access to old transactions

Account credit card payments online

Bill paying

Categorizing transactions and producing reports

Exporting banking data to popular money management software

Free checks, free foreign ATM use, and free online bill payment

Funds transfers

Instant approval for personal loans

Interactive guides to aid selection of a proper product

Interactive tools to design a savings plan, choose a mortgage, and/or
obtain online insurance quotes all tied to applications

IRA and brokerage account information

Loan status and credit card account information online

Online application for both checking and savings accounts

Online forms for ordering checks and issuing a stop payment

Online funding for checking accounts

Online mortgage and CD applications

Viewing digital copies of checks

Written guarantee against fraud and late payment

---

limitations, program size will definitely pose a challenge to online software distribution. McAfee Associates sells software online via the honor system.

The development of online copyright-protection schemes continues to be a challenging problem. If users need an encryption code to "unlock" software, backups may not be possible. However, the odds are in favor of electronic software distribution, as it provides an inexpensive, convenient, and speedy method of purchase and implementation [5,6].

3-7-8 HEALTH CARE

Electronic patient records on the Web could provide complete medical information and allow physicians to order lab tests, admit patients to hospitals, refer

Figure 3-12 Initial screen of National Discount Brokers.

patients to other doctors or specialists, and order prescriptions. Test and consultation results would be directed automatically to electronic patient records. The advantages of this approach include the fact that all patient information would be accessible in one central location. Another positive side of this application is that it would allow easy access to critical health information. Imagine a person who is far away from home and runs into a serious health problem due to injury or other causes. Any doctor in any location will be able to download the complete medical history of this individual and prescribe a suitable treatment in a short period. However, these systems have some disadvantages, such as problems with information privacy, accuracy, and currency.

Telemedicine <http://telemedtoday.com> may provide the medical profession with the ability to conduct remote consultation, diagnosis, and conferencing. This could result in major annual savings in travel costs and overhead for medical care professionals. As part of the information superhighway, a personal health information system (PHIS) could conceivably provide interactive medicine tools to the public. Public kiosks located in shopping malls would be equipped with user-friendly computer equipment for network access. Patients would be prompted through the diagnosis procedure by a series of questions.

Premature onset of disease could be minimized with this aggressive and proactive approach [2].

Virtual medicine on the Web may allow specialists at major hospitals to operate on patients remotely. Telepresence surgery, as this is called, would allow surgeons to operate all over the world without physically traveling anywhere. A robot would perform the surgery based on the digitized information sent by the specialist over the Internet. Robots would have stereoscopic cameras to create three-dimensional images for the surgeon's virtual reality goggles. Doctors would operate in a virtual operating room. Tactile sensors on the robot would provide position information to the surgeon so that he or she feels what the robot feels. Already, prescription drugs are sold online, and several web sites offer medical services [3].

Figure 3-13 shows the initial screen of WebMD Corporation that links health-care-related information systems and other supporting systems, such as eligibility, referrals, diagnostics, and so forth. WebMD provides the health-care industry with connectivity and a full suite of services that improve administrative efficiencies and clinical effectiveness. The company's products and services facilitate information exchange, communication, and transactions between the con-

Figure 3-13   The initial screen of WebMD Corporation.

sumer, physician, and health-care institutions. HEALTHteacher.com, as a part of WebMD, provides alternative approaches to improving school-based health education. HEALTHteacher.com provides a comprehensive, sequential K–12 health education curriculum that consists of almost 300 lesson guides that meet National Health Education Standards and provide skills-based assessment methods. HEALTHteacher.com is designed to address the significant health and behavioral issues facing today's youth and their classroom teachers. Information Box 3-3 reviews other applications of e-commerce in health care.

INFORMATION BOX 3-3

E-Commerce in Support of Health Care

E-commerce applications have been used in the health-care industry for many years. Currently, anyone can retrieve health-related documents from general media sites or get more specific information from specialty sites, such as the American Heart Association's web site <www.americanheart.org>. The site offers tips on reducing the risk of stroke and heart disease.

The new Organ Procurement Transport Network (OPTN) is a much more sophisticated way to use the Web for health-care purposes. The OPTN is a Web-based database that links over 50,000 patients to 460 transplant organizations. The network stores information that is relevant to the transplant needs of the patient, and it is used to coordinate the transportation of organs when a transplant is made. The Bergen Medical Imaging center (BMI) recently created another database that allows doctors to access the results of radiology tests from any computer with Web access. The system allows specialists from around the world to instantly view a patient's X rays. A company called Vicon Motion Systems that specializes in 3-D animation software is developing applications that will be used by surgeons to diagnose specific injuries and determine how to correct them. Vicon's software is known as motion capture; it records the movements of a model that is wearing magnetic sensors attached to its body. A surgeon will be able to map surgery plans by comparing the recorded movement of an injured limb with that of the computerized healthy one. NASA has already demonstrated a "virtual hospital" in which doctors can evaluate patients and even perform practice surgical procedures via the Web. Eventually, this system may be used to treat patients in remote areas, or even in space.

SOURCES: Kirk LaPointe (1996). "Use Your Computer to Become a Heart Specialist." *Calgary 1 Herald,* pg. D13, September 12; Anonymous (1998). "Internet Gaining as Tool for Medical Professionals." *Newsbytes,* April 24; Heather Clancy (1996). "Animation to Reach New Arenas—Developers Find Uses For Technology In Medical Field, Not Just the Entertainment Industry." *Computer Reseller News.* pg. 53, September 2.

3-7-9 POLITICS

In recent years the Web has become a major promotional tool for all major political contenders in races for the White House, the House of Representatives, the Senate, and other races. Political candidates use the Web to announce their platforms, their major differences with their opponents, their leadership styles, forthcoming debates, political events, and so forth. They even use the Web for fundraising.

The Web may empower voters and revitalize democracy. Twenty-first century citizens may vote using a computer connected to a communications network by a modem, resulting in increased participation. Part-time legislators may have remote access to Washington, and they may be able to remain geographically close to their constituents. Of course, an identification system will have to be in place, which could very likely use voice identification, face scan, finger image, or some other biometric verification technology. If such a system becomes available then security of voting application, results, and counting accuracy must be carefully analyzed. Currently, the U.S. House of Representatives is attempting to put all pending legislation online. Presidential documents can be found on the Web. Full-text versions of speeches, proclamations, executive orders, press briefings, daily schedules, the proposed federal budget, health-care reform documents, and the Economic Report of the President are available. There are a number of repositories of this information that can be found using search engines.

3-7-10 EMERGING APPLICATIONS

Businesses are using the Web in a multitude of creative ways. The owner of a New York neon sign company found African power transformer specifications by conducting a search at an electrical engineering college in South Africa. E-mail is used extensively for business applications. IBM engineers use the Web to communicate with other companies on development work rather than driving to each other's labs. Using the Web enhances cross-functional teams. In today's increasingly global environment, teams can be geographically dispersed and become incredibly flexible. The Web will serve as a powerful tool to bring these teams together with minimal cost.

Since 1991 the Internet Weather Channel has provided weather observations and forecasts by the University of Michigan. The information available includes temperature highs and lows, precipitation, sunrise and sunset, forecasts and extended forecasts, hurricane advisories, earthquake locations, tornado path reports, images of the latest eclipse, videos of famous blizzards, and air pollution modeling software. Both textual and graphical formats are available. In addition, Canadian and international reports are included [7].

Senior citizens are finding extended family on the Web. A newsgroup called SeniorNet has over 34,500 members globally, and seniors go online to chat with others and to obtain a rich new source of friends and information. Connecting with younger generations has been facilitated by Web links to schoolchildren. SeniorNet has been likened to the "equivalent of the old folks sitting around the village square." This "intellectual mobility" is particularly important for nonmobile seniors who are physically restricted. Two million seniors were recently identified as computer users. They are also using the Web to monitor investments, to track genealogy, to produce memoirs, and to perform Web research as a business. SeniorNet began as a small research project in 1986 and now serves as a major international nonprofit organization that has taught over 100,000 older adults to use computers and the Internet. With a global membership of more than 34,500 people, two thriving online communities, a network of over 180 locally run computer learning centers, and a variety of educational publications, SeniorNet offers comfort and community to a population that was initially neglected during the information revolution [1].

The vast majority of computer and peripheral manufacturers have web sites that not only contain information on their latest products, but also "driver download" areas that allow you to select your specific computer or peripheral and download the latest driver for that equipment. Drivers are small programs that enable different hardware and software programs to work with each other. For example, you may have to download and install a particular driver in order to enable your printer to work with certain software programs. The advantage to this is that you have online access to this information, giving you the ability to obtain bug fixes, capability enhancements, and so forth.

3-8 INDUSTRY CONNECTION: EBAY, INC.

eBay, Inc.
2145 Hamilton Avenue
San Jose, California 95125
Telephone: (408) 558-7400
Fax: (408) 558-7401
Web site address: <http://www.ebay.com>

Pierre Omidyar launched eBay on Labor Day in 1995. eBay is the world's largest personal online trading site. eBay created a new market: efficient one-to-one trading in an auction format on the Web. Individuals and large businesses use eBay to buy and sell items in more than 4,300 categories, including automobiles, collectibles, antiques, sports memorabilia, computers, toys, Beanie

Babies, dolls, coins, stamps, books, magazines, music, pottery, photography, electronics, jewelry, gemstones, and much more. As the leading consumer auction site, buyers are attracted to trade on eBay due to the availability of a large number of products and services. Similarly, sellers are attracted to eBay to conduct business with a great number of buyers. eBay provides over 4 million new auctions and 450,000 new items every day from which customers may choose. eBay provides a user-friendly site that even novices are able to use for trading. Many online instructions and help features walk customers through the entire bidding process. Some of the services offered by eBay include the following:

Free Insurance. If the customer feels that he or she has been defrauded and meets the insurance guidelines, the customer may file a claim for insurance. eBay is backed by Lloyds and will reimburse the customer up to $200, with a $25 deductible, if Lloyds deems that the customer has been a victim of fraud.

Safe harbor. This is eBay's comprehensive safety resource and protective arm. It provides fraud prevention and insurance and informs the customers about items that can and cannot be sold.

Escrow services. This service allows a buyer to place money in the custody of a trusted third party. The money is then paid to the seller once predefined sets of conditions are met. eBay uses the **i-Escrow** Company to provide this service to eBay customers.

Authentication. eBay has links to companies that provide authenticity of a product or service. Using this service, the customer can get a quick, preliminary opinion online regarding an item's authenticity before buying it. This service is currently available only for sports autographs and memorabilia. The customer can find out whether an item is genuine based on an independent authenticator's physical inspection. Alternatively, the customer can determine the physical condition of an item.

Investigations. The investigations team attempts to resolve reported cases of inappropriate trading behavior. eBay will consider the circumstances of an alleged offense and the user's trading history and records before taking action.

Dispute resolution. By using the services of the **Square Trade** dispute-resolution provider, eBay offers two services: a free Web-based forum that allows customers to attempt to resolve their differences on their own, or, if necessary, the use of a professional mediator.[1]

3-9   SUMMARY

This chapter first provided an overview of online auctions, their advantages and disadvantages, and introduced several reasons for their popularity. Com-

---

[1] This information was gathered from the company web site and other promotional materials. For detailed information and any update, contact the company.

monly used auction terminologies were introduced, including different types of auctions, such as consumer, B2B, English, Dutch, sealed-bid, double, and Vickrey second-price auctions. Major industry leaders in the auction world were introduced and important considerations for online auction site management discussed. The second part of the chapter explored the role of e-commerce in several service industries, including tourism and travel, publishing, real estate, higher education, online employment, banking, brokerage firms, health care, and politics. eBay.com was the industry connection. The materials presented in this chapter clearly highlighted the versatility of e-commerce and its phenomenal growth.

3-10 REVIEW QUESTIONS

1. What are the two major reasons why individuals participate in online auctions?
2. Why are online auctions so popular?
3. Name three popular online auction sites.
4. What are some of the reasons why eBay has maintained its leadership in consumer online auction market? Discuss.
5. What is proxy bidding? How does it work?
6. What is bid history? What is included in a bid history? Discuss.
7. What are some of the differences between consumer auctions and B2B auctions?
8. Who are some of the pioneers in B2B auctions? Discuss.
9. What are English auctions? How do they work?
10. What are Dutch auctions? How do they work?
11. What are sealed-bid auctions? How do they work?
12. What are double auctions? How do they work?
13. What are Vickrey second-price auctions?
14. What are some of the considerations for online auction site management? Discuss.
15. What is the role of e-commerce in travel and tourism?
16. What are some of the possible services offered by e-commerce in the tourism industry? Discuss.
17. What are some of the advantages of a traditional versus an online travel business? Discuss.
18. What are some of the services offered through online real estate companies?
19. What are some of the advantages of online real estate over traditional real estate companies? Discuss. What are some of the possible drawbacks? Discuss.

20. What services are offered through an online employment agency? What are some of the advantages of these online firms over traditional employment agencies? Discuss.
21. What services are offered through online banks? What are some of the advantages of online banking over traditional banking? What are some of the drawbacks? Discuss.
22. What services are offered through online brokerage firms? What are the advantages of these firms over traditional brokers? What are their shortcomings? Discuss.
23. Who are the key players in the online brokerage firms?
24. What are the advantages of online software distribution? What are the shortcomings? Discuss.
25. In what ways do politicians use the Web?
26. What are some of the health-care applications of the Web? What are the shortcomings?

3-11 PROJECTS AND HANDS-ON EXERCISES

1. Log onto the web site of the eBay Inc. at the following URL:

   <http://www.ebay.com>

   What services and products are offered by this company? Why has eBay been so successful in consumer auctions? Who are eBay's competitors? Discuss. What are some of the challenges for a company such as eBay? Discuss.
2. By referring to the materials presented in this chapter and reviewing the materials presented in the following sites and other sources, list two advantages and two disadvantages for each auction type.

   <http://www.agorics.com/auctions/auction6.html>
   <http://www.suite101.com/article.cfm/online_auctions/36527>

Auction type	Advantage	Disadvantage
Consumer		
Business-to-business		
English		
Dutch		
Sealed-bid		
Double		
Vickrey second-price		

3. By referring to the materials presented in this chapter and other sources, list two advantages and two disadvantages of e-commerce in the following four areas.

	Advantages	Disadvantages
Tourism		
Publishing		
Higher education		
Real estate		

4. Compare and contrast traditional and online banking. What are two advantages of online banking? What are two disadvantages? What are some of the obstacles that must be resolved before a full-feature online banking service can be implemented? Discuss.
5. The following sites provide comprehensive listings of terminologies used in online auctions. By referring to these sites and other sources, define the following commonly used auction terminologies:

<http://exchange.techsmart.com/scripts/glossary.asp>
<http://www.auctions.nytoday.com/scripts/FAQS.asp>

Auction agent
Proxy bidding
Maximum bid
Reserve price
Escrow

6. Log onto Tropical Island Vacations at the following web site:

<http://www.tropicalislandvacation.com>

What are some of the services and products offered by this company? What are some of the advantages of this online travel agency over a traditional travel agency? What are some of the disadvantages? Discuss.
7. Log onto Century 21 at the following web site:

<http://www.century21.com>

What real estate products and services are offered by this company? Who are this company's major competitors? How is an online realtor different from a traditional realtor? What are some of the advantages of each? What are some of the disadvantages? Discuss.
8. Mortgage Expo.com (mortgageexpo.com) lists more than 800 home lenders throughout the United Sates. Log onto the site and examine the offerings of a couple of these companies. What are some of the

differences between an online mortgage company compared to a traditional mortgage company? What are some of the advantages and disadvantages of each? Discuss.

9. Hotjobs.com <http://hotjobs.com> provides numerous employment opportunities. Log onto the site and examine its offerings. What are some of the differences between an online employment agency compared to a traditional employment agency? What are some of the advantages and disadvantages of each? Discuss.

10. National Discount Brokers is a highly successful online brokerage firm. Log onto the following web site and examine its offerings:

<http://ndb.com>

What are some of the differences between an online compared to a traditional brokerage firm? What are some of the advantages and disadvantages of each? Discuss.

11. Log onto the *Telemedicine Today* web site at the following URL:

<http://telemedtoday.com>

What are some of the materials discussed in this magazine? What is the role of the Internet and e-commerce in the health care industry? How might e-commerce applications and technologies improve the quality of health care? Discuss.

12. Sorcity.com <http://sorcity.com> and MaterialNet.com <http://www.materialnet.com> are two sites that provide reverse auctions. Log onto these sites and examine their offerings. What are some of the differences between regular auctions and reverse auctions? Which business type and application might benefit from reverse auctions? Discuss.

13. The homeowners.com web site provides all types of home-buying services. Log onto this site and calculate the mortgage payment for a $100,000 loan at an 8% interest rate and a 15-year payback period.

<http://homeowners.com/index2.html>

14. The following site provides diverse information on real estate services:

<http://www.escrow.com>

Log onto the site and examine its offerings. What are some of the differences between this company and Century 21 <http://www.century21.com>? What are some of their similarities? Discuss.

3-12 KEY TERMS

Banking, 100–101
Business-to-business auctions, 88
Consumer auctions, 87–88
Double auctions, 90
Dutch auctions, 89–90
English auctions, 88–89
Health care, 102–105
Higher education, 95–96
Online auction management, 91–92
Online auctions, 84–85

Online employment, 98–100
Politics, 106
Proxy bidding, 85
Publishing, 94–95
Real estate, 96–98
Sealed-bid auctions, 90
Software distribution, 101–102
Tourism and travel, 93–94
Vickrey second-price auctions, 90
Yankee auction, 89

REFERENCES

[1] <http://www.seniornet.org/press/000607.html>. Seniornet research report reveals similarities in Internet use between U.S. and Japanese seniors (date of Access April 12, 2001).

[2] Anonymous (August, 1994). "Heath Care on the Information Superhighway Poses Advantages and Challenges." *Employee Benefit Review,* pp. 24-29.

[3] Bazzolo, F. (May, 2000). "Putting patient at the center." *Internet Health Care Magazine,* pp. 42-51.

[4] Carter, Merkle (1999). "Internet Banking Incentives: What Online Services Are Financial Institutions Offering their Customers?" Bankino.com

[5] Cross, Richard (October, 1994). "Internet: The Missing Marketing Medium Found." *Direct Marketing,* pp. 20-23.

[6] Hayes, Mary (January 2, 1995). "Online Shopping for Software." *Information Week,* pp. 23-24.

[7] Notess, Greg, R. (October, 1994). "The Internet Weather Channel," *Database,* Vol. 17, No. 5, p. 95.

[8] Vickrey, William. "Counterspeculation, Auctions, and Competitive Sealed Tenders." *Journal of Finance,* Vol. 16 (March, 1961), pp. 8-37.

Chapter 4

Intranets and Extranets

Learning Objectives

After studying this chapter you should be able to do the following:

- Define the term *intranet* and compare and contrast it with the Internet and extranets.
- Outline major phases for the construction and successful maintenance of an intranet site.
- Discuss the importance of security and privacy issues in intranet and extranet development.
- Discuss intranet site marketing for promoting increased utilization.
- Discuss several major applications of intranets and extranets.

115

INFORMATION BOX 4-1

Intranets and Extranets in Action

An intranet is an effective solution for companies that need access to enterprisewide information on demand. The primary applications of an intranet include sales and marketing, product development, customer service and support, and human resources. Speed, ease of use, convenience, security, and cost effectiveness are some of the advantages of a corporate intranet.

VISA International estimates that it will save over 2 million pieces of paper as member banks are given access to the VISA intranet to transact online inquiries.

In June 1998, Lockheed Martin rolled out its intranet to over 170,000 employees spread among 640 domestic and 45 international locations.

Eli Lilly & Company, the pharmaceutical giant based in Indianapolis, has an intranet of more than 12,000 pages. It covers a broad range of information, from directory listing to product information and pension plans.

Intranet connection has become a major sales tool of Hewlett-Packard's sales force for acquiring product information, competitive intelligence, and ideas for winning sales pitches.

Some companies use intranets for regular e-mail and e-mail with multimedia attachments.

Boise Cascade, a paper and office product company, has recently launched its extranet as an alternative to the less flexible and more costly private networks it previously used.

In the near future, a significant portion of e-commerce will be conducted through extranets.

System security is one of the major concerns for establishing an operational extranet.

Wal-Mart has been an industry leader in the development of extranets. Using extranet technology, Wal-Mart has established a very close relationship with its suppliers. A true just-in-time inventory model has become a reality for Wal-Mart. Suppliers are able to find out about inventory status and deliver needed goods in a timely manner.

Polaroid Corporation is building an expansive extranet that gives suppliers limited access to its databases and makes 40% of its U.S. sales over an electronic data interchange (EDI) service. Polaroid has used EDI for 2 years and has connections to many major customers, including Wal-Mart Stores.

A popular example of an extranet is the Federal Express Tracking System. Using this system a customer can access FedEx's public site, enter his or her tracking number, and locate any package still in their system. Their package shipping service allows the customer to enter all the information needed to prepare a shipper form, obtain a tracking number, print the form, and schedule a pick-up.

INFORMATION BOX 4-2

Extranets in Action: Boeing Corporation

Boeing's rocket engine designers are using collaborative extranet applications to re-vamp how they build rocket engines. By doing this they have been able to cut de-velopment costs by a factor of 100. Costs were the foremost concern. Boeing's competitors had begun to import Russian-built rocket engines at sharply dis-counted prices. In some cases, those engines were selling for "not a lot more than freight for the engines," said Robert Carman, program manager for advanced propulsion at Rocketdyne. "We elected to build a new baseline engine to com-pete." That strategy presented a major challenge: to drastically reduce production cycles and cut costs by a factor of 100. To achieve this, Boeing needed to be more productive in the design phase by placing a strong emphasis on concurrent engi-neering with suppliers.

Prior to using the extranet, Boeing would contract with a supplier to build a particular part to a predetermined specification, requiring extensive upfront work. In the extranet pilot project, Boeing drafted engineers from supplier firms with-out specific roles in mind for them. The extranet yielded a more free-flowing cre-ative process that was tightly monitored through revisions because the extranet is a repository for project data. The results were dramatic, Carman said.

The product, normally made up of 140 different parts, was redesigned with only 5 parts. First unit costs or the cost to develop an initial version dropped from $1.4 million to $50,000. Design time was compressed from 7 man-years to less than 1 man-year. The engine is being tested now and will soon go into production.

SOURCE: Richard Karpinski, March 15, 1999, *InternetWeek*. Available: <http://www.internetwk. com/news0399/news031599-4.htm>

4-1 INTRODUCTION

Intranets support organizational or intrabusiness e-commerce-related activi-ties, and extranets support business-to-business (B2B) e-commerce. Due to their importance and versatility, this entire chapter is devoted to these two important topics. Intranet and extranet technologies have been effectively used in the e-commerce environment, and their popularity is on the rise. The chapter defines intranets and compares and contrasts intranets with the Internet and extranets. The chapter discusses in detail eight major steps for the development and main-tenance of a successful intranet program. These steps include establishing goals and problem definition, cost and benefit analysis, formation of the task force, construction of a prototype, assessing security and privacy issues, tool selection, implementation, and postimplementation audit and intranet site marketing. The chapter concludes with a detailed discussion of various applications of intranets and extranets in the business world, highlighting IBM Corporation as the industry connection.

4-2 WHAT IS AN INTRANET?

The excitement created by the Internet has been transferred to another growing application called intranets. In simple terms, whatever you do with the Internet you should be able to do with an organization's private network or intranet. A 2000 survey indicates that all fortune 500 companies either have established an intranet or are planning to do so very soon.

Since the computer's inception in 1946, medium- and large-sized organizations have used these machines to access timely, accurate, and meaningful information to gain a competitive advantage. Information systems have improved the efficiency and effectiveness of decision makers. Until 1995 the client–server model that promoted intracompany collaborative capabilities, such as e-mail and newsgroups, was the approach of choice for companies to support their growth. As will be discussed in Chapter 8, client–server describes the relationship between two computer programs in a network environment in which one program (the client) makes a service request from another program (the server), which fulfills the request. Internet technology has provided a worldwide connectivity for all types of organizations by improving the capabilities of client–server systems. The point-and-click approach for finding information using hypermedia has been well received by millions of workers and decision makers.

The creation and use of intranets is the next logical step in client–server technology. An intranet provides users with easy-to-use access that can operate on any computer regardless of the operating systems. Intranet technology helps companies disseminate information faster and more easily to both vendors and customers and can be of benefit to the internal operations of the organization. Although intranets are fairly new, they have attracted a lot of attention in a very short time.

The intranet uses Internet and Web technologies to solve organizational problems traditionally handled by proprietary databases, groupware, scheduling, and workflow applications. One should understand that an intranet is different from a local area network (LAN) or wide area network (WAN), although it uses the same physical connections. An intranet is an application or service (or set of applications or services) using the computer networks (the LANs and WANs) of an organization, which makes it different from LANs and WANs. The intranet is only logically internal to the organization. Intranets can physically span the globe, as long as access is specifically defined and limited to the specific organization's community of users behind a firewall or a series of firewalls. As will be discussed in Chapter 8, a LAN consists of two or more computers and other

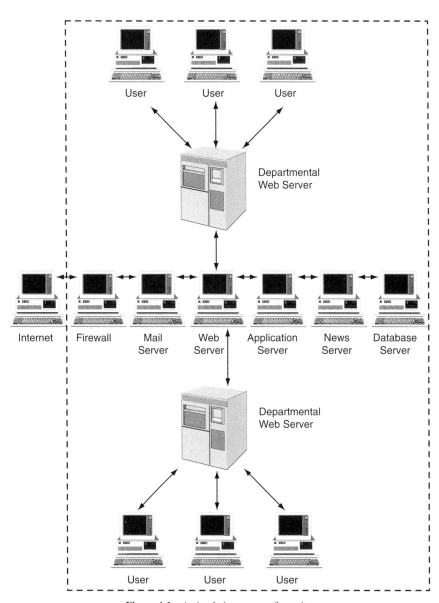

Figure 4-1   A simple intranet configuration.

peripheral equipment connected in close proximity. A WAN does not limit itself to a certain geographical area. It may span several cities, states, or even countries. Usually several different parties own it. LAN and WAN technologies are geographically oriented; intranet technologies are not.

Figure 4-1 illustrates a simple intranet configuration. As this figure indicates, all users in the organization have access to all the web servers. The system ad-

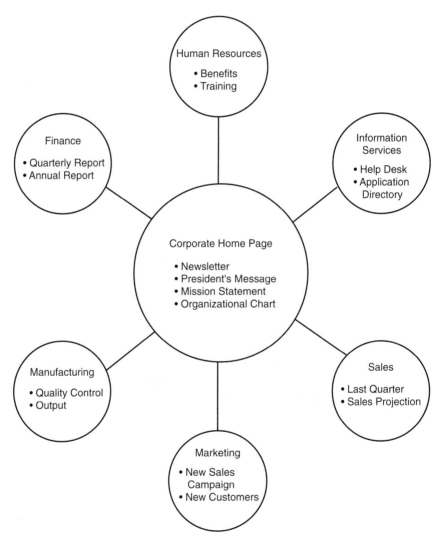

Figure 4-2   An organization intranet structure.

ministrator must define the degree of access for each user. They can constantly communicate with one another and post information on their departmental web servers. However, as the figure shows, a firewall (or several firewalls) separates these internal networks from the Internet (the worldwide network).

Within these departmental web servers, individual employees can have their own web pages broken down by department through a series of web pages. For example, the following departments each may include several web pages as parts of the organization's intranet program (see Figure 4-2):

- Finance
- Human resources
- Information services
- Manufacturing
- Marketing
- Sales

So what is an intranet? In simple terms, an intranet is a network within the organization that uses web technologies—Transmission Control Protocol/Internet Protocol (TCP/IP), hypertext markup language (HTML), file transfer protocol (FTP), hypertext transfer protocol (HTTP), extensible markup language (XML), and simple mail transfer protocol (SMPT)—to collect, store, and disseminate useful information throughout the organization. This information supports e-commerce activities such as sales, customer service, marketing, and so forth.

Employees can find internal information, and they can bookmark important sites by using an intranet. Furthermore, individual departments can create their own web sites (Figure 4-2) to educate or inform other employees about their departments by implementing intranet technology. For example, marketing can present the latest product information, while manufacturing can post shipping schedules and new product designs. The human resources department can post new jobs, benefit information, recent promotions, and 401K plan information. The finance and accounting departments can post cost information and other financial reports on their sites. The president's office might post the next company picnic on its site. This information collectively supports a successful e-commerce program.

4-3 WHAT ARE EXTRANETS?

Interorganizational systems (IOSs) facilitate information exchange among business partners. Some of these systems, such as electronic funds transfer (EFT) and e-mail, have been used in traditional businesses as well as in the e-commerce environment. Among the most popular IOSs are electronic data interchange (EDI) (discussed in Chapter 5) and extranets (discussed in this chapter). Both EDI and extranets provide a secure connection among business partners. Their role in B2B e-commerce is on the rise. These systems create a seamless environment that expedites the transfer of information in a timely matter.

Some organizations allow customers and business partners to access their intranets for specific business purposes. For example, a supplier may want to check inventory status or account balances. These networks are referred to as extranets. It should be noted that an organization usually makes only a portion of its intranet accessible to these external parties. Also, comprehensive security measures must ensure that access is given only to authorized users and trusted business partners.

For the purpose of this book I define an extranet as a secure network that uses Internet and Web technology to connect two or more intranets of business partners, enabling B2B communications. An extranet is a network service that allows trusted business partners to have secure access to information assets on another organization's intranet. Figure 4-3 illustrates a typical extranet configuration. Table 4-1 provides a comparison of the Internet, intranet, and extranet [15].

As discussed in this chapter, there are numerous real-life applications of extranets in the e-commerce world. One such example is Toshiba America, Inc. Toshiba has designed an extranet for timely order-entry processing. Using this extranet, more than 300 dealers can place orders for parts until 5 P.M. for next-day delivery. Dealers can also check accounts receivable balances and pricing arrangements, read press releases, and much more. This secure system has resulted in significant cost savings and improved customer service [20].

Another example of an extranet is the Federal Express Tracking System (see Figure 4-4) (www.fedex.com). Federal Express uses its intranet to collect information and make it available to customers over the Internet. The FedEx web site is one of the earliest and best known examples of an extranet—an intranet that is open to external users. The customer can access FedEx's public site and enter a tracking number to locate any package still in the system. Using this system, a customer can enter all the information needed to prepare a shipping form, obtain a tracking number, print the form, and schedule a pick-up.

Extranets provide highly secure, temporary connections over public and private networks between an organization and a diverse group of business partners outside of the organization. These groups may include the following:

- Customers
- Vendors
- Suppliers
- Consultants
- Distributors
- Resellers
- Outsourcers, such as claim processors, or those with whom the company is doing collaborative research and development (R&D) or other collaborative work, such as product design

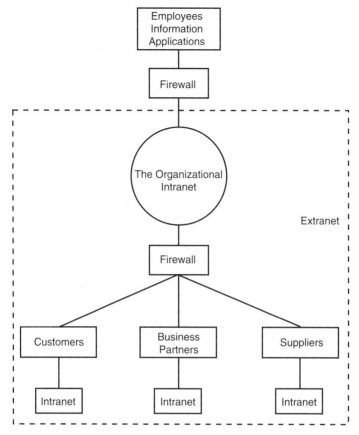

Figure 4-3 A typical extranet configuration.

Table 4-1

Comparison of the Internet, Intranet, and Extranet

	Internet	Intranet	Extranet
Access	Public	Private	Private
Information	Fragmented	Proprietary	Shared by close business partners
Users	Everybody	Members of an organization	Groups of closely related companies

Figure 4-4   FedEx extranet (www.fedex.com).

Extranets not only allow companies to reduce internetworking costs, but they also provide a competitive advantage, which leads to increased profit. A successful extranet program requires a comprehensive security system and management control. The security system should provide comprehensive access control, user-based authentication, encryption capability, and comprehensive auditing and reporting capabilities. (I discuss security issues and measures in detail in Chapter 11.)

An extranet offers an organization the same benefits that an intranet offers, while also delivering the benefits of being linked to the outside world. Some of the specific advantages of an extranet include the following:

• **Coordination**—An extranet allows for improved coordination among participating partners. This usually includes suppliers, distributors, and customers. Critical information from one partner can be made available so that another partner can make a decision without delay. For example, a manufacturer can coordinate its production by checking the inventory status of a customer.

• **Feedback**—An extranet enables an organization to receive instant feedback from its customers and other business partners. It gives the consumers an opportunity to express their views about products or services before those products or services are even introduced to the market.

• **Customer satisfaction**—An extranet links the customer to an organization. This provides the customer with more information about products and services and the organization in general. This also makes ordering products or services as easy as a click of the mouse. Expediting B2B e-commerce is definitely one of the greatest benefits of an extranet.

• **Cost reduction**—An extranet can reduce inventory costs by providing timely information to the participants of a supply-chain program. Mobil Corporation, based in Fairfax, Virginia, designed an extranet application that allows distributors throughout the world to submit purchase orders. By doing this, the company increases the efficiency of the operation significantly. It also expedites the delivery of goods and services [21].

• **Expediting communication**—Extranets increase the efficiency and effectiveness of communications among business partners by linking intranets for immediate access to critical information. A traveling salesperson can receive the latest product information from his or her hotel room before going to a sales meeting. A car dealer can provide the latest information to a customer on a new model without making several phone calls and going through different brochures and sales manuals.

A group of automakers, dealers, and financial institutions have jointly developed an extranet application, called automotive network exchange (ANX) to exchange sales performance and customer satisfaction statistics in nationwide dealerships. This system is expected to connect more than 15,000 dealerships. This interconnection will facilitate access to customer-specific data regardless of the customer location. This network enables the sales force to improve their sales performance by providing online access to promotional, inventory, and financial information useful for closing deals [25].

ANX has significantly expanded its operations in recent years. Now, some of the biggest companies in the world have been trading confidential designs and sensitive EDI documents using the network. With more than 300 trading partners online, another 150 waiting in the queue, and a new owner with financial support and a global presence, the ANX is set to expand into other industries, placing any company on the list of prospective candidates. Other industries targeted as possible ANX users include trucking, chemical, plastics, steel, and railroad industries. Individual companies also have expressed interest. For example, appliance maker Whirlpool Corporation says it is interested in using the ANX to trade with suppliers [9].

In a law firm, for example, an extranet can be used to leverage existing web technologies to create an interactive attorney–client data warehouse. For example, through the use of a web browser, clients and/or corporate counsel view the

status of a case, review current attorneys' fees and costs, and preview and com-
ment on other key data. Traditional methods of reporting this information required clients to pay for and wait for staffers to search through file cabinets to
find all those answers. An extranet allows a law firm to provide its clients with
cost-effective access to critical data—24 hours a day, 7 days a week [1].

Table 4-2 [11] lists other companies using extranet technologies. Other case
examples will be presented at the end of the chapter. Table 4-3 lists some of the
general applications of extranets by major sectors.

Table 4-2

Companies Successfully Using the Extranet Technologies

Cisco posts more than $11 million in orders daily from resellers using its extranet. This has
    resulted in significant savings in technical support, marketing, and distribution costs.

Dell Computer customizes access to its extranet through the use of its Premier Page program,
    which serves over 19,000 high-volume worldwide corporate customers. It automatically
    generates purchase orders and allows customers to track their purchases.

Federal Express's extranet allows customers to print shipping labels, request pick-ups, and track
    their shipments.

Ford Motor Company's extranet, called Ford Supplier Network, provides suppliers with frequent
    updates on their performance in quality ratings, on-demand delivery ratings, and recalls. It also
    provides information on product development process reengineering and customs data for
    international part orders.

General Electric's extranet used for bidding processes has reduced the purchasing cycle from 14
    days to 7. (An example of buyer-controlled B2B e-commerce)

Heineken USA, the North American distributor of Heineken products, has established an extranet
    called Heineken Operations Planning System (HOPS) that allows the 450 local distributors to
    access the information used by the company for inventory control.

Marshall Industries uses its extranet to manage its relationship with over 65,000 customers and
    over 100 suppliers throughout the world. Suppliers can monitor sales activities to allow for
    demand satisfaction. It also provides requests for quotation to its customers.

McDonnell Douglas uses an extranet to accommodate its document-distribution tasks. This has
    resulted in reductions in delivery time, errors, and document duplication.

Charles Schwab's extranet, called eSchwab, allows more than 400,000 customers to access a
    private web site daily for personalized account information, to conduct trades, and to take
    advantage of interactive financial tools.

Carson Wagonlit Travel offers an extranet to its travel agents. The extranet uses push technology
    from BackWeb to deliver relevant travel information that the agent can deliver to customers in a
    personalized way. The system ties together travel suppliers, agents, and customers.

Table 4-3

General Applications of Extranets by Major Sectors

Sector	Applications
Government	Electronic filing of Security Exchange Commission documents and tax documents
Manufacturing	Order status and online order placement by customers
Pharmaceutical	Gathering test data from different sources for drug testing conducted by researchers throughout the world
Service industries	Providing access to corporate databases, account information, and for transfer of funds to their customers
Transportation	Allowing customers to check the availability schedules for their truck, rail, and air fleets
Utilities	Allowing customers to access account and utilization status

4-4 THE INTERNET VERSUS INTRANETS

In Chapter 1 I explained the Internet in some detail. In this section I briefly highlight the similarities and dissimilarities between the Internet and intranets. The Internet is a public network. Any user can access the Internet assuming the user has an account with an Internet service provider (ISP). The Internet is a worldwide network, whereas intranets are private and are not necessarily connected to the World Wide Web (WWW). Intranets are connected to a specific company network, and the users are usually the company's employees. An intranet is separated from the Internet through a firewall (or several firewalls). Intranets usually have higher throughput and performance than the Internet and are generally more secure than the Internet.

Apart from the above-mentioned dissimilarities, the two have a lot in common. They both use the same network technology, TCP/IP, and they both use browsers such as Microsoft Internet Explorer or Netscape Navigator. They both use documents in HTML and XML formats, and both are capable of carrying documents in multimedia format. Also, they both use the Java programming language for developing applications. As will be discussed in Appendix A, Java is an application development platform that replaces PCs with simple network computers equipped with small memory and often no hard drive. Java applications normally reside on a server and are delivered to the client as needed, centralizing data storage on servers and easing client–computer administration. Java downloads nuggets of application code, known as applets, from server to client on demand, regardless of computer platform.

Table 4-4

The Internet versus Intranet[a]

Key feature	Internet	Intranet
User	Anybody	Employees only
Geographical scope	Unlimited	Limited to unlimited
Speed	Lower than intranet	Higher than Internet
Security	Lower than intranet	Higher than Internet
Technology used	TCP/IP	TCP/IP
Document format	HTML/XML	HTML/XML
Multimedia capability	Could be lower than intranet	Could be higher than Internet

[a]TCP/IP, Transmission Control Protocol/Internet Protocol; HTML, hypertext markup language; XML, extensible markup language.

Intranets may or may not use any of the technologies beyond HTML (i.e., Java programming, Java Applets, JavaScript or VbScript, Active X, Dynamic HTML) or XML. (These technologies are reviewed in Appendix A.) An advantage of an intranet is that since the organization can control the browser used, it can specify a browser that will support the technologies used. Beyond Web documents, the organization can also specify the use of the Internet phone, e-mail, videoconferencing, and other Web technologies supported by the chosen browser. Table 4-4 summarizes the similarities and dissimilarities of these two technologies.

4-5 DEVELOPING AN INTRANET SITE

Developing an intranet or extranet is similar to developing other e-commerce applications. This means that a formal life-cycle approach similar to the one introduced in Chapter 12 should be followed. The following phases are used to develop an intranet site [8]:

- Establishing goals and problem definition
- Cost and benefit analysis
- Formation of the task force
- Construction of a prototype
- Assessing the security and privacy issues
- Tool selection
- Implementation
- Postimplementation audit and intranet site marketing

4-5-1 ESTABLISHING GOALS AND PROBLEM DEFINITION

Prior to the implementation of an intranet, similar to other information systems projects, an organization must set goals for the project. What the organization is trying to achieve should be specified as precisely as possible. Establishing goals will enable a prospective organization to measure the degree of success or failure at a later date. The goals might include improving communications among the functional areas for better advertising campaigns, supporting sales activities, creating an organizationwide platform for e-commerce activities, improving inventory control, and so forth.

Several methods can be used to develop an intranet for an organization. An intranet can start small and grow. A company can try out an intranet pilot project to publish a limited amount of information, for example, personnel policies, on a single platform and measure the results. If the pilot is successful then additional content can be added and more departments and organizational units can participate.

During the problem-definition phase for building an intranet site, a likely area for deployment must be identified. The information flow and the needs within the organization must be identified. An area that has appeal to a broad user group should be chosen. This can be done by examining the company's newsletter, human resources procedural handbooks, employee benefits handbook, and competitive sales information. The next step is to identify the content source or authors who will be responsible for the intelligence behind the information and for delivering it. Some of this information may already be available in written or electronic forms; in other cases the entire content may have to be developed from scratch. To identify where the information resides is always a challenging task. Is it in a series of word-processing documents, spreadsheets, or database documents? Does it exist in the minds of the employees? Should it be collected from external sources?

4-5-2 COST AND BENEFIT ANALYSIS

Most organizations already have some kind of communications infrastructure in place. When this is the case, additional costs are minimal. However, if the infrastructure is not in place, this will be a major cost. (I will discuss this later in the chapter.) Table 4-5 summarizes the major costs associated with intranet development.

In most cases the benefits that an effective intranet provides outweigh its costs. An intranet can serve as a dynamic platform for collecting and disseminating critical information throughout the organization. This may improve the efficiency and effectiveness of the employees, and it may also improve morale. An

Table 4-5

Major Costs for Intranet Development

Initial content development

Further content development

Monthly maintenance

Network costs

Personnel salary and benefits

Server hardware

Software (network software and browsers, Web publishing software)

Application maintenance

Telecommunications hardware

Workstations and PCs

intranet can support many activities that in turn support an effective e-commerce program by creating an open platform for functional areas within the organization. An intranet is a critical component of an extranet that makes B2B e-commerce a reality.

Intranet technology can help employees reduce paper reports and unnecessary information. In a typical office, duplicated documents are floating all around. With an intranet only one copy, for example, a training manual, can be posted on the web server, and anybody interested can access the document electronically. Intranet technology allows different individuals to create and maintain relevant information and then make it available to all interested parties.

One of the most important benefits of an intranet is its ability to shift the control of information flow from the information creators to the information consumers. Intranet technology enhances information access by individual users from their desktops. This information may be standard forms, reports, minutes of meetings, new advertising campaigns, or the company mission statement, to name but a few.

The information transfers can also include the dissemination of training manuals and educational documents. Traditionally, organizations have spent significant time and money to train and educate their employees on new products, software, and e-commerce policies and procedures. With intranet technology, information can be found efficiently and distributed on demand, which will lead to changing the traditional education and training model. If the appropriate infrastructure is in place, current information content can be found and accessed when and where it is needed. As a result, an intranet can reduce both the time needed for training and the amount of information an employee is required to absorb at once [24]. (I discuss training applications of intranets in section 4-7.)

The intranet is based on "pull technology" through which employees and interested parties extract (pull) exactly what they need when and where they need it. This is the opposite of the traditional "push" technology in which information is delivered (pushed) despite not being asked for or requested. Although push technology is useful for applications, such as memo and policy distribution, this technology may significantly increase the network load. Too often workers are overloaded by information they cannot absorb [13]. Intranets can even reduce the flow of e-mail throughout the organization. For example, instead of sending an e-mail to all employees, the president of the company can post a message on the president's page and the employees can read it if they need to.

4-5-3 FORMATION OF THE TASK FORCE

Similar to the development of other information systems, the development of an intranet should include a task force. The task force creates broad support for this new technology and provides an opportunity for the involved parties to express their views. The participants of the task force should include representatives from the following departments and user groups:

- User groups (including finance, accounting, marketing, manufacturing, and personnel)
- Top management
- Hardware group
- Software group
- Legal department
- Graphics or art department

Each group should express its views and needs regarding intranet development. The representatives from the user groups are the most important participants of the task force. Their views must be carefully considered. The representative from top management needs to provide encouragement and financial support. Hardware and software specialists provide technical advice regarding the proper implementation and utilization of the system. They also help with the technical aspects and security issues. The legal department should provide advice regarding legal issues, copyrights, and privacy problems. If such a department does not exist in a particular organization, an external consultant should be hired.

The representative from the graphics or art department should provide advice regarding the look, feel, and aesthetics of the intranet site. Users will better receive a more professional-looking site. If such a department does not exist in a particular organization, an external consultant should be hired.

4-5-4 CONSTRUCTION OF A PROTOTYPE: PILOT IMPLEMENTATION

As with other information systems, the development of an intranet site should start small or be implemented as a pilot project and then be introduced to the entire organization. Organizations must determine whether information should be made available via a web server, e-mail, or through some other means. Many companies find that building Web interfaces to legacy information systems is a key application. With tools such as Purveyor's Data Wizard and HTML Transit, end users can build simple point-and-click access to legacy information systems without programming, making information available to nontechnical users through their Web browsers. Key database applications including access to customer records, product information, and technical problem tracking are good exercises for the pilot project.

Typically, organizations begin a pilot with existing content delivered via paper. It is important, for the sake of the pilot, to choose a candidate by which both the costs and results can be tracked and measured accurately. A company usually can directly measure the cost of duplicating and distributing copies of its employee benefits manual. When this traditional process is moved to an intranet site, the savings in direct costs can be taken directly to the bottom line, and the incremental costs of managing the content on the intranet server can be calculated and justified.

However, the costs of informal information publishing, such as a memo or table that provides a competitive product analysis, may not be directly measurable. In many organizations, these competitive tables are developed and distributed by staff people rather than production departments, and the direct costs are buried in other overhead expenses. Therefore, the move from traditional paper-based information flow to an intranet may not result in direct measurable cost savings. Once the value of intranet technology has been established through such a pilot, it can be expanded into other departments and functions. In addition, access to other legacy information systems can be provided, so that employees can search and update customer databases, check 401K balances, vacation days, or register for training classes. This pilot project should provide the entire organization with a better understanding of the usefulness of this powerful technology. It also provides the design team with opportunities to resolve problems before a full-scale implementation takes place.

4-5-5 ASSESSING THE SECURITY AND PRIVACY ISSUES

The development of intranets brings up certain organizational challenges, including security and privacy issues (discussed in detail in Chapter 11). Due to the importance of these issues, I mention them briefly here.

Security can be defined as providing access for authorized personnel to the organizational information. A security system protects data resources, the second most important resource (after human resources) in an organization. In the case of intranets, these authorized accesses are given to the users of the organizational intranet. At the same time a comprehensive security system must deny access to all others. Web servers allow system administrators to limit access rights by specific IP addresses for individual pages. This capability would potentially allow system administrators to set access to financial records or personnel files only for the workstations of authorized staff.

Security may include encryption at several levels. Web servers offer encryption for communications between the server and browser, effectively scrambling the message and preventing its interception. Encryption may also play a major role if the intranet application spans multiple organizations or locations. As will be discussed in Chapter 11, firewalls can provide comprehensive security measures, protecting an intranet from unauthorized users outside of the organization who try to access the system. Many companies require employees to use personal identification numbers and passwords that limit access to their information. E-mail confirmation sent automatically after any transaction can also guard against tampering.

Firewalls are among the most effective security measures for intranets. Firewalls are a combination of hardware and software systems that protect one part of a network from another, or protect an internal network from the outside world. A firewall can determine who will cross a network boundary. The organization can further control security by restricting file and directory level access using standard user privileges.

Hackers and other computer criminals (usually technically savvy outsiders), are the most serious threat to intranet security. A hacker may break into a corporate intranet just for fun or for a challenge. A cracker, who is sometimes an expert retained by a competitor to wreak havoc on a company's intranet, is another outside threat. In addition to outside threats, there is an increasing trend toward security breaches initiated by current and former employees [10]. It is estimated that insiders commit more than 70% of security threats. This makes the job of security protection a challenging one.

Intranet applications can either assist in maintaining an employee's privacy, or they can have the potential to invade his or her privacy if the designer is not careful. Privacy can be enhanced by the use of intranet applications for delivering sensitive information in an anonymous manner. For example, new raises or an overseas assignment can be delivered confidentially to the employee workstation. While the interoffice mail staff may pick through a document when they deliver a memo that is marked confidential, an intranet server treats all pages without similar bias or prejudgment. Employees can feel free to review the employee assistance program information at their desktops. They may browse information on maternity leave or sabbatical programs without fear of raising concerns of their supervisors or of personnel representatives. However, in a loosely secured network, all of this information and much more can get into the hands of unauthorized personnel. For these reasons, security issues and measures must be taken seriously. Guidelines introduced in Chapter 11 must be followed in order to keep intruders at bay.

4-5-6 TOOL SELECTION

Numerous basic intranet-publishing tools are available. Web servers, for instance, are available for a variety of platforms found in a typical organization, including Windows 3.1, Windows 95/98, Windows NT, Windows 2000, Macintosh, NetWare, VMS, UNIX, OS/2, and many others. An increasing number of tools enable the user to create HTML documents for intranet applications. Many software programs allow documents to be saved in HTML format, and tools are entering the market that allow large-scale migration of content from traditional word-processing format to HTML format. For example, documents created in Microsoft Word can be saved in HTML format. Slides created in Microsoft PowerPoint can be saved in HTML format.

Database tools such as Microsoft Access and Borland Paradox are available for developing comprehensive data tables to be used as part of the intranet contents. These tools allow nontechnical users to continue to create content in their familiar application and to transfer this content to the server without having to manipulate each file or document. Table 4-6 lists some of the popular Web publishing programs that can be used for a moderate cost. There are other popular

Table 4-6

Web Publishing Software

Adobe PageMill

Adobe SiteMill

Macromedia Backstage Designer

Macromedia Dreamweaver

Microsoft FrontPage

Netscape Navigator Gold

Netscape Composer

SoftQuad HotMetal Pro

Claris Home Page

Hot Dog Pro

programs that offer limited Web-authoring capabilities. Among the popular ones are the following:

- Corel NetPerfect
- Lotus FastSite
- Microsoft Publisher
- Microsoft Word

Sophisticated users can also create HTML documents manually through any text editor. Organizations can also use Java to develop software applications that can run on any computer. Java is an object-oriented programming language similar to Visual BASIC or C++ and can deliver the software functionality for a specific task as a small applet downloaded from a network. An applet is a small program that can be sent along with a web page to a user. They are usually interactive and perform different tasks on a web page. As a recent programming concept, object-oriented programming (OOP) is organized around "objects" rather than "actions." It emphasizes the manipulation of objects rather than the logic that manipulates these objects. In an OOP environment, first all the objects are identified and then their relationships established.

Java can run on any computer and operating system. It can run on a personal digital assistant (PDA), a subnotebook, or a mainframe. The operating systems include Windows, UNIX, and Macintosh OS.

To run Java applets, a computer needs a Java Virtual Machine (JVM). The JVM is a small program embedded in the web browsers that enables the computer to run Java applications. For example, a JVM is incorporated into Netscape's web browser software. Java programs are coded into bytecode (computer source code) in applets or applications that are downloaded and run through the Java Virtual Machine. JavaScript scripts are a text source code in web pages that are interpreted by the browser as the page is used. The JVM runs the bytecode and executes the Java applet instructions one-by-one and then performs the commands. Java capabilities allow the web server to pass information taken from HTML pages to programs that run outside of the server.

4-5-7 IMPLEMENTATION

There are three main activities during the implementation phase of intranet development [26]:

1. **Build the infrastructure.** This includes the interconnection of nodes (devices attached to a network such as workstations and PCs) and installing the software and browsers.

2. **Choose and set up the network operating system (NOS).** This may include one of the popular operating systems, such as Windows NT, Windows 2000, Novell NetWare, IBM OS/2, Macintosh OS, and so forth.

3. **Overlay the intranet onto the NOS.** This involves installing TCP/IP and browsers such as Microsoft Internet Explorer or Netscape Navigator, and so forth.

Intranets usually will run on a LAN (discussed in Chapter 8) in a client–server environment using the TCP/IP protocol (discussed in Chapter 8).

4-5-8 POSTIMPLEMENTATION AUDIT AND INTRANET SITE MARKETING

Similar to other information systems projects, an intranet site has to be revised for improvement. Because the information needs of decision makers are constantly changing, and hardware and software technologies are improving, an intranet site could be constantly improved in order to better respond to the needs of key decision makers. New hardware and software technologies should improve the flexibility and ease of use of the intranet site, and they should always be integrated to the existing system.

Let's say an intranet has been introduced and the initial results are positive. This last phase can assist the organization by significantly enhancing the efficiency and effectiveness of this new decision-making vehicle. The goal of selling an intranet site or application is to encourage all employees to use the site as a central communications tool. The company should focus on educating its employees on how an intranet will help them do their jobs better. In other words, intranet site marketing should educate employees and show them how this new tool can make them more efficient and effective. There are four parts of a good marketing plan or a good postimplementation audit program [23]:

- Involve top management
- Create awareness
- Provide ongoing education
- Introduce new features by active user participation

4-5-8-1 Involve Top Management

As I have said all along, top executives and senior managers are among the most important groups of people who can make or break any information systems project, including the introduction of an intranet. These individuals can provide both encouragement and support regarding the success of the intranet program. If these people use e-mail, for example, everybody else will start using e-mail. CEO and senior-level executives should be instructed on how to use the intranet site. The importance of the intranet must be explained to them. The benefits of using the intranet have to be focused on their needs. Some of the specific benefits of an intranet for executives may include the following:

- An efficient and effective way to communicate
- An effective way to control the operation of the organization at all levels
- A good way to keep in touch with the organization's operations while traveling
- A foundation for conducting B2B e-commerce

However, the complexity and technical operations of the intranet should be de-emphasized for the executives. The executives do not have to know how this technology works. They should be instructed how to navigate through the applications on the intranet, which may include sending their reports or organizational notices using e-mail [15].

4-5-8-2 Enhance Awareness

Employees have to be told that the site or application is available. Effective awareness campaigns should focus on the benefits of this new tool. Introducing the intranet as being similar to other technology applications may create resistance. The resistance can be expressed in a number of ways. Some employees may be skeptical; others will view the new tool as the latest toy; still others might complain that the new tool is one more thing added to their already overburdened workload. Ongoing education, encouraging active user participation, and including employees in the task force team should minimize these resistance issues. The existence of the site and its benefits should be advertised. Here are some methods for getting the word out [23]:

- Announce important events through the site.
- Have the site featured in the company magazine and/or newsletter.
- Have the site's availability mentioned in staff meetings.
- Place a banner in the cafeteria and in other meeting places.
- Put a flyer in all employee mailboxes.
- Send an e-mail message to all employees.
- Set up meetings with division managers and supervisors and discuss the intranet in detail.
- Conduct training programs to introduce the site's features

4-5-8-3 Provide Ongoing Education

The role of education and ongoing education in improving system acceptance is well documented throughout the information systems literature. One organization that I have experience with has gone beyond traditional educational methods. The organization not only provides traditional education with an instructor, lectures, and slides, they also provide CD-ROM-based education. They provide private tutorial on a one-on-one basis for employees who need this kind of personal attention. They have been very successful in introducing all types of information systems applications to a broad group of users with minimal technical background. As described later in this chapter, the intranet itself is a great training tool that the organization can use for future projects and applications.

Generally speaking, education and training depends on company size and the location of employees. For a single-location company, a member of the information system staff can visit departmental meetings and present the site. Users should be grouped and taught how to use a browser and how to navigate through the company's web site. A brief document explaining the intranet site should be passed out to all employees. The document should highlight the type of information that can be obtained from the site. Companies that have offices located throughout a large region should implement training through the intranet from its headquarters. Training should be short, simple, and to the point [23].

4-5-8-4 Introduce New Features by Active User Participation

As the intranet grows, different departments will put their information on the company's web site. As mentioned earlier, there are readily available Web publishing programs that enable employees to create their own web pages without knowing HTML programming syntax. One such package is Microsoft Front-Page. Most organizations now have one or more Web masters who assist employees in publishing their own web pages. The organization should distribute formal policies and procedures for publishing and maintaining Web materials. Guidelines such as the following may be helpful [23]:

- Use the established company style guide.
- Create documents that are grammatically correct and are in standard English.
- Develop materials that are appropriate for viewing by the entire organization.
- If access to the information is restricted, a user ID and password protection should be used.
- The information published must be legal and also should not be copy protected. In the case of copyrighted materials, the written permission of the copyright holder must be obtained.

4-6 APPLICATIONS OF THE INTRANET: AN OVERVIEW

A properly designed intranet can make the type of information listed in Table 4-7 available to the entire organization in a timely manner. This information directly or indirectly can support a successful e-commerce program.

Table 4-7

Possible Information Provided by the Intranet

401K plans	New product offerings
Budget planning	Newscast on demand to desktop, custom
Calendar events	filtered to client profile
Call tracking	Online training
Company mission statement and policies	Order placement
Competition data regarding the latest actions	Order tracking
taken by the competitors	Organizational charts
Contest results	Patient treatment sign-off
Customer information	Personnel policy
Department information	Press releases
Employee classified	Product catalog
Employee stock options	Project information
Equipment inventory	Salary ranges
Expense report	Sales tips
Facilities management	Software program tutorials
Industry news	Suggestion box
Job postings	Telephone listings
Job descriptions	Time cards
Leave of absence and sabbatical news	Training manuals
Maps	Training schedules
Medical benefits	Travel authorization
Meeting minutes	Upcoming functions
New hire orientation materials	

Many internal applications in use today can be easily converted to an intranet or supported using an intranet. Human resources applications, such as job information, name and phone number lists, and medical benefits can be displayed on a human resources web page. A finance web site might present information on time cards, expense reports, or credit authorization. Employees can easily access the latest information on a server. With e-mail, e-mail distribution lists, and chat lines, employees can easily retrieve meeting minutes.

The intranet also allows organizations to evolve from a calendar- or schedule-based publishing strategy to an event-driven or needs-based publishing strategy. In the past, companies published an employee handbook once a year. Traditionally, the handbooks would not be updated until the following year even though they may have been outdated as soon as they arrived on the users' desks. I have experience with several applications of this kind. Some of these organizations sent a few loose pages as an update every so often. The employee is supposed to add these additional pages to the binder. After a while these materials become difficult to go through to retrieve specific information.

With an intranet publishing strategy, information can be updated instantly. If the organization adds a new mutual fund to the 401K program, content on the benefits page can be updated immediately to reflect that change, and the company internal home page can include a brief announcement about the change. Then, the employees have the new information at their desktop as soon as they look up the 401K programs.

Intranets dramatically reduce the costs and time of content development, duplication, distribution, and utilization. The traditional publication model includes this multistep process:

- Creation of content
- Production of the draft
- Revision of the draft
- Final draft preparation
- Migration of the content to the desktop publishing environment
- Duplication
- Distribution

However, intranet technology reduces the number of steps to only two (it eliminates the duplication and distribution steps):

- Creation of content
- Migration of content to the intranet environment

Although content still needs review and approval regardless of medium used for delivery.

4-7 TRAINING APPLICATIONS OF THE INTRANET

Training is essential for any organization, including an e-business. Hardware, software, and procedures are constantly changing, and key personnel must be always aware of recent developments. An increasing number of organizations use the intranet to train their employees on new software, procedures, products, and so forth. Examples of companies that have successfully used intranets for this purpose include the following:

- Graybar
- Hewlett-Packard
- Intel
- Lawrence Livermore National Laboratory
- NCR

- Oracle
- Qualcomm
- Silicon Graphics
- Sprint

There are 10 good reasons to use an intranet for an effective training program [24]:

1. **Consistency:** With an intranet, every employee can view the same training materials. This will create balanced training for all participants.

2. **Pull versus push approach:** Too often, the company provides employees with more information than they can possibly absorb. A 90-page training manual that the company passes to employees may be viewed with dread. However, an intranet allows the company to provide access to as little or as much information as employees wish to pull onto their desktops.

3. **Interactivity:** Intranets provide two-way communication tools to create discussion groups.

4. **Ease of and low cost for updates:** The company can easily and inexpensively update online publications and training materials as frequently as needed by using various Web technologies.

5. **User-friendly interface:** If employees can easily get to the information they seek, they're much more likely to look for that information. The point-and-click approach provided by intranet training makes it a user-friendly environment.

6. **Centralization:** With an intranet, employees can access information from a central database at any time, and from any number of geographical locations. Self-training can be completed at home, in the office, or on the road. The process is also self-paced, which gives the trainee the opportunity to advance at his or her own desired speed.

7. **Simplicity in creation and maintenance:** Intranet sites can be created and maintained with a minimum of programming expertise.

8. **Keeping up with the workforce:** As more and more young employees enter the workforce, keeping up with technology will become increasingly important. The young workforce is used to being intellectually stimulated through electronic media. Intranet training provides them with such an opportunity.

9. **Flexibility:** An intranet can be an ongoing work in progress.

10. **Potential:** As the evolution of intranet sites continues, more and more features will emerge that expand its functionality.

The Washington State Department of Personnel handles human resources data consisting of more than 100 state agencies with 60,000 employees. Faced with increasing demand for reports containing analytical and operational data and tight fiscal constraints, the human resources department set out in July 1995 to create a system using Web technology to access data easily from its data warehouse. As a result, the human resources department has received positive feedback from the client agencies. Carol Wyckoff, the department's human resource business representative, says, "Most significantly, it has allowed a quick turnaround time in answering questions." Furthermore, other agencies said that intranet technology has increased their administrative efficiency [12].

Thomson Consumer Electronics (TCE) developed its intranet server for training purposes. Gary Fields, senior systems consultant for Web technologies at TCE, spent about 2½ years developing an intranet solution. Doghouse, an intranet server, helps TCE train its new employees by offering an essential source for information such as procedures, policies, and employee personal data pages, including pictures [17].

Silicon Graphics, Inc. (SGI), a manufacturer of high-powered workstations, used to send thick, hard-copy training manuals to all its employees. Some employees did not find these materials useful, so they did not use them. Duplication and distribution of these materials was a major expense for the company. The company solved the problem by using a CD-ROM. However, there was still a problem because not every desktop computer was equipped with a CD-ROM drive. Therefore, Silicon Graphics has begun to replace the CD-ROM distribution method with distribution of training materials via an intranet. Now everyone can access the programs whenever they want. The intranets benefit the company in reducing reproduction costs of training manuals. If the company wants to make a change to the program, it can do so at a central location. With an intranet, the company can make available all kinds of training documents, including product directions, sales tips, company history, new hire orientation materials, and software program tutorials [24].

Ramos & Associates, Inc., a workflow automation systems integrator, has used an intranet to train its employees. Of the 170 employees in the company, only 10 of them do not travel regularly, and at any one time there are usually fewer than 20 people at the corporate office. The intranet allows its people to access training materials whether they are at home or in a hotel room. In addition, the company can send audio interviews with top consultants and show video clips of new products and procedures [24].

4-8 MAJOR BUSINESS APPLICATIONS OF INTRANETS AND EXTRANETS

Table 4-8 provides several categories of popular intranet applications. These are only sample applications. Organizations can develop further applications within each category [5,6,7,14,18,19,22,26].

Table 4-8

Applications of Intranets and Extranets in Specific Areas

General category	Specific applications
Sales	Provides instant access to product information
	Places orders and checks status quickly and efficiently
	Provides technical background information regarding products, enabling sales agents to sell products with more confidence
Human resources	Online job postings
	Employment applications
	401K programs
	Training classes
	Forms
	Security policies
	Web policies
	E-mail policies
	Saves the cost of printing and distributing human resource information
Customer service	Increases the processing speeds by providing online information to sales people
	Provides up-to-date information on customer orders
Health services	Increases effective communication among physicians, hospitals, labs, insurance, and drug companies
Financial services	Provides the bulk of research reports and manuals on financial procedures
Manufacturing	Reduces the preparation time for assembly instructions
	Improves effective problem solving in the assembly process
	Carries data on quality measurement, such as defects, rejects, maintenance, training schedules, sales history, purchase orders, and quality
	Distributes technical drawings

4-9 APPLICATIONS OF INTRANETS AND EXTRANETS BY MAJOR COMPANIES

Numerous companies have successfully implemented intranets and extranets. Table 4-9 presents a summary of some applications of the intranets and extranets by selected companies. Domino's Pizza is one example. With the help of Fry Multimedia and Micro-Age, Domino's designed an intranet that utilizes a Lotus Notes-based groupware application. They first published the company's

Table 4-9

Applications of Intranets and Extranets by Selected Companies

Company	General applications
AT&T	Uses an intranet to integrate disparate billing systems from various AT&T business units, to provide interfaces to library services, internal research, and external news feeds, to provide a system for ordering office supplies, and to provide an interface for employee contacts of more than 300,000 employees
Avant Corporation	Uses an extranet to securely manage over 1,000 customer accounts, to reliably move large proprietary data files of semiconductor designs over the Internet, to delegate management of customer accounts and access permissions to account engineers and representatives without requiring an administrator's intervention
CIBA-GEIGY AG	Uses intranets and extranets to advertise surplus equipment available for other hospitals, to increase knowledge sharing among international units, and to improve the company's corporate culture by fostering a feeling of connection that spans countries.
Columbia/HCA Healthcare	Uses an intranet to provide an up-to-date corporate directory, to post physician resumes submitted via the intranet site, and to train employees on processes.
Federal Express	Uses an intranet to publish internal technology reports, personnel guidelines, tax forms, employee evaluations, and project management documentation, and to create an adjunct help desk support application to streamline customer support by information system
Ford Motor Company	Uses an intranet to provide information on benchmarking, auto show global market information, competitor news, and global product-cycle plans and patent information.
Fujitsu Corporation	Uses an intranet to support the needs of Fujitsu system engineers in research and development, as well as manufacturing to access a comprehensive set of resources and to provide an information service for Fujitsu's sales division.
Harley-Davidson	Uses extranets to create a link between the company and its dealerships. It is used for warranty-processing applications.
US West	Utilizes its Global Village intranets to streamline document distribution by sending e-mails and to integrate with a mainframe system to determine when new telephone facilities will be available.

(continues)

Table 4-9 (*continued*)

Home Depot	Uses an extranet to integrate data about sales, inventory, store productivity, and staffing from proprietary programs operating on different platforms. District managers receive dynamically updated store-performance reports, sales data, labor hours, and inventory statistics from their desktops. A salesperson at a store's information desk using the extranet can tell a customer when a customer's order will arrive or whether another store has a particular item. Executives at headquarters can check weekly sales for a certain district based on virtually up-to-the-minute data [2].
IBM	Uses an extranet to improve customer relations between IBM and its major clients. This system allows IBM to create secure, tailored web sites for their large customers such as Intel and Citibank. These sites provide the company access to pertinent news stories, current promotions and price lists, marketing messages, as well as a list of IBM client representatives who are associated with each company. This Lotus Notes/Domino application creates new sites based on options chosen by IBM. It also allows IBM to quickly update the sites as soon as new content becomes available. The application also includes a unique management interface, called Enterprise Sites Management Interface, to keep track of internal changes as well as feedback from web users [3].
The Sonesta International Hotels	The Sonesta International Hotels public web site is supported by an extranet application that allows each hotel manager in the Sonesta family to update, support, and process all the activity associated with their property. This allows each property manager the freedom to post last-minute travel specials, area activities and happenings, and special offers. Direct e-mail to customers alerts them to specials at the destinations they are most interested in visiting. The travel preferences of frequent customers are stored in the database, so that repeat reservations are always handled with the unique Sonesta care and attention [4].

phone directory and newsletter online. Once the intranet concept started to catch on companywide, they launched their core application called Contact Log. Contact Log tracks interactions between field representatives and store owners. Contact Log is one of the applications that the company has developed to deliver to the individual franchise owners the specific information they need. The individual employees can also benefit from Domino's intranet. They now have access to company calendars, policies, and a detailed document library. At any point, they are able to download any mission-critical information that they come across. The employees also have access to an online discussion forum to talk with management and fellow employees about any important management issues. Using the intranet has improved communication and coordination throughout the organization, which results in savings of time and money. The next phase of the intranet that Domino's plans to introduce will offer an online financial reporting system that will be directly linked to the company's Informix Data Warehouse.

4-10 INDUSTRY CONNECTION: IBM CORPORATION

IBM Corporation
500 Columbus Avenue
Thornwood, New York 10594
Telephone: (914) 742-5981
Fax: (914) 742-6123
Web site address: <http://www.ibm.com>

IBM was incorporated in the state of New York on June 15, 1911, as the Computing-Tabulating-Recording (C-T-R) Company. In 1924, to reflect C-T-R's growing worldwide presence, its name was changed to International Business Machines Corporation. IBM is the largest computer company in the world and is active in just about every aspect of computing and e-commerce. The American National Standards Institute (ANSI) in cooperation with IBM has developed the data encryption standard (DES) that is used throughout the world for encryption. DES incorporates the transfer of "keys" throughout computer networks, as well as the new "elliptical curve key," a microcomputer crypto algorithm. A key is a secret series of characters that enables a user to access a file, computer, and program or to decipher (decode) an encoded (encrypted) program, file, or password. A key (discussed in Chapter 6) enables secure business transactions over the Web. A customer uses a public key to encrypt and transfer information over the Web, and a business uses a private key to decrypt the transferred information. IBM is actively involved in e-commerce. IBM's most significant contribution in this area is the secure electronic transaction (SET) (discussed in Chapter 6). This technology was developed primarily for Visa and MasterCard to ensure instant confirmations for credit transactions over the Web. IBM offers numerous products and services effectively used in the e-commerce world. Some of the important security and e-commerce-related products and services offered by IBM that can be used with intranets and extranets include the following:

1. Antivirus software that detects and prevents intentional and sometimes un-intentional computer viruses. The detection technology effectively monitors a network and logs the presence of viruses for reference and tracking.

2. Crytolope Containers are secure delivery vehicles for any type of infor-mation (numbers, text, video, images, or animations) being transmitted over the Web. This unique technology also ensures the security of electronic commerce using DES. The container monitors access beyond the firewall and ensures that all the enclosed information is kept confidential.

3. Firewalls are a combination of hardware and software that screen out the incoming and outgoing information to and from the internal corporate network (discussed in Chapter 11). IBM firewalls selectively restrict requests for access to information resources by identifying the source and type of the request.

4. WebSphere B2B Integrator software combines IBM's integration and trans-action software technologies and is based on open XML technology. WebSphere B2B Integrator is built on IBM's WebSphere application server, its MQSeries messaging software, and open XML technology for the exchange of electronic contracts, called tpaML. IBM's open B2B software strategy enables businesses to integrate their own computing systems, linking operations, including supply-chain management and logistics, with their trading partners' systems.[1]

4-11 SUMMARY

This chapter introduced intranets and extranets as two of the growing appli-cations of the Internet and Web technology used in support of e-commerce. It compared and contrasted intranets with the Internet and extranets. The chapter provided a detailed discussion of the steps taken for the construction of an in-tranet site. These included establishing goals and problem definition, cost and benefit analysis, formation of the task force, construction of a prototype, assess-ing the security and privacy issues, tool selection, implementation, and postim-plementation audit and intranet site maketing. The chapter concluded with a de-tailed listing of various intranet and extranet applications and a sample of organizations that have been successfully using these technologies, highlighting IBM as the industry connection.

4-12 REVIEW QUESTIONS

1. How do you define an intranet? An extranet?
2. What are three differences between the Internet and an intranet?

---

[1] This information was gathered from the company web site and other promotional materials. For detailed information and any update, contact the company.

3. Generally speaking, is an intranet faster than the Internet? If yes, why? Discuss.
4. Do the Internet and an intranet use the same technology? Discuss.
5. What is the role of intranets and extranets in the e-commerce environment?
6. What are the steps for the development of an intranet?
7. What takes place during the problem definition phase of intranet development? Why must goals and objectives be defined in this phase? Discuss.
8. List three important costs and three important benefits of an intranet program.
9. It is generally believed that the costs of developing an intranet are relatively low compared with other information systems. Why is this claim true? Discuss.
10. Intranet technology is based on pull technology. What is the difference between pull and push technology? Why is pull technology more effective in the case of the intranet? Discuss.
11. Who should participate in the task force for intranet development?
12. Why should a representative from the legal department be included in the task force?
13. What is the role of the art department representative in the task force?
14. Why is it a good idea to design a prototype or introduce the intranet as a pilot? What are some of the advantages of this approach?
15. Why security and privacy issues must be carefully examined in the intranet development process?
16. How do you protect security and privacy issues for intranets and extranets? What are some of the available tools?
17. What are some examples of tools for developing the content of an intranet site?
18. What are some of the activities that will take place during the implementation phase of the intranet development process?
19. What are the purposes of intranet site marketing?
20. Why should top executives be involved in the intranet development process?
21. How does Dell Computer use intranets and extranets to gain competitive advantage? Discuss.
22. List 10 popular applications of intranets and extranets.
23. What are the sales applications of an intranet? What are its applications for human resources management?
24. Name four organizations that have been successfully using intranets/extranets. In which areas are these technologies used? Discuss.
25. What are some advantages of using an intranet for training? Discuss.

26. Federal Express has been successfully using extranet technology for several years. What are some specific applications of the extranet in this company? Discuss.

4-13 PROJECTS AND HANDS-ON EXERCISES

1. Log onto the web site of the IBM Corporation at the following URL:

    <http://www.ibm.com>

    What are some of the e-commerce products and services offered by this company? IBM uses intranets and extranets in its operations to gain competitive advantage. What are some of the applications of these technologies in IBM? What are some of the IBM's security products that can be used in intranets and extranets development? Discuss.

2. Log onto the following web site:

    <http://www.intranetjournal.com>

    By examining the materials presented in this site and other sources, answer the following questions:

    What are examples of Intranet strategy?
    What are examples of Intranet database tools?
    What are examples of Intranet software tools?

3. A large CPA firm has offices in Seattle, Portland, Oregon, San Francisco, Los Angeles, and San Diego. In each city there are five offices at the present time, and the company has been growing 25% per year for the past 5 years. The company plans to establish an intranet for all of its branches in these five cities. The initial contents of the intranet site include a detailed skill inventory of all the employees, passages of the past e-business consulting projects, and detailed listings of all the e-business-related firms in each city. They need your advice. Provide a detailed cost and benefit analysis for this project. Where should they start? Using the eight steps outlined in the chapter, provide a three-page recommendation to be submitted to the CEO of this firm. What are some of the future applications of an intranet as they relate to e-business consulting for this firm? What are some of the ongoing costs? What types of security systems should they implement? Should they develop this project internally or should they use outsourcing services? (The company does have a large management information system [MIS] department in San Francisco.) What are some of the advantages and disadvantages of each alternative? In the next 5 years they are

planning to serve as an outside consultant for one of the large national and international accounting firms. They are planning to open their intranet site for limited access to this new partner. What are some of the issues that must be considered for this future intranet–extranet application? Write down five of the most important issues that must be considered for this new partnership.

4. What are some of the applications of an extranet in B2B e-commerce? How is Home Depot using this technology? What is achieved by extranet applications in a national or international law firm? Discuss.

5. The following is an informative site for intranets. Log onto the site and examine its offerings. What are some examples of software used in intranet and extranet development? Discuss.

<http://intranets.com>

6. Federal Express provides a good example of an extranet. Log onto the following site and examine its contents. What are some of the competitive advantages of this extranet site for Federal Express? How does this site help FedEx to save money? How does this site improve customer service?

<www.fedex.com>

7. Telecom Information Resources provides links on intranets and telecommunications. Log onto the following site and review the latest on intranets and extranets development:

<http://china.si.umich.edu/telecom>

According to the materials presented in this site and other sources, how do you guarantee intranet repeat use? How do you measure intranet return on investment? According to this site, what are the latest on extranets? Discuss.

8. The following site is a commercial example of intranet solution (Citibank):

<http://www.citibank.com>

Log onto the site and examine its contents. What are some of the specific offerings of this program? How may an intranet such as this save costs? Discuss. How may an intranet such as this improve customer service? Discuss.

9. The following site is a commercial example of intranet solution (Charles Schwab):

<http://www.schwab.com>

Log onto the site and examine its contents. What are some of the specific offerings of this program? How may an intranet such as this save costs? Discuss. How may an intranet such as this improve customer service? Discuss.

10. The following site is a commercial example of an intranet solution (Texaco):

<http://www.texaco.com>

Log onto the site and examine its contents. What are some of the specific offerings of this program? How might an intranet such as this save costs? Discuss. How may an intranet such as this improve customer service? Discuss.

11. The following site is a commercial example of intranet solution (Sony Music):

<http://www.sonymusic.com>

Log onto the site and examine its contents. What are some of the specific offerings of this program? How might an intranet such as this save costs? Discuss. How may an intranet such as this improve customer service? Discuss.

12. The following site is a commercial example of intranet solution (St. John's University):

<http://www.stjohns.edu>

Log onto the site and examine its contents. What are some of the specific offerings of this program? How may an intranet such as this save costs? Discuss. How may an intranet such as this improve customer service? Discuss.

13. The intranet/extranet research center provides valuable information on various aspects of intranet/extranet development and utilization. Log onto the following site and by examining its content identify 10 specific applications of these two technologies in the e-commerce world.

<http://www.ibizcenter.com/extranets.htm>

4-14 KEY TERMS

REFERENCES

[1] Legal Web Technologies, LLC, Extranet <http://www.legalwebtech.com/extranet.htm> (Date of access: April 13, 2001).

[2] <http://cgi.netscape.com/comprod/at_work/customer_profiles/hd.html>. The Home Depot Provides Information Instantly to Managers and Employees 1999 Netscape, All Rights Reserved. (Date of access, April 13, 2001).

[3] Synaptic Communications, Inc., <http://www.synap.com/extranet.htm>. Extranet Applications, Copyright 2001, Synaptic Communications, Inc. (Date of access: April 16, 2001).

[4] <http://www.ibizcenter.com/extranets.htm>.

[5] Allerton, Haidee (1997, February). "Intranet News." *Training & Development,* pp.55-56.

[6] Anthes, Gary, H. (1997, January 6). "Community Intranet Gets Real-World Test." *Computerworld,* pp. 55-56.

[7] Bidgoli, Hossein (1999, Summer). "An Integrated Model for Introducing Intranets," *Information Systems Management,* vol. 16, no. 3, pp. 78-87.

[8] Bushaus, Dawn (2000, March 6). "Trade The ANX Way: The Automotive Network Exchange is moving into other industries with the goal of becoming the business-class Internet." Information Week Online. <http://www.informationweek.com/776/anx.htm>.

[9] Canterucci, Jim (1997, February). "Intranet Security." *Training & Development,* p. 47.

[10] Chan Stephen, and Tim R.V. Davis (2000, Winter). "Partnering on Extranets for Strategic Advantage." *Information Systems Management,* pp. 58-64.

[11] Cheng, Francis (1997, September 29). "State agency turns to an Intranet for easy access to its data warehouse," *InfoWorld,* p. 100.

[12] Croft, Brian (1996, July). "Ten Reasons to Use Intranet for Training." *Personnel Journal,* p. 28.

[13] DiDio, Laura (1997, January 27). "Network gives resort a lift: Sundance taps IntranetWare for LAN links." *Computerworld,* pp. 53, 56.

[14] Fletcher, Trina (1997, September 29). "Intranet Pays Dividends in Time and Efficiency for Investment Giant." *InfoWorld,* p. 84.

[15] Foster, Andrew (1997, September 29). "Worldwide Intranet Sparks Innovative and Enthusiastic Communication at TCE." *InfoWorld,* p. 98.

[16] Hibbard, Justin (1997, April 7). "Spreading Knowledge: Intranet Puts all of Arthur Andersen's Know-How in Hands of Consultants at Client Sites." *Computerworld,* pp. 63-64.

[17] Hibbard, Justin (1997, January 20). "GMAC Takes Fast Ethernet Route to Multimedia Intranet." *Computerworld,* pp. 8.

[20] Jones, Kevin (1998, February 9). "Copier Strategy as yet Unduplicated." *Interactive Week.*

[21] Maloff, Joel (1997, August). "Extranets" Stretching the Net to Boost Efficiency." *Net Guide Magazine.* <http://www.unc.edu/cit/guides/irg-50.html>

[22] Nash, Kim S. (1996, July 29). "BIONET: Intranet Helps Researchers Cross-Pollinate." *Computerworld,* p. 59.

[23] Rosen, Anita (1997). "Intranet Site Marketing." *Looking into Intranets & the Internet,* AMACOM: New York, pp. 170-174.

[24] Stevens, Larry (1996, July). "The Intranet: Your Newest Training Tool." *Personnel Journal,* pp. 27-32.

[25] Wagner, Mitch (1997, July 7). "Vertical Industries Rev Extranet Motors." *Computerworld,* p.8.

[26] Weinstein, Peter (1996, October). "Intranets: Time for a Web of Your Own." *Technology and Learning,* pp. 50-57.

Chapter 5

Electronic Data Interchange

Learning Objectives

After studying this chapter you should be able to do the following:

- Define electronic data interchange (EDI) as a fundamental technology used in the e-commerce environment.
- Discuss the historical development of EDI.
- Outline the six major steps for introducing EDI into an organization.
- Differentiate between value-added network (VAN)-based EDI and Internet-based EDI.
- Review some of the popular applications of EDI.
- Explain supply chain, supply-chain management, and the role of EDI and the Internet for improving the efficiency and effectiveness of supply-chain management.

INFORMATION BOX 5-1

Electronic Data Interchange in Spotlight

EDI refers to computer-to-computer transmission of business information between trading partners. The information should be organized in standard file formats or transaction sets.

EDI reduces paper consumption, eliminates data entry errors, speeds up transfer of business information, and facilitates just-in-time (JIT) processes.

EDI provides a controlled and effective means for organizations to exchange business transactions, such as orders and invoices, with their major trading partners.

As part of a presidential memorandum, all contracting offices throughout the federal government are, or will be, using EDI for all their procurement actions in the $2,500 to $100,000 range. Requests for quotes (RFQs), quotes, award notices, purchase orders, and invoices will all be sent via EDI.

EDIFACT is a standard endorsed by a United Nations committee to define EDI business documents. It is expected that this will eventually become the worldwide standard for EDI transmissions.

To implement EDI, two types of software are needed: communications software and translation software. Communications software is used to transfer data between the organization and its selected value-added network (VAN). Translation software is used to translate the EDI transaction from a format that can be used in the organization application and inversely translate the organization application format to an EDI transaction.

Internet-based EDI is gaining popularity due to its worldwide availability, lower cost, and ease of implementation.

INFORMATION BOX 5-2

Electronic Data Interchange in Compaq Computer

Compaq Computer is one of the largest manufacturers of PCs in the world, and it is active in most aspects of computing. Compaq utilizes EDI technology extensively, and it has reengineered its entire procurement process using EDI to make it faster and more accurate. According to Compaq, real-time data now flows 24 hours a day, 7 days a week between Compaq and raw materials suppliers. EDI is used to communicate to the suppliers when more raw materials are needed. In return, suppliers notify Compaq when shipments are made. Compaq customers also have their own reengineering projects that rely extensively on EDI. "We're looking at everything from pricing to stocking strategies to payment authorization," says Brent Gutzman of GE Capital Technology Management Services in Toronto. "Administration-wise, EDI can deliver huge costs savings. Other benefits are accuracy, and freeing up the time of professionals to plan for the future instead of the day-to-day."

Compaq began implementing EDI with U.S. suppliers in 1988. It has evolved into an essential business tool today. EDI helps Compaq keep costs competitive and deliver products when promised. This information technology also enables Compaq to purchase and receive JIT materials. According to Compaq, the benefits of EDI are as follows:

1. Improves accuracy and speed of information exchanged between companies
2. Reduces operational costs for customers, suppliers, and Compaq
3. Helps Compaq reduce cycle time to manufacture and deliver products
4. Improves Compaq customer service
5. Makes JIT manufacturing at Compaq possible
6. Moves customers, suppliers, and Compaq toward a "paperless" environment

Compaq continually reviews and adds new EDI transactions based on Compaq business initiatives, market needs, and recommendations from business partners. Currently, Compaq uses EDI for the following business applications:

1. Administration—product catalogs and price lists
2. Sales analysis—sales and inventory information
3. Purchasing/order management—orders, acknowledgments, order status, and changes
4. Shipping and receiving—shipping, notification, proof of delivery, and customs information
5. Billing—invoicing and statements
6. Payment applications—payment remittance

SOURCE: Compaq (2001). What Is EDI? <http://207.18.199.3/corporate/edi/edi-def.html> (Date of access, April 16, 2001).

5-1 INTRODUCTION

This chapter discusses electronic data interchange (EDI) as a growing technology used in the e-commerce environment. The chapter provides a definition of EDI, its applications, and its historical development throughout the world, especially in North America. The chapter reviews six major steps for introducing EDI into an organization, including (a) assessing the strategic value of EDI applications, (b) analyzing the advantages and disadvantages of EDI applications, (c) analyzing the EDI costs, (d) choosing a communication interface option, (e) compiling EDI standards, and (f) implementing EDI. The chapter introduces several popular applications of EDI and highlights several organizations that are successfully using EDI. The chapter concludes with an overview of supply chain and supply-chain management, the role of EDI and the Web for a successful supply-chain management program and business-to-business (B2B) e-commerce, and highlights Ariba, Inc., as the industry connection.

5-2   WHAT IS ELECTRONIC DATA INTERCHANGE?

Although computers have enabled companies to store, process, and retrieve data electronically since their inception, companies needed a more effective method to capture and transfer data at the source. This method was implemented by the extensive use of data communications.

Data communications can help companies transmit data electronically over telephone lines, other communications media, and the Web. These data can be directly entered into a trading partner's business application. However, data communications can only solve part of the problem. The data are captured first and then electronically transmitted. Some manual intervention will take place here.

Electronic data interchange was initially (1960s) developed for improving response time, reducing paperwork, and eliminating potential transcription errors. EDI represents the application of computer and communications technology to traditional paper-based business processes, supporting innovative changes in those processes. Similarly, EDI is the electronic exchange of business transactions, in a standard format, from one entity's computer to another entity's computer using a communications network. Figure 5-1 illustrates a typical EDI configuration. As this figure shows, EDI may use VANs (described later in the chapter) or the Internet in order to conduct electronic transactions with business partners.

In today's competitive business environment, most large companies and government agencies are committed to reducing expenses, increasing efficiency, and improving their business relationships with a limited number of key suppliers. EDI is one of the main technologies that help organizations achieve these goals. EDI is one of the oldest and most successful technologies used in B2B e-commerce.

EDI is a comprehensive set of standards and protocols for the exchange of business transactions in a computer-understandable format. This may cover applications such as the following:

- Acknowledgment of business transactions
- Financial reporting
- Inquiries
- Invoices

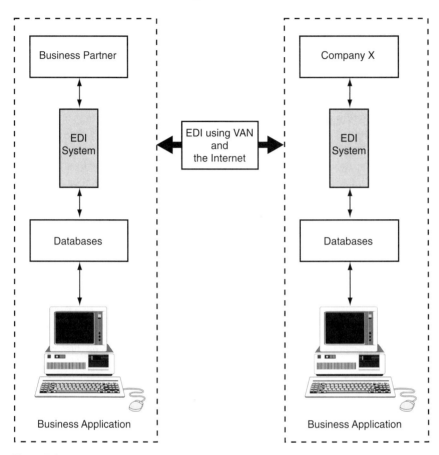

Figure 5-1 A typical electronic data interchange (EDI) configuration. VAN, value-added network.

- Order status
- Payments
- Pricing
- Purchasing
- Receiving
- Scheduling

EDI is commonly defined as an application-to-application transfer of business documents between computers using industry-defined standards. EDI is the closest option to processing a paperless business transaction. Many businesses use EDI to substitute their usual method of communication, where paper documents such as purchase orders, invoices, and/or shipping notices were physically carried from department to department, mailed or faxed from one organization to another, or manually reentered into the computer of the recipient. Also, organizations use EDI to electronically communicate, with documents and other types of information transmitted immediately and accurately into a computer-understandable format.

EDI is different from sending e-mail or sharing files through a network (LANs, WANs, or MANs), or through an electronic bulletin board. Using these communications systems, the format of the transmitted document must be the same for the sender and receiver. Otherwise effective communication will not take place.

When EDI is used, the format of the document does not need to be completely the same. When documents are transmitted, the translation software of EDI converts the document into an agreed upon standard. Once the document is received, translation software changes the document into the appropriate standard. An EDI message is held within two parts, known as envelopes. One envelope, called the outside envelope, contains the interchange control information to address the

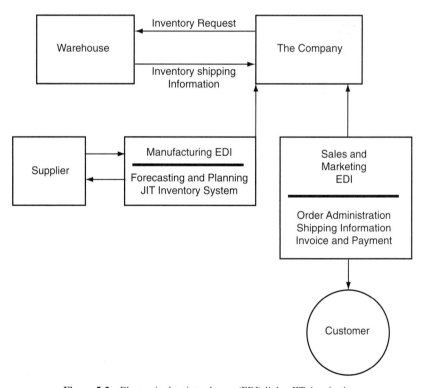

Figure 5-2   Electronic data interchange (EDI) links. JIT, just-in-time.

message being transmitted. The outside envelope can be compared to a common paper envelope that will send a letter. Another part of the EDI message is called the inside envelope (the content). The inside envelope consists of header information, which is the content of the document that is being transmitted, signature authentication, and error detection and correction information. This inside envelope can be compared to the content of a letter sent in a regular paper envelope.

For the purpose of this book we define EDI as a computer-to-computer exchange of business documents in a public- or industry-standard format using public or private networks among trading partners. This may include RFQs, purchase orders, invoices, and transaction balances. Figure 5-2 illustrates the EDI links in the organization.

5-3 HISTORY

The growth of EDI is mainly due to the introduction and growth of data communications. EDI has been in existence since the late 1960s and has gained popularity ever since. With improvements in the quality and affordability of data communications systems, EDI has become more attractive to all types of organizations. Experts in the field believe that the Internet will further enhance the applications and popularity of EDI in all types of organizations. Prior to the Internet era, EDI was very expensive, and only very large organizations could afford using it. The Internet, by providing an inexpensive connection and an open platform, has significantly improved the availability and affordability of EDI. Table 5-1 highlights some of the major events in the historical development of EDI applications [2,4,6,11,13,20].

5-4 INTRODUCING ELECTRONIC DATA INTERCHANGE INTO AN ORGANIZATION

As mentioned earlier, EDI can enhance an organization's competitiveness by expediting the delivery of information and reducing costs. Similar to other e-commerce applications, EDI utilization is a multifaceted process that involves detailed planning and other considerations. The following are the major steps that must be analyzed for proper introduction of EDI into an organization:

- Assessing the strategic value of EDI applications
- Analyzing the advantages and disadvantages of EDI applications
- Analyzing EDI costs
- Choosing a communication interface option
- Reviewing EDI standards
- Implementating EDI

In the following pages I provide a detailed explanation of these steps.

Table 5-1

Major Events in the Historical Development of Electronic Data Interchange Applications[a]

Year	Event
1968	Ten California banks form SCOPE to recommend specific rules and procedures for paperless payments and deposits using magnetic tapes. The transportation industry forms the TDCC, having recognized the problems of communicating with different formats, protocols, and media speed.
Mid-1970s	National Data Corporation, General Electric, and several other companies develop systems using their time-sharing networks for banks to store and for customers to retrieve balance and transaction information.
1975	The ACH network begins to process Social Security payments. Other nationwide applications include veterans' payments and military payrolls. Insurance companies begin to debit premiums and pay claims to individuals through the ACH.
1976	American Hospital Supply Corporation (now part of Baxter Healthcare Corporation) introduces ASAP, a proprietary computer order-entry system. Large suppliers such as Sears, JCPenney, and K-Mart develop proprietary standards for ordering from their suppliers.
1978	The U.S. Federal Reserve implements interregional exchange among automated clearinghouses. The major trade associations in the grocery industry commission Arthur D. Little, Inc., to study the feasibility of EDI among food manufacturers, distributors, and brokers. The study analyzes how electronic communications could make basic ordering and invoicing functions more efficient. It recommends the use of a store-and-retrieve system for communications and grocery industry adaptation of the TDCC message format system.
1978/1979	ANSI forms the ASC X.12 to develop uniform, variable-length, cross-industry standards. It builds on the message format system developed by the TDCC. The U.S. Federal Reserve begins processing debits through the night processing cycle, by providing banks with instructions to transfer funds through the ACH. Companies can make deposits in remote locations late in the day and use those funds in their central accounts the next morning. The NACHA board of directors appoints a task force to study corporate trade payments.
1981	The AIAG, a nonprofit trade association, is formed by members of middle management in vehicle manufacturing companies and their suppliers. NACHA introduces the first corporate trade payment formats: CCD and CTP. Banks begin to sell corporate trade payments through the ACH network as an alternative to regular checks.
1982	JEDI is formed to combine dictionaries. EDI pilots are developed in Canada under the auspices of the Grocery Products Manufacturers of Canada and another by the drug industry. The Public Warehousing Industry develops WINS.
1983	ANSI X.12 publishes its first standards; ANSI X.12 standards become common standard for cross-country standards. Canadian grocery industry adopts modified version of UCS message standard (to allow metric trades).
1984	The West European Technical Assessment Group produces an EDI standard that later becomes the basis for EDIFACT.

(continues)

160

Table **5-1** (*continued*)

1985	EDI Council of Canada formed.
1986	General Motors announces a program to pay its suppliers electronically.
1987	The U.S. Treasury Department starts a program to replace an annual volume of 80 million vendor check payments with ACH payments. NACHA implements the CTX format as a cooperative effort with ASC X.12. ASC X.12 and Grocery Industry discuss possible merger. WINS and UCC propose merging standards. ISO 9737 (international syntax) is approved.
1988	The AIAG realizes that U.S. auto makers and their suppliers need a standard, developed by ANSI.
1989	Canadian Inter-Financial Institutions EDI Committee forms, responsible for establishing standards for financial institutions exchanging transactions with each other through EDI.
1992	Canadian Payments Association approves standards and guidelines applicable to EDI transactions. These standards collectively govern the exchange of EDI transactions between Canadian financial institutions that are members of the Canadian clearing system.
1993	The Department of Defense implements a variety of pilot EDI systems at a number of buying installations. As a result of these early efforts, the Department of Defense spearheads the conversion effort at the federal level to EDI by developing the infrastructure for the process and conducts a variety of training events over the next 2 years.
1995	The ISO/IEC JTC1/SC30 is established. ISO, representing more than sixteen countries from Europe, Pan America, and Asia, announces the availability of reference models for open-EDI, which is the new framework for coordinating standards development. This reference model is an alternative method to the traditional EDI standards development process, which is slow and cumbersome. The committee has worked on this project for 3 years, and has reached its first goal of making this reference model available for worldwide review and ballot. Reaching this milestone allows the open-EDI concept to be openly shared and standards to be established in a structured manner.
1996/1997	The UN's CEFACT and ANSI's ASC X.12 create prototypes of model-generated EDI standards and discuss the institutional changes necessary to implement model-driven standards development and maintenance process.
1998	The use of Internet for EDI transactions is considered as an alternative to traditional methods for communications.
2005	According to Jupiter Communications, business-to-business e-commerce online will approach $6.3 trillion (estimates).

^aSCOPE, Special Committee on Paperless Entities; TDCC, Transportation Data Coordinating Committee; ACH, Automated Clearinghouse; ANSI, American National Standards Institute; ASC, Accredited Standards Committee; NACHA, National Automated Clearinghouse Association; CCD, Cash Concentration or Disbursement; CTP, Corporate Trade Payment; JEDI, Joint Electronic Data Interchange; WINS, Warehousing Industry Network Standards; UCS, Uniform Communications Standards; EDIFACT, EDI For Administration, Commerce, and Transport; CTX, Corporate Trade Exchange; UCC, Uniform Code Council; AIAG, Auto Industry Action Group; ISO/IEC JTC1/SC30, International Standards Organization/International Electrical Committee Joint Technical Committee/Standards Committee 30; CEFACT, Center for Facilitation of Practices and Procedures for Administration, Commerce, and Transport.

5-4-1 ASSESSING THE STRATEGIC VALUE OF APPLICATIONS

EDI could be viewed as a part of total quality management (TQM) and business process reengineering (BPR) programs. TQM, BPR, and EDI are closely related. Organizations can benefit from recognizing this relationship. TQM is a management philosophy aimed at creating an organization committed to continuous process improvement and customer satisfaction. EDI represents an innovative method of meeting and exceeding customer expectations. Effective use of EDI by suppliers results in better availability of information and greater cost savings through operational efficiencies. EDI creates a link between suppliers and customers, reducing the time required for responding to changing market conditions [19].

BPR typically involves close scrutiny of the core business activities and effective design of those activities. EDI represents a process change in the sense that electronic documents are used instead of paper documents. However, the effect of EDI on business processes is really much more pervasive and often requires changes in work practices. The successful implementation of EDI can involve redesigning other information systems applications and related work structures.

Given that EDI results in changes and modifications in hardware and software infrastructure for electronic business, this infrastructure can then be used to reengineer organizational processes. The EDI network between the companies provides an opportunity to reengineer additional business processes to utilize the electronic channels. E-mail communication, alliances for marketing products, creation of the virtual organization, and product distribution are some of the bases for successful B2B operations, and these applications could benefit from this infrastructure.

EDI often requires that information systems personnel accompany sales personnel on customer visits to understand customer requirements or to answer questions from customers regarding EDI. This change in roles of information systems personnel has implications for training. Information systems personnel must be trained in how to interact with customers and in other marketing issues. Marketing personnel, who must sell the EDI applications, must be trained in information systems issues. This training is critical to the success of the EDI partnership, both internal and external to the company. The full potential of EDI as a strategic tool is often overlooked because many firms view EDI as a tool for maintaining market share. EDI is usually perceived as a method of reducing paperwork and inventory cost. Other impacts of EDI utilization include quick response time, greater accuracy gained from reduction in data entry, improved cash flow, improvements in the customer–supplier relationship, and improvements in productivity.

The development of EDI applications in the workplace has largely evolved from a desire to improve efficiency in order processing and billing. For these applications, management views the benefits gained from EDI utilization as operational in nature. The introduction of EDI provides a method for electronically handling the customer–supplier transfer of data. Customers request and/or receive goods, services, and data in a standardized format through established policies and procedures. Using electronic journals, companies can easily monitor the performance of suppliers in providing the goods and services requested.

Successful EDI implementation encourages better allocation of resources for the suppliers and customers because of availability of timely information. Suppliers often adopt JIT processes along with EDI to serve customers.

With a sound agreement between trading partners, a manufacturer can determine the current sales and inventory levels of their customers (distributors). Therefore the manufacturer can forecast accurate future sales and plan production and their own purchasing accordingly. Vendors often find it difficult to provide JIT information via paper, so they utilize EDI, which allows them to promptly receive orders from customers and transmit those orders to manufacturers. EDI will significantly improve the transfer of information in the customer–manufacturer chain and makes JIT delivery a reality. Information availability helps in tactical control of the manufacturing process at the supplier level and evaluation of supplier performance at the customer level. For effective and efficient implementation of EDI, companies must understand the significance of EDI as a competitive tool and a major technology for a successful B2B implementation. The following strategies must be carefully evaluated [19]:

1. **Differentiation strategy:** Differentiation is the attempt to obtain above-average profits by providing unique services to customers. The chemical industry has used EDI to offer inventory control for its customers. The chemical supplier is connected directly to the customer's inventory database. Using a remote automated program, periodic checks by the supplier signal the customer's need for raw materials. These raw materials are then automatically ordered for the customer by the supplier's computer program. Delivery of the materials is handled by the supplier and subsequently billed electronically to the customer. By using this system, the supplier can anticipate a shipment, and the customer can reduce the chance of running out of inventory. Periodic review of the customer database for sales data helps the chemical company anticipate customer needs. Suppliers who are capable of such service may use this technology to differentiate themselves from those who do not. Naturally, a broad range of businesses wanting to achieve the same strategic objective can adopt this kind of application. As discussed in Chapter 4, some organizations use extranets to achieve the same objective.

2. **Cost leadership strategy:** Cost leadership strategy is the attempt to obtain below-average cost by using EDI and other technologies and procedures.

EDI can provide low-cost delivery of products and services. At an operational level, EDI serves the company by providing paperless ordering and receiving applications. Time saving from the absence of rekeying equates to efficiency gains. Faster preparation and transfer of invoices and payments resulted in faster turnover of accounts receivables.

3. **Innovation strategy:** Innovation strategy is the attempt to provide new services to the customers by using EDI and other technologies. Financial institutions are constantly seeking methods of providing new services to their clients. The financial application in cash management can also be considered as an innovative strategy. A financial institution, for instance, initiated an EDI application to provide loan and scholarship payments for students. Students may receive money from several sources to complete their education, including scholarships and loans from private companies or government agencies. Many times these checks must go directly to the school to pay tuition, and transactions are handled manually. The balance then goes to the student for other related expenses. In an effort to simplify the process, the bank receives loan and scholarship payments from multiple sources to perform clearinghouse activities for educational institutions. Students receive their checks or direct deposits from one financial institution. After direct tuition payments have been made, the financial institution receives the benefits of having its name on all checks issued from this process and of acquiring the names and addresses of all students serviced. This activity represents a new service provided for the university (and existing customers) and an innovative method of obtaining a new student customer base for the financial institution.

4. **Growth strategy:** Growth strategy is the attempt to grow above average by using EDI and other technologies. The chemical company mentioned earlier is presently expanding its service. Faced with reduced staff and escalating business opportunities, the company is employing EDI to manage the changes. Manufacturing multiple products across dispersed geographical regions has forced the chemical company to develop a corporate growth strategy that includes implementation of EDI. EDI has facilitated the link between the different divisions of the company, allowing for economies of scale in purchasing across divisions. Some customers are also forcing the chemical company to be EDI proficient, awarding contracts to those companies that meet the stated EDI requirements with the fewest errors in processing. Thus, growth of business could be linked to EDI. Introduction of new EDI-based products and services by financial institutions can also be viewed as a growth strategy.

5. **Alliance strategy:** Alliance strategy is the attempt to establish an alliance with diverse companies in related industries in order to improve competitiveness and reduce cost by using EDI and other technologies. Financial institutions have taken a lead in developing alliance strategies. One company has formed an alliance with a VAN vendor to produce a financial EDI application. The applica-

tion combines accounts payable and receivables with electronic funds transfer (EFT). This includes information exchange between banks or other financial institutions, which results in debits and credits and automated clearinghouses. The application will be jointly owned and operated for the benefit of both parties in the alliance, providing a complete package of products and services required by prospective financial EDI customers.

5-4-2 ANALYZING THE ADVANTAGES AND DISADVANTAGES

Similar to other information systems and e-commerce applications, EDI could present a series of advantages and disadvantages to a typical organization. The extent of these advantages and disadvantages may vary from organization to organization and from application to application. However, for the most part, an EDI application offers the following advantages and disadvantages.

5-4-2-1 Advantages

If properly designed and integrated, EDI offers numerous benefits outlined in Table 5-2 [7,10,16,20,24].

5-4-2-2 Disadvantages

An EDI system may include some disadvantages compared with traditional systems. A proper implementation may eliminate or at least minimize some of these advantages. The following lists some of these disadvantages [1,5]:

1. **Concentration of control:** The strength of the internal control structure provided by segregation of duties and structured management reporting may be reduced or weakened in an EDI environment because the number of people is reduced. EDI causes management to rely more heavily on computer systems and places control in the hands of fewer individuals, potentially increasing risk. While effective automated controls can reduce the potential for human errors, the impact of any control deficiencies will be greater and could include overpayment, over- and understocking, and over- and underproduction.

2. **Data processing, application, and communications errors:** Errors in computer processing and communications systems may result in the transmission of incorrect trading information or the reporting of inaccurate information to management. Application errors or failures can also result in significant losses to trading partners.

3. **Potential loss of management and audit trails:** In some cases, EDI transaction data may not be maintained for a long period of time. Without proper consideration of legal and auditing issues, the entity may not be able to provide

Table 5-2

Electronic Data Interchange Advantages

Accelerates the order–invoice–payment cycle from days or weeks to hours or minutes

Decreases paperwork

Expands the organization customer base

Improves accuracy of information transfer

Improves customer service

Improves response and access to information

Improves communications

Improves cost efficiency

Improves customer service

Improves quality through improved record keeping, fewer errors in data entry, reduced processing delays, less reliance on human interpretation of data, and minimized unproductive time

Improves the competitiveness of an organization

Improves the speed of transaction processing

Improves the speed of information transfer

Increases business opportunities through wider diffusion of procurement information

Offers process improvement and quality assurance benefits through improving the way in which companies handle information

Provides timely and accurate information for decision making

Reduces data entry costs

Reduces inventory

Reduces mailing costs

Reduces personnel requirements

Simplifies order entry and processing

Simplifies accounting and billing

adequate or appropriate evidence, in hard copy or on magnetic media, for the legal dispute to be resolved favorably or for the audit to be completed cost effectively. Backup of the transactions must be made and maintained to guard against this possible problem.

4. **Reliance on third parties:** The organization will become more dependent on third parties to ensure security over transactions and continuity of processing. Also, EDI may share the same kinds of security threats associated with any electronic data communications and other e-commerce applications. A number of potential risks include the following:

- Confidential information could be exposed to unauthorized third parties, possibly competitors.

- Third-party staff could introduce invalid and/or unauthorized transactions.
- Transactions could be lost because of disruptions of data processing at third-party network sites or en route to the recipient partner, causing business losses and inaccurate financial reporting.

5. **Reliance on trading partner's system:** In facilitating JIT and quick response systems, EDI creates a dependence on the trading partner's computer system. Errors, security breaches, and processing disruptions in the trading partner's system may have an impact on the client's business operations.

6. **Total systems dependence:** All EDI transactions entered by an entity could be corrupted if the EDI-related application became corrupted. If the errors remained undetected, there could be an impact on cash flow, noncompliance with contractual obligations, and adverse publicity and loss of business confidence by customers and suppliers. Undetected errors in transactions received from trading partners could cause losses from inappropriate operating decisions.

7. **Unauthorized transactions and fraud:** Increased access to computer systems can increase the opportunities to change an entity's computer records and those of its trading partners, enabling significant fraud to be committed. Where payment transactions are automatically generated by the system, payments can be manipulated or diverted, or they can be generated in error or at the wrong time intervals. The benefit of human experience in identifying unusual or inconsistent transactions is reduced with electronic or EDI transactions, which are less subject to visual review.

5-4-3 Analyzing Costs

There are several different types of costs associated with implementation of EDI. Table 5-3 summarizes these costs [1,19].

5-4-4 Choosing a Communication Interface Option

EDI transactions are transmitted either directly between the organizations and their trading partners or through third parties called VANs and public networks, such as America Online, CompuServe, Prodigy, and the Internet. The VAN serves as an electronic clearinghouse or post office, routing messages between trading partners and holding them until the recipient is ready for them. The EDI transmission process commonly involves three phases [1,8,20]:

1. The application interface includes passing the electronic transactions to (or extracting them from) the appropriate business application system. It is the critical link between the EDI translator and the business's own internal processing.

Table 5-3

Major Costs of Electronic Data Interchange

Hardware costs associated with the installation of the system. This may vary from organization to organization and depending on the type of hardware chosen, including mainframes, minicomputers, or microcomputers.

Legal and other costs associated with setting up trading partner relationships

Security costs

Software costs associated with the installation. The costs of EDI software for a minicomputer or mainframe can be significant, depending on the comprehensiveness of the installation.

System development costs that vary according to the extent to which EDI is being implemented

Telecommunications costs, accessing, and using value-added or other types of networks

Training, which includes training employees to change their existing work practices

Personnel costs

---

2. The EDI translator performs formatting (or reformatting) of the data into an agreed-upon EDI data format and passes them to the data communications interface. All transaction data must pass through this process to be sent from or received by the organization.

3. The communications interface includes the transmission and reception of EDI documents electronically. It presents the media that all EDI transactions go through.

There are four common types of communications networks that a company can choose from. Which option should be selected depends on the strategic goals of a particular organization. These options include the following:

1. In **point-to-point connections,** EDI partners establish a direct computer-to-computer link through a private network. In this case all partners must use the same standards and conventions for setting up formats for various transactions, conform to specified speed, and be responsible for developing and monitoring their individual systems. This option has been popular with government agencies and U.S. car makers. Table 5-4 summarizes the advantages of this option, and Table 5-5 summarizes the disadvantages of this option.

2. In VANs, EDI partners do not deliver messages directly to each other; instead they use a VAN as a sort of "post office" for holding and forwarding messages. The sender transmits data to the VAN; that, in turn, determines the intended recipient for the transaction and places the data in the recipient's electronic mailbox. The data remain in the mailbox until the intended recipient retrieves them. A VAN usually provides dependable and secure service and is a more cost-

Table 5-4

Advantages of Point-to-Point Connection

It allows the organization to control the access to the network.

It allows the organization to use and enforce a proprietary software standard in dealing with all trading partners.

The sponsoring organization controls the system. Therefore, there is no reliance on third parties for computer processing.

With the absence of a third-party handling data, the timeliness of delivery can be improved.

effective alternative compared to point-to-point connections. It also provides services such as storing and forwarding messages, detecting and correcting errors, and message encryption and decryption [1,28].

VAN providers such as Sterling Commerce (Dublin, OH), GEIS, and IBM Global Networks are planning to introduce a new generation of Internet Protocol (IP)-based EDI. This new EDI would interconnect legacy systems in industries and companies that have not had the resources to utilize traditional EDI. For example, Sterling Commerce, which has 1,600 employees, over 30,000 EDI customer sites worldwide, and 20 years' experience in building EDI solutions, recently started two new business units to implement Internet-based EDI solutions. The company has inexpensive PC-based software for a "Commerce Catalog," which can be used to build EDI-enabled, IP-based electronic catalogs. These can be used to develop EDI-customized order forms and other types of EDI-enabled documents [1,28].

Sterling has also developed the Commerce Connection, a package of IP-based software applications for EDI materials. They have simple Internet-like browsers and offer quick IP-based network access. Web technology promises to eliminate

Table 5-5

Disadvantages of Point-to-Point Connection

A higher initial cost for communication networks

A need to establish the point-to-point connection with each trading partner

Limited business partnership

Computer scheduling issues

Hardware and software compatibility

Need for standard protocols

many of the complications of EDI, as it was implemented on mainframes in various flavors of UNIX and in proprietary VANs.

GEIS launched an initiative recently when it established a partnership with Netscape, called Actra, to integrate EDI with Netscape's Navigator browser technology. GEIS's role is to establish and stabilize the standards to add security, interoperability with EDI systems, and functions like certification of Internet B2B transactions. These features should make EDI more acceptable over the Internet with a moderate cost.

Table 5-6 summarizes the advantages of VANs, and Table 5-7 lists some of the disadvantages.

3. **Proprietary networks** are used in some industries, such as health care and banking. In these cases industry-specific networks have been developed that allow the transmission of EDI transactions [27].

4. **Internet-based EDI** or the **open EDI option** uses the Internet to transmit EDI transactions. Figure 5-3 illustrates this configuration. As this figure illustrates, Company X sets up a purchase order using its internal application program. Next, EDI software translates the purchase order from the internal format to the standard ANSI X12 or EDIFACT. The formatted data must be encapsulated using Multipurpose Internet Mail Extensions (MIME). The encapsulation processing is similar to putting the data in an electric wrapping. To ensure the security and integrity of data it must be encrypted using an encryption algorithm (discussed in Chapter 11). These formatted and encrypted data are routed over the Internet using simple mail transport protocol (SMTP) (introduced in Chapter 9). On the receiving end, the reverse process takes place, the "stripping" task. The data contents are taken out of the wrapping and then decrypted. The actual EDI content is extracted from the message body using MIME rules. These data

Table 5-6
Advantages of Value-Added Networks

In some cases, the VAN provides value-added services, such as converting the application format to a standard format; the partner sending the data does not have to reformat it.

It reduces communication and data protocol problems, as most VANs have the appropriate facilities to deal with diverse protocols. The fact that the sender and receiver are not directly connected eliminates the need to agree on and implement a common protocol.

It reduces scheduling problems, since senders and receivers do not directly communicate; the receiver can, at its convenience, request delivery of the information from the VAN.

The mailbox facility of the VAN allows one trader to deal with many partners without establishing numerous point-to-point connections.

The VAN can provide increased security and can act as a network firewall to protect the entity.

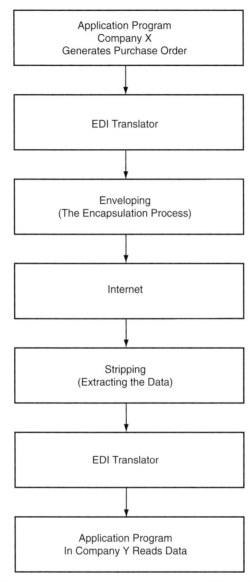

Figure 5-3 Internet-based electronic data interchange (EDI) configuration.

Table 5-8

**Advantages of Internet-Based Electronic
Data Interchange**

Higher transmission speed
Lower cost
Worldwide connectivity
Platform independent
Ease of use infrastructure
Broader market

are passed to the EDI translator, which reformats it so that the recipient's (Company Y) application program can read it [31,33].

Internet-based EDI is a growing new alternative to VANs and proprietary networks because it provides several unique advantages, as outlined in Table 5-8. Table 5-9 lists some of the disadvantages of this Internet-based EDI, and Table 5-10 highlights some of the providers of Internet-based EDI.

5-4-5 Reviewing Standards

In a growing economy, EDI standards are fundamental to enhance development and to reduce overall costs. EDI initially developed along industry-specific lines, with each industry developing its own standards. Due to the increased use of EDI, cross-industry common standards became a necessity. The goal of standardization is to enable dissimilar computer systems, with dissimilar data structures and formats, to be able to communicate with one another with minimum human intervention. By agreeing to use common standards, companies can program their computers only once, per standard, to send messages, and once to re-

Table 5-9

Disadvantages of Internet-Based Electronic Data Interchange

Overall security concern
Inability to provide audit logs and third-party verification of message transmission and delivery

Table 5-10

Some Providers of Internet-Based Electronic Data Interchange

Advanced Data Exchange (ADX, formerly The EC Company)

Ariba, Inc.

Commerce One

DynamicWeb Enterprises

IPNet

Proxicom

VanTree

---

ceive. The larger the number of companies using common standards, the greater the benefits for all the participants [32].

Standards and protocols are the common language spoken when dealing with trading partners, defining the format of the transaction and the way in which the transaction is communicated. Generally speaking, it will be a generic, comprehensive protocol, agreed by a sufficiently wide user community. The alternative will be for each industry to support at least three standards: (a) the standard for its own industry, (b) the X.12 North American standard, and (c) the EDI For Administration, Commerce, and Transport (EDIFACT) European standard. The two main EDI standards include American National Standards Institute (ANSI) X.12 and UN/EDIFACT.

Numerous proprietary standards have been established in various industries such as the following [32]:

- London Insurance Market Network (LIMNET) for the insurance industry
- Society for Worldwide Interbank Financial Transactions (SWIFT) for the banking industry
- Organization for Data Exchange Through Tele-Transmission for European (ODETTE) automotive industry
- Data Interchange for Shipping (DISH) for European transportation industries
- Reinsurance and Insurance Network (RINET)
- Trading Data Communication (TRADCOMS) in the United Kingdom

In addition, there are company-specific standards, such as Ford-Net from Ford of Europe or the proprietary rules from Siemens in Germany.

5-4-6 IMPLEMENTATION

There are basically two types of EDI implementation [1]:

1. Stand-alone EDI. In this type of implementation, a small pilot project with only a microcomputer interface is designed. Transactions are often printed, manually reviewed, and rekeyed for entry into the application system. Thus, there is a small change in the workflow (small audit impact).

2. Integrated. In this type, application-to-application EDI with the integration of the receiver and sender's computer systems (for example, order processing, fulfillment, and payment) is implemented.

EDI implementation goes through three phases: (a) preimplementation, (b) implementation, and (c) postimplementation audit [3,20,32].

During the **preimplementation** phase, the organization's current position must be carefully identified. Questions such as the following must be asked:

• Does the organization have any vendors, clients, or business partners that are currently using EDI? If so, the organization can use them to help support implementation.

• Who is the right person to "champion" the EDI project? Similar to other e-commerce projects, someone (preferably from top management) who has fairly broad experience and contacts within the organization should champion the project.

A design team should be organized. This team is similar to the task force discussed in Chapter 4. At the very least the team should include representatives from the management information systems (MIS), legal, and accounting departments. Representatives from production and purchasing departments will add more strength to the team. Whoever leads the team should preferably report to the CFO or another high-level financial executive. This individual should feel that he or she has a personal stake in making sure the EDI project is successful. He or she will be best able to quantify and understand the benefits that EDI will bring to the organization.

The final step in preimplementation is to set a strategic direction and make an implementation plan. The organization needs to identify the areas of the business that can most benefit from EDI. A plan should be laid out, preferably with dates, to implement the entire project. Project management tools such as Gantt charts and Program Evaluation Review Technique (PERT) would be very helpful.

There are several ways to **implement** EDI. The basic process is as follows:

1. Identify the organization's potential trading partners.

2. Identify the types of documents the organization will exchange with those trading partners.

3. Acquire some expert advice or training in setting up the organization's specific EDI transactions.

4. Choose the EDI software. There are many options available, and features and prices vary. Make sure the organization's receives what it needs. If one of the organization's trading partners is already using specific software that should be considered. Talk to other companies in the same field and observe what they are using. Also contact one or more of the EDI consulting firms. There are plenty of resources and products available.

5. Choose a communication method. Communication takes place in three primary ways: direct dial-up, Internet, and VANs. As explained earlier, a VAN is a service provider that provides one type of private and secure e-mail box for your corporation. Many commercial VANs are available (most of the major telephone companies provide such services). The costs for their services vary, so several options should be examined. The cheapest service is not necessarily the best. Secure and consistent access is of prime importance.

6. Coordinate setup with your trading partners and make sure you are all using the same version or release of the EDI software, and that the protocol of transmittal and confirmation is agreed upon. The transactions you choose partially dictate what you can and should do. At this stage all the trading partners should be identified. The full benefits of EDI are not realized if the organization only identifies a small number of trading partners.

7. Prioritize the implementation process. The organization must make sure to identify where the greatest benefits will be gained and implement those areas first. Because EDI is relatively new, the benefits generated from this application may be different from other information systems applications. A new and significantly different way of doing business, EDI is going to create a cultural change in the business; it is not just an improvement project.

The **postimplementation audit** is at least as important as preimplementation and implementation. The organization should review how things went and plan for the future. The organization should realize that even though a number of trading partners have been secured and several areas are online, there will be more work in the future. The organization should put together a permanent EDI team to ensure future growth. This team will be responsible for making sure that EDI continues to run as smoothly as it did during a well-planned implementation.

The organization should review the implementation process and evaluate how the system is working. The team should evaluate how much money is being saved and exactly where. They should evaluate the number of transactions that the system processes and the satisfaction of the trading partners. The team should look for other areas where the organization can use newfound EDI expertise to continue to improve the organization's competitiveness.

5-5 ELECTRONIC DATA INTERCHANGE IN ACTION: AN OVERVIEW

The number and diversity of EDI applications is well documented throughout the literature. In this section I review some of the popular applications and the organizations that use these applications [17,18,22] (see Table 5-11). Information Box 5-2 presented at the beginning of the chapter discussed EDI applications of Compaq Computer.

Table 5-11

**Some Organizations Using
Electronic Data Interchange**

Alcoa

BancBoston Mortgage Co.

Bank of America

British Airways

Carter Hawley

Chrysler Corp.

Department of Defense

DuPont

Federal Government

Ford Motor Co.

General Electric

General Motors

JCPenney

K-mart

MCI Communications

Mobil

Nestle Distribution Co.

Price Club Canada

RJR Nabisco

Rockwell International

United Parcel Services (UPS)

United States Custom Service

Veterans Administration

Wal-Mart Stores

Whirlpool Corp.

5-5-1 DuPont Corporation

The DuPont Corporation of Wilmington, Delaware, exports more than 200 shipments yearly originating from many commercial centers within the company. The company's forwarders generate 2,000 telex messages and produce a total of 30,000 pages of related information daily. The cost of producing and storing this information is estimated at $20 million annually. Although EDI can serve as a catalyst for operational improvements throughout a company, for many, such improvements need to start with the initial automation of processes and procedures that are still paper- and people-intensive. DuPont's solution is called XT or Export-TRIMS (Transportation Rate/Route Information Management System) with export rating, routing, payment, and shipment information files among other modules. With information provided by the material and logistics department and with shipment specifications, the system presents available routings, including carriers, exit ports, and types of services available.

Inquiries can be made based on various parameters, such as export control numbers and hazardous material controls, and the system audits for duplicate shipment payments. Compatible with other corporate systems, XT is credited with enhancing the company's competitive position in the global marketplace [30].

5-5-2 Federal Government

The U.S. government is trying to reduce paperwork by using various applications of EDI. The U.S. Custom Service, for example, is attempting to gain maximum electronic linkage between its headquarters and the import community, using its Automated Commercial System to exchange trade data. The paperless environment for cargo clearance is an achievable goal. Ultimately, there will be no hard-copy forms involved in the import of foreign merchandise. Import brokers can use EDI to send entry forms to the agency and get clearance for certain shipments before the ship ever reaches the port. This means that millions of dollars in duties and fees can be sent quickly to the Treasury Department, where they can start earning interest rather than waiting days or even weeks for paperwork to clear. The Defense Department wants to migrate its acquisition and logistics operations to EDI and paperless applications by 2002. The goal is to set up programs that can support EDI throughout a project's life cycle [9,26].

5-5-3 General Motors

General Motors (GM) Corporation has introduced an invoiceless payment system where all invoices will be paid electronically by using EDI and EFT. This occurred mainly because several financial institutions set up third-party EDI networks. EFT, a special type of EDI, is a money transfer system that banking and financial institutions provide worldwide. In addition, the automobile industry was one of the early supporters of EDI and helped promote the number of EDI users by adopting EDI for business, with thousands of EDI transactions occurring each day. GM sees many advantages for using this technology:

1. Cost effectiveness: An EDI transaction costs less than traditional methods.
2. Speed: EDI eliminates five-day mailing time for business documents.
3. Reliability: Transaction acknowledgments help ensure the delivery of information.
4. Flexibility: EDI transactions are not restricted to paper forms. Information may be added or deleted as required.
5. Expandability: Additional transactions can be easily added.

In the United States, GM considered paper reduction a strong motivating factor for EDI introduction. Implementation began in its payments system, where the organization was spending $4 billion per month, using 400,000 checks to 2,000 suppliers. Complete implementation of EDI was reported to be capable of saving $200 to $500 in costs per vehicle produced [1,29]. In addition, GM began linking suppliers in West Germany, Spain, Italy, Belgium, and the Netherlands to the company's central European computer system in Antwerp, Belgium.

5-5-4 HEALTH-CARE INDUSTRIES

Electronic medical claims have revolutionized the way health-care organizations conduct business and provided direction for the next generation of EDI technology in the health-care industry [21]. In 1995, the state of New Jersey released a report on the Healthcare Information Networks and Technologies (HINT) project. HINT is the only available independent report that details the impact of EDI on the health-care industry. The HINT survey results support the popular view that provider groups that submit information electronically benefit as follows:

- A lower average cost per claim than paper-based claims.
- A lower average rejection rate for both initial claims and follow-up claims than paper-based claims.
- A shorter turn-around time on accounts receivable than paper-based claims.

Generally speaking, every segment of the health-care industry reported cost savings, lower claim-rejection rates, and faster payment as a result of using EDI.

The survey revealed that hospitals save 15%, pharmacies save 24%, physicians save 35%, laboratories save 37%, and payers save 37% by using EDI. In addition, hospitals reported 47% fewer rejected initial claims and 45% fewer rejected follow-up claims as a result of using EDI. Physicians' experienced 21% fewer rejected initial claims and 20% fewer rejected follow-up claims. Laboratories, pharmacies, and payers averaged 27% fewer rejected initial claims and 30% fewer rejected follow-up claims. The survey also concluded that electronic claims were paid considerably faster than paper-based claims. By submitting electronic claims instead of paper-based claims, hospitals saved 29 days in collecting accounts receivable, with a 44% improvement in cash flow; physicians saved 30 days in collecting accounts receivable, with a 52% improvement in cash flow, according to HINT survey results [15].

5-5-5 MOBIL CORPORATION

Proxicom, the leading provider of Internet-based business solutions, and Mobil Corporation recently announced the deployment of a revolutionary Internet-based EDI solution. This will help Mobil Corporation to conduct business more effectively with its more than 300 lubricant distributors. Proxicom implemented an extranet application adhering to EDI's X.12 standard while allowing for a paperless exchange of business documents using the Internet.

Mobil Corporation is a leading oil, natural gas, and petrochemical company with operations in more than 125 countries. Mobil Corporation distributors can now submit purchase orders directly through their web browsers without the complexity and cost of a traditional EDI system. In addition to placing orders via their Internet connection, distributors will be able to execute product buy backs and receive invoices and transaction acknowledgments. This solution is the future of B2B e-commerce. As mentioned earlier, Internet-based EDI is faster and considerably less expensive than traditional systems. Mobil Corporation has secured a competitive advantage by embracing the Internet to create new values for their distributors while incorporating their specific business rules. Through the extranet, Mobil has strengthened their distribution channels and increased the profit potential for all the involved parties. EDI over the Internet offers Mobil Corporation and its distributors a tremendous business advantage. The Internet vastly extends what Mobil can accomplish compared with more traditional systems. Mobil gains innovative, easy ways to communicate and work with their distributors, while saving time and money. Proxicom has been instrumental in helping Mobil Corporation to define an Internet strategy and in developing a workable solution [23].

5-5-6 TRANSPORTATION INDUSTRIES

Ocean shipping is becoming a crucial link in all of the important international trade sectors, and a new EDI network promises to transport the industry's customers into the age of paperless business, while saving time and money. The ocean transport industry is counting on EDI to link all international trades. The difference between booking cargo with an ocean carrier by phone or by EDI is significant. For example, the cost of a phone and fax booking is around $3, while the same booking by EDI costs 5 cents [25].

In the rail industry, the Industry Reference Files will allow customers to get stationmaster, rail regulations, and the rail route information. It will also allow for the information to be passed from company to company along the rail routes of the United States. The rail industry uses 70 transaction sets, which deal with every aspect of rail transport from bills of ways to financial EDI for transaction settlement [12].

The air transportation industry has finished the first year of using a UN/EDI-FACT message suite for passenger processing. EDIFACT is the United Nations-sponsored EDI standard for global commerce. The interactive UN/EDIFACT messages being used are connecting computer reservations with the airlines. Also, EDI is used in the fuel and corporate purchasing ends of the airline industry as well as in the air cargo industry [12].

5-6 WHAT IS A SUPPLY CHAIN?

A supply chain includes the integrated network of suppliers, transportation companies, and brokers providing materials and services to customers (businesses and consumers). The important links in a supply chain in a manufacturing organization may include the following (see Figure 5-4):

- Suppliers
- Purchasing departments
- Manufacturing facilities
- Distribution systems
- Customers

An effective supply chain performs the functions of procurement of materials, transformation of these materials into intermediate and finished products, and the distribution of these finished products to customers. Supply chains exist in both service and manufacturing organizations, although the complexity of the

Suppliers	Manufacturing Facilities	Distribution Center	Customers

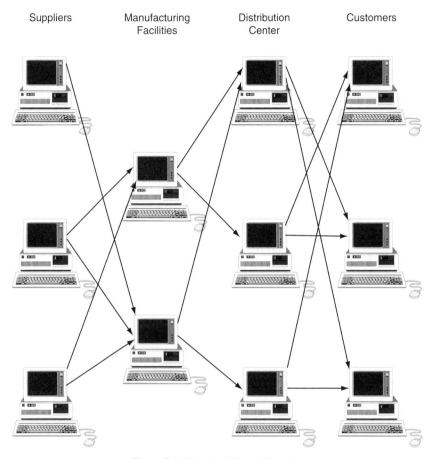

Figure 5-4 Supply-chain configuration.

chain may vary significantly from industry to industry and organization to organization [14].

5-7 SUPPLY-CHAIN MANAGEMENT AND BUSINESS-TO-BUSINESS E-COMMERCE

Supply-chain management is the process of active participation and interaction with suppliers and other companies in the supply chain to improve products, services, procedures, and processes using information systems solutions. Some of the activities in supply-chain management in a manufacturing firm may include the following:

- Procurement of materials
- Transformation of these materials into intermediate and finished products
- The distribution of these finished products to customers

Achieving customer satisfaction, expediting the delivery of products and services, and reducing the cost of manufacturing and distribution are some of the main goals of a successful supply-chain management program. For example, in a furniture-manufacturing firm, supply-chain management includes all the activities from the acquisitions of raw materials (wood) to the delivery of finished furniture delivered to the customer's door. An effective supply-chain program should include the following:

- Control of the physical flow of products
- Manufacturing of products
- Management of the shop
- Inventory management, including a fully integrated work-flow-driven order-fulfillment system
- Delivery of products

The Internet and EDI play a significant role in improving the efficiency and effectiveness of the entire supply-chain management process. EDI and the Internet could expedite the delivery of accurate and relevant information throughout the entire supply chain including the following:

- Order administration
- Shipping information
- Invoice and payment information
- Inventory management
- Sales forecast and planning

Four key decisions in supply-chain management are as follows:

- Location (where to locate the manufacturing facilities)
- Inventory (methods for improving the efficiency and effectiveness of inventory management, such as JIT)
- Production (what to produce and how much to produce)
- Transportation (selection of the optimum transportation systems that reduces the cost and expedites the delivery process)

Dell Computer has modified the supply chain from a "push" to a "pull" style manufacturing process, altering the supply chain to provide Dell with a competitive advantage. Dell sells directly to customers, eliminating extra steps (middlemen) between the manufacturer and the customer. Using this model not only has Dell reduced cost, it has also reduced inventory, manufacturing, and delivery time, which significantly improves Dell's competitiveness.

5-8 INDUSTRY CONNECTION: ARIBA, INC.

> Ariba, Inc.
> 11625 Rainwater Dr.
> Alpharetta, Georgia 30004
> Telephone: (678) 336-2900
> Fax: (678) 336-2920
> Web site address: <http://www.ariba.com>

Ariba, Inc., is a leading provider of B2B solutions and services. Ariba provides a comprehensive and open commerce platform to build B2B marketplaces, manage corporate purchasing, and electronically enable suppliers and commerce service providers on the Web. The Ariba B2B Commerce Platform offers a single system for managing the buying, selling, and marketplace e-commerce processes. Ariba offers a rapid-deployment, flexible e-procurement solution that focuses on helping companies execute their business strategy. Ariba Buyer applications help organizations optimize, manage, and leverage all aspects of their strategic buying. Some of the products and services offered by Ariba are as follows:

Ariba Buyer is Ariba's answer to the procurement needs of today's global enterprises. Companies use Ariba Buyer as a solution to buy both direct and indirect goods, acquire services, and to track travel costs and other expenses. The application redefines the buying process, reducing costs, eliminating inefficiencies, and speeding up transaction flow from end-to-end.

Ariba Marketplace is a flexible, rapid-deployment solution for market makers of all kinds that is suitable for all types of B2B exchanges—from horizontal procurement marketplaces to highly specialized vertical marketplaces and commodity exchanges. The application bridges traditional buy-side and sell-side solutions. Ariba Marketplace provides an all-in-one solution that makes it easy for market makers to deploy online trading communities rapidly and effectively.

Ariba Dynamic Trade is Ariba's highly configurable, fully integrated auction and exchange application. The solution delivers the full range of dynamic pricing mechanisms, auction, bid–ask exchange, and reverse auction in a flexible architecture. Ariba Dynamic Trade is highly configurable and supports such B2B trading situations as multitier channel relationships, approved vendor lists, price and bidder confidentiality, time sensitivity, and differing quality or support levels.

Ariba Commerce Services Network provides sourcing, liquidation, supplier content, and directory services, secure transaction routing, multiprotocol exchange of transaction information, payment services, and logistics. Ariba's set of network-based commerce services helps businesses streamline their supply chain and seize new revenue opportunities. Offered both directly and through partnerships with other leading service providers, these services allow businesses to take maximum advantage of online B2B trade.[1]

5-9 SUMMARY

This chapter provided a detail discussion of EDI as a growing application and technology used in B2B e-commerce. The chapter provided definition, applications, and historical development of EDI throughout the world, particularly in North America. The chapter introduced six major steps for a proper introduction of EDI in an organization. These steps included (a) assessing the strategic value of EDI applications, (b) analyzing the advantages and disadvantages, (c) analyzing the costs, (d) choosing a communication interface option, (e) setting EDI standards, and (f) implementating EDI. The chapter introduced several popular applications of EDI and reviewed several organizations that have been successfully using EDI. The chapter concluded with a discussion of supply chain and supply-chain management and the role of the Internet and EDI in B2B e-commerce, highlighting Ariba, Inc. as the industry connection.

5-10 REVIEW QUESTIONS

1. What is EDI? What are some of the differences between EDI and data communications in general? Discuss.
2. How did EDI start?
3. What are some of the important milestones in EDI development?
4. What is the role of the Internet in further development of EDI applications?
5. What are some of the strategic values of EDI applications?
6. What are the relationships of EDI, TQM, and BPR? Discuss.
7. What are three main advantages of EDI?
8. What are three main disadvantages of an EDI system?

---

[1] This information was gathered from the company web site and other promotional materials. For detailed information and any update, contact the company.

9. Are the advantages and disadvantages of EDI the same for all the applications and organizations or do they vary? Discuss.
10. What are some of the costs of EDI implementation?
11. How is Compaq Computer using EDI? What are some of the EDI applications in this company? Discuss.
12. When it comes to the selection of a communications interface option, how many choices are there? What are some of the advantages and disadvantages of these various options?
13. What are some of the components of an EDI system?
14. Why is Internet-based EDI gaining popularity? What are some of the advantages of this type of EDI? What are some of the disadvantages? Who are some of the providers of this service?
15. What are EDI standards? Why should an organization choose a standard? What are some of the popular options?
16. What are some of the choices for the implementations of EDI? Discuss.
17. List ten popular applications of EDI in B2B e-commerce.
18. What are some examples of companies who have successfully implemented EDI?
19. What has EDI done at DuPont? At Mobil Corporation?
20. What has EDI done in the transportation industry? In the health-care industry?
21. In your opinion, will the popularity of EDI increase or decrease in the near future? Discuss.
22. What is supply chain? Who are some of the main players in a supply chain of a manufacturing organization? Discuss.
23. What is supply-chain management? What is the role of EDI and the Internet for an effective supply-chain management program? Discuss.

5-11 PROJECTS AND HANDS-ON EXERCISES

1. Log onto the web site of the Ariba, Inc., at the following URL:

    <http://www.ariba.com>

    What are some of the software products and services offered by this company? What are some of the specific e-commerce solutions offered by this company? Discuss. Who are some of Ariba's major competitors?
2. A new automotive discount retailer is planning to use EDI in dealing with its suppliers. They need your help. Provide a detail cost and benefit analysis statement for this organization. What are some of the advantages of EDI for this organization? What are some of the disadvantages? Discuss.

3. Compare and contrast extranets, EFT, and EDI. You may want to refer to the materials presented in Chapters 4 and 6 for background information. Which industry may benefit the most from each technology? What is the role of each technology in a successful B2B e-commerce implementation? Discuss.

4. What are some of the advantages of EDI for academic institutions? How is the transportation industry benefiting from EDI? The health-care industry? Discuss.

5. Texas Instruments is a major user of the Internet-based EDI. Research this company and prepare a one-page report on the applications of EDI in this company. What are some of the advantages of the Internet-based EDI compared with VAN-based EDI? Discuss.

6. What are some of the protocols used in Internet-based EDI? What is the encapsulation process? What is the stripping process? What is the role of SMPT? Discuss.

7. The following web sites provide comprehensive information on Medicare and health-care EDI.

<http://hedic.org>
<http://www.officemed.com/home.htm>
<http://www.hcfa.gov/medicare/edi/edi.htm>

Log onto each site and examine its contents. What are some of the advantages of EDI in Medicare? How may EDI improve patient care? Discuss. Based on the materials presented in these sites and other sources, prepare a two-page report on the applications of EDI in the health-care industry. Are these applications unique? Could the same application be applied to other industries? Discuss.

8. The following sites provide comprehensive information on EDI.

<http://fox.nstn.ca/~cottier/overview/EDI/edi.html>
<http://www.ptxecrc.com/edi.htm>
<http://www.seagate.com/support/edi/ediguid6.html#WHATISEDI>

Log onto each and examine its contents. What are the latest in EDI? What are the advantages of Internet-based EDI compared with traditional EDI? Discuss.

9. The following web sites provide comprehensive information on supply-chain management:

<http://www.manufacturing.net/magazine/logistic/pointpgs/webex.htm>
<http://www.ascet.com/ascet/sp/spHP.html>
<http://www.manufacturing.net/scl>
<http://silmaril.smeal.psu.edu/misc/supply_chain_intro.html>
<http://www.ebnonline.com/supplychain>

By reviewing the materials presented in these sites and other sources, prepare a two-page report on supply-chain management. How has e-commerce improved supply chain? What is the role of EDI for a successful supply-chain management program? Discuss.

10. The following web site provides comprehensive information on EDI service providers.

<http://www.dir.ca.gov/dwc/EDIvend.HTM>

By reviewing the materials presented in this site and other sources, provide 10 criteria for choosing an EDI service provider. In your opinion, what are the most important criteria before choosing a provider?

5-12 KEY TERMS

REFERENCES

[1] American Institute of Certified Public Accountants (AICPA) (1996). *Auditing Procedure Study: Audit Implication of EDI,* AICPA, New York, pp. 7-21.

[2] American Institute of Certified Public Accountants (AICPA) (1996). *Auditing Procedure Study: Audit Implication of EDI,* AICPA, New York, pp. 55-58.

[3] Chan, Sally, Govindan, Marshall, Richard, John Y., Takach, George S., and Wright, Benjamin (1995). *Information Technology Division: EDI Management, and Audit Issues,* American Institute of Certified Public Accountants (AICPA), New York, p. 2.

[4] Chan, Sally, Govindan, Marshall, Richard, John Y., Takach, George S., and Wright, Benjamin (1995). *Information Technology Division: EDI Management, and Audit Issues,* American Institute of Certified Public Accountants (AICPA), New York, pp. 7-9.

[5] Chan, Sally, Govindan, Marshall, Pichard, John Y., Takach, George S., and Wright, Benjamin (1995). *Information Technology Division: EDI Management, and Audit Issues,* American Institute of Certified Public Accountants (AICPA), New York, pp. 22-28.

[6] Comaford, Christine (1966, October 14). "Taking Care of Business the Net Way: Electronic Data Interchange; Mission Critical; Internet/Web/Online Service Information; Column," *PC Week,* Vol. 13, No. 41, p. 69.

[7] Davey, Tom (1997, September 22). "They are still sold on EDI." *InformationWeek,* No. 649, pp. 153-157.

[8] Dearing, Brian (1995, November). "How EDI Is Driving VAN Growth in Europe; Electronic Data Interchange and Value-Added Network Operators: Industry Trend or Event," *Telecommunications,* Vol. 29, No. 11, p. 62.

[9] "Digital or Else: Defense Department Wants to Migrate Acquisition and Logistics Operations to EDI and Paperless Application by 2002." *Government Computer News* (1997, September 1), Vol. 16, No. 26, p. 60.

[10] "Electronic Data Interchange (EDI)." *Automatic I.D. News* (1997, March 15), p. 20.

[11] "EDI Modeling Would Change ASC X.12 Procedures: Standards Groups Stake Future On IDEF, Contemplate Implementation." *EDI News* (1997, September 15), Vol. 11, No. 19.

[12] "EDI News Short Takes . . ." *EDI News* (1997, October 27), Vol. 11, No. 22.

[13] "GE Unveils European TradeWeb Web-Based EDI System." *Newsbytes* (1997, October 27).

[14] Handfield, Robert B., and Ernest L. Nichols, Jr. (1998). "Introduction to Supply Chain Management." Prentice Hall, Upper Saddle River, NJ.

[15] Hansen, Bruce (1996, January). "Electronic data interchange: Exploring the benefits of full-service EDI networks," *Healthcare Financial Management,* Vol. 50, No. 1, pp. 64-66.

[16] Joseph, Gilbert W., and Engle, Terry J. (1996, July). "Controlling an EDI Environment: Electronic Data Interchange." *Journal of Systems Management,* Vol. 47, No. 4, p. 42.

[17] Jilovec, Nahid (1997, August 29). "Call centers using EDI, CTI, imaging and workflow, *Midrange Systems,* Vol. 10, No. 13, p. 033.

[18] Kerstetter, Jim (1996, June 24). "Livermore Labs, Bank of America Debut Secure EDI: Electronic Data Interchange; Pilot Project Almost Complete; Technology Information." *PC Week,* Vol. 13, No. 25, p. 10.

[19] Kumar, Ram, and Crook, Connie W. (1996, March). "Educating senior management on the strategic benefits of electronic data interchange." *Journal of Systems Management,* Vol. 47, No. 2, p. 42.

[20] Lankford, William M., and Riggs, Walter E. (1996, March), "Electronic Data Interchange: Where Are We Today?" *Journal of Systems Management,* Vol. 47, No. 2, p. 58.

[21] Lummus, Rhonda R. (1997, May). "The Evolution to Electronic Data Interchange; Are There Benefits at All Stages of Implementation?" *Hospital Material Management Quarterly,* Vol. 18, No. 4, pp. 79-83.

[22] Mahabharat, C.T. (1997, September 10). "India-Exporters Body Sets Up EDI Service Center." *Newsbytes.*

[23] McLean, Va. (1997, March 10). "Proxicom and Mobil Introduce New Internet-Based Electronic Data Interchanges," *PR Newswire.*

[24] Montana, John (1996, July). "Legal issues in EDI; Electronic Data Interchanges; Legal Issues." *Records Management Quarterly,* Vol. 30, No. 3, p. 39.

[25] "Ocean Shipping Gets Easy with Interactive EDI Other Modes of Transportation Show Interest Too," *EDI News* (1997, October 27), Vol. 11, No. 22.

[26] Olsen, Florence (1996, August 12). "Electronic data interchange hits a home run; at the Veterans Affairs Department and the Treasury; Government Activity." *Government Computer News,* Vol. 15, No. 20, p. 1.

[27] "Proprietary UPS EDI system could put customers in a bind." *EDI News* (1997, August 18), Vol. 11, No. 17.

[28] Puttre, John (1997, August). "Can Internet Standards Bring EDI to Everyone? Electronic Data Interchange." *Business Communication Review,* Vol. 27, No. 8, p. 23.

[29] Thierauf, Robert J. (1990). *Electronic Data Interchange in Finance and Accounting,* Quorum Books, Connecticut, pp. 12-16.

[30] Thierauf, Robert J. (1990). *Electronic Data Interchange in Finance and Accounting,* Quorum Books, Connecticut, p. 63.

[31] Tucker, Michael Jay (1997, April). "EDI and the Net: A profitable partnering; electronic data interchange; includes related article on EDI's detractors; Internet/Web/Online Service Information," *Datamation,* Vol. 43, No. 4, p. 62.

[32] Whipple, Larry C. (1997, June). "Electronic Data Interchange: Making It Happen; Discover What EDI Is, and What It Takes to Implement It in Your Business." *Database Web Advisor,* p. 48.

[33] Wilde, Candee (1997, March 17). "New Life for EDI: The Internet may help electronic data interchange finally meet expectations." *InformationWeek.*

Part II

Electronic Commerce Supporting Activities

Chapter 6

Electronic Payment Systems

Learning Objectives

Ater studying this chapter you should be able to do the following:

- Review electronic payment systems (EPS).
- Compare and contrast electronic payment systems with traditional payment systems.
- Elaborate on electronic funds transfer (EFT) as one of the earliest electronic payment methods.
- Explain payment cards, including smart cards.
- Discuss electronic cash, electronic checks, and electronic wallets.
- Explain tools and technologies for secure EPS.
- Elaborate on some of the commercial examples of EPS.

INFORMATION BOX 6-1

Electronic Payment Systems in Action

Flooz is an online gift currency sent by e-mail. The recipient spends it, just like money, at the online store of his or her choice.

Electronic commerce modeling language (ECML) was created by several industry leaders. Some of the key participants are American Express, AOL, Compaq, CyberCash, Discover, IBM, MasterCard, Microsoft, Novell, Sun Microsystems, Trintech, and Visa. ECML provides simple guidelines for Web merchants and enables digital wallets from multiple vendors to automate the exchange of information between consumers and merchants. More consumers will find shopping on the Web easy and compelling. ECML allows merchants to interoperate with a number of wallet solutions, and this makes shopping on its web site easier for consumers.

E-coins are electronic tokens issued by eCoin.net that can be used to pay for online goods and services. They are used for micropayment transactions.

E-check has been in active use for U.S. Treasury payments within the United States, and it is under further development in Singapore.

Clickshare is an electronic cash system for the magazine and newspaper industry. It can be used for micropayment transactions.

CheckFree provides online payment processing services to both large companies and consumers. It provides electronic bill payment processing services to more than 350 financial institutions.

About 95% of all online purchases were made with credit cards in 1999; however, this could change as software developers and electronic payment services unveil a variety of new payment options

More than two-thirds of the nation's six billion Automated Clearing House (ACH) payments are processed each year through CheckFree's ACH software and services. The fact that customers are reluctant to disclose their credit card numbers directly to e-businesses is promoting the use and development of electronic payment systems (EPS). EPS increases convenience and reduces costs to sellers, buyers, and the banking industry.

"Scrip," a different version of e-cash, is issued by third-party organizations, such as Beenz.com. Scrip could be "earned" by visiting certain web sites and then spent on items from e-businesses that support this kind of currency.

Some of the popular e-cash companies include CheckFree, Clickshare, Cyber-Cash, Digicash, eCoin.Net, and MilliCent.

Smart cards eventually will replace most of the contents of credit cards, debit cards, student identifications, parking cards, driver licenses, work IDs, public transportation tickets, public phone payments, photographs, and even cash.

Digital signature is an authentication technique that enables the sender of a message to attach a code that guarantees the source and integrity of the message.

INFORMATION BOX 6-2

CyberCash: A Major Player in Electronic Payment Systems

CyberCash, started in April 1995, is one of the leaders in electronic payment systems (EPSs). Its products and services are free to merchants and customers. Cyber-Cash collects fees from the banks processing their credit cards. Because of the volume of transactions it handles with various banks, CyberCash charges merchants wholesale rates of 2–9 cents per transaction, with an average fee of 5 cents per transaction. In addition, because all transactions between merchants and CyberCash are transmitted over the Web, merchants don't have to pay for costly leased lines or dial-up connections to banks.

The merchant transaction entry component is the CyberCash Merchant CashRegister, which can be used with any storefront software installed on any NT or Unix-based web server. CyberCash offers its consumers Wallet, which can be downloaded by the customer from the merchant's web site or from CyberCash's site. However, depending on how a merchant has set up its site, a customer has the choice of using a secure sockets layer (SSL)-based browser or the secure Cyber-Cash Wallet to make a credit card purchase. (SSL will be discussed later in the chapter.) Once the merchant receives the purchase request and returns a summary of the order to the customer, the customer then verifies the information and clicks the "Pay" button to send the packet of information back to the merchant. Cyber-Cash also supports secure electronic transaction (SET) (discussed later in the chapter).

When the CyberCash server receives the purchase information packet, it strips out the order information, and the payment information is digitally signed and encrypted. The merchant cannot see the customer's credit card information, which enhances security should someone hack the merchant's web server for credit card numbers. CyberCash then moves the transaction behind its firewall and off the Web. It then unwraps the packet within a hardware-based crypto box, reformats the transaction, and forwards it to the merchant's bank over dedicated lines. The merchant's bank then forwards the authorization request to the issuing bank via the card associations or directly to the credit card company. The approval or denial code is sent back to CyberCash, and the entire process takes between 15 and 20 seconds to complete.

Because the merchant doesn't maintain transaction information, reports must be accessed from CyberCash's database via the merchant's administrative server.

SOURCES: <http://www.cybercash.com>; Lisa L. Sweet, *Internet Business,* February 9, 1998.

6-1 INTRODUCTION

This chapter starts with an overview of electronic payment systems (EPSs) and then compares and contrasts EPSs with traditional payment systems. The chapter explores electronic funds transfer (EFT) as one of the oldest EPSs. Four types of payment cards, including credit cards, debit cards, charge cards, and smart cards, are introduced, and current and future applications of smart cards are presented. Electronic cash and checks are discussed and compared and contrasted with traditional cash and checks. The chapter presents a discussion on various tools and technologies for secure EPSs, including digital signatures, authentications, public key cryptography, certificates, certificate authorities, the secure sockets layer (SSL), secure hypertext transfer protocol (HTTP) digital signatures, and public and private key secure electronic transmissions (SET). (Other security issues and measures will be discussed in Chapter 11.) The chapter introduces electronic wallets, micropayment, and other payment systems and concludes with two popular commercial examples of electronic payment systems, including Mondex e-Cash and NetChex debit check card, highlighting Microsoft Corporation as the industry connection. EPSs are in their introductory phases, and their use should become more widespread in parallel with e-commerce expansion. In the near future their popularity and acceptance should increase.

6-2 ELECTRONIC PAYMENT SYSTEMS: AN OVERVIEW

In traditional brick-and-mortar establishments, a customer sees a product, examines it, and then pays for it by cash, check, or credit card (see Figure 6-1).

In the e-commerce world, in most cases the customer does not physically see the actual product at the time of transaction, and the method of payment is performed electronically. Therefore, issues of trust and acceptance play a more important role in the e-commerce world than in traditional businesses as far as payment systems are concerned.

EPSs utilize integrated hardware and software systems that enable a customer to pay for the goods and services online. Although these systems are in their infancy, some significant progress has been made. The main objectives of EPS are to increase efficiency, improve security, and enhance customer convenience and ease of use. As shown throughout this chapter, there are several methods and instruments that can be used to enable EPS implementation (see Figure 6-2.)

As mentioned previously, in conventional businesses customers pay for goods

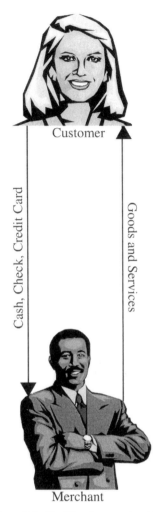

Figure 6-1 Traditional payment systems.

and services by cash, check, or credit cards. Online shoppers may use one of the following EPSs to pay for goods and services purchased online:

• Electronic funds transfer (EFT) involves electronic transfer of money by financial institutions.

• Payment cards include stored financial value that can be transferred from the customer's computer to the merchant's computer.

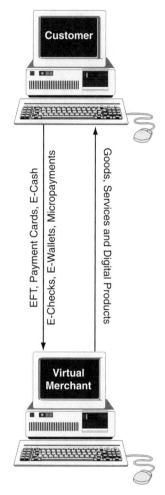

Figure 6-2   Electronic payment systems. EFT, electronic funds transfer.

• Credit cards are used by charging against the customer credit and are by far the most popular method used in EPSs.

• Electronic money (e-money or e-cash) is standard currency converted into an electronic format to pay for online purchases.

• Electronic gifts are one way of sending electronic currency or gift certificates from one individual to another. The receiver can spend these gifts in their favorite online stores provided they accept this type of currency.

• Online payment of monthly utility, Internet, or phone bills.

- Smart cards include stored financial value and other important personal and financial information used for online payments.
- Electronic wallets (e-wallets) are similar to smart cards in that they include stored financial value for online payments.
- Micropayment systems are similar to e-wallets in that they include stored financial value for online payments; however, they are used for small payments, such as pennies and fractions of pennies.

Although these groups appear to be distinct, there is some overlap among them. For example, e-wallets can be classified as payment cards when they are used to store credit card information or as e-money when they store electronic currency. When the industry matures, this duplication in naming and function should be resolved.

6-3 ELECTRONIC FUNDS TRANSFER

Electronic funds transfer (EFT) is one of the oldest EPSs and is used for transferring money from one bank account directly to another without any paper money changing hands. EFT is the foundation of the cashless and checkless society where checks, stamps, envelopes, and paper bills are eliminated. The most popular application of EFT is the direct deposit option used by millions of workers in the United States. (Please note different names may be used outside of the United Sates.) Instead of receiving a paycheck and depositing it into an account, the money is deposited to an account electronically. The Federal Reserve's Fedwire and New York Clearing House Interbank Payment Systems (CHIPS) are two major users of EFT systems.

Customers, companies, and government agencies use EFT for all kinds of applications. EFT is considered to be a safe, reliable, and convenient way to conduct business. Direct deposit is used for payroll, travel, and expense reimbursements, annuities and pensions, dividends, and government payments such as Social Security and veterans benefits. Other types of EFT are frequently used for bill payments, retail purchases, Internet purchases, corporate payments, and treasury management, and for the disbursement of food stamps and other government cash assistance.

In broad terms EFT refers to any transfer of funds initiated through an electronic terminal, including credit card, ATM, Fedwire, and point-of-sale (POS) transactions. It is used for both credit transfers, such as payroll payments, and for debit transfers, such as mortgage payments. Many utility companies and sport clubs also use EFT. The advantages of EFT include the following:

- Reduced administrative costs
- Increased efficiency

- Simplified bookkeeping
- Enhanced security

At present, acceptance of this system has not been widespread. (Please note that acceptability of payment methods varies between countries.) Banks process EFT transactions through the Automated Clearinghouse (ACH) network. ACH is a secure network that connects all U.S. financial institutions. For electronic payments, funds are transferred electronically from one bank account to the billing company's bank, usually within 24 hours of the scheduled payment date.

Another common application of EFT is for money transfer among banks and other financial institutions. When a customer pays for goods and services by checks, the merchant collects these checks (assuming the checks are accepted) and sends them to its bank. The bank credits the merchant account and then sends these checks to the clearing department. The clearing department separates the checks by banks and transfers them to a clearinghouse. At this point, banks transfer checks among themselves. The customer's bank eventually receives the check and debits the customer account. In some cases these checks are sent back to the customer, which marks the end of the process. If there are not sufficient funds in the customer's account, then the check is sent back to the merchant bank. The merchant must pay for the fee involved in the nonsufficient funds process and has to settle this with the customer or write it off as a bad check.

The U.S. government monitors EFT compliance through Regulation E of the Federal Reserve Board, which implements the Electronic Funds Transfer Act (EFTA). Regulation E governs financial transactions with EPSs, specifically with regard to disclosure of information, consumer liability, error resolution, record retention, and receipts at electronic terminals [1].

6-4 PAYMENT CARDS

Payment cards are the most popular instrument for electronic payment transactions and they include the following:

- Credit cards
- Debit cards
- Charge cards
- Smart cards

6-4-1 CREDIT CARDS

Flatbush National Bank began issuing payment cards in 1947; Diners Club was first issued in 1950 and American Express in 1958. The other major players in the credit card environment are MasterCard, Visa, and Discover. There are two types of credit cards on the market today: (1) those issued by credit card companies (e.g., MasterCard and Visa) and major banks (e.g., Wells Fargo and Bank of America), and (2) those issued by department stores (e.g., May Company), and oil companies (e.g., Chevron). Because businesses benefit tremendously from these company cards and they are cheaper to operate, they are widely issued to and used by a broad range of customers. Businesses offer incentives to entice customers to open an account and receive one of these cards.

Credit cards are issued based on the customer's credit history, income level, and total wealth. The credit limit ranges from a few hundred dollars to several thousands of dollars. The customer uses these cards to purchase goods and services or obtain cash from the participating financial institutions. The customer is supposed to pay his or her debts during the payment period; otherwise interest will accrue.

Two limitations of credit cards are their unsuitability for very small or very large payments. It is not cost-justified to use a credit card for small payments. Also, due to security issues, these cards have a limit and cannot be used for excessively large transactions.

6-4-2 DEBIT CARDS

Debit cards function similar to checks in that the charges will be deducted from the customer's checking account. The real advantage for the merchant is the speed at which the merchant collects these charges. The advantage to the customer is the ease of use and convenience. They also keep the customer under his or her budget because they do not allow the customer to go beyond his or her means.

6-4-3 CHARGE CARDS

Charge cards are similar to credit cards except they have no revolving credit line, so the balance must be paid off every month. Credit, debit, and charge card methods of payments have been successfully utilized in the pre-Internet era, and they are often used in the e-commerce world as well. Some of the reasons for their popularity in the e-commerce world are their availability (most customers own one of these cards), ease of use, and acceptance by most customers.

To use these cards as an online payment system, a well-defined process is followed. The diagram in Figure 6-3 illustrates this process. A brief description follows.

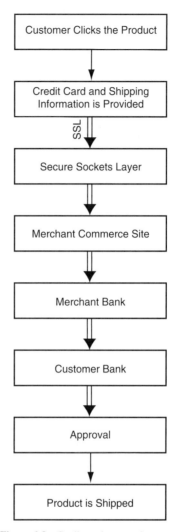

Figure 6-3   Credit card approval process.

1. A customer using his or her browser clicks on a product on the merchant's web site and adds it to an electronic shopping cart.

2. The customer provides the shipping instructions and credit card information.

3. The detailed payment information is displayed for the customer to review. A transmission technology known as secure sockets layer (SSL) (discussed later

in the chapter) protects the payment and shipping information while it is in transit.

4. This encrypted information is transmitted to the merchant's commerce site.

5. The server software adds the merchant identification to the information transmitted.

6. The secure payment request is transmitted over the Web to the merchant bank.

7. The merchant bank transmits this information to the customer's bank for authorization.

8. The customer's bank sends approval for payment to the merchant's bank, and if approved, the process is terminated and the merchandise shipped. This entire process (not including shipment) takes less than 30 seconds!

6-4-4 SMART CARDS

Smart cards have been actively used in Europe, Asia, and Australia for many years. Their acceptance is slowly increasing in the United States. They have been extensively used in the telecommunications industry for years. Due to their multipurpose functions, their popularity in the United States is also on the rise. A smart card is about the size of a credit card, made of a plastic with an embedded microprocessor chip that holds important financial and personal information. The microprocessor chip is loaded with the relevant information and periodically recharged. Figure 6-4 illustrates an IBM smart card.

Smart cards are broadly classified into two groups: contact and contactless. A **contact** smart card must be inserted into a special card reader to be read and updated. This type of smart card contains a microprocessor chip that makes

Figure 6-4 An IBM smart card <http://www.pc.ibm.com/europe/europeglobaloptions/smartcard_id.html>.

contact with electrical connectors to transfer the data. A **contactless** smart card can be read from a short distance using radio frequency. This type of smart card also contains a microprocessor chip and an antenna that allows data to be transmitted to a special card reader without any physical contact. This type of smart card is useful for people who are moving in vehicles or on foot. They are used extensively in European countries for collecting payment for highway tolls, bus fares, train fares, parking, admission fees to movies, theaters, plays, ferry crossings, and so forth.

The microprocessor chip can process different types of information, and therefore, various industries use them in different ways. Smart cards can accommodate a variety of applications that allow the customer to make purchases from a credit account, debit account, or stored value on the card. These cards can even have multiple applications operating at the same time. For example, the customer could have a frequent flyer program working on the same card as the customer debit or credit account. This enables the customer to earn points in his or her favorite program. Other services allow the customer to participate in frequency or loyalty programs with merchants, including storing hotel reservation preferences on the smart card.

Several computer manufacturers, including Compaq and Hewlett-Packard, are developing keyboards that include smart card slots that can be read like bank credit cards. A smart card can be programmed for different applications. Some cards contain programming and data to support multiple applications, and some can be updated with new applications after they are issued. Smart cards can be designed to be inserted into a slot and read by a special reader or be read at a distance, such as at a toll booth. IBM, Microsoft, Schlumberger, and Bull are among the major players in smart card development and utilization. Smart cards can be disposable or rechargeable. A popular example of a disposable smart card is the one issued by telephone companies. After using the prespecified amount, the card can be discarded. Some of the current and future applications of smart cards are summarized in Table 6-1.

Some of the advantages of smart cards include the following:

- Cannot be easily duplicated
- Can store many types of information
- Convenience (portable and do not occupy much space)
- Could include high security
- Low cost to issuers and users
- High accuracy of information

Lack of universal standards for their design and utilization and low consumer acceptance are among the disadvantages of smart cards. However, these disadvan-

Table 6-1

Current and Future Applications of Smart Cards

Electronic cash

An ID card when logging onto an Internet service provider

An ID to an online bank

A dial connection on a mobile telephone that is charged on a per-call basis

Admission to hospitals to provide personal information without filling out a form

Buying gasoline

Paying for parking at meters

Paying to get on subways, trains, or buses (popular in Europe)

Purchases on the Web

Telephone calls

In universities as identification and for campus purchases

---

tages should be resolved in the near future, and smart card applications are expected to increase.

6-5 ELECTRONIC CASH

Electronic cash (e-cash) is a secure and convenient alternative to bills and coins. This payment system complements credit, debit, and charge cards and adds additional convenience and control to everyday customer cash transactions. E-cash usually operates on a smart card. As discussed earlier, a smart card is a small plastic card similar to an ordinary credit card, which includes an embedded microprocessor chip. The microprocessor chip stores cash value and the security features that make electronic transactions secure.

E-cash transactions usually require no remote authorization or personal identification number (PIN) codes at the point of sale. This is because e-cash is transferred directly from the customer's desktop to the merchant's site. E-cash can be reloaded onto the card's microprocessor chip as frequently as needed. Using e-cash the customer has two options: a stand-alone card containing e-cash, or a combination card that incorporates both e-cash and debit. E-cash can be transferred over a telephone line or over the Web. The microprocessor chip embedded onto the card keeps track of the e-cash transactions.

When used, e-cash is transferred directly and immediately to the participating merchants and vending machines. Similar to regular cash, e-cash enables transactions between customers without the need for banks or other third parties. Mondex, a subsidiary of MasterCard (Mondex Canada Association) is a good example of e-cash. Information Box 6-3 further explains the specific applications and benefits of Mondex e-Cash. The following paragraphs explain how a typical e-Cash system works:

1. A customer or merchant signs up with one of the participating banks or financial institutions.

2. The customer receives specific software to install on his or her computer. The software allows the customer to download "electronic coins" to his or her desktop. The software manages the electronic coins. The initial purchase of coins is charged against the customer's bank account or against a credit card.

3. When buying goods or services from a web site that accepts e-cash, the customer simply clicks the "Pay with e-cash" button. The merchant's software generates a payment request, describing the item(s) purchased, price, and the time and date. The customer can then accept or reject this request. When the customer accepts the payment request, the software residing on the customer's desktop subtracts the payment amount from the balance and creates a payment that is sent to the bank or the financial institution of the merchant, and then is deposited to the merchant's account. The interesting aspect of the entire process is its prompt turnaround time (within a few seconds). The merchant is notified and in turn ships the goods.

6-6 ELECTRONIC CHECKS

An electronic check (e-check) is a new payment instrument that combines high-security, speed, convenience, and processing efficiencies for online transactions. An e-check is an electronic version of a paper check. It uses the same legal and business protocols associated with traditional paper checks. Theoretically, it can be used in any transaction where paper checks are used today. It shares the speed and processing efficiencies of all-electronic payments. An e-check can be used by large and small organizations, even where other electronic payment solutions are too risky or not appropriate. The key advantages of e-checks are as follows:

- Fast check processing
- Very low transaction cost
- Rapid and secure settlement of financial obligations

E-check is the result of cooperation among several banks, government entities, technology companies, and e-commerce organizations. The Financial Services Technology Consortium (FSTC), whose e-check project is currently being

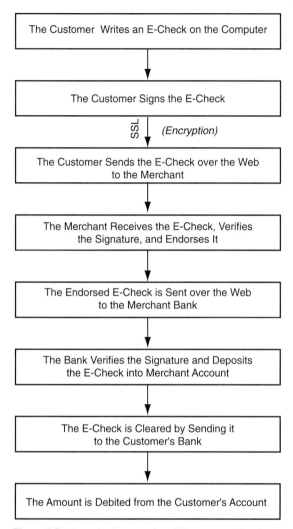

Figure 6-5   An e-check transaction. SSL, secure sockets layer.

used by the U.S. Treasury in a two-year pilot program, developed the technology used to standardize the implementation of e-checks. As mentioned earlier, e-check conforms to the familiar and well-established legal infrastructure and business processes associated with paper checks. It is the first and only electronic payment mechanism chosen by the U.S. Treasury to make high-value payments over the public Internet. E-check has been in active use at the U.S. Treasury; it is also under further development in Singapore and is being considered for many online transactions. Figure 6-5 shows an e-check transaction.

6-7 SECURE ELECTRONIC PAYMENT SYSTEMS' INFRASTRUCTURE

In order to ensure the integrity and security of each electronic transaction, the FSTC's e-check technology and other EPSs utilize some or all of the following security measures. It should be noted that a number of these measures are used in other applications as well. For example, authentication is used for other security purposes, such as when logging onto a network, digital signatures are used for formal contracts, and so forth.

I discuss various security issues and measures in detail in Chapter 11. In this chapter I explain the following seven measures and technologies that are directly related to EPSs:

- Digital signatures
- Authentication
- Public key cryptography
- Certificate authorities
- SSL
- Secure HTTP digital signatures
- Public and private key secure electronic transmission (SET)

6-7-1 DIGITAL SIGNATURES

A digital signature is an electronic rather than a written signature that can be used by an individual to authenticate the identity of the sender of a message or of the signer of a document. The U.S. government now accepts these signatures and gives them the same rights and privileges as written signatures. This law was passed in June 2000. E-check technology also allows digital signatures to be applied to document blocks, rather than to the entire document. This allows part of a document to be separated from the original, without compromising the integrity of the digital signature. This technology would also be very useful for business contracts and other legal documents transferred over the Web.

6-7-2 AUTHENTICATION

Authentication is the process of verification of the authenticity of a person and/or a transaction. As explained in Chapter 11, there are many tools available to confirm the authenticity of a user; for example, passwords and ID numbers are used to allow a user to log onto a particular site.

6-7-3 Public Key Cryptography

Cryptography is the process of protecting the integrity and accuracy of information by converting (encrypting) data into an unreadable format, called cipher text. Only those who possess a private key can decipher (decrypt) the message into plain text. Public key cryptography uses two keys, one public and one private, to encrypt and decrypt data, respectively. Generally, a designated authority issues this public–private key combination. The cryptographic certificates used with an e-check enable a check payee to determine the validity of the signature. Public key cryptography uses a pair of keys, one private and one public. In comparison, private key cryptography uses only one key for encryption. The advantage of the dual-key technique is that it allows the businesses to give away their public key to anyone who wants to send a message (sending a credit card number, for example). The sender can then encrypt the message with the public key and send it to the intended businessperson over the Internet or any other public network; the businessperson can then use the private key to decrypt the message. Naturally, the private key is not publicly known [6].

6-7-4 Certificates

Certificates provide a mechanism for establishing confidence in the relationship between a public key and the entity that owns the corresponding private key. A certificate can be thought of as similar to a driver's license. A driver's license is accepted by numerous organizations both public and private as a form of identification. This is mainly due to the legitimacy of the issuer, which is a government agency. Because organizations understand the process by which someone can obtain a driver's license, they can trust that the issuer verified the identity of the individual to whom the license was issued. Therefore, the driver's license can be accepted as a valid form of identification.

6-7-5 Certificate Authorities

In the e-commerce world, certificate authorities are the equivalent of passport offices in the government that issue digital certificates and validate the holder's identity and authority. Certificate authorities are similar to a notary public, a commonly trusted third party.

6-7-6 SECURE SOCKETS LAYER

The SSL protocol introduced by Netscape Corporation provides a relatively secure method to encrypt data that are transmitted over a public network such as the Internet. SSL provides security for all Web transactions, including file transfer protocol (FTP), HTTP, and Telnet-based transactions. It provides an electronic wrapping around the transactions that go through the Internet. All the major web server vendors, including Microsoft and Netscape, support SSL. The open and nonproprietary nature of SSL is what makes it the preferred choice for TCP/IP application developers for securing sensitive data. Similar to any other security measure, SSL is not perfect. For example, the protocol is vulnerable to attacks on the SSL server authentication. Despite its vulnerabilities, when properly implemented, SSL can be a powerful tool for securing Web-sensitive data. SSL offers comprehensive security by offering authentication and encryption at the client and server sides. It operates between the transport and the application layers in the network stack and uses both public and private key cryptography.

Transport and application layers are two of the layers in the network stack in the open system interconnection (OSI) reference model. OSI is a seven-layer architecture defining the method of transmission of data from one computer to another through a network. It is used to describe the flow of data between the physical connection to the network and the end user application. It standardizes levels of service and types of interaction for computers exchanging information through a network. Each layer in the architecture performs a specific task. (1) The **application** layer is application dependent and performs different tasks in different applications. (2) The **presentation** layer formats the message. (3) The **session** layer is responsible for establishing a dialogue between computers. (4) The **transport** layer is responsible for generating the receiver's address and ensuring the integrity of the messages sent. (5) The **network** layer is responsible for message routing. (6) The **data link** layer oversees the establishment and control of communications link. (7) The **physical** layer specifies the electrical connections between the computer and the transmission medium [5].

Both public and private key cryptography techniques have been around for a long time. Authentication begins when a client requests a connection to an SSL server. The client sends its public key to the server, which in turn generates a random message and sends it back to the client. Next, the client uses its private key to encrypt the message from the server and sends it back. All the server has to do at this point is decrypt the message using the public key and compare it to the original message sent to the client. If the messages match, then the server knows that it is from the client communicating with the intended client. To implement SSL in a web server, the following steps are followed:

1. Generate a key pair on the server.
2. Request a certificate from a certification authority.
3. Install the certificate.
4. Activate SSL on a security folder or directory.

It is not a good idea to activate SSL on all the directories because the encryption overhead created by SSL decreases system performance. One important drawback of SSL is that certificates and keys that originate from a computer can be stolen over a network or by other electronic means. One possible solution to this weakness is to use hardware tokens instead. Hardware tokens improve security tremendously because these tokens are more difficult to steal and they can be customized to individual users. This can be done in a number of ways, including using biometric techniques discussed in Chapter 11, such as fingerprint or retinal scan matching.

Some of the advantages of SSL include the following:

- **Authentication:** Allows Web-enabled browsers and servers to authenticate each other.
- **Limits access:** Allows controlled access to servers, directories, files, and services.
- **Protects data:** Ensures that exchanged data cannot be corrupted without detection.
- **Shares information:** Allows information to be shared by browsers and servers while remaining out of reach to third parties.

Some of the disadvantages of SSL include the following:

- **Uses simple encryption:** This might increase the chances of being hacked by computer criminals.
- **Only point-to-point transactions:** SSL handles only point-to-point interaction. Credit card transactions involve at least three parties: the consumer, the merchant, and the card issuer. This limits its all-purpose applications.
- **Customer risk:** Customers run the risk that a merchant may expose their credit card numbers on its server; in turn, this increases the chances of credit card frauds.
- **Merchant's risk:** Merchants run the risk that a consumer's card number is fraudulent or that the credit card won't be approved.
- **Additional overhead:** The overhead of encryption and decryption means that secure HTTP (SHTTP) is slower than HTTP.
- **U.S. federal restrictions:** U.S. federal restrictions on the export of encryption technology mean that SSL products can't be approved for international distribution unless they are severely weakened. This may limit the appeal of SSL for transactions with international customers.

6-7-7 SECURE HYPERTEXT TRANSFER PROTOCOL DIGITAL SIGNATURES

The term *digital signature* generally applies to the technique of appending a string of characters to an electronic message that serves to identify the sender or the originator of a message (the authentication function). In other words, digital signature includes any type of electronic message encrypted with a private key that is able to identify the origin of the message. Some digital signature techniques also serve to provide a check against any alteration of the text of the message after the digital signature was appended (the seal function). Early concerns were focused on the problem of the recipient being able to ensure that the message received was genuine and unaltered. However, there was reason to consider the potential legal problem of proving at a later time that the intended recipient did not himself alter the message to use as bogus evidence. This later capability (the integrity function) is of great interest in cases where legal documents are created using such digital signatures. Finally, privacy and confidentiality are of significant concerns in many instances where the sender wishes to keep the contents of the message private from all but the intended recipient.

6-7-8 Public and Private Key Secure Electronic Transmission

The SET protocol imitates the current structure of the credit card processing system and replaces every phone call or transaction slip of paper with an electronic version. This can generate a large number of data packets. The SET protocol offers packets of data for all these transactions, and each transaction is signed with a digital signature. This makes SET the largest consumer of certificates, and it makes banks by default one of the major distributors of certificates. IBM and GTE have announced plans to help banks offer certificates to their customers; this promises to be a significant market for developers of these large databases.

One of the most active debates in the SET community is over who will pay for the SET certificate-revocation list. Certificate revocation is an essential part of the certificate process. There are several reasons why a certificate must be revoked before it expires. For example, a user might change organizations or lose his or her key pair, or an e-commerce site using SSL may discontinue its operations. In all these cases, the certificate needs to be revoked before it expires so that it cannot be used intentionally or unintentionally. The SET protocol forces a transaction processor to check the lists regularly to catch transactions that might be generated by a lost or stolen certificate. In order to simplify the process of keeping the lists current and synchronized, the protocol defines a fingerprint to be a hash of the latest revocation list. A hash function accepts a variable-size message as input and generates a short fixed-sized tag as output. The transaction processors can compare fingerprints to ensure that their copy of the list matches the latest master list.

The following steps describe a typical flow of SET protocol messages through a SET transaction (see Figure 6-6).

1. The certificate authority issues certificates to cardholder.
2. The customer (cardholder) initiates a purchase.
3. The merchant requests authorization.
4. The cardholder authorization is provided.
5. The merchant ships products.

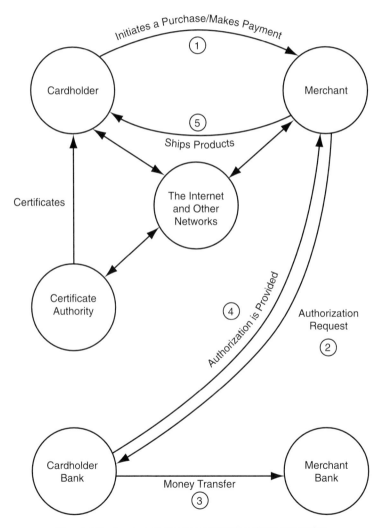

Figure 6-6 A secure electronic transmission (SET) transaction.

The confidentiality of messages in the SET payment environment is accomplished through encryption of the payment information using a combination of public key and private key algorithms. In general, public and private key cryptographic algorithms (the process of transforming readable text into ciphertext and back again) are used together to encrypt the actual message contents with a short private key, which is distributed securely via the public–private key pair.

The most important property of SET is that the credit card number is not revealed to the vendor. However, the SET protocol, despite strong support from Visa and MasterCard, has not emerged as a leading standard. The two major reasons for lack of widespread acceptance are (1) the complexity of SET and (2) the need for the added security that SET provides. However, this might change in the future as encryption technology becomes more commonly utilized in the e-business world.

Some of the **advantages** of SET include the following:

- No opportunity for anyone to "steal" a credit card.
- Neither a person "listening in" nor a merchant can use the information passed during a transaction for fraud.
- Flexibility in shopping; if you have a phone you can shop.

Some of the **disadvantages** of SET include its complexity and high cost for implementation.

6-8 ELECTRONIC WALLETS

Electronic wallets (e-wallets) are commercially available for pocket, palm-sized, handheld, and desktop PCs. They offer a secure, convenient, and portable tool for online shopping. They store personal and financial information such as credit cards, passwords, PINs, and much more. In most cases they offer complete file compatibility between the Windows CE handheld or palm-sized PC and the desktop. This feature provides extra convenience and security for a typical customer.

Microsoft Wallet is a popular example of an e-wallet on the market. To acquire Microsoft Wallet, you first should establish a Microsoft Passport. Microsoft Passport consists of several services including the following [3]:

- A "single sign-in" service that allows the customer to use a single name and password at a growing number of participating e-commerce sites.
- A "wallet" service that the shopper can use to make fast online purchases.
- A "Kids Passport" service that helps you to protect and control your children's online privacy.

After establishing a Passport, you then use it to establish a Microsoft e-wallet. E-wallets can be used for micropayments (discussed in the next section) and are very useful for frequent online shoppers. They also eliminate reentering personal information on the forms, resulting in higher speed and efficiency for online shoppers.

6-9 MICROPAYMENT AND OTHER PAYMENT SYSTEMS

Micropayments are used for small payments on the Web, usually payments under five dollars. Some experts predict that this type of payment will grow substantially for purchasing digital products on the Web. The process is similar to e-wallet technology where the customer transfers some money into the wallet on his or her desktop and then pays for digital products by using this wallet. Imagine you are only interested in one article from a professional journal or a chapter from a scientific book. Or you may be interested in listening to one song from a CD. Or you may want to subscribe to an online magazine for a short period. Using micropayment you will be able to pay for these digital products on the Web. There are many vendors involved in micropayment systems. IBM offers micropayment wallets and servers. IBM micropayment systems allow vendors and merchants to sell content, information, and services over the Web, for amounts as low as one cent. It provides universal acceptance and offers comprehensive security. This micropayment system can be used for billing by banks and financial institutions, telecommunications, Internet service providers (ISPs), content providers (offering games, entertainment, reference information, archives, reviews, and consumer information), service providers (offering fax, e-mail, or phone services over the Web), and by premium search engines and specialized databases.

Qpass sells content from publishers such as *The Wall Street Journal* Interactive Edition on a short-term or per-article bases. **Cybergold** allows users to purchase digital content such as software, video files, and MP3-based songs. Figure 6-7 illustrates the initial screen of Cybergold. Other examples of micropayment systems are the following:

Flooz is an online gift currency sent by e-mail. The recipient spends Flooz, just like money, at the online store of their choice.

1ClickCharge assists customers to download a wallet and prepay for a block of micropurchases by credit card.

Trintech offers NetWallet and ezCard, which provide customers with simple and secure e-commerce payment instruments. It does not require buyers to download a wallet; it bills micropayments to the consumer's ISP account.

Millicent is a micropayment system implemented by Digital Equipment

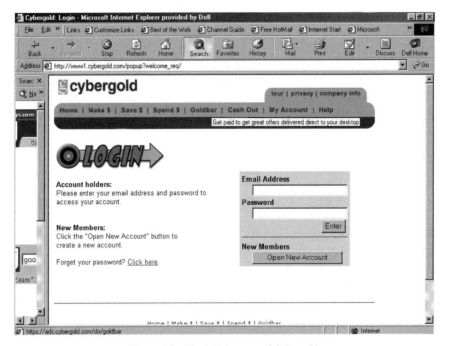

Figure 6-7   The initial screen of Cybergold.

Corporation (now merged with Compaq), started in 1999 in Japan, with wallets starting at 1000 yen and payments as small as 5 yen (approximately $0.04).

The **AuricWeb** system allows ISPs to document online transactions along with other user statistics.

CyBank adapts telephone-billing models. It uses prepaid cards and metered charges to Internet purchases.

Electronic gifts are one way of sending electronic currency or gift certificates from one individual to another. Electronic gifts are similar to regular gifts only they are transferred on the Web from the sender to the receiver. Electronic gifts are available from just about all major online stores, and their acceptance is on the rise. Paid for by credit card, they are usually nontransferable. Flooz, PayPal, and Emoneymail are examples of electronic gifts. PayPal and Emoneymail transfer funds to a recipient chosen by the sender. To use PayPal and Emoneymail, the user is supposed to establish an account. Also, PayPal charges a service fee. These options are only practical for transferring a small amount of money without the recipient using or obtaining a credit card.

Clickshare is another popular micropayment system. Using Clickshare the customer can purchase information, music, video, software, and other digital

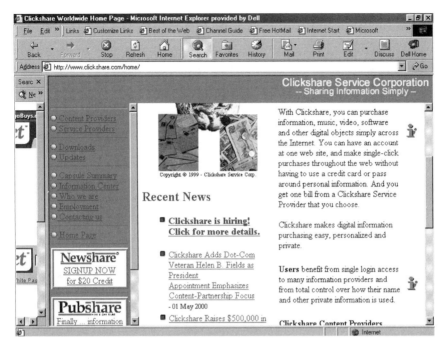

Figure 6-8   Initial screen of Clickshare.

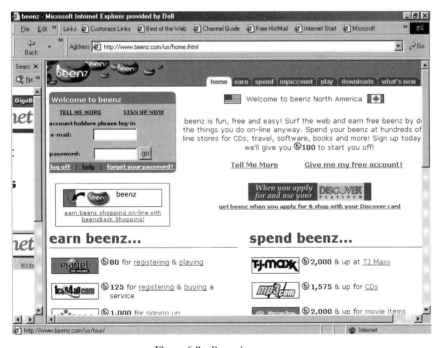

Figure 6-9   Beenz home page.

products and services over the Web. You get one bill from a Clickshare service provider that you choose. Figure 6-8 shows the initial screen of Clickshare.

Beenz, E-gold, and **Mypoints** are other examples of currency used in the e-commerce world. Figure 6-9 shows the Beenz home page.

Information Box 6-3 introduces Mondex e-cash, and Information Box 6-4 presents NetChex debit check card as two commercial examples of EPSs.

INFORMATION BOX 6-3

Commercial Example of Electronic Payment Systems: Mondex E-Cash

Mondex e-cash is an example of e-cash that provides a secure and convenient alternative to bills and coins. The Mondex e-cash payment system complements credit, debit, and charge cards and adds greater convenience and flexibility to everyday customer cash transactions. Mondex e-cash operates on a smart card (explained earlier). The microprocessor chip on the card stores cash value and the security features. Similar to cash, Mondex e-cash transactions require no remote authorizations or PIN codes at point-of-sale terminals because Mondex e-cash is transferred directly from the buyer to the seller. Mondex e-cash can be reloaded onto the card's microprocessor chip as frequently as desired. Customers can request either a standalone card containing Mondex e-Cash or a combination card that incorporates both Mondex e-cash and debit.

The Mondex e-cash function can be issued on its own or, soon, as part of a group of products on a multifunction card. The MULTOS (multipurpose operating system) smart card operating system makes this possible, allowing the card issuer and cardholder to combine a number of services on a single card that meets the specific lifestyle requirements of the customer. For example, the cardholder might choose to have one card that combines Mondex e-cash, debit, credit, and various retailer loyalty programs, all in one. Mondex e-Cash offers several advantages:

1. It can be transferred over a telephone line or over the Web.
2. The microprocessor chip maintains a private and up-to-date receipt of the card's last ten Mondex transactions.
3. E-cash can be locked onto the card's microprocessor chip with a code chosen by the customer. When locked, the cash value stored on the card and the card's transaction records cannot be accessed.
4. When used, e-cash is transferred directly and immediately to the merchant, vending machine, or other participating organizations.
5. Like cash, e-cash enables transactions between individuals without the need for banks or other third-party intervention.

Sources:<http://www.mondex.ca/eng/welcome/whatismondex.cfm?pg=welcome>; <http://www.mondex.com>

INFORMATION BOX 6-4

Commercial Example of Electronic Payment Systems: NetChex Debit Check Card

NetChex (National Check Exchange) is the first Internet debit check card. It allows Internet users the convenience of shopping online without the need for a credit card. The money is deducted directly from the customer's U.S. checking accounts electronically. It provides secure, reliable, real-time electronic transaction processing for any size online business.

The NetChex program allows businesses and consumers to purchase goods and services online utilizing their personal or business checking accounts electronically. The NetChex program is linked directly to the customer's existing checking account, allowing the customer to purchase freely as if using a credit card. NetChex offers its merchants and cardholders the NetChex Desktop Wallet that allows cardholders to fill in online merchant forms with one click of a mouse. Cardholders can use the wallet to store personal and payment information securely on their desktop. The customer simply drags the NetChex check card or credit card from the wallet to the merchant checkout form and that finalizes the process. This payment system offers several advantages:

1. The customer does not need to open a new account; an existing account can be used.
2. This method offers additional security, because no account number is transferred over the Web.
3. It may be cheaper than other EPSs, because no additional hardware and/or software is needed to use this system.

SOURCE: The first Internet Debit Card System for the eCommerce Industry. <http://www.netchex.com/> (Date of access, April 19, 2001).

6-10 INDUSTRY CONNECTION: MICROSOFT CORPORATION

> Microsoft Corporation
> One Microsoft Way
> Redmond, Washington 98052
> Phone: (425) 882-8080
> Fax: (425) 936-7329
> Web site address: <http://www.microsoft.com>

Microsoft was founded in 1975 by Chairman and CEO William H. Gates III (then a 20-year-old sophomore at Harvard) and Paul Allen (then a Honeywell employee). Microsoft stock went public on March 13, 1986. Microsoft is the world's largest software company and is actively involved in all aspects of desktop computing. It is best known for its disk operating system (DOS), Windows operating system, and application software, including Word, Excel, Access, and PowerPoint. Microsoft introduced Windows 3.0 in 1990. Windows is the most popular operating system for PC and PC-compatible computers. In 1993 Windows NT was released for mission-critical corporate applications. Future plans at Microsoft are to incorporate voice-enabled computing into the next generation of Windows products. In 2000, in response to antitrust and unfair competition allegations from the U.S. Department of Justice, a federal judge ruled that the company should be broken up. The company is appealing the decision. Microsoft's current lines of e-commerce-related products and services are as follows:

- **Electronic wallet (e-wallet)** and **Passport** are EPSs accepted and used by many e-commerce sites (further explained earlier in this chapter)
- **Internet Information Server,** a powerful web server (further explained in Chapter 9)
- **Windows 2000 Server,** a multipurpose network operating system for businesses of all sizes
- **Windows 2000 Advanced Server,** the operating system for e-commerce applications
- **Windows 2000 Datacenter Server,** the operating system for high-demand applications
- **Exchange Server,** a full-featured work-group communications application
- **Site Server Commerce Edition** analyzes site usage.
- **Proxy Server,** a software application that serves as an intermediary between a workstation user and the Internet so that the enterprise can ensure security and administrative control
- **Internet Explorer,** a leading Internet browser (explained in Chapter 1)
- **FrontPage,** a powerful HTML translation editor for developing web pages and other HTML applications (will be briefly explained in Appendix A)
- **MSN,** an Internet portal that combines Web services and capabilities to form a rich online experience and the world's largest provider of free Web-based e-mail with Hotmail
- **Windows DNA** is Microsoft's platform for building and deploying interoperable Web solutions. It is the precursor of the NET Enterprise Servers, Microsoft's comprehensive family of server applications for building, deploying, and managing scalable, integrated, Web-based solutions and services.
- **Visual Studio,** a graphical programming language mostly used with Internet applications.[1]

---

[1]This information was gathered from the company web site and other promotional materials. For detailed information and any update, contact the company.

6-11 SUMMARY

This chapter started with an overview of EPSs and compared and contrasted EPSs with traditional payment systems. The chapter explored EFT as one of the oldest EPSs. Four types of payment cards were introduced, including credit cards, debit cards, charge cards, and smart cards, and current and future applications of smart cards reviewed. Electronic cash and checks were discussed and compared and contrasted with traditional cash and checks. The chapter presented a discussion of various tools and technologies for secure EPSs, including digital signatures, authentication, public key cryptography, certificates, certificate authorities, SSL, secure HTTP digital signatures, and public–private key secure electronic transmission. Other security issues and measures will be discussed in Chapter 11. The chapter concluded with a discussion of electronic wallets and micropayment systems and introduced two popular commercial examples of EPSs, including Mondex e-cash and NetChex debit check card, highlighting Microsoft Corporation as the industry connection. EPSs are in their introductory phases of development, and they should become more widely used in parallel with e-commerce expansion. In the near future their popularity and acceptance should increase.

6-12 REVIEW QUESTIONS

1. What instruments are used to pay for goods and services in a mortar-and-brick business?
2. Which EPS is the oldest?
3. What are some of the applications of EFT? Who are the major users of EFT?
4. What are some examples of payment cards? What are some of the differences between a credit card and a charge card?
5. Who are some of the issuers of credit cards?
6. What are two major types of credit cards on the market today?
7. What are some of the advantages of EFT?
8. When was the first credit card issued? Which institution issued the first credit card?
9. What are some of the major steps for credit card approval? How is this process enhanced over the Web? Discuss.
10. What is a smart card? Why are these cards called "smart"? Discuss.
11. What are some of the current and future applications of smart cards?
12. What is e-cash? What are some of the differences between an e-cash and regular cash?
13. How does an e-cash system work?
14. What is an e-check? How does it work? Discuss.
15. What is a digital signature? How does it work?

16. What is authentication? How is it done over the Web?
17. What is public key cryptography? How does it work?
18. Who are certificate authorities?
19. What is SSL? How does it work? Who are some of the key players in SSL development and utilization? Discuss.
20. What are some of the advantages of SSL? Disadvantages? Discuss.
21. What are secured HTTP digital signatures? How do they work? Discuss.
22. What is SET? How does it work?
23. What are some of the advantages of SET? Disadvantages? Discuss.
24. What are e-wallets? How do they work? Who are some of the key players in e-wallet development?
25. How does Microsoft Passport work? Discuss.
26. What are micropayments? How do they work?
27. What are some examples of micropayment systems?
28. What are some advantages and disadvantages of PayPal? Of payment by utility?
29. What are some of the EPSs offered by Mondex? Discuss.
30. What is NetChex debit check card? How does it work? Discuss.

6-13 PROJECTS AND HANDS-ON EXERCISES

1. Log onto the web site of the Microsoft Corporation at the following URL:

   <http://www.microsoft.com>

   What are some of the e-commerce products and services offered by this company? How does Microsoft Wallet work? What is Microsoft Passport? What are some of the features of Windows 2000 Server? What are some of the differences among Windows 2000 Server, Windows 2000 Advanced Server, and Windows 2000 Datacenter Server? Discuss.

2. By referring to the materials presented in this chapter and other sources, complete the following table.

	Advantage(s)	Disadvantage(s)
Electronic funds transfer		
Credit cards		
Debit cards		
Charge cards		
Smart cards		
Electronic cash		
Electronic check		
Electronic wallets		
Micropayment systems		

3. The following site provides comprehensive information on e-Wallets:

<http://www.iliumstore.com/ewallet2.html>

By examining the materials presented in this site and other sources, write a one-page report on e-wallets. How does an e-Wallet work? For what types of transactions is this medium most useful? What are some of the shortcomings of this medium? Discuss.

4. The following site provides comprehensive information on Microsoft Wallet and Passport:

<http://memberservices.passport.com/HELP/MSRV_HELP_whatis.asp>

Log onto the site and review its contents. How is Microsoft Wallet different than other e-wallets?

5. The following site provides comprehensive information on Digicash:

<http://www.digicash.com>

By examining the materials presented in this site and other sources answer the following questions:
   a. How is Digicash different than other EPSs?
   b. What are some of the advantages and disadvantages of this medium?

6. The following sites provide current information on various e-commerce issues including EPS:

<http://www.ecompany.com>
<http://ilearn.senecac.on.ca/homepage/Tim.Richardson/iec802/payment802.htm>
<http://www.fstc.org/projects/echeck/index.shtml>

By examining the materials presented in these sites and other sources, prepare a one-page report on the latest developments in EPSs. Why have electronic payment systems not become as popular as they were expected? Discuss.

7. The following sites provide current information on digital signatures:

<http://www.digsigtrust.com>
<http://www.abanet.org/scitech/ec/isc/dsg-tutorial.html>
<http://www.abanet.org/scitech/ec/isc/dsg-toc.html>

By examining the materials presented in these sites and other sources, answer the following questions:
   a. What are some of the advantages of digital signatures compared to traditional signatures?
   b. What are some of the shortcomings of digital signatures?
   c. What are some of the legal challenges that must be overcome before this technology really takes off? Discuss.

8. The following sites provide current information on SET:

<http://www.setco.org>
<http://www.setco.org/set_specifications.html>

By examining the materials presented in these sites and other sources, answer the following questions:
a. What are some of the strengths of SET?
b. What are some of its limitations?
c. Why has SET not become as popular as it was expected?
9. By consulting the materials presented in this chapter and other sources, compare and contrast SET and SSL. Which technology is more popular now? Which one may become more popular in the near future? Discuss.

6-14 KEY TERMS

Authentication, 206–207
Certificates, 207
Certificates authorities, 207
Charge cards, 199–201
Credit cards, 198–199
Debit cards, 199
Digital signatures, 206
Electronic cash (e-cash), 203–204
Electronic check (e-check), 204–206
Electronic funds transfer
  (EFT), 197–198
Electronic payment systems
  (EPS), 194–197

Electronic Wallets (e-wallets), 212–213
Micropayments, 213–216
Mondex e-Cash, 216
NetChex debit check card, 217
Public key cryptography, 207
Public and private key secure
  electronic transmission
  (SET), 210–212
Secure Hypertext Transfer Protocol
  (HTTP) digital signatures, 209–210
Secure sockets layer (SSL), 208-209
Smart cards, 201–203

REFERENCES

[1] NACHA. <http://www.nacha.org> The Electronic Payments Association, Copyright by NACHA, 2000, (Date of access, April 19, 2001).
[2] <http://www.echeck.org> (Date of access, April 19, 2001).
[3] <http://www.passport.com/Consumer/default.asp?PPlcid=1033> Microsoft Passport Home © 1999–2001 Microsoft Corporation. All rights reserved. (Date of access, April 19, 2001)
[4] <http://www.beenz.com/us/home.ihtml> beenz a new kind of money, © 2001 beenz.com, Inc., all rights reserved. (Date of access, April 19, 2001).
[5] Bidgoli, Hossein (2000). "Handbook of Business Data Communications: A Managerial Perspective." Academic Press, Inc., San Diego, California.
[6] Kaufman, C., R. Perlman, and M. Speciner (1995). "Network Security: Private Communication in a Public World." Englewood Cliffs, NJ: Prentice Hall.

Chapter 7

Marketing and Advertising on the Web

Learning Objectives

After studying this chapter you should be able to do the following:

- Review various features of marketing and advertising on the Web and compare and contrast it with traditional marketing.
- Discuss the Web as a marketing tool.
- Understand basic Web marketing terminology.
- Elaborate on methods for promoting an e-commerce site.
- Explain different Web marketing and advertising tools, such as banner ads, newsgroups, message boards, and so forth.
- Discuss the strengths and weaknesses of various Web marketing and advertising tools.
- Discuss the role of intelligent agents in Web marketing and providing better customer service.
- Outline the ingredients of an effective marketing and advertising program.

INFORMATION BOX 7-1

Facts and Figures about Web Marketing

PointCast (now Infogate.com) sends news and sports information to users based on their individual needs.

Through its EntryPoint, PointCast delivers the information crucial to Internet users through personalized alerts, a news and stock ticker, and one-click access to the most useful resources and shopping destinations on the Web.

Dell and Gateway Computers' web sites allow a customer to enter the exact specifications for a new computer, which is then delivered in a few days.

More than 85% of web surfers use search engines to find what they are looking for on the Web. Therefore, registering an e-commerce site with popular search engines and using the right keyword in the page (body and title) is crucial. If the web masters and web designers do not use the right keyword, the site may not show up among the top listings; therefore, the page may not be seen by a potential visitor.

American Airlines, using Broadvision's intelligent agent, offers personalized web pages for each of its registered travel-planning customers. This results in customer loyalty.

ZineZone.com <http://zinezone.com> collects information about its visitors and creates profiles that are used to push personalized advertisement.

Netzero offers free Internet access in exchange for viewing ads.

Cybergold <www.cybergold.com> and Goldmine <www.goldmine.com> connect you with advertisers who pay to read ads and navigate the Web.

Wayfarer <http://www.wayfarer.com> offers a web-casting solution with a variety of data delivery methods, which allows administrators and supervisors to restrict content delivered to users' desktops.

Web advertisements should be pleasant looking and targeted to specific groups or individual customers.

Page-loading speed has a direct correlation with the number of visitors viewing the page; therefore, complex graphics and large tables should be avoided at least in the initial page.

Intelligent agents and shopping bots are increasingly used in the e-commerce world to assist customers in finding the cheapest possible prices. They are also a marketing tool for collecting relevant information regarding customers' purchasing habits and the sites they usually visit.

INFORMATION BOX 7-2

Data Warehouse and Call Centers Improve Marketing Efforts at KeyCorp

By employing an IBM business intelligence solution, KeyCorp was able to consolidate all customer data into a single dedicated data warehouse—allowing marketing executives in all areas of the organization to access customized data about each of their 7 million customers. The solution improved marketing and cross-selling potential through faster and more accurate delivery of actionable business information to remote sales personnel.

This system enables marketing and sales professionals to access customer information in a dedicated data warehouse. "Today, KeyCorp has moved from just 'direct mail marketing' to leveraging all the channels through which customers interact with us," stated Lyn Kennedy, vice president of data mining. The result—KeyCorp now nurtures a web of new directions in which to expand and grow.

Because the solution provides information access at any time of day, KeyCorp also has been able to implement 24-hour-a-day, 7-day-a-week call centers. "In a call center, you need to reduce the amount of time someone is on a call—so the rep needs to be able to pull information up at the time the call comes in," noted Kennedy. The system has also helped KeyCorp's marketing team to determine which products are profitable and which are not. Unprofitable products have subsequently been discontinued.

Additionally, the new solution has helped the bank target its marketing. Communications are now sent to customers most likely to respond to them. As a result, direct mail response rates have jumped to as high as 5–10% from the 1–2% previously experienced. "We need to show results," Troy D. Thomas, Senior Vice President, customer warehouse, says. "With the data warehouse, we can do better marketing and cross-selling, so the reps can focus on sales—not on collecting information about their customers."

The solution has also enabled KeyCorp's marketers to segment customers demographically, based on the products they currently have and on the portability of those products. The solution's sophisticated modeling and knowledge discovery techniques enable the user of this information to target customers as leads for particular offers. "We still do a great deal of product-focused marketing, but we're also doing a lot more relationship-based marketing with this new suite of tools," Thomas says.

Some of the specific benefits of the system are as follows:

1. Enabled implementation of call centers 24 hours a day, 7 days a week.
2. Helped marketing team separate unprofitable products from profitable ones.
3. Increased direct mail response rates by an average of five times.
4. Allowed marketers to demographically segment customers and target them for particular offers.

SOURCE: <http://www-3.ibm.com/e-business/casestudy/24220.html> IBM United States, e-business case studies, (Date of access April 20, 2001).

7-1 INTRODUCTION

This chapter starts with an overview of marketing and advertising on the Web, then discusses the Web as an effective marketing tool. The chapter introduces basic Web marketing terminology and outlines different methods for promoting an e-commerce site. Different advertising and marketing tools on the Web include banner ads, discussion lists, e-mail and registering e-mail, links on other web sites, newsgroups, online classified advertisements, message boards and special interest malls, splash screens, spot leasing, intelligent agents, and push technology. The chapter discusses the growing popularity of intelligent agents, including four well-known types: mail agents, World Wide Web and navigational agents, Usenet and Newsgroup agents, and shopping agents. The chapter concludes with a series of guidelines for an effective marketing and advertising program, highlighting America Online–Time Warner, Inc. as the industry connection.

7-2 MARKETING AND ADVERTISING ON THE WEB: AN OVERVIEW

The Web offers several technologies and applications that could enhance customer service, marketing, and advertising efforts with a moderate cost. The Web could improve customer service by sending e-mail for order confirmation, product announcements, and order tracking. The Web provides customer service through corporate web sites, integrated call centers, online help desks, and online customer service.

In recent years, customers have used corporate web sites for many different applications: downloading forms, software patches, printer drivers, minor upgrades to an existing software, and receiving prompt answers to frequently asked questions (FAQs). All of these features have improved customer service and lowered costs for both the corporation and its customers.

Customers, by using online catalogs, are able to conduct product searches and compare and contrast different features of different products. The Web assists in online customer research. Just about all legitimate data about customers can be collected directly or indirectly through cookies, intelligent agents, and online questionnaires. As discussed later in this chapter, intelligent agents are rule-based software that can be used effectively in the e-commerce environment. Intelligent agents can be used for customer service, offering the customer the lowest possible price using shopping agents, or learning about customer behavior, shopping patterns, and preferences. Online customer data can be collected very fast and with minimum cost.

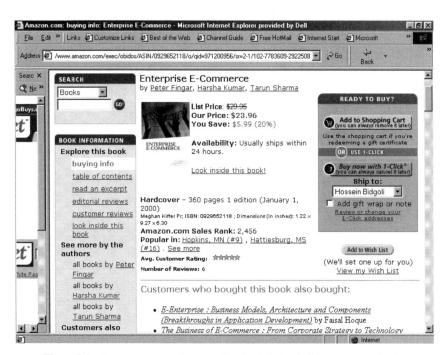

Figure 7-1 Amazon.com sample screen showing links to similar e-commerce books.

Target marketing can be economically conducted on the Web with minimum cost. The following is an example of target marketing. If, for example, you purchase a French CD from Amazon.com, then every time that you log onto this particular site, you will receive an alert when a new French CD or a French book has become available. It is logical and highly likely that you may buy another French CD or you might be interested in French literature, since you have already shown some interest in French language. Another good example is the relevant links on many online bookseller sites. For example, if you go to Amazon.com and purchase an e-commerce book, on the same screen you see links to other e-commerce or e-commerce-related books that individuals who purchased this e-commerce have also purchased. Figure 7-1 is a sample screen from Amazon.com that shows these relevant links to the buyer of *Enterprise E-Commerce*.

7-3 THE WEB AS A MARKETING TOOL

Marketing is perhaps the best-suited major business function for utilizing the power of the Web. The Web puts large and small organizations on the same footing. Regardless of size or financial strengths, any business can sell goods and services through the Web. Users have already divided themselves into interest or newsgroups complete with e-mail addresses. However, the traditional approach to marketing will not work on the Web. Because of the democratic atmosphere, consumers are on the plus side of the power balance. They can respond individually to a marketing attempt or they can spread the word to their associates. If they approve, everything is fine; however, if they disapprove, consumers have the power in this medium to wreak havoc with an ill-fated marketing attempt. Users unhappy at receiving material from catalog companies have flooded them with messages not to do it again. Marketers, therefore, should only post concise messages to applicable newsgroups that are relevant to a company's campaign. Appropriate newsgroups should be identified before attempting contact. Martin Nisenholtz has suggested the following six guidelines for Internet advertising [1].

1. Never send intrusive messages.
2. Express permission of the user is required prior to selling consumer data.
3. Advertise only in designated newsgroups.
4. Use full disclosure to conduct direct selling or promotions.
5. Obtain the consumer's informed consent when conducting research.
6. Internet communications should never be used to conceal activities.

Passive advertising is used successfully by businesses. Bulletin boards can be set up, and minimal investment is required to cover the hardware and software costs. An alternative would be to publish advertisements through an Internet service provider (ISP) such as AOL, a directory such as Yahoo!, or a search engine such as AltaVista.

The medium perhaps best suited for advertising on the World Wide Web is establishing a home page. Thousands of companies, including Cadillac, Dell Computer, Gateway, Microsoft, Novell, Apple Computer, Cisco Systems, and IBM have established home pages for corporate and corporate-sponsored advertising. The advantage is that marketing messages are individually tailored for each customer. Companies such as Apple, IBM, Novell, Microsoft, and Schlumberger are making product information, press releases, e-mail directories, and financial information available via the Web. Some of the soft drink manufacturers now include a URL address on their cans or bottles that a customer can access for additional information on the product, such as information related to the ingredients, nutritional facts, and so forth. Online malls or shopping centers are growing in number. Buyers are able to buy almost every product from a growing number of online malls. These malls include many businesses, from a coffee store to a marine equipment shop.

Because business use of the Web is still very much in the introductory stage, to date, small advertisers are producing the majority of online advertising, and the present situation has been compared to the early days of cable TV. However, in the near future the introduction of interactive television (ITV), video on demand, cable modems, and digital subscriber lines (DSL) will result in increased popularity and business usage of the Web.

Newsgroups (further discussed later in this chapter) are one of the best advertising areas on the Web. For example, if a business wanted to advertise a dog food, they could post their advertisement in newsgroups that are interested in dogs.

As Figure 7-2 shows, the Web serves as a strong marketing tool for all types of organizations regardless of their size and the types of products and services that they sell. Any organization using the Web can advertise all over the world and sell 7-days a week, 24-hours a day [4].

Gathering marketing data through the Web could enhance the marketing efforts of any organization. An organization using these data will be able to customize a particular product or service to the specific needs and requirements of a prospective buyer. Marketing data can be collected through various tools available on the Web with moderate cost. E-mail, online questionnaires, online forms, newsgroups, discussion lists, cookies, and intelligent agents are among the popular tools that can be used for this purpose. One common application of this type of data collection is filling out the renewal form of a magazine. With a few mouse clicks, the subscriber is able to renew a magazine subscription online. Because these data are collected online, the publisher can utilize these data immediately and conduct different types of analyses, including determining the status of the subscriber, the accuracy of the data, and so forth.

Figure 7-2   The Web as a marketing tool.

Selling traditional products through the Web has become a reality in recent years. Online stores are able to offer a variety of choices, convenience, and in many cases lower prices. With the introduction of e-wallets, e-cash, and other electronic payment systems (EPSs) (discussed in Chapter 6), customers are able to pay for these products and services with enhanced security and convenience. EPSs such as e-Wallet enable the customers to fill out online forms with a few mouse clicks, enhancing the customer's convenience. This is basically transferring the old retail model to the Web and taking advantage of all the technologies and applications that the Web offers in order to generate revenue.

Selling digital products is a new way that businesses can generate revenue with moderate expenses. Downloading a piece of software, a song, a magazine article, or a movie are some examples. With the increased popularity of cable modems, DSLs, higher bandwidth, and tighter security measures, these applications are expected to increase dramatically. Also, as introduced in Chapter 6, micropayment systems will enable e-businesses to sell a digital product as low as a penny or even lower and still make a profit (without paying any fees to credit card companies.)

Online marketing experiments are becoming popular applications of Web marketing. Marketers are able to reach a wide geographic base and collect marketing data with no or moderate cost. These marketing data can be used for testing various experiments, such as the attractiveness of an advertising campaign or the strengths and weaknesses of a marketing medium, with moderate costs.

The Web provides unparalleled support for marketing-mix data (product, price, promotion, and place). The **product** component is concerned with the type of products and services that an e-business plans to sell. These products and services could be brand new or an enhancement over existing products and services. The enhancements might be price, features, and usability. The **price** component is concerned with the most suitable price for the product or service. Overpricing and underpricing are both unacceptable. In the case of overpricing, nobody buys the product or service, and in case of underpricing, the e-business will not make any money. Collecting online data and analyzing a competitor's offerings should help the e-business to establish a reasonable price for its products or services. The **promotion** component objectives are to inform, persuade, and remind customers regarding new products and services. Promotions persuade customers to buy products or services, remind them about new offerings, and encourage repeat sales. Web technology should be able to do this with moderate costs. The **place** component is concerned with the mechanisms that the e-business uses to get products and services to customers. In many cases, the Web provides virtual storefronts for some customers that otherwise could not have been able to do any transaction with a particular e-business. Customers in remote or rural areas or customers who are immobile and unable to shop in traditional stores are some examples.

The data related to the four components of marketing mix can be collected very rapidly with moderate cost. A web site such as CyberAtlas (www.cyberatlas. com) provides information about Web demographic, geographic, and usage patterns and the cost of developing a web site for various purposes. Figure 7-3 shows the initial screen of this site. Table 7-1 provides other Web resources for conducting successful Web marketing and advertising [2].

The Web provides mass **customization and personalization** with moderate cost. PointCast, for example, delivers customized news and financial data to every single customer based on his or her specific needs. Amazon.com displays specific recommendations based on the customer's previous purchases. These kinds of services are very expensive in traditional marketing. The Web provides e-businesses with the infrastructure to participate in this new paradigm shift. The e-business can move from providing general products or services to providing products or services customized to a customer's needs, tastes, and preferences. To provide mass customization, two technologies are commonly used.

1. **Push technology** (discussed in more detail later in the chapter)—The customer is automatically provided with information by being sent to the right place.

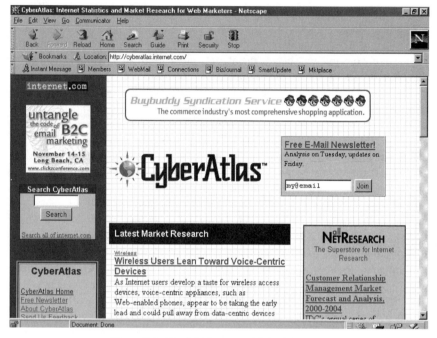

Figure 7-3   The initial screen of CyberAtlas.com.

This is similar to television or radio, where the broadcaster sends information over the airwaves and the consumer chooses the channel of his or her choice. The Web can further refine this, by sending the relevant information to the customer workstation, in a one-on-one format.

2. **Pull technology** (discussed in more detail later in the chapter)—The customer must express a need in order to receive information. This is similar to an automated teller machine (ATM) in a bank, where the customer inputs his or her password and then receives account information specified by the customer. As explained later in the chapter, various services on the Web are able to implement this strategy very effectively with moderate cost.

The Web serves as a **virtual storefront.** This virtual storefront can effectively convey the unique offerings of an e-commerce site to prospective visitors. This virtual storefront can be easily modified to reflect the new offerings of the site. Customers can browse through the site at their own pace to find special products and services. Figure 7-4 shows the initial screen of Ticketmaster.com, Figure 7-5 shows the initial screen of Buy.com, and Figure 7-6 shows the initial screen of AutoTrader.com. Each storefront has different goals and objectives, and each one conveys a different message to its perspective customers. Log onto these

Table 7-1

Resources for Successful Web Advertising and Marketing

1. ActiveMedia <http://www.activemedia.com>
   Provides current survey of trends in the Web marketplace, spending per web site, and so forth.

2. AdBase.Net <http://www.adbase.net>
   Provides interactive media directory for advertising and marketing opportunities on the Web.

3. Ad-Guide.com <http://www.ad-guide.com>
   Provides guide to Internet advertising and marketing.

4. ClickZ <http://www.clickz.com>
   Provides various resources for Web advertisers.

5. Electronic Marketing <http://www.america.net/~scotth/mktsite.htm>
   Lists numerous resources regarding e-marketing.

6. EMarketer <http://www.emarketer.com/404.htm>
   Provides e-advertising report, free weekly newsletter, list of top e-business sites, new e-marketing strategies, and other online business resources.

7. EZine Factory <http://www.ezinefactory.co.za>
   Provides the most recent Web marketing techniques. Teaches techniques that increase a site's chance of being listed among the top 10 in various search engines and directories.

8. Internet Directory <http://www.windsorbooks.com/adsites>
   Provides free list of classified ads sites.

9. Internet Resources for Online Promotions <http://jlunz.databack.com/resources.htm>
   Provides all sorts of Web marketing materials.

10. Nua Internet Surveys <http://www.nua.ie/surveys/index.cgi?f=FS&cat_id=2>
    Provides various resources for online statistics and trend analysis.

11. OLAF.net <http://www.olaf.net>
    This is an online advertising forum offering news, opinions, links, and sources about online advertising and marketing, technology, interactive industry, trades, management, creative research, and so forth.

12. SearchZ <http://www.clickz.com>
    Provides a guide to online marketing, advertising, and e-commerce.

13. AD RESOURCE <http://adres.internet.com>
    Provides Internet advertising and promotion resources.

14. Internet.com <http://internet.com>
    Provides diverse internet advertising and promotion resources.

sites and browse through them to see how effectively they are using the Web for diverse business purposes.

Matching products and services to customers' needs is a strong feature of Web marketing. The internal search engines available on many of e-commerce sites allow the customer to search for a specific product and service. The customer can even specify a particular taste and mood, and an online music store can find the right CD for the customer. As mentioned earlier, sites such as

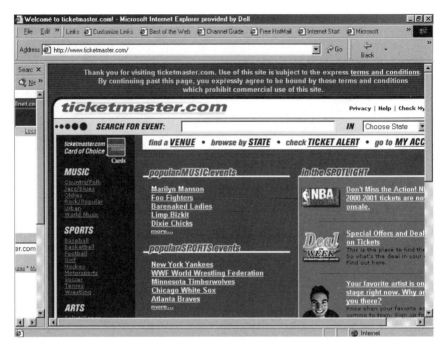

Figure 7-4   The initial screen of Ticketmaster.com.

Figure 7-5   The initial screen of Buy.com.

Figure 7-6   The initial screen of AutoTrader.com.

Amazon.com display recommendations as soon as you log onto the site based on your previous purchases.

The Web allows the e-businesses to be in a close contact with their customers. Using e-mail and the company web site, the e-business and its customers are in close contact. Customers can freely express their opinions regarding the products and services sold by a prospective e-commerce site. A good example of this type of communication can be seen in an e-commerce site such as Amazon.com, which allows its customers to review a recently purchased book. In other words, the Web provides an open forum for customers.

7-4 WEB MARKETING TERMINOLOGY

To better understand Web marketing and advertising, some commonly used terminology should be defined.

Ad impression: One surfer viewing one ad.

Banner ad: These commonly appear on popular web sites. They are typically 468 x 60 pixels in size, with simple animation. By clicking on these banner ads, either a surfer is transferred to another web site or a short marketing message is displayed.

Click: This is the opportunity for a surfer to click on a URL or a banner ad and be transferred to another web site or to view a marketing message, as recorded by the web server.

Cost per thousand (CPM): The majority of Web and e-mail media is priced based on a cost per thousand (CPM) model. For example a $125 CPM means it costs $125 per 1000 ad impressions.

Cost per click (CPC): The cost for every click on an advertisement. For example $1.25 CPC means that for every click that an advertiser receives, the advertiser is supposed to pay $1.25 for it to the sponsoring site.

Click ratio: This indicates the success of a banner ad in attracting surfers to click on the ad. For example, if a banner ad receives 2000 impressions and there are 400 clicks, the click ratio is 20%.

Click through rate (CTR): This is computed by taking the number of clicks a given advertising program received divided by the total impressions bought. For example, if a customer buys 100,000 impressions, and gets 20,000 clicks, the CTR is 5% (20000/100000 = 5%).

Cookie: A cookie is information that a web site puts on the surfer hard disk so that it can remember something about the surfer at a later time and date. This information is used to record the surfer preferences when using a particular site, his or her surfing habits, and pattern of surfing.

Hit: Every element of a requested page (including text, graphics, and interactive items) is counted as a hit to a server. Hits are not the preferred unit of site traffic's measurement because the number of hits per page varies widely depending on the number of graphics, the type of browser in use, and the size of the page.

Meta tag: A special hypertext markup language (HTML) tag that provides information about a web page. Unlike normal HTML tags, meta tags do not affect how the page is displayed in a browser. Instead, they provide information such as what the page is about, which keywords represent the page's content, the designer of the page, and how often the page is updated. This information is very important, especially the keywords that identify the page, because most search engines and directories use this information when building their indexes. Again, this information has a direct correlation with the top listing of the page in a search engine and directory.

Page view (PV): One surfer viewing one web site page.

7-5 METHODS FOR PROMOTING AN E-COMMERCE SITE

For an e-business to sell its products and services, it first must bring customers and visitors to its site. Regardless of the elegance and substantial investment in an e-commerce site, customers and surfers do not visit the site randomly. The e-commerce site must be aggressively marketed using the following techniques:

1. Register the e-commerce site with all search engines and directories. For the most part this service is free; the site can be listed in popular search engines and directories such as Yahoo!, Lycos, HotBot, and Excite, or in industry-specific sites. For example, if the site sells insurance, then it is advisable to register the site with online auto dealers or with online mortgage companies. When the site is registered, the location of the keyword in the site (whether it's in the body or in the heading) and the frequency of the word's use will have direct effect on the ranking of a page. The e-commerce site must make sure that the search engine lists the site among the top 10; otherwise, the chances of being seen by many surfers is low. A typical surfer usually looks at the top 10 to 20 listings after conducting a Web search. Different search engines and directories have different ways of searching for keywords, titles, and the text included in the page. Therefore, the web master and web designer need to make sure that they understand how each search engine and directory searches the registered sites and how it creates its index. Table 7-2 lists popular search engines and directories that can be used for registering an e-commerce site.

2. Promote the e-commerce site using banner and other Web advertising methods on popular search engines, directories, and Web portals. As discussed later (section 7-6-2), banners are effective ways to promote a site or a product.

Table 7-2

Major Search Engines and Directories for Listing an E-Commerce Site

AltaVista
Direct Hit
Excite
Google
GoTo
HotBot
Infoseek
Lycos
MSN
Netscape
Search.com
WebCrawler
Yahoo!

These banners can be displayed on popular search engines, Web portals, and directories. Table 7-3 lists popular search engines, directories, and Web portals.

3. Print the e-commerce domain name on all printed and written forms, company cars, and equipment (if there are any). This may include company letterhead, envelopes, business cards, business cars, trucks, and so forth.

4. Market the e-commerce site to existing customers. Current customers will be the first to appreciate the added convenience of online business. And they may pass the word to their friends and families.

5. Join online discussion groups and promote the site to people already interested in the company's offerings.

6. Exchange URL links with other web sites that offer companion products or services. Many web sites provide free links to other sites as a service to their visitors. For example, it would be a good idea for an insurance company to include a link in an online car dealer or in an online mortgage company.

7. Participate in free ad banner exchanges. Some companies and sites offer services, which allow ad banners to be freely exchanged with comparable sites. Your company agrees to carry banner advertising in exchange for other sites carrying your company ad banners.

8. Use e-mail lists to send out notices or newsletters on the company's products and services.

9. Offer giveaways.

10. Offer contests.

11. Offer quizzes.

12. Offer coupons.

13. Display the results of popular sport matches and lotteries.

Items 9 through 13 provide rich content for the e-commerce site and encourage visitors to come back to the site.

Table 7-3

**Major Search Engines, Web Portals,
and Directories**

Yahoo!

Excite

AltaVista

Lycos

America Online

Sidewalk

Infoseek

7-6 ADVERTISING AND MARKETING THE PRODUCTS AND SERVICES OF AN E-COMMERCE SITE

To promote its products and services, an e-commerce site may use a combination of traditional and Web marketing tools. Each technique has advantages and disadvantages and may be suitable for a specific type of business. Naturally advertising methods that have the potential to reach the highest number of potential customers are more expensive.

7-6-1 TRADITIONAL MARKETING AND ADVERTISING TOOLS

Table 7-4 lists traditional media that can be used to promote an e-commerce site. For example, a TV commercial can be very effective during popular shows and programs such as the Super Bowl; however, commercials are extremely expensive and usually beyond the budget of many e-commerce sites. Newspapers and magazines could be effective, especially if the e-commerce site has a traditional business in place already.

7-6-2 BANNER ADS

A banner ad is usually a graphic image that displays the name or identity of a site or is an advertising image. Typically a banner is 468 × 60 pixels in size and includes simple animation. Advertisers sometimes count banner "views," or the number of times a banner graphic image was downloaded over a period of time. A banner can be clickable, which will transfer surfers to another site, or

Table 7-4

Traditional Media Used for Advertising

Magazines

Newspapers

Posters

Press releases

Radio

TV commercials

Word of mouth

just static, which shows some relevant information about a site, product, or service offered by the e-commerce site. A banner ad is the equivalent of a TV ad with much less cost. However, TV ads in popular shows will potentially attract a lot more customers than banner ads. Where to put a banner ad is similar to placement of TV ads. For example, if the site is selling insurance, then the banner ad should be placed in an online car dealer site or in a bank or a mortgage company. Also, it should be placed on sites that attract large traffic. The cost of banner ads varies with the popularity and the traffic that the sponsoring site carries. For example, putting a banner ad in Yahoo! is a lot more expensive than other less popular sites. Figure 7-7 shows a screen from the Dell Computer site, which displays three clickable banners on the top of the screen and one on the lower left of the screen.

7-6-3 DISCUSSION LISTS

Discussion lists provide a strong advertising medium. An e-business can subscribe to one or several discussion lists and post relevant information regarding

Figure 7-7   Several banner ads displayed on Dell Computer's web site.

Table 7-5
Discussion List Resources

Name	Offerings
I-Advertising <http://www.i-advertising.com>	An interactive global community specific to the Internet advertising industry.
Email discussion groups/lists and resources <http://www.webcom.com/impulse/list.html>	Provides comprehensive information resources about e-mail discussion groups and lists.
Online advertising discussion list <http://www.o-a.com>	Focuses on professional discussion of online advertising strategies, results, studies, tools, and media coverage.
Publicly accessible mailing lists <http://paml.net>	Allows the user to search for a particular discussion list or browse by list name or subject.
Tile.Net—lists <http://tile.net/lists>	Provides listings of all listserv discussion groups by description, name, subject, country, and sponsoring organization.

its products or services. However, the organizations must first conduct careful analysis and find the most suitable list that might be interested in the offerings of the e-commerce site. Table 7-5 lists several resources to find suitable discussion list resources.

7-6-4 E-MAIL AND REGISTERING E-MAIL

E-mail is used for product announcements, shipment confirmations, order confirmations, and general correspondence with customers. Successful e-businesses register the customer's e-mail and other relevant information using online forms. Capturing this information could be essential for repeat sales. As an example, consider an e-business that sells flowers, greeting cards, and toys. An automatic e-mail system can alert a customer that a particular birthday is coming up. With a mouse click the customer can order a greeting card, toys, or flowers.

E-mail could be quite effective for repeat sales, reminding the customer for the next purchase or for the next visit. Many products and services are purchased on a regular basis, such as dog and cat food, pool supplies, and visits to a beauty salon. A customer can be alerted to reorder these items or that the next visit or appointment is coming up. However, with all these advantages, e-mail must be used with caution. Customers should not be bombarded with unnecessary e-mails. If a customer gets irritated, that sale and the customer may be lost.

7-6-5 LINKS ON OTHER WEB SITES

An e-business could create a partnership with other e-businesses for link exchange agreements. Your site creates a link to another site, and that site creates a link to your site. An e-commerce site can create a revenue-sharing program with other e-commerce sites. For example, Amazon.com offers other web sites 15% of a book sale when a customer purchases a book through a link to Amazon.com. The Yahoo! Store includes built-in tools to help you create and manage revenue sharing links. The same strategy can be used for banner exchange.

7-6-6 NEWSGROUPS

A newsgroup can serve as a powerful advertising medium. A newsgroup is a discussion about a particular subject consisting of notes written to a central Internet site and redistributed through Usenet. Usenet is a collection of notes on various subjects that are posted to servers on a worldwide network. The subjects and topics discussed in newsgroups range from animal shelters to the newest cure for cancer. Posting on these newsgroups is free. There are thousands of newsgroups, and it is possible for a group of users to form a new newsgroup if they so desire. Before joining and posting to these newsgroups, the e-business must do some analysis and read the frequently asked questions (FAQs) of a particular newsgroup. Newsgroups are organized into subject hierarchies, with the first few letters of the newsgroup name indicating the major subject category and subcategories represented by a subtopic name. Many subjects have multiple levels of subtopics. Major subject categories include the following:

- Comp (computers)
- News
- Rec (Recreation)
- Sci (Science)
- Soc (Society)

To use newsgroups as an advertising medium, after a short message you may post the URL of the e-commerce site. Direct advertising should be avoided as it may not be appealing to the participants of a newsgroup.

7-6-7 ONLINE CLASSIFIED ADVERTISEMENTS

Many sites such as Yahoo! allow customers to put classified ads on their sites for free or for a small fee. Also many newspapers have online versions where an e-commerce site can advertise with a portion of the fee they pay for newspaper ads. Specific sites also include classified ads; this is common in online real estate sites. Buyers and sellers of homes and commercial properties can advertise in these sites for free or for a small fee. These sites charge higher fees to banks, mortgage, and insurance companies to advertise.

7-6-8 Message Boards and Special Interest Malls

Message boards and special interest malls usually serve as an area to list a product and service. A product and or service can be listed in several of these message boards throughout the Web. Before you list a product or service, a comprehensive search must be conducted in order to find the most suitable message board for the intended product or service. Figure 7-8 is an example of special interest mall.

Figure 7-8   An example of a special interest mall.

7-6-9 SPLASH SCREEN

A splash screen is an initial web site page used to capture the surfer's attention for a short period, which usually leads the surfer to the e-business web site. The splash screen can display the e-business's corporate image and brand. In some cases it displays a message to the surfer indicating the requirement for viewing a page, such as the browser type and the specific software. By using multimedia effects, this advertising medium could be very effective for attracting visitors to an e-commerce site.

7-6-10 SPOT LEASING

Search engines and directories such as Yahoo! offer a space (spot) on their web site that can be leased by any business for advertising purposes. The term of the lease and fee vary from site to site. Spot leasing is similar to banner ads with one major advantage. Banner ads change at different times; the leased spot appears in the same place and is permanent during the contract period. The disadvantage of this approach is its size, which is very small and may be difficult to see; therefore, visitors may miss it. Another disadvantage is its high cost, especially in high-traffic sites such as Yahoo!.

7-6-11 INTELLIGENT AGENTS: AN OVERVIEW

Intelligent agents or bots (short for robots) are applications of artificial intelligence and are gaining in popularity, particularly in the e-commerce world. Imagine that you, as a busy executive, return from a business trip and find over 60 e-mail messages waiting for you. What do you do with all these e-mail messages? Let's say you have time to go through seven of these messages now. What would be the 7 most important e-mails that you should choose from these 60 messages? An intelligent agent may come to your rescue. A sophisticated mail agent can prioritize all your e-mail messages and can even respond to some of them while you were gone. It can sort your messages by date, name, or subject. They can also be sorted into different folders. Some mail agents can even page the user's pocket pager to alert him or her that a particular mail has arrived.

So what is an intelligent agent? Different people define intelligent agents differently. For the purpose of this book, we define an intelligent agent as a combination of hardware and software that is capable of reasoning and rule-based meaning, by following a series of well-defined rules, the system is capable of performing certain tasks. For example, in our e-mail example, the agent may delete an e-mail message if it was received before or after certain dates, related to a specific topic, or came from a particular source.

Some of the important capabilities of a sophisticated intelligent agent are as follows [3]:

- **Adaptability.** This is the ability to learn from prior knowledge and go beyond what has been given previously.
- **Autonomy.** This is the ability to be goal-directed, proactive, and self-starting.
- **Collaborative behavior.** This is the ability to work with other agents to achieve a common objective.
- **Humanlike interface.** This is the ability to interact with users in a language similar to natural language.
- **Mobility.** This is the ability to migrate in a self-directed way from one platform to another.
- **Reactivity.** This is the ability to selectively understand and act in a given situation.

Most intelligent agents in use today fall short of these capabilities. However, research has been steady, and much improvement is expected to be seen in the near future. Intelligent agents perform many tasks in the e-commerce environment. One important application of this software platform is for Web marketing. Intelligent agents can collect relevant information about customers, such as items purchased, customer profile, address, age, gender, purchase history, expressed preferences, and implicit preferences. This information can be effectively used by the e-business to better market its products and services to customers. These software agents are called **product-brokering agents.** They alert the customer about a new product or a new release of a product. Agents of Amazon.com have been doing this successfully in recent years. Some of the major vendors of this software agent include the following:

- Broadvision
- Firefly Network
- Net Perceptions
- PerSonaLogic

These software agents are also assisting Web marketing with smart or interactive catalogs, also called "virtual catalogs." Although this technology is in its introductory phases, it appears very promising. A smart catalog will display a description and structure of a product based on the customer's prior experience and preferences. Currently, Stanford's Center for Information Technology (CIT) is working with IBM, Hewlett-Packard, and National Semiconductor to further develop smart catalogs.

The CIT project has specified a number of goals for these catalogs. It envisions that these catalogs will be kept up-to-date and created dynamically from source material, and they will be searchable by content using common concepts (similar to human behavior) rather than navigated through links. They will also be cross searchable and referenced so that suitable entries satisfying a query (a user request) can be found in multiple catalogs.

There are several categories of intelligent agents or bots on the market. Some of the popular types include the following:

- Mail agents
- World Wide Web navigational agents
- Usenet and newsgroup agents
- Shopping agents

The screen illustrated in Figure 7-9 highlights major categories of intelligent agents or bots. However, it should be noted that most of these agents (bots) are not truly intelligent because they do not possess the capabilities outlined above. It is expected that their capabilities should be improved in the near future, and they should be able to demonstrate more of the above-mentioned "intelligent" capabilities.

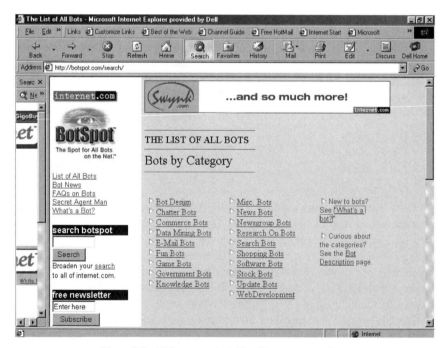

Figure 7-9   Major categories of intelligent agents or bots.

7-6-11-1 Mail Agents

As discussed earlier, mail agents perform many activities related to an e-mail program. A typical mail agent may perform the following tasks:

- Generate autoresponse messages
- Generate specific autoresponse messages
- Selectively forward incoming messages
- Create e-mail messages based on the content of incoming messages

Snoop (Smaller Animals Software, Inc., Raleigh, NC) is a commercial example of a mail agent. It can be used with any Messaging Application Program Interface (MAPI)-based clients. MAPI is a Microsoft Windows program interface that enables a user to send e-mail from within a Windows application. The e-mail can also include attachments. Microsoft Outlook and Exchange are the two popular MAPI clients. For the best performance, Snoop should be used with clients that have a continuous connection to their server.

7-6-11-2 Worldwide Web Navigational Agents

World Wide Web Navigational agents allow the user to navigate through the vast resources available on the Web, providing better results in finding information. These agents can navigate the Web much faster than we can, and they gather more consistent information. They can serve as search engines, site reminders, or personal surfing assistants.

PriceScan <http://www.pricescan.com> is a commercial example of a shopping agent that finds the lowest computer prices. PriceScan shows you all competitive prices. BestBookBuys.com <http://bestbookbuys.com> is another example of a shopping agent.

7-6-11-3 Usenet and Newsgroup Agents

Usenet and newsgroup agents have features that are specific to newsgroups. They provide sorting and filtering functions. They can access specific groups and send and receive information.

FAQFinder <http://infolab.cs.uchicago.edu/faqfinder/tst> is an automated question-answering system that uses the files of FAQs associated with many Usenet newsgroups. FAQFinder will take a user's query on any topic, tries to find the FAQ file most likely to yield an answer, searches within the file for similar questions, and returns the given answers.

DogPile <http://www.dogpile.com/index.html> searches the Web using several search engines including Yahoo!, Lycos, Excite, WebCrawler, InfoSeek, and many more and provides requested information.

7-6-11-4 Shopping Agents

Shopping agents are similar to World Wide Web Navigational agents and are capable of doing comparison shopping and finding the best price for a specific item. One of the best-known shopping agents on the Internet is the Bargain Finder <http://www.bargainfind.com>, a project developed by Andersen Consulting Research and Development. This agent performs price-comparison shopping for compact disks. The following are popular examples of shopping agents:

<www.jango.com>
<www.mysimon.com>
<www.comparisonshopping.net>
<www.agentsoft.com> (AgentSoft is now a subsidiary of Alcatel)

7-6-12 PUSH TECHNOLOGY

The Web works based on pull technology, meaning the user searches the Web to find (to pull) information. In most cases this is adequate; however, for the marketing of certain products and services, push technology would be more suitable. This means relevant information will be pushed to the user based on his or her prior inquiries, interests, or specifications. Using this technology, marketing information, product lists, prices, and product updates will be directly updated in real time and sent to the customers. Push technology can be effective for both business-to-consumer (B2C) and business-to-business (B2B) marketing. As an example, a car manufacturer may send the latest information on new models, prices, features, and other related information to all of its dealers in real time. This could be a major cost saving, and it certainly improves business relations and customer service.

Several software vendors, as part of their e-commerce solutions, support push technology. Among the popular ones are PointCast, Marimba Castanet Tuner, AirMedia Live, First Floor, BackWeb, Diffusion, and NetDelivery.

1. **PointCast** <www.pointcast.com> is among the earliest push technology providers and specializes as the Internet news network. Some of the channels of information that the user can subscribe to include headline news, stocks, sports, and weather. The contents are gathered from major organizations such as CNN, *People Magazine,* Reuters, and *Time.*

2. Marimba's **Castanet Tuner** <http://www.marimba.com> lets users set up a transmitter to send information channels to subscribers. Content delivered to the various channels of the Castanet Tuner can be in the form of applications or web pages.

3. **AirMedia Live** <www.airmedia.com> uses wireless technology to deliver broadcast content by radio. The simplicity and low cost of wireless technology

has attracted lots of attention. AirMedia focuses mainly on news, sports, stocks, and weather but also provides other types of information. Some of the channels that the user can subscribe to include CNN, Reuters, MovieLink, and the Weather Channel.

4. **First Floor** <http://www.firstfloor.com> uses intelligent agents to interactively monitor and distribute documents.

5. **BackWeb** <http://www.backweb.com> allows users to pick from many channels to receive news, multimedia, cartoon, and audio announcements, which download onto the computer desktop.

6. **Diffusion** <http://www.diffusion.com> is targeted at B2B communications, allowing desktop-generated information (product lists, price lists, and other relevant information) to be distributed to the subscribers in their preferred media (web pages, e-mail, or fax) in a specified format.

7. **NetDelivery** <http://www.netdelivery.com> is the pioneer of the concept of *Community Marketing,* which links people with common interests and shared attitudes to organizations that offer relevant information, products, and services via the Web.

7-7 GUIDELINES FOR AN EFFECTIVE ADVERTISING AND MARKETING PROGRAM

To conclude my discussion on marketing and advertising on the Web, I offer the following suggestions that may help you to put together an effective Web marketing and advertising plan. If the organization has a plan in place already, these guidelines may serve as a checklist.

1. Define the strategic goals and objectives of the organization as it relates to Web marketing and advertising. The e-business has to carefully define the types of products and services that will be sold through the site. Who are the competitors? Where are these products and services going to be sold (in local, national, or international markets)? What are some of the added benefits of your products and services compared to the competition? Is it price? Customer service? Or both? These factors should be highlighted in the marketing campaign.

2. Establish a budget, measure the effectiveness of the advertising and marketing campaign, and take corrective actions if the goals are not achieved.

3. All the methods discussed in section 7-5 should aggressively be utilized to promote the e-commerce site (summarized in Table 7-6.)

4. Use all or a combination of Web marketing tools discussed in section 7-6 and summarized in Table 7-7.

5. Keep the customers at your site and encourage them to explore and browse. Bringing customers to the site is the first step. A more important task is to keep

Table 7-6

Methods for Promoting an E-Commerce Site

Register the e-commerce site with all the search engines, directories, and Web portals.

Promote the e-commerce site using banner and other Web advertising methods on popular search engines, directories, and Web portals.

Print the e-commerce domain name on all printed and written forms, company cars, and equipment (if there are any).

Market the e-commerce site to your existing customers.

Join online discussion groups and promote the site to people already interested in the company's offerings.

Exchange URL links with other web sites that offer companion products or services.

Participate in free ad banner exchanges.

Use e-mail lists to send out notices or newsletters on the company's products and services.

Offer giveaways.

Offer contests.

Offer quizzes.

Offer coupons.

Display the results of popular sport matches and lotteries.

Table 7-7

Web Marketing Tools

Traditional marketing and advertising tools

Banner ads

Discussion lists

E-mail and registering e-mail

Links on other web sites

Newsgroups

Online classified advertisements

Message boards and special-interest malls

Splash screen

Spot leasing

Intelligent agents

Push technology

the customers at the site, encouraging them to browse and shop. This can be done in a number of ways. Customer service, a help desk, availability of a live operator (in case), a clear return policy, a clear statement regarding security concerns, ease of navigation, and the look and appearance of the site all help to keep the customers at the site and encourage them to return. 1-800-Flowers offers visitors three methods to buy: telephone, retail shops, and through the Web. This flexibility encourages the customers to visit the site again. Personalization of the site as experienced by companies such as American Airlines is also very helpful. Amazon.com and eBay are two examples of e-businesses that offer excellent customer service. These services encourage customers to return to the site again and again.

6. Make electronic catalogs available to your customers. Electronic catalogs enable customers to browse through diverse groups of products and services and compare prices and features. In addition, they offer the following advantages compared with traditional catalogs:
- Lower costs
- Higher speed of navigation by the customers
- Multimedia options, such as animation, video, and audio
- Easier updating
- Availability of virtual (interactive) catalogs that could match the product to the customer's taste and preferences.

7. Use the services of marketing and advertising agencies. Now that you know what constitutes an effective marketing and advertising program, either create it internally or outsource it to agencies that provide these kinds of services. Table 7-1 presented several Web resources for successful Web advertising and marketing. Table 7-8 lists additional sources that could provide these needed services for a fee.

Table 7-8

Marketing and Advertising Agencies

Ad-up <http://www.ad-up.com>

Answerthink <http://www.thinkinc.com>

Deadlock Design <http://deadlock.com>

Gobeyond <http://www.gobeyond.com>

K2 DESIGN, INC <http://www.k2design.com>

Online and Multimedia Marketing Group <http://www.ommgroup.com>

7-8 INDUSTRY CONNECTION: AMERICA ONLINE–TIME WARNER, INC.

America Online Time Warner, Inc.
22000 AOL Way
Dulles, Virginia 20166
Telephone: (703) 265-1342
Fax: (703) 265-2135
Web site address: <http://www.aol.com>

Founded in 1985, America Online (AOL), Inc., is the largest Internet service provider (ISP) and the world's leader in interactive services, Web brands, Internet technologies, and e-commerce services. AOL's Interactive Marketing department delivers advertisers a comprehensive portfolio of brands, services, and demographics. AOL's brands bring together the largest community of consumers in cyberspace. Thousands of advertisers and marketers have made AOL's family of brands a key part of their marketing mix, taking advantage of the branding, shopping, and e-commerce opportunities that these brands offer. Nine unique services, each with distinct features, content, and services, make up AOL's family of brands. AOL, Inc. operates AOL, with more than 26 million members, and CompuServe, with more than 2.8 million members, the company's two worldwide Internet services. With purchase of Netscape, AOL has a strong presence in the browser market and many e-commerce products and services. (Netscape was introduced in Chapter 1). AOL, through strategic alliance with Sun Microsystems, develops and offers easy-to-deploy, end-to-end e-commerce and enterprise solutions. Its merger with Time Warner was finalized in January 2001. This merger will deliver comprehensive content to many different platforms. Products and services offered by selected AOL brands include the following:

ICQ is a user-friendly Internet tool that informs the user who's online at any time and enables the user to contact them if so desire. ICQ does the searching for the user, alerting the user in real time when they are logged on. With ICQ, the user can chat, send messages, files, and URL's, and play games.

AOL Instant Messenger (as briefly introduced in Chapter 1) allows the user to talk to family and friends on the Web. It is faster than e-mail and cheaper than long-distance phone. It is available to everyone (AOL users and nonusers.)

Digital City, Inc. provides a comprehensive guide to going out and finding all types of information in the largest U.S. cities for business and entertainments.

Mapquest provides maps, driving directions, live traffic reports, yellow and white pages, travel, and city guides.

AOL.com serves as a comprehensive Web portal that offers AOL mail, chat, search, weather information, stocks, and much more.[1]

7-9 SUMMARY

This chapter started with an overview of marketing and advertising on the Web, then discussed the Web as an effective marketing tool. The chapter introduced basic Web marketing terminology and outlined different methods for promoting an e-commerce site. Different advertising and marketing tools on the Web were discussed including banner ads, discussion lists, e-mail and registering e-mail, links on other web sites, newsgroups, online classified advertisements, message boards and special interest malls, splash screen's, spot leasing, intelligent agents, and push technology. The chapter discussed the rising popularity of intelligent agents, including four popular types: mail agents, World Wide Web and navigational agents, Usenet and newsgroup agents, and shopping agents. The chapter concluded with guidelines for an effective marketing and advertising program, highlighting America Online–Time Warner, Inc. as the industry connection.

7-10 REVIEW QUESTIONS

1. What are some of the differences between traditional marketing and Web marketing? Why is the Web a suitable medium for marketing efforts? Discuss.
2. How is target marketing done on the Web? Why and how is it easier to conduct target marketing on the Web than in traditional marketing? Discuss.
3. What are some of the tools available on the Web for collecting marketing data?
4. How does the Web make selling some traditional and digital products an easier task compared with traditional brick-and-mortar companies? Discuss.
5. How does the Web enhance marketing experiments? Discuss.
6. How does the Web support marketing-mix efforts? Discuss.
7. How does the Web support a successful advertising and marketing program? (Hint: see Table 7-1.)

---

[1]This information was gathered from the company web site and other promotional materials. For detailed information and any update, contact the company.

8. How does the Web support mass customization and personalization efforts? Discuss. What are the roles of pull and push technologies in this effort? Discuss.

9. How does the Web support matching products and services to customers' needs? Discuss.

10. How does the Web provide an open forum between the e-business and its customers? What are some of the technologies and applications used to achieve this? Discuss.

11. What is some of the commonly used Web marketing terminology? What is CPM? CPC? CTR?

12. What is the role of meta tags in a web page's being listed among the top 10 in search engines or directories? Discuss.

13. What is included in a meta tag?

14. What are some of the popular methods for promoting an e-commerce site?

15. What are some of the traditional marketing and advertising media that can be used to promote an e-commerce site?

16. What are banner ads? What are their advantages? Disadvantages?

17. What are discussion lists? How are they used as a marketing tool in the Web environment?

18. What are some of the discussion list resources? (Hint: see Table 7-5.)

19. How are e-mails used as a marketing and advertising tool? How does registering e-mail work for generating repeat sales?

20. What are newsgroups? How do they work as a marketing tool?

21. How do you locate online classified ads?

22. What are splash screens? What is the difference between a splash screen and a banner ad?

23. What is spot leasing? How is it different than banner ads?

24. What is the role of intelligent agents in Web marketing? What are some of the characteristics of intelligent agents? Discuss.

25. What are some of the popular types of intelligent agents?

26. What are some of the tasks that an intelligent agent can perform? Discuss.

27. What are virtual (interactive) catalogs? What is the role of intelligent agents in designing these virtual catalogs?

28. What is push technology? What is its role in Web marketing?

29. What are some examples of software platforms that support push technology?

30. What advice could you provide for keeping customers at an e-commerce site?

31. In your own terms, list 10 recommendations for designing an effective Web marketing and advertising program.

7-11 PROJECTS AND HANDS-ON EXERCISES

1. Log onto the web site of the AOL at the following URL:

   <http://www.aol.com>

   What are some of the e-commerce products and services offered by this company? What is the significance of the merger between AOL and Time Warner? Why has AOL become such a major force in online advertising? What are some of the differences between AOL and other ISPs? Discuss.

2. By referring to the following sites and other sources, write a two-page report on marketing and advertising on the Web:

Jupiter Communications	<www.jup.com>
Net buyer	<www.netbuyer.com>
Morgan	<www.ms.com>
Project 2000 at Vanderbilt University	<www2000.ogsm.Vanderbilt.edu>
Internet Advertising Bureau	<www.iab.net>

   What are some of the major differences in using the Web as an advertising medium versus traditional media? What are some of the advantages? What are some of the disadvantages? Discuss.

3. The following sites provide all sorts of Web user demographics:

Commercenet	<www.commerce.net>
A. C. Nielson Media Research	<www.nielsenmedia.com>
The U.S. Census Report	<www.census.com>
GVU	<http://www.cc.gatech.edu/gvu>
NUA	<www.nua.ie>
Network Frontiers	<www.netfrontiers.com>

   By examining the materials presented in these sites and other sources, write a one-page report on Web demographics. Who are the prime users of the Web? (Gender, age group, occupation, nationality, and so forth.) How might a marketer use this information for an effective marketing program? Discuss.

4. The following sites provide comprehensive information on electronic catalogs:

   <http://www.autopart.com/radiatorinfo/catalog.htm>
   <http://www.dscp.dla.mil/subs/ecat.htm>

   By referring to this site and other sources write a one-page report on electronic catalogs. What are some of the advantages and disadvantages of this medium? Compare and contrast electronic catalogs with paper catalogs.

5. The following sites offer free coupons:

<www.hotcoupons.com>
<www.supermarkets.com>
<http://totallycoupons.com>

Log onto these sites one-by-one and examine their offerings. What are some of the incentives for these sites to offer free coupons? How effective are free coupons for enticing customers to visit a store? What are some of the advantages and disadvantages of this type of promotion?

6. The following site reviews the CIT's Work on Smart and Virtual Catalogs:

<http://meta2.stanford.edu/cit/cit-catalog-work.html>

By referring to this site and other sources, write a one-page report on virtual catalogs. What are some of the advantages and disadvantages of this medium? Compare and contrast virtual catalogs with electronic catalogs and traditional catalogs.

7. The following sites provide comprehensive definitions of Web marketing terminologies.

<http://list-advertising.com/terms>
<http://whatis.techtarget.com/WhatIs_Definition_Page0,4152,211535,00.html>

By referring to these sites and other sources define the following Web marketing terminologies:

Ad impression
Banner
Campaign
Click
Click rate
Clickthrough
CPC
CPM

8. The online firm Netcreation provides e-mail marketing services:

<http://www.netcreations.com>

By examining the material presented in this site and other sources, compare and contrast e-mail marketing versus traditional marketing. What are some of the advantages and disadvantages of each? Which one is more effective? Discuss.

9. DoubleClick specializes in putting banner ads on web sites. By examining the material presented in this site and other sites listed below, write a one-page report on banner advertising:

<http://www.doubleclick.com>
<http://www.bcentral.com/?leindex>
<http://www.coder.com>

What are some of the advantages and disadvantages of this medium? Discuss.

10. The following site from the Department of Advertising, the University of Texas at Austin, provides all sorts of Web marketing and advertising resources:

<http://advertising.utexas.edu/world/Internet.html>

Based on the materials presented in this site and its related links, what is the latest in Web advertising? Which Web advertising tool is the most effective?

11. Internet Shopping Network is one of the largest online malls. Log onto the following site and examine its contents.

<www.internet.net>

What are some of the advantages and disadvantages of using online malls such as this for advertising?

12. Infogate.com (formerly PointCast) is an intelligent agent that uses "push technology."

<www.infogate.com>

By examining the materials presented in this site and other sources, write a one-page report on push technology. What is the role of this technology in a successful e-commerce program? What is the role of this technology in Web marketing? Discuss.

13. BestBookBuys.com finds the cheapest price of a book that is being sold on the Web. Log onto the following site and find out who sells one of your textbooks with the lowest price.

<http://bestbookbuys.com>

14. One of the best-known shopping agents on the Internet is the Bargain Finder. Log onto the following web site, and try to buy an item and compare prices.

<http://www.cdrom-guide.com/bargainfinder.htm>

How does this price compare with the one found in project #13 above?

15. The following site provides comprehensive information on popular intelligent agents on the market:

<http://botspot.com/search>

By examining the materials presented in this site and other sources write a two-page paper on the role of intelligent agent technology in e-commerce. What is the role of this technology in Web marketing? Discuss.

16. BottomDollar (www.bottomdollar.com) is a shopping agent that claims to find the lowest prices on the Web in categories such as books, movies, CDs, and so forth. Log onto the site and do some comparison shopping. Compare these prices with those found in project #13 above.

7-12 KEY TERMS

Ad impression. 235
Banner ads. 235, 239–240
Click, 236
Click ratio, 236
Click through rate (CTR), 236
Cookie, 236
Cost per click (CPC), 236
Cost per thousand (CPM), 236
Discussion lists, 240–241
E-mail and registering e-mail, 241
Hit, 236
Intelligent agents, 244–248
Links on other web sites, 242
Mail agents, 247
Marketing mix, 231
Message boards and special interest malls, 243

Meta tag, 236
Newsgroups, 242
Online classified advertisements, 242–243
Page view, 236
Product-brokering agents, 245
Pull Technology, 232
Push technology, 231–232, 248–249
Shopping agents, 248
Smart catalog, 245
Splash screen, 244
Spot leasing, 244
Traditional marketing and advertising tools, 239
Usenet and newsgroup agents, 247
World Wide Web navigational agents, 247

REFERENCES

[1] Cross, Richard (1994, October). "Internet: The Missing Marketing Medium Found." *Direct Marketing,* pp. 20–23.

[2] Department of Advertising, The University of Texas at Austin <http://advertising.utexas.edu/world/Internet.html>

[3] Etzioni, Oren, and Daniel S. Weld (1995). "Intelligent Agents on the Internet: Fact, Fiction, and Forecast." *IEEE Expert* 10(4), pp. 44–49.

[4] Strauss, Judy, and Raymond Frost (1999). "Marketing on the Internet: Principles of Online Marketing." Upper Saddle River, NJ: Prentice Hall.

Part III

Implementation and Management Issues in Electronic Commerce

Chapter 8

Technologies and Applications to Support Electronic Commerce

Learning Objectives

After studying this chapter you should be able to do the following:

- Define local, wide, and metropolitan area networks.
- Understand the differences between a peer-to-peer and a server-based local area network.
- Discuss public networks and virtual private networks.
- Define packet-switching and circuit-switching networks.
- Explain client–server computing and its major architectures.
- Discuss wireless and mobile networks.
- Review wireless e-commerce.

INFORMATION BOX 8-1

Spotlight on E-Commerce-Enabling Technologies

E-mail and corporate intranets are among the most common application of local area networks (LANs).

Groupware applications, including e-mail, messaging, scheduling, calendaring, and task and workflow management utilities, are becoming very popular.

According to the International Telecommunications Union (ITU), more than half the population of the world has never made a telephone call. Global teledensity is currently less than 2%. Wireless access will help all developing societies to increase their teledensity, thereby yielding a higher gross domestic product. This may increase the popularity of wireless e-commerce applications.

Doctors and nurses in hospitals are more productive because handheld or notebook computers with wireless LAN capability deliver patient information instantly. This may increase wireless e-commerce applications in hospitals and medical facilities.

For developing countries, wireless networks offer a short-cut to the rapid achievement of high-market penetration and accelerated prosperity.

In a wireless environment, portable computers use small antennae to communicate with radio towers in the surrounding area. Satellites in near-earth orbit pick up low-powered signals from mobile and portable network devices.

Some of the prime advantages of mobile networks are lower capital expenditures and long-term operating costs, easy installation, fewer risks and less damage to the environment, and easier ability to meet future market growth.

Wireless networks are particularly useful for isolated areas, buildings, and for professionals who are in continuous movement, such as nurses and doctors.

Wireless networks provide all the functions of wired networks, without the physical constraints of the wire itself.

Network managers implement wireless LANs to provide backup for mission-critical applications running on wired networks.

IBM has signed agreements to further its wireless e-commerce strategies with these seven leading wireless and Internet companies in the U.S. and Europe: Nokia, Motorola, Palm Inc., Cisco Systems, Intel, Ericsson, and Symbian Ltd. These companies will work with IBM to develop and market integrated products for wireless e-commerce.

INFORMATION BOX 8-2

E-Commerce in Action: Wal-Mart Stores, Inc.

Wal-Mart Stores, Inc. is improving their suppliers' access to their sales and inventory data, replacing dial-up connection with frame relay and a customized Web front to ensure an uninterrupted flow of goods to over 3,400 stores worldwide. One project, called the Vendor Frame Network, connects about 20 of Wal-Mart's largest suppliers to its frame relay backbone via permanent virtual circuit (PVC) connection. Wal-Mart suppliers, which include companies such as Mattel, Procter & Gamble, and Warner-Lambert, run customized applications that give them real-time access to sales, inventory, and forecasting data about their specific products. These data are housed on Wal-Mart mainframes and NCR Teradata servers in Tulsa, Oklahoma. A security system of filters, firewalls, permission, and field-level security in the applications prevents vendors from accessing data about one another's products. Wal-Mart also has added a Web-based front end to its RetailLink system, which provides suppliers with access to the data repository. Wal-Mart has also added redundancy to its frame relay network to boost reliability. The retailer has set up dual PVCs to assure continuous uptime for the network that links stores, distribution centers, and other facilities. Wal-Mart uses information technology to gather sales results, gross margins, payroll, and other data for all its stores. The individual stores use the information to write schedules and maintain inventory tracking. New initiatives include a voice-based filing system for the grocery distribution centers designed to eliminate product-labeling costs. Order information is sent via radio frequency to a portable unit worn by the order selector. Wal-Mart uses AT&T's 3600 supercomputer, allowing the following:

- Wal-Mart merchandisers can access a database and make decisions on replenishment, examine consumer-buying trends, perform analyses, change prices, and generally react to changing business factors at any time.
- Major suppliers can access detailed daily sales information from any Wal-Mart store. (2,500 suppliers have access only to information concerning their merchandise in Wal-Mart's database.)

Other e-commerce applications in Wal-Mart chain include the following:

- Automated distribution
- Computerized routing
- Radio-frequency tagging
- Electronic data interchange (EDI)

SOURCE: Janah, Monua. "Wal-Mart Links to Suppliers—Frame Relay and Web Front End Replace Dial-Up Connections To Boost Data Access." *Information Week* October 5, 1998.

8-1 INTRODUCTION

This chapter discusses some of the technologies and applications that support e-commerce operations. Technologies discussed in this chapter and Chapter 9 collectively provide the platform needed for the implementation of e-commerce applications. The chapter first introduces local area networks (LANs) as the foundation for any client–server application, including intranets, extranets, e-mail, and various groupware applications. The chapter then explains peer-to-peer (PTP) and server-based LANs and reviews wide area (WAN) and metropolitan area (MAN) networks. Public networks and virtual private networks (VPN) are discussed, and different types of client–server models are explained, including two-tier, three-tier, and *n*-tier architectures and thin and fat clients. The chapter reviews wireless and mobile networks and wireless e-commerce, as their popularity is on the rise, highlighting Cisco Systems, Inc., as the industry connection.

8-2 WHAT IS A LOCAL AREA NETWORK?

A LAN is the foundation of any client–server application, such as intranets and extranets, and consists of two or more computers and other peripheral equipment connected in close proximity. Usually a LAN is limited to a certain geographical area, such as a building, and is privately owned and does not use public carriers. The geographical scope of a LAN can be a single office, a building, or an entire campus. The typical speed of LANs varies from 10 megabits per second (Mbps) to 1 gigabit per second (Gbps). There are two types of LANs: wired and wireless. Wired LANs utilize wires (otherwise known as conducted media), such as twisted-pair, coaxial, and fiber-optic cables. Wireless LANs utilize radiated media, such as microwave, spread spectrum radio, and broadcast radio. To establish a LAN, careful planning and a thorough assessment of the information needs of a particular organization are required. The hardware, software, and personnel costs must be carefully calculated and compared and contrasted with the benefits that a LAN system will offer [1, 2].

LANs can be broken down into two basic models: **peer-to-peer** and **server-based.** Many important criteria, such as the size of the network, security, cost, the number of platforms and protocols that must be supported, and LAN administrative overhead, are critical considerations when deciding which network model to implement. The following information will help you to differentiate the advantages and disadvantages of these two models.

8-2-1 WHAT IS A PEER-TO-PEER LOCAL AREA NETWORK?

Peer-to-peer networks are the easiest types of LANs to install and maintain as there is no central or dedicated server. Peer-to-peer networks allow computers to access files on each other's hard drives, share peripherals such as printers and modems, and share access to applications such as e-mail, all while each PC remains usable as a workstation. To implement a peer-to-peer network, all you need to do is install a network operating system (NOS), network adapters, and wiring and connect the workstations using an inexpensive hub. A hub is a device that acts as a LAN's wiring center (a point at which many cables come together and join so they can communicate). Microsoft's Windows 95/98 and Artisoft's LANtastic are examples of peer-to-peer networking products. Figure 8-1 illustrates a peer-to-peer LAN.

Generally speaking, the peer-to-peer LAN model is a good solution when the environment consists of 10 or fewer workstations, file and printer sharing needs are limited, security is not a major consideration, and when the need is high for a simple solution that works well for a single platform, single protocol, low volume, and low cost. One weakness of the peer-to-peer model is that because all of the computers are equal, every user must be an effective administrator of the computer they use. If a user's workstation locks up or is inadvertently shut down, all other workstations won't be able to access the locked-up station. Also, because part of a workstation's CPU and memory resources must be devoted to file and peripheral sharing tasks, workstation performance can be degraded.

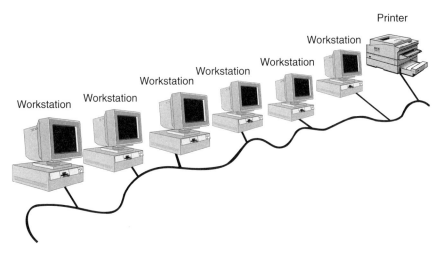

Figure 8-1 A peer-to-peer local area network.

8-2-2 What Is a Server-Based Local Area Network?

A server-based LAN has a central computer that provides application, file, security, and communications services. Novell NetWare, Microsoft NT/2000, Banyan Vines, Apple Computer AppleShare, and IBM LAN Server are examples of server-based networking products.

Generally, the server-based network model is a good solution when the environment consists of more than 10 workstations, file and printer sharing needs are high, security precautions are warranted, and the need for a larger, multiplatform or protocol, high-performance, fault-tolerant network is needed. A server-based solution is also well suited for environments where there are a high level of network-intensive operations, such as database serving, application serving, and file and print serving. One intrinsic weakness of the server-based model is that it is more complex, usually requiring the devoted time and attention of a dedicated LAN administrator. Figure 8-2 illustrates a server-based network.

8-2-3 Which Model Should You Implement?

To decide which model (peer-to-peer or server-based) to implement, you must consider the strengths and weaknesses of each model, taking into consideration the unique needs of the users whom the LAN will serve. For example, if hardware and administrative overhead costs are the most important concerns, the peer-to-peer model provides a good solution. Alternatively, if reliability and se-

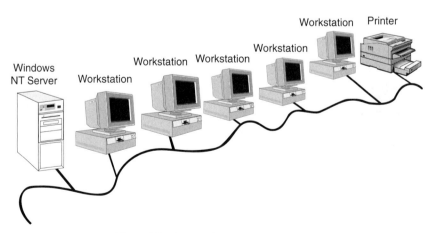

Figure 8-2   A server-based local area network.

curity are the top considerations, the server-based model may be the best choice. A detailed analysis requires establishing a weighting or ranking system for each criterion.

Finally, you should keep in mind that the criteria outlined above are only generalizations. Most peer-to-peer networks can handle as many as 100 clients, and server-based solutions are appropriate for very small workgroups (less than 10 workstations) where security considerations are high. Some peer-to-peer networking products, such as Artisoft's LANtastic, offer provisions for upgrading to a dedicated server when and if the need arises. If you ever have to change from a peer-to-peer to a server-based network environment, most of the network interface cards and cabling will still work.

8-3 WHAT IS A WIDE AREA NETWORK?

A wide area network (WAN) does not limit itself to a certain geographical area. It may span several cities, states, or even countries. Usually several different parties own it. The geographical scope of a WAN can be intercity or across international borders. The speed of WANs varies from 28.8 Kbps to 100 Mbps. As an example of a WAN system, consider a company that has its headquarters in Washington, D.C., and 40 offices in 40 states. With a WAN system, all these offices can be in continuous contact with the headquarters and can send and receive information. Remote data entry becomes a real possibility in a WAN system. An airline reservation system is another example of a WAN. You can reserve an airline ticket in the United States and pick it up in Asia or Africa.

A WAN uses dedicated or switched connections to link computers and other devices in geographically remote locations that are too dispersed to be directly connected to LAN media. These wide area connections can be made either through public or private networks built by the organizations they serve. A WAN may utilize many different technologies. For example, it may use different communications media (twisted-pair, fiber-optic, or coaxial cable, or satellite and microwave), terminals of different sizes and sophistication (workstations, PCs, and notebooks), multiplexers, concentrators, and so forth. A multiplexer (also called a mux) is a hardware device that allows several devices to share one communication channel. A concentrator is another device that combines data from several workstations onto a single communication line. Although multiplexers and concentrators perform similar functions—combining data on a communication line—the devices have different characteristics and are used in different configurations. Multiplexers, for instance, must be used in pairs, whereas concentrators are used alone. Similar to workstations, concentrators also support some processing and data storage functions, which may not be available in all multiplexers. However, more and more, multiplexers are supporting some of these advanced features, and the gap in the processing capability of the two devices has been narrowing. Figure 8-3 illustrates a WAN system.

Typical WANs use one or several routers, which send traffic from the local network over the wide area connection to a remote destination. A router is a network interconnection device and the related software that connects two network systems. The two connecting systems can be different; however, they must use a common routing protocol. The router is connected either to an analog line or a digital line. Routers are connected to analog lines via modems or to digital lines via a channel service unit and/or data service unit (CSU/DSU). The CSU/DSU is the WAN equivalent of an enhanced and sophisticated network interface card (NIC) in a LAN. The type of carrier service determines the exact type of equipment the WAN will need for an optimum operation.

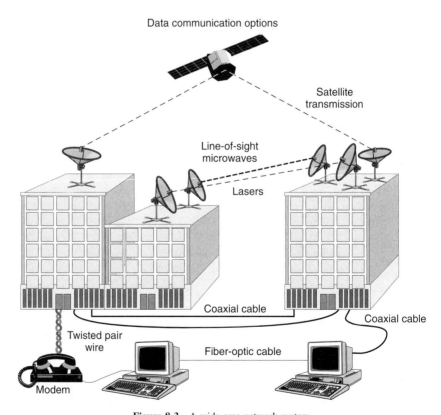

Figure 8-3   A wide area network system.

8-4 WHAT IS A METROPOLITAN AREA NETWORK?

A committee of the Institute of Electrical and Electronic Engineers (IEEE) has developed specifications for a public, independent, high-speed network that connects a variety of data communications systems, including LANs and WANs in metropolitan areas. This new set of standards defines what is called a **metropolitan area network** (MAN). This network is designed to deliver data, video, and digital voice to all organizations within a metropolitan area. The geographical scope of a MAN usually covers a city and contiguous cities. The speed of MANs varies from 2 Mbps up to 100 Mbps. Several companies are involved in developing the MAN system, including Bell Atlantic, AT&T, and QPSX Communications, Ltd., of Australia. A MAN is a relatively new class of network; it is a public citywide LAN that makes large-scale resource sharing a possibility. Figure 8-4 illustrates a typical MAN, showing how a MAN connects several LANs to each other.

Many companies designed LANs as a logical way to connect workstations, personal computers, printers, and other peripheral devices throughout an organization. Now that the LANs are in place, users are calling for connectivity between LANs in other buildings or across town. Dedicated T3 (44.736 Mbps), fiber distributed data interface (FDDI), or Gigabit Ethernet technology are increasingly used for this connectivity.

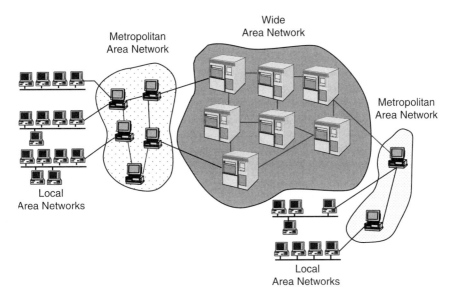

Figure 8-4   An example of a metropolitan area network.

Table 8-1

Comparison of Local, Wide, and Metropolitan Area Networks[a]

	LAN	WAN	MAN
Ownership	Usually one party	More than one party	One to several parties
Speed[b]	10 Mbps to 1 Gbps	28.8 Kbps to 100 Mbps	2 Mbps to 100 Mbps
Scope	A building to a campus	Intercity to international	One city to several contiguous cities

[a]LAN, local area network; WAN, wide area network; MAN, metropolitan area network.
[b]Mbps, megabits per second; Kbps, kilobits per second; Gbps, gigabits per second.

LAN

MAN

WAN

Figure 8-5   Local (LAN), metropolitan (MAN), and wide (WAN) area networks.

MANs use digital backbone that bridge LANs and WANs and act as a data communications link between the two. This type of system is a necessary medium that optimizes the midrange of resource-sharing networks. LANs are most efficient at short-distance resource sharing and communications, and WANs provide distance but are relatively slow. Therefore, a MAN is a logical setup that makes the most of both these technologies. There are three important features that distinguish MANs from LANs or WANs:

1. **Size.** The network size falls intermediate between LANs and WANs. A MAN typically covers an area of between 5 and 50 km. Many MANs cover an area the size of a city, although in some cases MANs may be as small as a group of buildings or as large as the South Side of Chicago.

2. **Ownership.** A MAN is not generally owned by a single organization. Either a consortium of users owns the MAN communications links and equipment, or a single network provider sells the service to users. This level of service provided to each user must therefore be negotiated with the provider of the MAN services, and some performance specifications are normally dictated.

3. **Speed.** A MAN often acts as a high-speed network to allow sharing of regional resources (similar to a large LAN). It is also frequently used to provide a shared connection to other networks using a connection to a WAN. Most MANs run at speeds between 2–100 Mbps. Table 8-1 compares LANs, WANs, and MANs, and Figure 8-5 illustrates these three networks.

8-5 PUBLIC NETWORKS

Public networks are the wide-area telecommunications facilities owned by common carriers and resold to users by subscription. These common carriers include the following:

- Local exchange carriers (LECs)
- Interexchange carriers (IXCs)
- Value-added carriers (VACs)
- Value-added networks (VANs)

In order to choose a carrier, the following important criteria must be carefully analyzed:

- Carrier reputation and quality of service
- The capacity of service
- Flexibility of the service (switched versus dedicated circuits)
- Reliability of the service (error rates and circuit failures)

LECs include companies such as the Regional Bell Operating Companies (RBOCs), GTE, and other companies that handle local telephone and telecommunications connections.

An **IXC** is a long-distance telecommunications carrier, such as AT&T, World-Com, and US Sprint. Customers choose an IXC based on its offerings, prices, and the geographical area covered.

VACs, such as CompuServe Information Services and GE Information Services, often provide WAN services as a sideline to their core business. Typically, a VAC has a national private data network (PDN) established for its own use, and it resells the excess capacity of that PDN to customers. Using the PDN saves the user the trouble of acquiring the various carrier services and setting up his or her own switching equipment because the switching is done in the carrier's network. The VAC also handles the management and maintenance of the WAN services, and it may even be able to do some protocol conversion for the customer.

A **value-added network (VAN)** is a common-carrier facility available to the public that is able to send and receive information over publicly and privately owned networks. These networks, capable of routing messages through switching equipment, provide computer services and access to databases. They not only transmit information, but also change its characteristics or enhance it; this is the feature that distinguishes VANs from WANs. WANs transmit data essentially unchanged, whereas VANs provide supplementary databases, electronic mail, network management, electronic data interchange (EDI), and security features. EDI (as discussed in Chapter 5) is one of the prime users of VANs.

8-6 VIRTUAL PRIVATE NETWORKS

A virtual private network (VPN) is a new type of VAN that runs on the Internet and appears to the user as a private network. The provider of a VPN service takes the user data, encrypts them, and sends them the to their destination over the Internet. The sender and receiver are the only two parties on the VPN. The main advantage of VPN is its relative low cost. The two major disadvantages are lack of standardization among various providers and a relatively slow transmission speed.

VPNs are one method of providing the security needed by an extranet, but there are others, including simple user name or password access and dedicated leased line access. A VPN is a secure hybrid network that utilizes both public and private resources. A user may lease media and configure a VPN on an as-needed basis. Using this configuration, some traffic may be transferred using a public network and some may be transferred over the private network. In the Windows NT (2000) operating system, Microsoft includes software for VPN with enhanced security features including authentication. Alternatively, VPNs can be used for intranets and other network applications. The key feature of VPNs is providing a secure virtual "private" network using the resources of the "public" Internet for whatever application the organization wants to use. VPNs are an alternative to private leased lines or dedicated integrated services digital networks (ISDN) lines, T1 lines, and so forth. A remote user may use VPN for

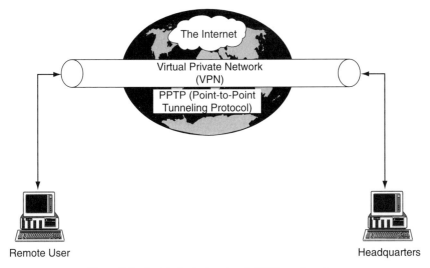

Figure 8-6 A virtual private network (VPN) configuration.

a secure connection to the computing facilities of the parent company or a business partner (see Figure 8-6). The steps are outlined as follows:

1. The user may use an ordinary telephone line, ISDN, or digital subscriber line (DSL) to connect to the Internet. The ISDN can network telephones, PCs, mainframes, printers, and fax machines using ordinary twisted-pair telephone line and digital transmission technology to send voice, data, and images over the same line. DSL is a common carrier service and is promoted as one of the high-speed access capabilities to remote LANs and the Internet, providing speeds of up to 51 Mbps. DSL provides both traditional voice transmission and high-speed full-duplex digital data transmission.

2. The Internet service provider (ISP) creates a virtual private tunnel using a tunneling protocol such as Microsoft's point-to-point tunneling protocol (PPTP).

3. The message is transferred through the VPN.

4. The connecting router at the receiving side receives the message, removes the tunneling protocol, and delivers the plain message to the right workstation.

8-7 PACKET SWITCHING AND CIRCUIT SWITCHING: DEFINITIONS

Using **packet switching,** a message is transmitted by dividing it into fixed-length packets and then sending the individual packets to their destination.

Connections don't need to be established before data transmission begins; in other words, no virtual circuit is needed. A virtual circuit is made of a series of logical connections between the sending and receiving stations. Using packet switching, the connection is made after both stations exchange information and agree on communication variables that establish and maintain the connections. Virtual circuits can be temporary, lasting for a specific time period, or permanent. The special software creates a virtual circuit in such a way that users think they have a dedicated point-to-point leased circuit. Packets may be sent over different paths and may arrive at their destination in a different order. At the destination, the packets are automatically put back into the proper order. Because there is no predefined virtual circuit, packet switching can increase or decrease bandwidth as required, and therefore it can handle high volume in packets very effectively. Taking advantage of the multiple paths of the network, packet-switching services can route packets around failed or congested lines. The best example of the packet-switching technique is the Internet. The packet switching technique allows multiple parties to use the same network at the same time. TCP/IP software must be installed on all computers connected to the Internet. The Internet packets are called datagrams. The timer and acknowledgment features of TCP assure the delivery of all datagrams on the Internet. Also, TCP eliminates duplicate datagrams.

Using **circuit switching,** an electrical connection between the sender and receiver nodes is established based on demand for exclusive use of the circuit until the connection is terminated. Using the circuit-switching process, physical circuits are created, maintained, and terminated for individual point-to-point or multipoint connections. A **point-to-point connection** uses a communication line to connect one node or workstation to a host computer. In a multipoint connection, several nodes or workstations share one communications line. Telephone connection is an example of the circuit-switching technique.

Whether to choose circuit-switching or packet-switching services depends upon two factors:

- The type of traffic that the network generates
- The allocated budget

If the traffic generated on the network is time sensitive, such as those generated by video applications, a circuit-switched service is the preferred option. However, the high cost of this option should be considered. On the other hand, if some delays can be tolerated, packet-switching services are more economical than circuit-switched services, and they also provide adequate reliability.

8-8 CLIENT–SERVER MODEL

To better understand the client–server model, a brief discussion of distributed data processing (DDP) is helpful. DDP solves two of the major problems associated with centralized and decentralized processing configurations: lack of responsiveness in centralized processing and lack of coordination in decentralized processing. DDP has overcome these problems by maintaining centralized control while decentralizing operations.

In DDP, the processing power is distributed among several locations. Databases, processing units, or input–output devices may be distributed. A good example is a newspaper publishing business, in which reporters and editors are scattered throughout the world. Reporters gather news stories throughout the world, enter them into their terminals, edit them, and using a communications medium, forward them to the editor in charge. The reporter and the editor can be thousands of miles apart. Since the mid-1970s, with advancements in networking and microcomputers, this type of data-processing configuration has gained popularity. Some of the unique advantages of a DDP system include the following:

- Access to unused processing power by an overused location
- Design modularity—computer power can be added or removed based on need
- Distance and location independence
- More compatible with organizational growth by adding workstations
- Redundant resources as a security measure—if one component fails, a redundant component will take over.
- Resource sharing, such as expensive high-quality laser printers
- System reliability—failure of a system can be limited to only one site.
- User orientation—the system is more responsive to user needs.

Some of the disadvantages of DDP include dependence on communications technology, incompatibility of equipment, and a more challenging network management.

Intranets and extranets are implemented using a client–server model. Using this model, client software runs on the local computer and communicates with the remote server, requesting information. A server is a remote computer somewhere on the network that provides information based on requests. (I discuss server platforms in more detail in Chapter 9.) For example, consider the request that I make from my PC on my desk to the campus database server. My request is, "DISPLAY THE NAMES OF ALL THE E-COMMERCE MAJORS WITH A GPA GREATER THAN 3.8." The database server receives my request and processes it, and it might respond with the following three names (see Figure 8-7):

Alan Jones
Morvareed Smith
Nooshin Jackson

Usually in the most basic client–server configuration, a client sends a request (usually in SQL format) and the server responds (see Figure 8-7). The client can

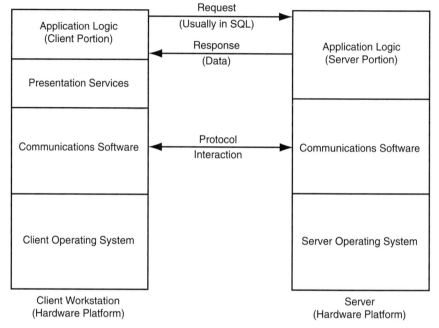

Figure 8-7   Classic client–server architecture. SQL, structured query language.

be smart or dumb, fat or thin (explained in section 8-8-3). The most significant advantage of client–server architecture is its scalability. Client–server architectures can be scaled horizontally or vertically. Horizontal scaling means more workstations (clients) can be added or deleted, and vertical scaling means the system can be migrated to larger and faster servers with minimum impact on the client–server architecture.

To better understand client–server architecture, the following three terms should be defined:

- Presentation
- Application
- Data management

The **presentation** logic is concerned with how data are presented to the client. Microsoft Windows Graphical User Interface (GUI) is an example of presentation software. **Application** is the software that processes the request for the user. This may entail processing a return on investment for an e-commerce project or processing the overdue payment for a specific account. **Data management** is responsible for the data management and storage operation of the client–server architecture. The real issue in client–server architecture is how to divide these three functions between the client and server.

8-8-1 Two-Tier Architecture

Two-tier architecture is known as the traditional client–server model. In this configuration, a client (tier one) directly communicates with the server (tier two), usually through a structured query language (SQL) query with no intervening server. This architecture is very effective in small workgroups (about 50 clients). Using this configuration, the client maintains most or all software applications and presentation logic, and the server maintains the data and data management logic. Application development speed, simplicity, and robustness are some of the main advantages of a two-tier architecture. On the downside, since the majority of the application logic is on the client side, changes in the application processes, logic, and rules will require significant modification on the part of the client, resulting in major upgrade and modification costs. However, this depends on the application and may not be true in all cases. Figure 8-8 illustrates this architecture.

For a typical dialogue between the client and server, the following events usually take place:

1. The user runs the client software to create a query.
2. The client accepts the request and formats it so that the server understands it.

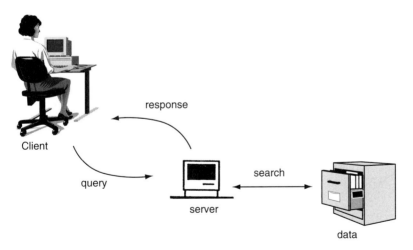

Figure 8-8 A two-tier client–server architecture.

3. The client sends the request to the server over the network.
4. The server receives and processes the query.
5. The results are sent to the client.
6. The results are formatted and presented to the user in an understandable format.

8-8-2 THREE-TIER AND N-TIER ARCHITECTURES

In a two-tier architecture, the presentation logic is always on the client and the data management on the server. But the specific location for the application is not defined. It could be on the client, the server, or it could be split between the two. If application software is placed on the client, a change in the data management software requires modification of the software for all the clients, a costly venture.

A three-tier architecture attempts to balance the workload between the client and the server with moderate hardware requirements. A three-tier (multitier) architecture removes the application processing from both the client and the back-end server and places it on the middle-tier server by itself while leaving the presentation on the client and the data management on the back-end server (see Figure 8-9). Improving network performance is one of the primary advantages of this architecture. However, the network management using this architecture is more challenging; there would be more network traffic, and it would be more difficult to program and test software in an n-tier architecture because more devices must communicate to respond to a user request. Figure 8-10 illustrates an n-tier architecture.

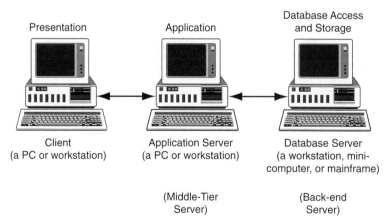

Figure 8-9   A three-tier architecture.

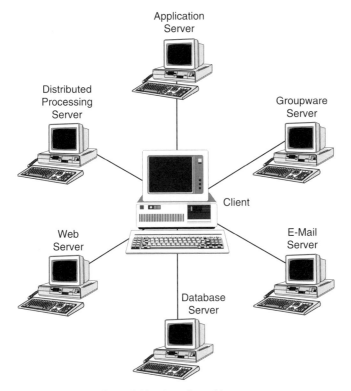

Figure 8-10   An *n*-tier architecture.

8-8-3 THIN CLIENTS VERSUS FAT CLIENTS

The terms *fat client* and *thin clients* are used to distinguish the amount of processing power at the desktop. Fat clients offer more processing power at the desktop compared with thin clients. In a two-tier architecture, the client is often provided with the ability to handle both presentation and application processing. In multitier architecture the client can be thin or fat, with processing distributed onto one or more application servers and data server on the back end. Thin clients offer the following advantages:

- Improved reliability
- Improved flexibility
- Improved ease of upgrades

- Improved security
- Less opportunity for users to change or modify anything on their PCs (resulting in less headache for the network manager)

As mentioned earlier, intranets are implemented using the client–server model. A web browser will be installed on each employee's PC or workstation. The client computer would then access the company's intranet web site to gather information. The local office would have a mail and proxy server (software for replicating and filtering Web content). The proxy server caches the most frequently accessed web pages from outside the intranet and will even check and automatically update those pages. This increases the speed of accessing those pages and reduces the traffic on the Internet link. Because the local pages are stored on local servers, that access should be reasonably quick. If the mainframe is used as a web server, then it is like any other server. Periodically, the proxy server will call up the central enterprise server and download the most requested web pages. The proxy server can also act as an entry point into the intranet through the firewall from the outside Internet. A proxy server saves connection time and network costs. The mail server forwards all mail to the people located in the local office and saves all the mail addressed to people who are not available locally [3,4,5].

8-9 WIRELESS AND MOBILE NETWORKS

As briefly mentioned in Chapter 2, e-commerce applications using mobile and wireless networks are expected to increase significantly in the near future. Mobility, flexibility, ease of installation, and cost are some of the prime advantages of mobile networks. These systems are particularly effective when there is no infrastructure in place. This is true in many developing nations and in old buildings that have not been designed with the right wiring and the Internet connection. The following are some of the drawbacks of mobile networks:

- Insufficient throughput
- Limited range
- In-building penetration problems
- Vulnerability to frequency noise

Some of these disadvantages will probably be resolved in the near future; in particular, throughput is expected to increase.

There are different definitions of mobile or wireless computing. Mobile computing may simply mean using a laptop away from the office, or it may mean using a modem to access the corporate network from a client's office. Neither of these activities requires wireless data communications. Wireless LANs (WLANs) usually refer to a proprietary LAN. The term is also used in some publications to describe any wireless network, meaning connectivity through wireless media. As described earlier, LANs are used in a limited geographical area and are usually owned by a single entity. WLANs have the same features and characteristics except they use wireless media, such as infrared light and radio frequency. Figure 8-11 illustrates a wireless notebook computer connecting to a wired LAN. The WLAN in the figure uses a small wall-mounted transceiver to connect to the wired network. The transceiver establishes radio contact with the portable network device. The transceiver or receiver can be mounted on a wall, physically attached to the device, or built in.

Numerous vendors and manufacturers crowd the wireless data communications field. The industry has entered the growth stage of the product life cycle, so there are many competitors and rapid changes. Wireless technologies generally fall into two groups:

1. WLANs are rapidly becoming established as an important alternative to wired LANs in many circumstances. WLANs, similar to their wired counterpart,

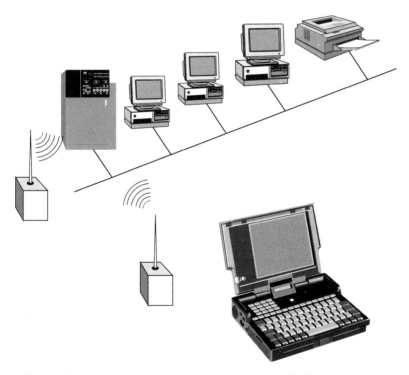

Figure 8-11 A wireless notebook computer connecting to a wired local area network.

are characterized by a single ownership and coverage in a limited geographical area.

2. Wireless WAN data communications cover a broad base not usually covered by WLANs. They include the following:

- Cellular networks
- Cellular digital packet data (CDPD)
- Paging networks
- Personal communications systems (PCS)
- Packet radio networks—ARDIS and RAM Mobile Data
- Broadband personal communications systems (BPCS)
- Satellite networks
- Microwave networks

These technologies enable computing devices to communicate with other devices or networks at any time or at any location bases. They feature a central protocol in which a system's transmitters and receivers communicate with user devices. There are two major differences between WLANs and wireless WANs:

1. Wireless WANs have greater distribution, and they have one owner and many nonowner users. Many users coexist on the same system, and available technology enables these systems to connect users virtually around the globe.

2. Usually WLANs use transmitters and receivers owned by the organization, which the network operates. Wireless WANs utilize public carriers such as AT & T, Sprint, WorldCom, and local telephone companies to send and receive data.

Both WLANs and wireless WANs have a single all-important commonality. They rely on the radio frequency (RF) spectrum as the medium through which they communicate. Spectrum refers to an absolute, continuous range of frequencies.

Cellular phone systems have a three-part architecture (see Figure 8-12):

1. Base stations send and receive transmissions to and from subscribers.

2. Mobile telephone switching offices (MTSO) transfer calls between national or global phone networks and the base stations.

3. System users (subscribers) connect to the base stations using mobile communications devices, such as handheld phones, car phones, notebooks, personal digital assistants (PDAs), pen-based computers, palmtops, and portable data-collection devices.

Mobile devices register with the system by subscribing to a carrier service. Every provider acquires one or more licenses for certain geographic areas. A single provider may own a national or even global network license, but each geographic area is administered separately. Roaming occurs when a mobile unit is outside the coverage area and must use an alternative provider.

The most important driving force in the growth of cellular network use was its total compatibility with the public phone system. This feature gave cell

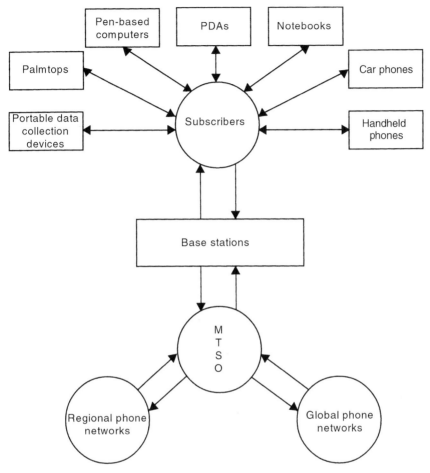

Figure 8-12 Cellular networks architecture. MTSO, mobile telephone switching offices; PDA, personal digital assistant.

phones tremendous value as soon as they became commercially available in 1983. Even if a user had no one else to reach on another cellular phone, he or she could still call every wired phone in the world.

Time division multiple access (TDMA) is a digital technology that divides each channel into six time slots. Each user is allocated two slots, one for transmission and one for reception. This method increases the efficiency of the system by 300%, as it allows three calls to be carried on one channel. The number of time slots can be increased significantly, thus increasing the number of calls on the channel. Two TDMA protocols are presently available in limited areas in the United States, DCS-800 and IS-136.

The second digital technology is code division multiple access (CDMA). This protocol transmits multiple encoded messages over a wide frequency and then decodes them at the receiving end. The current standard improves network capacity over advanced mobile phone system (AMPS) by a factor of 10, and like TDMA, can be further improved.

AMPS is still the primary system in the United States, but the digital systems are growing rapidly because of improved capacity, voice quality, encryption capability, and their ability to integrate with other digital networks. Digital, however, is not as universal as AMPS, and the two digital systems are not compatible. For this reason digital devices are built to be compatible with analog AMPS. In the long run, it is probably desirable that the United States adopts a single digital standard. As long as AMPS is the primary technology for many phones, it needs to be maintained. In the future, however, it would be wasteful to maintain an analog backbone just so that differing digital systems could communicate with each other. Likewise, it would be annoying to consumers if their cell phones couldn't talk to all cell phones using the other digital protocol because there was no analog bridge.

8-10 WIRELESS E-COMMERCE: A SECOND LOOK

As briefly discussed in Chapter 2, mobile commerce (m-commerce) is one of the fastest growing subfields of e-commerce. International Data Corporation (IDC) predicts that by 2003, 61.5 million people in the United States will be equipped with wireless Internet capabilities, up from 7.4 million in 1999. According to Arc Group, the number of wireless customers browsing the Internet using their handsets will total over 600 million by 2005, and the study predicts the total number of mobile users will reach more than one billion worldwide, exceeding the number of fixed Internet users.

Unofficially, wireless e-commerce (m-commerce) has been in existence for many years, and it is more recognized due to the recent success of wired e-commerce. Mobile communications and wireless networks have been utilized by workers to order parts, check inventories, assist customers, and dispatch technical personnel more efficiently. Major communications companies are already making e-commerce efforts in North America, Europe, and Asia. Motorola and IBM are in partnership to create an open, scalable voice and data framework for ISP and application service providers (ASPs) to develop and access wireless software and services. Many of the new wireless phones already include Web-browsing capabilities. Lack of software at the phone companies prevents them from conducting e-commerce.

All cellular systems can be used to conduct wireless e-commerce operations. A user must have equipment tailored to the technology. Modems are available for analog cellular, TDMA, CDMA cellular, and for CDPD. One method may be more suitable than another based on the data communications applications.

Wireless application protocol (WAP) initiated by Ericsson, Motorola, and Nokia, provides standards for wireless Internet use on digital mobile phones, pagers, PDAs, and other wireless devices, such as Palm. WAP is a specification for communication protocols to standardize the way that wireless devices, such as cellular telephones and radio transceivers, can be used for Internet access, including e-mail, the World Wide Web, newsgroups, instant messenger, and Internet Relay Chat. Information Box 8-3 highlights features of wireless networking that will soon be available.

INFORMATION BOX 8-3

E-Commerce Features That Will Soon Be Available

You, as a busy executive, step off a plane in New York City and turn on your personal communicator. The device is an electronic organizer with an integrated wireless modem. Here's what you receive via a wireless network, based on your personal profile:

1. E-mail that you've designated for wireless transmission from your corporate server or ISP.
2. A list of concerts in New York that you can immediately purchase tickets for wirelessly.
3. A list of half-price theater tickets that you can purchase immediately.
4. Seating charts for concerts, plays, etc., so you can check the location of your seats before you purchase a ticket.
5. A list of sales on men's or women's clothing, and the ability to request photos of the products and purchase the clothing immediately.
6. Your financial "net worth": savings and checking account balances, your six most recent credit card purchases—and your spouse's most recent purchases, the current value of your stocks and bonds, with the ability to transfer funds, purchase stocks, and pay bills, wirelessly.
7. A map of midtown Manhattan, with your bank's ATMs pinpointed.
8. The headlines and first paragraphs of very specific news articles.
9. The five-day weather forecast for New York.
10. A list of movies, times, and locations in New York, and the ability to reserve a seat in some theaters.
11. Today-only discount coupons for shopping at Macy's, Border's, and several computer stores.
12. You should be able to download your favorite song on your personal communicator.

SOURCE: Wireless E-Commerce: A New Business Model. Copyright © 1999 Wireless Internet & Mobile Computing.<http://home.earthlink.net/~aareiter/wireless2.htm> (Date of Access: April 24, 2001).

8-11 INDUSTRY CONNECTION: CISCO SYSTEMS, INC.

> Cisco Systems, Inc.
> 170 West Tasman Drive
> San Jose, California 95134-1619
> Phone: (408) 526-4000
> Fax: (408) 526-4100
> Web site address: <http://www.cisco.com>

Cisco Systems, Inc., is the world leader in networking and data communications equipment. Founded in 1984 by a small group of Stanford University computer science graduates, Cisco Systems went public in 1990. Their objective was to make connecting different computers together easier. Cisco hosts the largest Internet commerce site in the world. After shipping its first product in 1986, Cisco has increased its revenue over 100-fold and has acquired more than 60 companies.

Cisco's products comprise a broad selection, including routers, LANs, MANs, WANs, switches, web site management tools, e-commerce, and Internet applications (just to name a few). It is the closest you can get to one-stop shopping for a complete, end-to-end networking solution.

According to Cisco Systems, its e-commerce solution provides a framework for strategies and tactics to successfully conduct business online. A complete e-commerce solution includes the commerce engine or server and the associated commerce-enabling services. Cisco's full-service e-commerce solution model consists of six major components:

- **Preorder/lead management/online marketing:** all of the pretransaction functions
- **Online ordering/customer service:** the order-related components of online transactions
- **Financial services functions:** the actual transaction-related functions
- **Service contract functions:** provides customers with the ability to check on and order services
- **Logistics/fulfillment:** fulfillment/distribution functions
- **Postorder management/nontechnical customer support:** order status, invoicing, returns, parts replacement

Selected e-commerce-related products and services include the following:

Micro Webserver is a flexible web server that organizations can purchase in order to establish an Internet presence or provide a corporate intranet. (Chapter

9 provides a detailed discussion on various web server platforms.) This product includes built-in security and is accompanied with a form builder and a file transfer utility. Both Microsoft Internet Explorer and Netscape Navigator can effectively interact with this product.

PIX Firewall series delivers comprehensive security and high performance for corporate intranets. The PIX firewall allows corporations to protect their internal networks from outside intruders. (Firewalls as a major security measure in the e-commerce world will be discussed in Chapter 11.)[1]

8-12 SUMMARY

This chapter discussed some of the technologies and applications that support e-commerce operations. The chapter introduced LANs as the foundation for any client–server application, including intranets and extranets. Also explained were peer-to-peer and server-based LANs, WANs, and MANs. Public networks and VPNs were briefly discussed and different types of client–server models explained, including two-tier, three-tier, and n-tier architectures and thin and fat clients. The chapter highlighted the rising popularity of wireless and mobile networks and wireless e-commerce and highlighting Cisco Systems, Inc., as the industry connection.

8-13 REVIEW QUESTIONS

1. What is a LAN? What are two features that distinguish a LAN from a WAN?
2. What is the role of a LAN in e-commerce operations?
3. What is resource sharing? How does a LAN allow an organization to share computing resources? Discuss.
4. What are the differences between peer-to-peer and server-based LANs? Discuss.
5. What is a WAN? What are some of the differences between a MAN and a WAN? Discuss.
6. What is a MAN? What are some of the differences between a LAN and a MAN? What are some of the characteristics of a MAN? Discuss.
7. What are the speeds of LANs, MANs, and WANs? Which is the fastest? Which is the slowest? Discuss.

[1]This information was gathered from the company web site and other promotional materials. For detailed information and any update, contact the company.

8. What is packet switching? What is a virtual circuit?
9. What is circuit switching? What are some of the criteria used for choosing circuit switching over packet-switching services?
10. What are three classes of common carriers? What are some of the offerings of each group?
11. What is a value-added network (VAN)? Is it among the common carriers or private networks? Discuss.
12. What are some of the applications of WANs and MANs? Discuss.
13. What are some of the reasons for the popularity of mobile computing?
14. How do you define mobile or wireless computing?
15. Who are some of the current and future users of mobile computing? What is the role of mobile networks in e-commerce operations? Discuss.
16. Aside from being wireless, what are some other differences between wireless and wired networks?
17. What are two advantages of wireless networks compared with wired networks? What are two disadvantages? Discuss.
18. Why is m-commerce growing so fast? What does m-commerce offer that is not offered by other e-commerce categories? Discuss.
19. What types of businesses may gain the most from e-commerce?
20. Which devices will be used in the m-commerce environment? Discuss.

8-14 PROJECTS AND HANDS-ON EXERCISES

1. Log onto the web site of the Cisco Systems, Inc. at the following URL:

   <http://www.cisco.com>

   What are some of the e-commerce products and services offered by this company? What specific Cisco products and services are utilized in the e-commerce infrastructure? What is the role of Cisco Systems products and services in e-commerce security? Discuss.

2. The following sites provide current information on wireless or mobile commerce (m-commerce):

   <http://www.ecommercetimes.com/news/articles/991104-6.shtml>
   <http://mobileinfo.com>
   <http://www.mobileipworld.com>
   <www.televend.com>

   By examining the materials presented in these sites and other sources, explain the advantages and disadvantages of m-commerce. Why might this e-commerce category become popular? What does it offer that other e-commerce categories do not offer? Discuss.

3. The following site provides current information on WAP Forum:

<http://www.wapforum.org>

By examining the materials presented in this site and other sources, prepare a one-page report on the latest on WAP. What are some of the current limitations on wireless e-commerce? Discuss.

4. Phone.com is a major player in wireless e-commerce:

<http://www.phone.com/index.html>

Log onto the site and examine its contents. What are some of the products and services offered by this company used in e-commerce? Discuss.

5. Palm, Inc. is one of the major players providing devices used in the wireless e-commerce environment. By examining the materials presented in this site, examine the role of devices such as Palm in m-commerce. Who are other major players in this market?

<http://www.palm.com>

6. By examining the materials presented in the chapter and other sources, list two advantages and two disadvantages of a peer-to-peer and server-based LANs.

7. By examining the materials presented in the chapter and other sources, list two characteristics of LANs, WANs, and MANs.

8. By examining the materials presented in the chapter and other sources, list two characteristics of two-tier and three-tier client–server architectures.

9. By visiting the computer center of your school or an organization that you are familiar with, list all the hardware and software needed to establish a LAN. By interviewing the network administrator of this school or organization, find out the applications of LANs in this location. What types of security systems are being used? What are some of the e-commerce applications running on this LAN? Discuss.

8-15 KEY TERMS

REFERENCES

[1] Bidgoli, Hossein (2000). "Handbook of Business Data Communications: A Managerial Perspective." Academic Press, Inc.: San Diego, CA.

[2] Panko, Raymond R. (2001). "Business Data Communications and Networking," (3rd ed.). Prentice Hall; Upper Saddle River, NJ.

[3] Rosen, Anita (1997). "Client-Serve Model." *Looking into Intranets & the Internet,* AMACOM: New York, pp. 34–37.

[4] Stallings, William (2001). "Business Data Communications" (Fourth Edition, Prentice Hall, Upper Saddle River, NJ.

[5] Stamper, David A. (2001). "Local Area Networks" (3rd ed.). Prentice Hall: Upper Saddle River, NJ.

Chapter 9

Infrastructure for Electronic Commerce

Learning Objectives

After studying this chapter you should be able to do the following:

- Define Transmission Control Protocol/Internet Protocol (TCP/IP).
- Explain the functions of TCP and IP.
- Review different server platforms.
- Explain how a web server works.
- Elaborate on the features and capabilities of Apache HTTP Server, Microsoft Internet Information Server, and Netscape Enterprise Server as three of the most popular web server applications.
- Discuss the important criteria for choosing a web server.

289

INFORMATION BOX 9-1

Applications and Facts about the E-commerce Infrastructure

RapidSite is a virtual hosting service that runs on a personalized version of Apache.

Linkbot Developer Edition is a Web content-analysis solution that enables web developers to analyze and optimize their content for integrity, effectiveness, and reliability.

Among the different types of web sites, storefront and content delivery sites place the most stress on their platforms.

The Common Gateway Interface (CGI) allows interactivity between a client and a host operating system through the Web via hypertext transfer protocol (HTTP). It is a standard for external gateway programs to interface with information servers, such as HTTP or web servers.

High availability, a combination of responsiveness and reliability, is an important requirement for any e-commerce site.

Netscape Enterprise Server supports encryption and secure sockets layer (SSL) technologies to ward off eavesdroppers and intruders. Using the restrict access option, the web developer can limit access by user, group, IP address, or host or domain name.

Lynx is a full-featured World Wide Web browser for users on both UNIX and virtual memory system (VMS) platforms.

Opera is an advanced Internet or intranet browser for PCs.

United Parcel Service's Online Tools make it possible to add state-of-the-art shipping and logistics capabilities to your e-commerce web site or enterprise applications.

To create dynamic content tools such as Java, JavaScript, Perl, C/C++, and active server pages (ASP) are used. Web servers are designed with certain objectives in mind, including accepting network connections from browsers, retrieving content from disks, executing local CGI programs, transmitting data back to the client browser, and performing these tasks with the highest possible speed.

E-Commerce in United Parcel Service (UPS)

United Parcel Service (UPS) is the largest package delivery company in the world. UPS delivers an average of 12 million packages per day and serves more than 200 countries throughout the world. For mass-distribution shipping, and for customers outside the United States, UPS uses Online Envoy software. This software is available in five languages: English, Spanish, German, French, and Italian. The software simplifies and speeds up shipping and allows customers to track their packages via the Internet. UPS uses a network system that connects 3,000 UPS distribution sites worldwide and supports over 300 system applications, 90,000 PCs, 2,100 LANs, and 12 mainframes. The network supports all of UPS's information services, including voice, data, and imaging communications to employees, business partners, and half a million customers. UPS uses a combination of telecommunications technologies, such as cellular, public frame relay, the Internet, and satellite pathways. Services include custom clearance, real-time package tracking, just-in-time shipment coordination, financial transactions, systems integration, e-mail, and Internet access. UPS reconfigured its private-line telecommunications to provide capacity for new services and to respond to changing needs. UPS has been operating private telecommunications networks in more than 16 European countries for over 10 years. Joining forces with IBM, UPS created a software program that will help automate shipping functions for selling goods over the Web. This UPS/IBM Home Page Creator is a pilot program allowing customers to access UPS's Internet-based package-tracking service as well as to create their own e-commerce web sites. UPS's strategic marketing plan is to use this program to retain its customers by providing "an easy, end-to-end buying, selling, and delivery processing application." UPS expanded its relationship with iCat, HP, SUN Microsystems, and leading ISPs to develop iCat Lemonade Stand. This program is targeted toward small business commerce that wishes to build an Internet commerce presence with no upfront investment, small monthly fees, and an easy-to-use product. Users can access an iCat Lemonade Stand site using an Internet browser, design their store, add and update their product information, and select shopping cart options. Merchants can create unlimited products, prices, descriptions, and pictures. They can also accept payment via credit card, check, and COD, and process orders and print sales reports via e-mail or a browser. UPS also joined alliances with AT&T to offer end-to-end solutions for e-commerce via a reliable AT&T Internet backbone. Their offering includes a "highly flexible set of hosting and transaction services" and "simplifying the process of setting up a secure storefront." Other UPS alliances include Harbinger, with Harbinger's Trusted Link Instant Net Presence, an inexpensive commerce-enabled web site. Lotus Domino Merchant is another product of UPS' alliance with Lotus (an IBM company). This product "provides a single infrastructure for messaging, allowing the e-commerce system to be seamlessly integrated with other workflow applications."

SOURCE: E-commerce at UPS. <http://www.ec.ups.com>
(Date of access: April 24, 2001) Copyright © 2000–2001, United Parcel Service of America, Inc. All rights reserved.

9-1 INTRODUCTION

This chapter defines the Transmission Control Protocol (TCP)/Internet Protocol (IP) as one of the most important protocols used in the e-commerce world. The chapter reviews major functions of TCP/IP, including dynamic host configuration protocol (DHCP), serial line Internet protocol (SLIP), point-to-point protocol (PPP), point-to-point tunneling protocol (PPTP), file transfer protocol (FTP), and hypertext transfer protocol (HTTP). The chapter reviews important server platforms in the e-commerce world and then discusses the operations of web server software. Three of the most popular web server software applications will be discussed in some detail, including Apache HTTP Server, Microsoft Internet Information Server, and Netscape Enterprise Server. The chapter concludes with an overview of the important criteria for choosing a web server, highlighting Oracle Corporation as the industry connection.

9-2 TRANSMISSION CONTROL PROTOCOL/INTERNET PROTOCOL: AN OVERVIEW

TCP/IP is one of the most popular protocols used in the e-commerce world today. TCP/IP is a networking protocol that provides communication between networks made up of computers with diverse hardware architectures and operating systems. In other words, the TCP/IP architecture facilitates connectivity in diverse environments. Though an industry standard suite of protocols providing communications in heterogeneous environments, TCP/IP is, however, a de facto standard. De facto standards are usually defined by proprietary products rather than public specifications. These standards are based on products that enjoy widespread acceptance in the industry but are not generally recognized by one of the official standards-setting bodies.

The TCP segment of the protocol makes sure that packets get through to the other end. TCP keeps track of what is sent and retransmits anything that did not successfully get through. If any text item is too large for one datagram (the text being sent), TCP will split it up into several datagrams and make sure that all the datagrams arrive correctly and are reassembled in their proper sequence.

TCP/IP's primary advantage is its interoperability, or ability to link disparate platforms, computers, and peripheral devices. In addition, TCP/IP is a routable networking protocol and provides access to the Internet. It was the first protocol developed by a group of users and vendors under government sponsorship rather than by a standards organization. It was developed faster than those standards developed through a standards body and led the way for vendor consortiums and changed the way standards are developed today.

TCP/IP originally was intended for Internet-related communications; however, over time it addressed a variety of issues, such as portability, and became the standard protocol for UNIX-based network communications. It could be used on just about any kind of computer. It includes two major protocols: the TCP, which operates at the Transport layer, and the IP, which operates at the Network layer.

TCP/IP is a protocol suite that deals with data transmission and communications. The U.S. Department of Defense developed TCP/IP to interconnect hosts on ARPANET, PRNET (packet radio), and SATNET (packet satellite) computer networks. After these three networks were phased out, TCP/IP continued to grow in use due to its flexibility and ease of use. TCP/IP now can be found on almost every type and size of computer. TCP/IP is the most important component of Internet and intranet technology. Internet servers use a group of IP applications. The log information maintained by the computer converts the unique IP address from the host name (such as www.microsoft.com) to a number (such as 207.68.156.51), which is easier for a computer to manage and understand. (Actually, computers further translate the IP address into its binary equivalent!) The computer changes this log into a routing table. A computer uses IP to access the Internet. Each computer connected to the Internet has a list of closely located computers saved in a routing table that is continually updated. This table maps the network topology by calculating how far away the network is in "hops," which are routers that stand in between and determine which router the computer needs to use to send a packet to a network that is not directly connected to it. A packet is a unit of data sent across a network. An Internet packet is usually called an IP datagram. The address resolution protocol (ARP) is the actual mechanism that maps the IP address to physical addresses. ARP will find the new location and change this location in its table if a server is moved. This way, the client does not need to know where sites are located or how to get to a site.

TCP/IP has a hierarchy of servers. A root server is at the top of hierarchy, followed by a domain server, the local server, and finally the client. Clients are limited by the size of the connection of servers they need to go through. For example, a client might have fast access to any information within its local server, but it might have slow access when getting information from a domain name server such as com, edu, or gov. (For a detailed discussion on domain name systems, consult Chapter 1.) IP assigns a unique Internet address that is managed by the IP layer for each computer. This address is used by the IP protocol to allow hosts and workstations to communicate with each other. The IP application on the computer maintains a log of all IP addresses known to that computer [9,10,11,12,13].

9-3 FUNCTIONS OF TRANSMISSION CONTROL PROTOCOL

The primary functions of the TCP are to establish a virtual circuit between hosts, provide message integrity, ensure sequenced and acknowledged packet delivery, and regulate the flow of data between the source and destination nodes. A virtual circuit is a temporary transmission circuit in which data packets are routed between two points. Special software creates a virtual circuit in such a way that users think they have a dedicated point-to-point leased circuit. Packets may be sent over different paths and may arrive in different order. At the destination the packets are automatically put back into proper order.

9-4 FUNCTIONS OF THE INTERNET PROTOCOL

The IP was designed to support the global public network and is responsible for packet forwarding. To perform this task, it must be aware of the different data link protocols available and the optimum size of each packet. Once it recognizes the size of each packet, it must be able to break the data into the right size packets.

An IP address consists of four bytes, or octets (32 bits, when using IP version 4), and is divided into two parts: a network address and a node address. This 32-bit address space equates to approximately 4.3 billion addresses. Computers on the same network must use the same network address. However, each computer on the network must have a unique node address. IP networks combine both the network and node addresses into one IP address number; for example, 131.255.0.0 is a valid IP address.

Network addresses can be either Class A, Class B, Class C, Class D, or Class E (although addresses in Class D and Class E are reserved for special use). These classes correspond to the number of network IDs and host IDs allowed within a range of the total IP address space. Classes help hosts determine which portion of the IP address is the network address and which portion of the IP address is the node address.

Class A only uses the first octet to designate the network ID, and it uses the remaining three octets for the designation of the host ID. Class A provides for 16,777,214 hosts per network. Because this address class allows for such a large number of possible hosts per network, these addresses are only given to organizations that need to provide access to an extremely large number of hosts. In fact, few, if any, of these addresses remain, because they were assigned to organizations (mostly universities and the military) years ago.

Class B uses the first and second octets to designate the network ID, and it uses the remaining two octets for the designation of the host ID. Class B provides for 65,534 hosts per network. This class of address is designed for medium to large networks, and, although they are not easy to come by, a few of these addresses are probably still left.

Class C uses the first three octets to designate the network ID, and it uses the remaining octet for the designation of the host ID. Class C addresses allow for a maximum of 2,097,152 network addresses. This class of address is designed for small networks that only need to support a limited number of hosts. Because so many Class C addresses are available, they are the easiest type to obtain. However, because of the recent growth of the Internet, even organizations that want to obtain Class C addresses must be able to show that they have a need for the entire block of 254 host addresses. If an organization needs more IP addresses than a single Class C will allow, but not enough to justify issuing a Class B address, multiple Class C address blocks can be issued.

Class D is used for multicasting. Multicasting is used to send information to a number of registered hosts. These hosts are grouped by registering themselves with local routers, using a multicast address from the Class D range of addresses. Finally, Class E is an experimental class of addresses that is reserved for future use.

To understand IP addressing and classes, you have to understand how routers make routing decisions. A *router* is a network interconnection device and related software that connects two network systems that control the traffic flow between networks. As mentioned before, IP addresses are composed of 4-byte values or octets. The part that is the network address and the part that is the node address is determined by what class the IP address belong to, for example, the following:

- 255.0.0.0 is an example of a Class A address; the first byte is fixed and the organization assigns the last three bytes, resulting in more than 16,000,000 addresses available to user.
- 255.255.0.0 is an example of a Class B address; the first two bytes are fixed and the organization assigns the last two bytes, resulting in more than 65,000 addresses available to user.
- 255.255.255.0 is an example of a Class C address; first three bytes are fixed and the organization assigns the last three bytes, resulting in 254 addresses available to user. (IP addresses cannot end in 0 or 255).

The network address identifies the network that all workstations on the network belong to, and the node address identifies the specific workstation in the network. Obviously, Class A networks can accommodate far more node (workstation) IP addresses than Class B or C networks. Similarly, a Class B network can accommodate more node IP addresses than a Class C network.

To illustrate this process, let's say that a node receives a message from an application. The TCP attaches a header to the message and passes it down to the IP. The node's IP address determines whether the destination computer is a member of the local network or if it is outside of the local network. If the address is on the local network, then the IP passes the message to the local network routing device, which transports the message to the proper node. If the destination is a node on another network, the IP finds the best path to the destination and

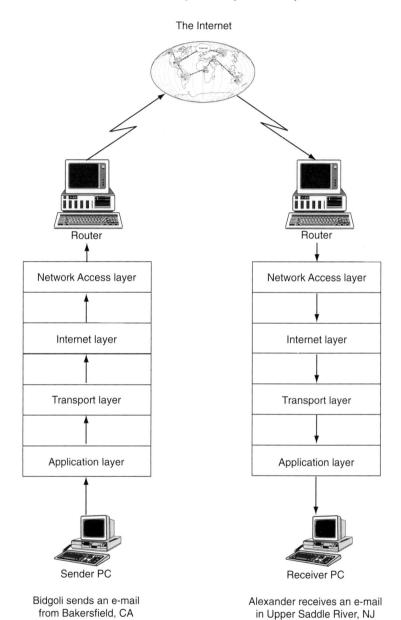

The Internet

Router   Router

| Network Access layer | | Network Access layer |

| Internet layer | | Internet layer |

| Transport layer | | Transport layer |

| Application layer | | Application layer |

Sender PC   Receiver PC

Bidgoli sends an e-mail   Alexander receives an e-mail
  from Bakersfield, CA   in Upper Saddle River, NJ

Figure 9-1   Transmission Control Protocol/Internet Protocol connection.

forwards the message to the next router along that path. Each router that the message encounters along the way is called a hop. Every time the packet is sent to another router, that router looks at it and decides what path it should take next until it finally arrives at the destination node. When it arrives at the destination router, the TCP decodes the header, checks for errors, and sends it to the destination computer. Figure 9-1 illustrates the path taken by a message going from the sender to the receiver.

9-5 TRANSMISSION CONTROL PROTOCOL/INTERNET PROTOCOL SERVICES

The TCP/IP protocol suite provides for a number of useful services including the following:

- Dynamic host configuration protocol (DHCP)
- Serial line internet protocol (SLIP)
- Point-to-point protocol (PPP)
- Point-to-point tunneling protocol (PPTP)
- File transfer protocol (FTP)
- Hypertext transfer protocol (HTTP)

9-5-1 DYNAMIC HOST CONFIGURATION PROTOCOL

DHCP was designed by the Internet Engineering Task Force (IETF) to provide a robust method of dynamic IP address allocation that would ease the initial configuration of client computers while reducing the required administration overhead. DHCP is a protocol that automates and simplifies the assignment of TCP/IP addresses to workstations on the network. This service enables the assignment of dynamic TCP/IP network addresses on a first-come-first-served basis, based on a specified pool of available addresses. When a network client that is configured for DHCP logs onto the network, it searches the network for a DHCP server. The function of the DHCP server is to maintain a pool of all available IP addresses and assign them to requesting computers on the network while ensuring that no duplicate IP addresses exist. When the workstation's request (called a "lease request") is broadcast to all addresses on the network (called a "DHCP discover message") and received by the DHCP server, the next available TCP/IP address is assigned to it from the pool of available addresses for that network session. The amount of time that the address remains assigned to the particular client is called the "time to live" (TTL) and can be configured based on the specific circumstances of the network environment. For example, in a network environment of 25 users and only 15 available TCP/IP addresses, the TTL parameter can be set to a short period, such as 1 day. This would assign the address to the client for 1 day, after which the address is returned to the pool for a new assignment. On the other hand, where there is no shortage of available TCP/IP addresses, the network administrator may set the TTL parameter to a longer time period. When a lease expires, a DHCP server can reassign the address to another computer. A client computer can indicate that it wants to extend the lease period simply by indicating that it is still using the address. The IETF is considering the DHCP service as a proposed open standard.

9-5-2 SERIAL LINE INTERNET PROTOCOL

SLIP was originally developed for the UNIX environment and is still widely used among Internet service providers (ISPs). Computers that have been previously configured to communicate with each other use SLIP. For example, your ISP may provide you with a SLIP connection to give you access to the Internet. SLIP does not provide for error checking, flow control, or security features. SLIP is a reasonably fast, low-overhead service that is typically used to connect to UNIX hosts and ISPs. Because of the reduced overhead tasks that SLIP must accomplish, it is a good protocol to use in situations where a faster data transmission speed is needed with little emphasis on data accuracy.

9-5-3 POINT-TO-POINT PROTOCOL

PPP addresses many of the shortcomings of SLIP, such as providing the ability to encrypt logons and support for additional transport protocols. PPP performs error checking and recovery functions and can handle synchronous as well as asynchronous communications. PPP is optimized for low-bandwidth connections and is a more efficient protocol than SLIP. In **synchronous transmission,** several characters are blocked together in parallel for transmission. At the beginning and end of each block, there are empty bits, but these bits make up a small percentage of the total number of messages. Synchronous transmission is used to reduce overall communications costs. In **asynchronous transmission,** each character is sent serially (one at a time) through a medium as an independent message. Each message is one character long, and the character is preceded by a start bit and ended with a stop bit. This type of transmission is more expensive than synchronous transmission; however, it is more accurate. PPP is optimized for low-bandwidth connections, such as those commonly used by users connecting to an ISP over a slow modem, and is generally a more efficient protocol than SLIP. Of course, this additional capability means that PPP comes with a higher overhead than SLIP. PPP is a good protocol to use in situations where data accuracy is important and fast data transmission speeds are not as important.

9-5-4 POINT-TO-POINT TUNNELING PROTOCOL

PPTP is a protocol that creates secure connections between private networks over the network. PPTP allows corporations to create secure connections between private networks over the public Internet through private "tunnels." Privately leased communication lines can now be replaced by secure PPTP connections. PPTP is also being considered by the IETF as a new standard. PPTP is a good protocol to use where the need for data security and privacy is high. For example, e-mail transmitted over the Internet can be captured and fall into the wrong hands. Corporations that need to communicate regularly can confidently do so over the Internet without worrying about the security of the messages transmitted by establishing a PPTP connection between the connecting networks. Benefits of PPTP include lower administrative, transmission, and hardware costs than other solutions for establishing a secure connection between private networks.

9-5-5 HYPERTEXT TRANSFER PROTOCOL

HTTP is the World Wide Web (WWW) application layer transport protocol that allows for the transfer of HTML documents over an intranet or the Internet, and which responds to actions like a user clicking on hypertext links.

9-5-6 FILE TRANSFER PROTOCOL

FTP is used for file transfers between a local hard drive and an FTP server. FTP is the simplest way to transfer files on the Internet. Common applications of the FTP protocol include downloading programs and files from FTP servers and uploading web pages to web servers. FTP is commonly used to transfer web page files from their creator (from your computer) to the computer that acts as the server (to your ISP) for everyone on the Internet. It is also used to download programs and other files to your computer from other servers. You can use FTP with a simple command line interface from the MS-DOS prompt or with a commercial program that offers a graphical user interface.

Anonymous FTP is a method for giving users access to files so that they don't need to identify themselves to the server. Using an FTP program or the

FTP command interface, the user enters "anonymous" as a user ID. Anonymous FTP is a common method to get access to a server in order to view or download files and programs that are in the public domain (accessible to anybody free of charge).

9-6 SERVER PLATFORMS: AN OVERVIEW

There are several different servers available, and each one performs a specific task in the e-commerce world. The popular server platforms include the following:

• Application servers store computer applications, which users can access from their workstations.
• Commerce servers allow users to "shop" on the Internet and are configured to allow secure electronic financial transactions.
• Database servers are configured to store vast amounts of data for access from user workstations.
• Disk servers contain large-capacity hard drives and enable users to store files and applications for later retrieval.
• Fax servers contain software and hardware components that allow users to send and receive faxes from their workstations.
• File servers contain large-capacity hard drives and enable users to store data files for later retrieval.
• Mail servers are configured to allow users to send, receive, and store e-mail.
• Print servers are configured to allow users to print to network printers.
• Proxy servers are used to store previously accessed web pages, making later retrieval much quicker.
• Remote access servers (RAS) allow remote users to connect to network resources, such as network file storage, printers, and databases.
• Web servers are configured to store HTML pages for access over the Internet.

9-6-1 APPLICATION SERVER

An **application server** is a server program that resides in the server (the physical location) and provides the business logic for the application program. The server program is a program that provides its services to the client program that resides either in the same computer or on another computer on the network. The application server is a second (or middle) tier of the three-tier structure in a client–server architecture (discussed in Chapter 8). The client's request first goes to the web server, which then sends the required query information to the application server. The application server then sends the response back to the web server after taking an appropriate action. The web server then sends the requested and processed information back to the client.

Application servers are mainly used in web-based applications that are based on three-tier client–server architecture as follows (see Figure 9-2):

- First tier: A graphical user interface (GUI) at the client workstation
- Second tier: Application server and a set of application programs
- Third tier: Back end, database server (usually a structured query language [SQL] server)

NetDynamics (Sun), Oracle WAS (Oracle), and Domino (Lotus) are three popular examples of application servers.

9-6-2 COMMERCE SERVER

Commerce servers deal with buying and selling goods and services. This software runs some of the main functions of e-commerce operations, such as product display, online ordering, and inventory management. The software works in conjunction with online payment systems (discussed in Chapter 6) to process payments.

9-6-3 DATABASE SERVER

The **database server** performs database management tasks. A user may send a request to the database server; usually an SQL server processes the request and sends the results back to the user. For example, the user may request a listing of all the e-commerce majors with their associated grade-point averages at California State University. The SQL server processes all the records in the database server and selects all the e-commerce majors, calculates their GPAs, and sends the selected records back to the user's workstation.

9-6-4 DISK SERVER

A **disk server** includes one or more hard disks that can be used by one or several workstations. A disk server is actually a file server with attached disks. Using this technology, a disk drive is divided among several users. New workstations typically come equipped with 8–9-gigabyte (Gb) hard disks. IBM and

Figure 9-2   Application server configuration. GUI, graphical user interface; SQL, structured query language.

other PC vendors recently announced a breakthrough in hard disk technology that will allow them to produce disk drive capacities of 100 Gb for servers, 60 Gb for desktop workstations, and 14 Gb for notebook computers. These breakthroughs, combined with the decreasing cost of hard-disk technology has led to workstations with extremely high-capacity disk drives, making the disk server less common.

9-6-5 FAX SERVER

A **fax server** manages fax traffic into and out of the network, by sharing one or more fax modem boards. Using special software, users can send and receive faxes from their workstations. This is much more efficient than printing a document, carrying it to the fax machine, and faxing it manually. Using fax software, the document stays in its electronic format the entire time, saving time and resources. Users "print" a fax simply by selecting the fax printer when printing a document. The fax software then requests the destination fax number, and the document is transferred from the fax server to a modem for transmission via a standard peripheral fax machine.

9-6-6 FILE SERVER

A **file server** allows remote workstations to access files and application software stored on their hard disks. Programs stored on file servers are executed through file-server program access. In this case, the application program is downloaded over the network to the client workstation, and it is executed on the client workstation. This is suitable for small application programs; however it may not be a suitable approach for larger and more complex programs.

9-6-7 MAIL SERVER

A mail server sends, receives, stores, and manages e-mail across the network. Unlike the regular post office that is only open on certain days and hours, mail servers work around the clock, 7 days a week, 24 hours a day, to deliver e-mail throughout the network in a timely manner. Simple mail transfer protocol (SMPT) for outgoing mail and post office protocol (POP) for incoming mail are two of the most common protocols used by the majority of e-mail programs. The SMPT protocol specifies the exact format of an e-mail message and describes how e-mail must be managed. SMPT provides services to users connected to a LAN. POP is responsible for retrieving e-mail from a mail server. Internet message access protocol (IMAP) is a more recent protocol that may replace POP, as it offers additional features and advantages, including user management of mail on the server. Other popular protocols include extended simple mail transfer protocol (ESMTP), authenticated post office protocol (APOP), and multipurpose Internet mail extensions (MIME). MIME informs a web browser what type of document is being sent. Such type of identification is not limited to simple graphics (gif or Jpeg) or HTML. In essence, more than 300 MIME types are distributed with the Apache Web Server (introduced later in the chapter) by default in the **mime.types** configuration file.

9-6-8 Print Server

A **print server** is responsible for handling printing tasks. Print servers can service several printers, regulating who can print, to which printer print jobs are sent, the priority of print requests, and so on. Depending on its size and complexity, a network can have more than one print server.

9-6-9 Remote Access Server

RAS (pronounced "razz") are specially configured to allow remote users to dial-in or connect to the network from remote locations. A single RAS may support one or several remote connections simultaneously. This capability is becoming increasingly important due to the changing nature of work requirements. More and more corporate users who travel are demanding access to file and print services while they are on the road. RAS servers provide this capability, keeping traveling executives and corporate employees in touch with vital information even though they may be far from the office.

9-6-10 Proxy Server

A **proxy server** is a software application that serves as an intermediary between a user workstation and the Internet so that the enterprise can ensure security and administrative control. A proxy server is part of a gateway server that separates the enterprise network from the outside network and a firewall server that protects the enterprise network from outside intrusion. To a user, the proxy server is invisible; all Internet requests and returned responses appear to be directly associated with the addressed Internet server. By caching previously accessed web pages, proxy servers also significantly decrease the amount of time required to redisplay requested resources. This is how a proxy server works:

1. A proxy server receives a request for an Internet resource from a user. For example, the user may request a web page from the Microsoft web site. The proxy server looks it up in its local cache of previously downloaded web pages. If it finds the page, it returns it to the user, and this marks the end of the operation.

2. If the page is not in the cache, the proxy server requests the page from the appropriate server on the Internet. When the page is returned, the proxy server forwards it on to the requesting user.

One main advantage of a proxy server is its cache capability. If one or more web pages are frequently requested, these pages are most likely available in the proxy's cache, which will improve the response time.

9-6-11 WEB SERVER

A **web server** stores documents (usually in multimedia format) that can be accessed with browsers such as Microsoft Internet Explorer or Netscape Navigator. Web servers are discussed in more detail later in this chapter.

9-7 HOW DOES A WEB SERVER WORK?

The diagram presented in Figure 9-3 illustrates the basics of a web server operation. The following example highlights this operation.

1. A user (as an example) using his or her web browser requests a document (books.htm) by entering the following:

<http://www.CSUB.edu/~hbidgoli/books.htm>

The browser and the server communicate using the HTTP protocol (as described earlier in the chapter) to respond to the user request to the web server.

2. The web server looks for the document in the file system (in the storage device).

3. The web server retrieves the document from the storage device.

4. The web server forwards the document to the browser.

5. The browser displays the requested page on the user's screen.

What we just described works for basic HTML documents and simple graphical files; in other words, this process serves static contents. These are contents that do not change as the document is being retrieved. When dynamic pages are requested, the web server follows a different path. Dynamic pages are created based on the user input. Let's say the calculation of a mortgage or the calculation of the price of several books purchased from an online bookstore is the requested information.

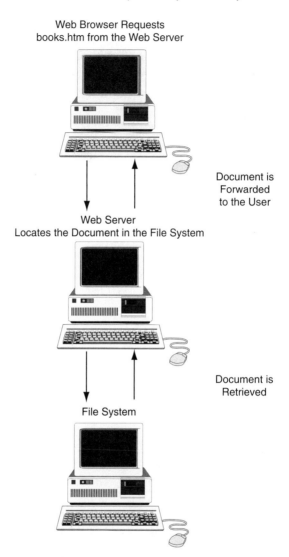

Web Browser Requests
books.htm from the Web Server

Document is
Forwarded
to the User

Web Server
Locates the Document in the File System

Document is
Retrieved

File System

Figure 9-3 Basic web server operations.

The most common standard for handling dynamic pages is Common Gateway Interface (CGI). This standard dictates how a web server should run pages locally and transmit their output through the web server to the user's web browser that is requesting the dynamic page. (See Figure 9-4.)

CGI is a method or convention for passing data back and forth between the server and the application. It is part of the Web's HTTP protocol, a standard

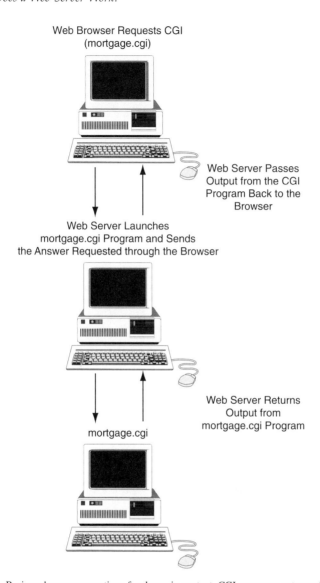

Figure 9-4 Basic web server operations for dynamic content. CGI, common gateway interface.

way for a web server to pass a web user's request to an application program and to receive data to forward to the user. A CGI program is any program designed to accept and return data that conform to the CGI specifications. These programs can be written in many different languages, including Visual Basic and Java. CGI programs are the most common way for web servers to interact dynamically with web users. The majority of web pages that include forms use a CGI program to process the form's data once they are transmitted. An alternative method to provide dynamic feedback for web users is to include scripts or programs that run on the user's PC rather than the web server. A script is similar to macros used in many languages, which include a list of commands and instructions that can be executed without user intervention. As will be introduced in Appendix A, these programs can be Java scripts, Java applets, or ActiveX control. These technologies are collectively known as client-side solutions, whereas the use of CGI is known as a server solution, as the processing takes place on the web server.

Because each time a CGI script is executed, a new process is started, this might slow down the server. This is considered a drawback of CGI processing. A more efficient solution, at the same time more difficult to implement, is to use the server's application program interface (API), such as Microsoft IS (Internet Server) API. Developers write programs that filter requests and get the correct web pages for different users by using Microsoft ISAPI interface. ISAPI is a set of Windows program calls that let the user write a web server application that will run faster than a CGI application. Another alternative is to use Netscape Server API (NSAPI).

9-8 WEB SERVER: A SECOND LOOK

As mentioned briefly in section 9-6-11, a web server stores documents that can be accessed with browsers. In other words, a web server is a computer system that delivers web pages. A web server has two major components: web server software, such as Apache, and web server hardware, such as Sun Ultra Enterprise. A web server has an IP address. For example, if you enter the following URL, **http://www.apnet.com/infosys,** in your browser such as Microsoft Internet Explorer, the browser sends a request to the server whose domain name is **apnet.com,** the server then retrieves the page named **infosys** and sends it to the requesting browser. Any computer can be configured to be a server; however, a computer with high speed, a large RAM, and large disk storage capacity is preferred. For a computer to be configured as a server, the web server software must be installed first and then it must be connected to the Web. As you will see later in this chapter, many web server software applications are available on the market. Some are free, such as Apache, and some must be purchased, such as Microsoft Internet Information Server and Netscape Enterprise Server. Figure 9-5 illustrates a typical configuration of a web server.

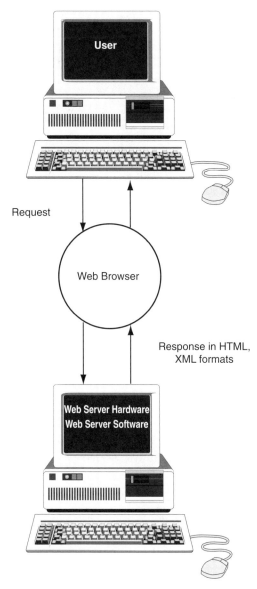

Figure 9-5 A typical web server configuration. HTML, hypertext markup language; XML, extensible markup language.

9-9 WEB SERVER SOFTWARE AND TOOLS

As mentioned earlier, a web server is a computer program that stores HTML documents (and other multimedia file formats) that can be accessed with browsers such as Netscape Navigator or Microsoft Internet Explorer. A web server uses the client–server model (explained in the last chapter) and the HTTP protocol and serves a group of files that collectively form a web site. The web users must install an HTTP client in their PCs or workstations in order to be able to access a web site. Every computer on the web that contains a web page must have a web server program. Table 9-1 lists the top ten web servers on the market.

In the following pages we explain some of the features of Apache HTTP Server, Microsoft Internet Information Server, and Netscape Enterprise Server. Apache and Microsoft own more than 70% of the server market share.

9-9-1 APACHE HTTP SERVER

Apache is a freely available web server that is distributed under an "open source" license. Rob McCool developed Apache while he was working at the University of Illinois at the National Center for Supercomputing Applications (NCSA). A UNIX-based server application, Apache runs on most popular platforms, such as Linux, Solaris, and Digital UNIX. Apache includes a built-in search engine and HTML authoring tools and supports FTP. Many modules are available as part of the Apache HTTP server, and the number of these modules

Table 9-1

Top 10 Web Servers

Apache
Microsoft-IIS
Netscape Enterprise
Rapidsite
Zeus
Thttpd
WebLogic
WebSitePro
Stronghold
WebStar

Source: [1].

or patches is increasing almost on a daily basis. Apache provides comprehensive security features, including password authentication and digital certificates. (Digital certificates were discussed in Chapter 6, and passwords are discussed in Chapter 11.) Access can be restricted by domain name, by IP address, or by a user ID. Apache also supports the SSL protocol (discussed in Chapter 6). To become more familiar with the many features of this powerful web server, log onto Apache's web site [3]. Figure 9-6 illustrates the initial screen of the Apache web site.

9-9-2 MICROSOFT INTERNET INFORMATION SERVER

Microsoft Internet Information Server (IIS) consists of a group of Internet servers (Web, HTTP, and FTP) and other capabilities for Microsoft's Windows NT and Windows 2000 Server operating systems. Figure 9-7 lists the major Microsoft server platforms.

With IIS, Microsoft's goal is to play a major role in the Internet server market. Microsoft IIS offers a set of programs for building and administering web

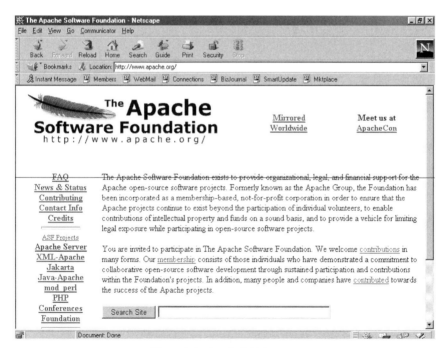

Figure 9-6 Apache initial screen.

Figure 9-7   Major Microsoft server platforms [4].

sites, a search engine, and support for writing Web-based and HTML applications that access databases. According to Microsoft, IIS is closely integrated with the Windows NT and 2000 servers in a number of ways, resulting in faster web page serving. A corporation that buys IIS can create pages for web sites using Microsoft's Front Page Web authoring tool.

Developers can also write programs that filter requests and get the correct web pages for different users by using Microsoft ISAPI interface. ISAPI is a set of Windows program calls that allow the user to write a web server application that will run faster than a CGI application. CGI is the method or convention for passing data back and forth between the server and the application. It is part of the Web's HTTP protocol. It is a standard way for a web server to pass a web user's request to an application program and to receive data to forward to the user.

IIS includes comprehensive security features and is relatively easy to install. Working closely with the Microsoft Transaction Server, IIS accesses databases and provides control at the transaction level. IIS also works with Microsoft's Netshow in the delivery of streaming audio and video, delayed or live.

Microsoft NetShow Theater Server is a powerful and flexible streaming media solution for delivering high-quality Moving Picture Experts Group (MPEG) video. NetShow Theater Server extends the streaming media services of Windows NT server to much higher bandwidths, allowing the user to deliver full-motion, full-screen video with high performance across high-bandwidth networks.

Microsoft includes special capabilities for server administrators designed to appeal to ISPs. All services and users can be administered from a single console. Components can be easily added as "snap-ins" that the user didn't initially install. Also, individual users can customize the administrative windows for access. For detailed information on this powerful server, consult the Microsoft web site [5].

9-9-3 NETSCAPE ENTERPRISE SERVER

Netscape Enterprise Server is a high-performance, scalable web server software for deploying large-scale web sites. Enterprise Server adds site and content management tools and incorporates a strong web development platform. Enterprise maintains users and groups in a .DBM file separate from the Windows NT domain. In order to add a user to multiple groups, you must first add the user, then go back and edit the user's profile. It also includes comprehensive documentation explaining various features of this powerful web server. Some of the major capabilities of Enterprise Server are as follows:

- Automatic recovery
- High performance and scalability for dynamic and secure content
- Workgroup-based content publishing management
- Sophisticated searching
- Lightweight Directory Access Protocol (LDAP) support. LDAP is a software protocol that enables any user to locate organizations, individuals, and other resources such as files and devices on the Web, intranets, or extranets.
- Intelligent agents (explained in Chapter 7) that launch from web server events

Enterprise Server runs under Windows NT and many versions of UNIX, such as Solaris. The management interface runs from any browser that supports frames and JavaScript. As explained in Appendix A, JavaScript applets are stored sets of instructions and are included as a part of a standard HTML document, allowing the user to manage the server remotely from any client or platform. Enterprise provides various options for mapping and forwarding URLs and supports URL redirection to directories on other servers. For large web sites, Enterprise supports hardware and software virtual servers. A virtual server is a server at someone else's location that is shared by multiple web site owners so that each owner can use and administer it as though they had complete control of the server. Hardware virtual servers must share the same server configuration but can have different IP addresses, and software virtual servers must share an IP address but can have different configurations. To host multiple virtual servers with different addresses and configurations, the user must install a separate instance of Enterprise for each virtual server.

By supporting NSAPI, CGI, and JavaScript, Enterprise offers a powerful, and yet an open development platform. The powerful LiveWire module comes with Site Manager and Application Manager. Site Manager includes tools for tracking all site elements and verifying internal and external hyperlinks. It also includes various web site templates for creating a complete web site from scratch. It also includes an application manager that allows the user to create, modify, debug, and run a Web application. The Debug option is very useful for tracing and debugging script codes. Using LiveWire and Navigator Gold, the user can create a site, develop and compile scripts, and deploy the application to any destination directory on your server. Figure 9-8 shows the instructions for installing Netscape Enterprise Server. For more information on Netscape Enterprise Server consult the following sources [7,8].

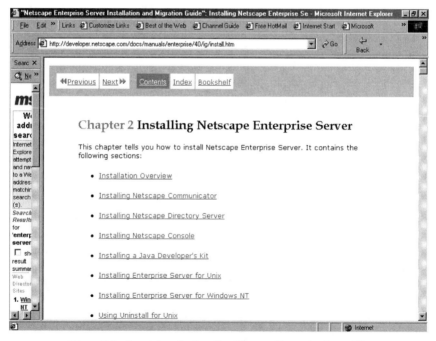

Figure 9-8   Instructions for installing Netscape Enterprise Server [6].

9-10 IMPORTANT CRITERIA FOR CHOOSING A WEB SERVER

As discussed in Chapter 12, many small and medium-sized organizations outsource their e-commerce sites. By employing web hosting services, these organizations leave the selection and maintenance of the optimum web server platforms to the hosting company. However, most large organizations and some of the medium-sized organizations choose their own hardware and software platforms in order to run their virtual storefronts. The following discussion of hardware and software applies only to those companies that are trying to establish their own server platforms. The following criteria must be carefully examined before deciding on a server platform.

1. Scalability. Will the platform grow with your company both horizontally and vertically?

2. Bandwidth. The response time and the information-carrying capacity of an e-commerce site is very important. Particularly with the increasing popularity of the multimedia documents, the bandwidth plays a very important role. The platform chosen must be responsive to the ever-increasing bandwidth demand.

3. Operating system. The platform chosen and the operating system that supports the platform is very important. Windows NT (2000), Linux, Unix, and Novell NetWare are among the popular operating systems in use today.

4. Static versus dynamic pages. Static pages are those HTML documents that are not changing as a user requests them. On the other hand, dynamic pages are changing as a user requests them. Dynamic pages put a heavier load on the web server platform, and this issue must be considered.

5. Security supports and features. A sophisticated web server must support important security protocols such as SSL, authentication, and user logins.

Table 9-2

Popular Benchmarking Alternatives for Web Server Software

NetBench (Ziff-Davis)

SeverBench (Ziff-Davis)

WCAT (Microsoft)

WebBench (Ziff-Davis)

WebStone (Mindcraft)

Table 9-3

Major Web Server Software Providers

Apache

Ariba

Commerce One

I2 Technologies

IBM

Microsoft

Netscape

Oracle

SAP

Sun

FTP, search engine features, data analysis, and site management are other important features of a sophisticated web server that should be considered before choosing the final candidate.

Benchmarking tools can assist you in choosing a more suitable web server for e-commerce operations. These tools provide the user with a rigorous and objective method to compare and contrast similar features of each platform against each other. They also put the entire package to test and assist the user in choosing the one that meet certain criteria. Table 9-2 lists several popular benchmarking software applications for web server performance evaluation.

Table 9-3 lists major Web server software providers and Table 9-4 lists some of the major server hardware vendors.

Table 9-4

Major Web Server Hardware Vendors

Compaq

Dell

IBM

Hewlett Packard

Sun Microsystems

9-11 INDUSTRY CONNECTION: ORACLE CORPORATION

> Oracle Corporation
> Redwood Shores, California 94065
> Telephone: (650) 506-7000
> Fax: (650) 506-7200
> Web site address: <http://www.oracle.com>

Lawrence J. Ellison, Oracle's Chairman and Chief Executive Officer, founded Oracle Corporation in 1977. Oracle is the world's leading supplier of software for information management, and the world's second largest independent software company (after Microsoft). Oracle offers its database tools and application products, along with related consulting, education, and support services, in more than 145 countries around the world. It is the world's largest supplier of relational database management systems. Oracle software runs on PCs, workstations, minicomputers, mainframes and massively parallel computers, as well as on personal digital assistants (PDAs) and set-top devices. Oracle's Internet-enabled solutions provide a variety of capabilities:

- An Internet-ready platform for building and deploying Web-based applications
- A comprehensive suite of Internet-enabled business applications
- Professional services for assisting in formulating an e-business strategy, as well as in designing, customizing, and implementing e-business solutions

In addition to various relational database software and services, Oracle offers a broad range of e-commerce products and services. The following categories summarize Oracle's offerings for e-commerce implementation:

Oracle *i*Marketing allows businesses to create real-time, targeted promotions and product recommendations on their e-commerce sites.

Oracle *i*Store provides a comprehensive, scalable, and secure environment for creating, managing, and personalizing Internet-based storefronts to sell both products and services.

Oracle *i*Payment is an electronic payment software solution that e-commerce developers can use to "payment-enable" their Web or client–server applications. It can accept payment instructions from nearly any e-commerce application and route payment data to and from third-party or proprietary payment systems.

Oracle *i*Support is a comprehensive, Web-based customer care system that enables merchants to proactively provide customer service and support in a self-service environment by offering immediate online order status and inventory check capabilities, order history, invoices, payment history, and online interactive forums. The following are just a sample of some of the Oracle e-business products and services:

- Application Server
- Integration Server (This is a comprehensive platform that provides an organization with a method to utilize the Internet, intranets, and client–server technologies while preserving investments in existing mainframe networks.)
- Enterprise Manager (This automates routine database administration and handles license and configuration management and database replication scheduling.)
- WebDB (This is a browser-based software for developing and deploying enterprise portals.)
- Jdeveloper (This is a full-featured application development tool that offers integrated support for building end-to-end e-business applications for the Internet.)
- E-business Portals
- E-business Suite[1]

9-12 SUMMARY

This chapter defined TCP/IP as one of the most important protocols used in the e-commerce world. The chapter reviewed the major functions of TCP/IP, including DHCP, SLIP, PPP, PPTP, FTP, and HTTP. The chapter highlighted important server platforms in the e-commerce world and then discussed the operations of web server software. Three of the most popular web server software packages were discussed in detail, including Apache HTTP Server, Microsoft Internet Information Server, and Netscape Enterprise Server. The chapter concluded with an overview of the important criteria for choosing a web server and introduced popular web server software and hardware platforms, highlighting Oracle Corporation as the industry connection.

9-13 REVIEW QUESTIONS

1. What is TCP/IP? Why has this protocol become so popular? Discuss.
2. Who sponsored the development of this protocol?

---

[1]This information was gathered from the company web site and other promotional materials. For detailed information and any update, contact the company.

3. What are some of the specific tasks performed by TCP? By the IP? Discuss.
4. What are Class A, Class B, and Class C addresses? Who assigns these addresses?
5. What is a router? What is its function?
6. What is the DHCP? What is its function?
7. What is SLIP? What is its function?
8. What is PPP? What is its function?
9. What is PPTP? What is its function?
10. What is HTTP? What is its function?
11. What is FTP? What is its function?
12. What is an anonymous FTP? What is its function?
13. What is an application server? What is a typical configuration of an application server?
14. What is a commerce server? What does it do?
15. What does a database server do?
16. What is a mail server? How does it work?
17. What are some of the differences between a mail server and the regular mail services handled by the U.S. Postal Service? Discuss.
18. What are some of the popular mail server protocols?
19. What are some of the functions of a RAS?
20. What is a proxy server? What does it do?
21. How does a web server work?
22. What are some of the differences between a static page and a dynamic page? Which type puts a heavier load on the server platform? Discuss.
23. What are some of the popular web server software packages on the market?
24. What are some of the features of Apache HTTP Server? Discuss.
25. What are some of the features of Microsoft Internet Information Server?
26. What are some of the features of Netscape Enterprise Server?
27. What are some of the criteria for choosing web server software? Discuss.
28. Who are some of the major web server software providers?
29. Who are some of the major web server hardware providers?

9-14 PROJECTS AND HANDS-ON EXERCISES

1. Log onto the web site of Oracle Corporation at the following URL:

<http://www.oracle.com>

What are some of the e-commerce-related products and services offered by this company? Who are some of the competitors of Oracle in the e-commerce space? Discuss.

2. Log onto the web site of UPS at the following URL:

<http://www.ups.com>

How is UPS using information technology in general and e-commerce in particular to stay ahead of the competition? Who are some of UPS's business partners?

3. The following sites provide comprehensive discussion on server operations:

<http://webcompare.internet.com/webbasics>
<http://www.ecommercetimes.com/news/articles2000/000713-3.shtml>

By referring to the materials presented in these sites and other sources, prepare a two-page report on web server operations. How does a web server handle static contents? How does it handle dynamic contents? Discuss.

4. The following web sites provide current information on popular web servers:

<http://www.netcraft.com/survey>
<http://www.apache.org>
<http://keyword.netscape.com/keyword/Netscape+Enterprise+Server>
<http://serverwatch.internet.com/hardware>
<http://www.zdnet.com/pcmag/stories/reviews/0,6755,2551182,00.html#>

By referring to the materials presented in these sites and other sources, identify the top four Web servers. What are the bases for this classification? What are some of the major criteria used for this selection? Discuss.

5. The following site provides valuable information on e-commerce infrastructure:

<http://www.zdnet.com/pcmag/stories/reviews/0,6755,2551182,00.html>

By examining the materials in this site and other sources, prepare a one-page report on e-commerce infrastructure. In your opinion, what is included in the infrastructure? Discuss.

6. Benchmarking techniques are used to measure the performance of web server software. Log onto the following site that provides examples of these benchmarking tools and review descriptions of these tools:

<http://webcompare.internet.com/bench.html>

Why are there so many of them? What criteria do you use to choose one of these products among these competing products?

7. Linkbot Pro will automatically scan a web site, for more than 50 potential types of problems, and generates graphical reports detailing errors that need to be fixed. In which stage of e-commerce operations a product such as this might be useful?

<http://www.watchfire.com/products/linkbot.htm>

8. The following site provides several e-commerce case studies:

<http://www.ibm.com/e-business/crm/case_studies/bancolombia.phtml>

Review these case examples and try to see if there are common goals among these different implementations. How can you apply these experiences to specific e-commerce operations?

9. The following sites provide comprehensive information on Web browsers:

<http://browserwatch.internet.com>
<http://www.stars.com/Software/Browsers>

By referring to the materials presented in these sites and other sources, identify three browsers (in addition to Internet Explorer and Navigator) in use. In which particular platform are these browsers used? Why do these browsers own such a small market share compared to Internet Explorer or Navigator? Discuss.

9-15 KEY TERMS

Anonymous FTP, 299–300
Apache HTTP server, 310–311
Application server, 300–301
Commerce server, 301
Database server, 301
Disk server, 301, 303
Dynamic host configuration
  protocol, 297–298
Fax server, 303
File server, 303
File transfer protocol, 299–300
Hypertext transfer protocol, 299
Internet protocol (IP), 292–293,
  294–297

Mail server, 303–304
Microsoft Internet Information
  Server, 311–313
Netscape Enterprise Server, 313–314
Point-to-point protocol, 298–299
Point-to-point tunneling protocol, 299
Print server, 304–305
Proxy server, 304
Remote access server (RAS), 304
Router, 293
Serial line Internet protocol (SLIP), 298
Transmission Control Protocol
  (TCP), 292–294
Web server, 305–309

REFERENCES

[1] http://www.netcraft.com/survey, June 2000, The Netcraft Web Server Survey. Copyright © Netcraft 1995–2001. (Date of access April 24, 2001).

[2] http://serverwatch.internet.com/reviews/web-rapidsite.html, September 26, 2000, internet.com, ServerWatch. Copyright 2001 internet.com Corp. All rights reserved. (Date of access April 24, 2001).

[3] <http://www.apache.org> The Apache Software Foundation (Date of access April 24, 2001).

[4] <http://microsoft.com/servers> Microsoft Servers, © 2001 Microsoft Corporation. All rights reserved. (Date of access April 24, 2001).

[5] <http://microsoft.com> Microsoft, © 2001 Microsoft Corporation. All rights reserved. (Date of access April 24, 2001).

[6] <http://home.netscape.com/enterprise/v3.6/index.html> Netscape Enterprise Server, © 2000 Netscape. All rights reserved. (Date of access April 24, 2001).

[7] <http://developer.netscape.com/docs/manuals/enterprise/40/ig/install.htm> Chapter 2 Installing Netscape Enterprise Server © Copyright © 1999 Sun Microsystems, Inc. Some preexisting portions. Copyright © 1999. Netscape Communications Corp. All rights reserved. (Date of access April 24, 2001).

[8] Alwang, Greg (1997). "Netscape Enterprise Server." PC MAGAZINE ONLINE Copyright © 1997 Ziff Davis Inc.

[9] Bidgoli, Hossein (2000). "Handbook of Business Data Communications: A Managerial Perspective." Academic Press, Inc., San Diego, CA.

[10] Comer, Douglas E., and David L. Stevens (2001). "Internetworking with TCP/IP, Vol. 3: Client-Server Programming and Applications, Linux/Posix Sockets Version, 1/e." Prentice Hall, Upper Saddle River, NJ.

[11] Houde, Dave, and Tim Hoffman (2001). "TCP/IP For Windows 2000, 1/e." Prentice Hall, Upper Saddle River, NJ.

[12] James, Scott D. (2001). "Introduction to the Internet, 3/e." Prentice Hall, Upper Saddle River, NJ.

[13] Stevens, Richard (1994). "TCP/IP Illustrated, volume 1." Addison-Wesley, Menlo Park, CA.

Chapter 10

Personal, Social, Organizational, Legal, Tax, and International Issues

Learning Objectives

After studying this chapter you should be able to do the following:

- Explain various negative impacts of information technology and e-commerce.
- Discuss privacy, crime, fraud, and health issues.
- Discuss various issues related to electronic mail, censorship, and electronic publishing.
- Explain social division, copyrights, and legal issues related to e-commerce.
- Discuss tax and international issues in the e-commerce world.

Personal, Social, Organizational, Legal, Tax, and International Issues of E-Commerce in a Snapshot

Doctors in 23 African nations use the Web to assist in each other's diagnostics and treatment of patients.

Peer tutoring on the Web brings students together from all over the world.

Cellular theft and phone frauds have become major crimes.

On February 24, 1998, Vladimir Levin, a 30-year old computer hacker from Russia was sentenced to 36 months in prison for the first publicly known e-bank robbery. He defrauded Citibank of more than $3 million.

On September 10, 2000, the Western Union computer was attacked by hackers. To protect customers' accounts, Western Union temporarily took its system off line.

G-7 nations and Russia have agreed to crack down on computer and Internet crimes.

Some companies are using filtering software such as Microsystems Cyber Patrol to block certain web sites.

Spoofing (when a hacker imitates another person and uses that person's identity to gain access), eavesdropping (gathering passwords), and physically stealing are three popular methods used by computer hackers for stealing computer data.

Students with disabilities may benefit significantly from distance learning and the courses that are offered over the Web.

The Internet will eliminate or reduce distribution services, such as postal services, phone communications, video stores, supermarkets, travel agents, and grocery stores. This may result in significant job losses in these groups.

The most common misuse of the Internet has been repeated visits to adult-oriented web sites by minors.

Trading sexually explicit pictures is widespread on the Web.

More than 80% of all images posted on Usenet are pornographic.

Numerous local and regional Internet service providers now offer filtering software.

The Internet Tax Freedom Act in the United States created the moratorium on e-commerce taxation, which expires in October 2001. It provides the following:

1. There should be no new taxes on Internet access services.
2. There should be no multiple or discriminatory taxes on e-commerce.

In addition, the act created the Advisory Commission on Electronic Commerce.

Software programs such as "cookies" and profiling systems are able to track and record surfers' page-viewing preferences, habits, product selections, and demographic information.

The government's first Internet-related regulation was the Children's Online Privacy Protection Act of 1998, which restricts children's data collection.

The Federal Trade Commission (FTC), the Commerce Department, and the Network Advertising Initiative (NAI) are currently working together to come up with a set of voluntary privacy rules that would restrain online profiling. Once the firms publish the agreements, the FTC will enforce them as trade principle laws.

> ### INFORMATION BOX 10-2
>
> #### Vulnerabilities in the E-Commerce World
>
> In February 2000, a computer hacker breached the security of SalesGate, an Internet Management Services company and other web sites, stealing credit card numbers and posting them on the Web. The cracker, whose web page was titled "Curador, The Saint of E-Commerce," posted some 6000 credit card numbers and claimed to have more than 23,000 credit card numbers. Among other sites that Curador attacked were Feelgoodfalls.com, Promobility.com, and Shoppingthailand.com.
>
> On February 18, 2000, the FBI's web site was hit with its second denial-of-service attack, which lasted several hours.
>
> Online auctions generate nearly half of the complaints received by the U.S. government's new Internet Fraud Complaint Center that collects and analyzes consumer complaints. Other major types of complaints reported to the center are security and commodities complaints 16.9%, credit card complaints 4.8%, identity theft 2.9%, loss of business opportunities 2.5%, professional service complaints 1.2%, and travel scams 0.3%.
>
> The following are other e-commerce vulnerabilities that should be observed and controlled:
>
> - Internet gambling
> - Alcohol sales on the Web
> - Pornography on the Web
> - Protecting the family and young children using e-commerce services and products
>
> SOURCES: Linda Rosencrance and DeWayne Lehman, (2000, March 6). "Cracker Steals Credit-Card Data." PC World.com, *Computerworld;* Margret Johnston, (2000, August 29). "Actions Lead Internet Fraud List." IDG News Service, PC World.com.

10-1 INTRODUCTION

The chapter begins with a general discussion of the negative effects of information technology (IT) and e-commerce. This includes IT and e-commerce impacts on workplace, privacy, crime, fraud, and health issues. The chapter provides a detailed discussion of data-collection issues on the Web, electronic mail, censorship, electronic publishing, and the possible social division created by IT and e-commerce. The last part of this chapter concentrates on copyrights, patents, piracy, and legal issues of IT and e-commerce, and it concludes with a discussion of tax and international issues in the e-commerce world, highlighting Symantec Corporation as the industry connection. The materials presented in this chapter should be carefully examined before introduction of any e-commerce applications to an organization, and when legal matters are involved attorneys and lawyers should be consulted. Consideration of these issues should improve the chances of successful e-commerce implementation and should reduce the negative impacts of this powerful and growing technology.

10-2 NEGATIVE EFFECTS OF INFORMATION TECHNOLOGY AND E-COMMERCE: AN OVERVIEW

In earlier chapters, I discussed the positive effects of IT in general and e-commerce in particular. No one can discount the positive impact of IT, which is well documented throughout the literature. Organizations around the world spend billions of dollars every year on these growing technologies to stay ahead of competitors. Consumers and organizations have reported significant savings by using various e-commerce applications. Nevertheless, some negative issues of these growing technologies deserve careful attention. These personal, social, legal, organizational, and health issues are not so severe as to require banning IT and e-commerce, but any undesirable aspects should be addressed. To eliminate or reduce negative effects, careful planning is required [8].

10-3 IMPACTS ON THE WORKPLACE

There is no doubt that IT has eliminated some clerical jobs. At the same time, ITs have created many new jobs for programmers, systems analysts, database administrators, local area network (LAN) managers, network engineers, web masters, home page developers, e-commerce specialists, chief information officers (CIOs), and technicians. In the e-commerce world, new jobs such as web designers, Java programmers, home page developers, and web troubleshooters have been created. Some argue that the jobs eliminated have been clerical, whereas the jobs created are mostly technical and require extensive training. Others advocate that ITs and e-commerce have reduced production costs and, therefore, have improved and increased the purchasing power of consumers, resulting in a stronger economy.

ITs definitely have a direct effect on the nature of the jobs performed by different workers. Telecommuting and some e-commerce applications, for example, will enable a significant portion of the work force to perform their duties from their homes. By means of telecommunications technology, a worker can use a personal computer and send and receive data to and from the main office. Using this technology, organizations have the opportunity to utilize the best and most cost-effective human resources available in a broad geographical region. ITs have made some jobs more interesting by taking over the repetitive and boring tasks. As a result, ITs have enabled some workers to be more satisfied with their jobs.

ITs have created "job de-skilling" by performing technical tasks such as computer automated design (CAD) for designers. In some situations, job skill content decreases over time, for example, as with a machinist who depends on ITs to perform the technical aspects of the job. At the same time, ITs have created "job upgrading"; think of the secretaries who now use computers to perform word-processing tasks. One skilled worker may end up doing the job of several workers. For example, by using word-processing and mail merge programs, a secretary can generate thousands of letters, thereby eliminating the need for additional secretaries. As another example, consider electronic message distribution that enables a secretary to distribute a message throughout the entire organization with a click of the mouse! As yet another example, consider mass-marketing efforts often used in the e-commerce environment for product announcements. Millions of customers can be reached with a minimal cost. In cases of job upgrading, the ideal is to train some of the existing employees to perform the newly created jobs; for example, clerical staff may be trained to create simple web pages. However, this is only possible to a point. It would be very difficult to train a clerical worker and change his or her duties to a Java programmer.

The effect of ITs and e-commerce on organizational structure may be varied. ITs can change the organizational structure of a company from a pyramid to a star structure. In a pyramid structure, three distinct layers of management exist: lower (operational), middle (tactical), and upper (strategic). A star structure consists of only decision makers and unskilled labor; it eliminates middle management personnel. In this case, ITs perform the jobs of middle managers. In another instance, ITs may reinforce the existing structure (the pyramid) by providing timely and accurate information for key decision makers, thus creating a better control mechanism for them. This may lead to a highly centralized organization. It can also lead to greater empowerment of line, operational, and tactical employees, creating a more decentralized organization. The end result depends on the "discretion" of the organization and its culture.

Another organizational impact of e-commerce is the possible creation or the promotion of virtual organizations. The increasingly popular *virtual organization* concept refers to the network of independent companies, suppliers, customers, and manufacturers connected by various information systems technologies to share skills, costs, and access to one another's markets [12]. A virtual corporation is a temporary network of several companies assembled to exploit a specific opportunity. No hierarchy, central offices, and organizational chart are necessary.

The virtual corporation is a temporary network of companies that come together quickly to exploit fast changing opportunities, costs, talents, resources, and access to global markets that can be shared in a virtual organization. In such a scenario, each participant can contribute information or skills for which they have the most expertise. The technology for implementation of a virtual corporation is very similar to telecommuting facilities. It utilizes various communications, the Internet, e-commerce, and computer technologies.

Dual Corporation delivers its products to the customers with the appearance of a highly integrated company. The virtual corporation, in fact, consists of a company that faces the customer and a network of other companies that cooperate to achieve what none of them would achieve alone. Using this strategy, each participant concentrates on what each party does best. This limits the risks and investment necessary to finish a project. Some of the advantages of the virtual corporation concept include the following [15]:

- Greater customer focus
- Higher customer responsiveness
- Reduced cycle times for new product introduction
- Lower cost
- Customization of mass-market products for every customer
- Financial flexibility
- A company can change its parents in the virtual coalition. This has operational flexibility.

Companies like MCI, Xerox, and Apple Computer have already used virtual organization concepts. This concept has assisted them to bring new products to market faster and generate higher sales per employee. Banks also use virtual organizations to market their financial products to diverse customers. Banks underwrite certificates of deposits, brokerages underwrite securities, and insurers underwrite annuities. Here, the bank can act as a virtual corporation and provide these services by making arrangements with these parties. If properly structured, the virtual corporation should provide benefits to all parties that participate [9,15].

In 2000, Amazon.com and Toys-R-Us announced a partnership to sell toys online. Toys-R-Us brings the merchandising and traditional toy retailing expertise, and Amazon brings selling online expertise. Also in early 2001, Dell, Microsoft, and Unisys Corporation announced a partnership to design a voting system for several U.S. states. Microsoft offers software, Dell offers hardware, and Unisys serves as the systems integrator. These examples use the principles of virtual organizations: no one company can do it alone, but collectively they can. In all of these partnerships, the Web plays a major role.

10-4 PRIVACY ISSUES

Managers in some organizations are now able to monitor an employee's performance, number of errors, speed of work, and time away from the desk by using computerized systems. The Internet and e-mail have added a new dimension to the meaning of privacy and private information in the office. Naturally, some workers are concerned about their privacy [19].

Much private data are stored at doctors' and attorneys' offices, on online order forms, and within financial institutions. This information is entered into computerized databases. Misuse and abuse of this information can have serious consequences. Who should have access to this information and to what extent is a question that must be resolved by information systems practitioners. Organizations should establish comprehensive security systems (discussed in Chapter 11).

When we think of what privacy means, most of us can give examples of things that we have become accustomed to. This includes such things as personal mail, bank account balances, and telephone conversations, especially since most of us now have private lines. We also assume that our personal life, as opposed to our career image, is private. In general, it is difficult to define privacy. In terms of electronic information, we probably all agree that a person should be able to keep personal affairs to his or herself. We also would like to know how information about us is used. With this somewhat elusive definition of what we think should be private, the use of electronic databases by federal and state governments, credit agencies, and marketing companies represents an invasion of our privacy. Unfortunately, ITs and e-commerce have been at the center of all of these important issues.

The number of computerized databases is increasing rapidly. In the United States, the top three credit-rating companies, TRW, Equifax, and Trans Union Credit Information, have records of more than 160 million individuals (and the number is increasing). About 85 federal databases have more than 300 million records on 120 million people. Although these companies are fairly reputable, that is, they supply information only to people who will use it for the intended purpose, there are a number of smaller companies that buy the information from one of the big three and use it in ways that were never intended. These credit agencies, called "superbureaus" will sell information to anyone who will pay for it. This is clearly illegal, but enforcement of federal laws has been very lax. Perhaps you have experienced the situation that, after joining a particular organization, for example, a credit agency, you begin receiving letters and other communications from other organizations. This makes you wonder how they got your address. Or you might have requested some information from an online car dealer, and then you receive e-mail from car insurance and other mortgage companies. How did your e-mail address get to the insurance company?

Advances in computer technology are making it easy to do what was impossible not long ago. Information in many databases can be cross-matched to create "profiles" of individuals and to even predict their behavior. This behavior is determined by individual transactions with various educational, financial, governmental, professional, and judicial institutions. Major uses of this information include direct marketing and credit check services for potential borrowers or renters. The author is familiar with a case that puts this discussion in perspective. An individual applied for insurance from a reputable insurance company. In the application, the applicant answered no to the question, Do you smoke? Apparently, the individual had purchased cigarettes several times, and this information had been documented through the club card used to do shopping from one of the grocery stores in the area. The insurance application was rejected because the insurance company found out that the applicant was a smoker. Later it was proven that the applicant had been buying cigarettes for an elderly relative living with the applicant. This case raises three major questions:

1. How did the information collected from the club card get to the insurance company?
2. How does the insurance company verify the accuracy of the collected information?
3. How is the denied applicant compensated financially and emotionally?

The social security number is the most common way to index and link these databases. However, a person's name can be used as well. A consumer's credit card purchases, charitable contributions, insurance information, movie rentals, mail order pharmacies, and other services that do not require a social security number can be tracked. Through credit bureaus, the social security number can be determined and a wealth of information may be obtained. This too is mainly used by direct marketing agencies.

To the individual, the result of all this information sharing is most commonly seen as increased "junk mail" (via regular mail or e-mail.) There are much more serious privacy issues to be considered. Should the information provided to a company, for example, to XYZ Bank to help a customer establish a credit record, be repackaged (i.e., linked with other databases), it may end up being used for less noble reasons.

The first governmental linking of large databases in the United States took place in 1977. The Department of Health, Education, and Welfare (HEW) decided to root out those people collecting welfare who were also working for the government. (It is illegal to collect welfare while being employed.) By comparing records of welfare payments and government payroll records, officials were able to identify these individuals. In this case, those persons abusing the system were discovered, so it can be concluded that the system worked.

Governmental efforts to match computer database records have expanded to more than 2 billion records in 110 programs. The Housing and Urban Development Department (HUD) has records that indicate whether mortgage borrowers are in default on federal loans. This information was made available to large banking institutions, such as Citibank, to add to their credit files on individuals. This led Congress to pass the first of several laws intended to protect individual rights of privacy of credit records.

There are several federal laws that regulate the collection and more specifically the use of information on individuals and corporations. However, these laws are all very narrow in scope and full of loopholes.

The 1970 Fair Credit Reporting Act bars credit agencies from sharing credit information with anyone but "authorized customers." An "authorized customer" is anyone with a "legitimate need." The term *legitimate* is not defined in the act [7].

Users and employees alike would like to be provided with legal software and hardware controls for protecting their private information. For example, they should be provided with controls that they could use to decide whether or not they want to provide personal information on the Web. To eliminate or at least minimize the invasion of privacy, organizations should adhere to the guidelines outlined in Table 10-1.

Many Internet users are concerned that their privacy is in jeopardy when they go online. Programs such as cookies, Java, and JavaScript may record the user's journey around the Web. One company that is attempting to resolve this issue is Anonymizer.

Anonymizer **<http://anonymizer.com>** based in San Diego, California, provides online privacy services. Anonymizer has offered users the ability to surf the Web in a private and anonymous fashion since 1996. According to Anonymizer, its proxy servers currently load over a million pages per day for its subscribers and free users. Anonymizer free services provide a facility that will hide the user Internet protocol (IP) address and remove cookies, Java, and JavaScript while the user surfs the Web. Anonymizer Window Washer removes the user tracks from a computer.

Table 10-1

Guidelines for Minimizing the Privacy Issues

Access to personal information should be limited to individuals that have proper authorization.

Careful data collection, inputting, and periodic verification must be used to ensure the accuracy of data.

Careful steps must be taken to ensure that data are accurate.

Collected data should only be used for the intended purpose, unless the user has consented.

Erroneous data must be corrected or deleted.

Individuals should be able to review their records and correct any inaccuracies.

Information should be kept for the amount of time needed for the specified purpose.

Only the data needed for the specified purpose should be collected.

There must be a well-defined purpose for collecting and maintaining the Internet user data.

Figure 10-1   The initial screen of Anonymizer.

Figure 10-1 shows the initial Anonymizer screen. For example, if you enter **www.yahoo.com** and press Go in the Anonymizer screen, after a few seconds you will see the screen presented in Figure 10-2. As you see in this figure, the Anonymizer hides the user IP address and serves as a filter. This process will stay in effect as long as all the URLs are entered through the Anonymizer screen. As soon as you directly enter a URL, the Anonymizer will disappear and the protection will go away. Using Anonymizer may slow down the connection and surfing speeds.

Software packages, such as PersonaValet (PrivaSeek, Inc), Idcide (IDcide, Inc.), and Freedom (Zero-Knowledge) provide security features to Web users. IDcide and PersonaValet let the user decide which information can be revealed. Free to consumers, PersonaValet provides access to popular online sites while putting users in control of their personal information online. Businesses can benefit by co-branding PersonaValet, receiving access to highly targeted consumers' data that are available by their consent.

Freedom allows the user to create online anonymous profiles called *nyms*, which use encryption technology to disguise the user's identity. Figure 10-3

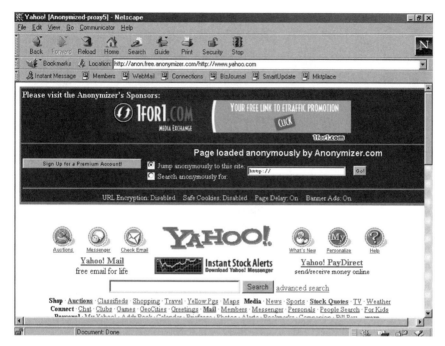

Figure 10-2   Logging onto Yahoo.com using Anonymizer.

shows the initial screen of Freedom. Figure 10-4 shows the initial screen of PersonaValet. Figure 10-5 shows the initial screen of Idcide.

However, this type of technology may have some drawbacks, since it may cover up criminal activities. For example, e-Bay often contends with sellers who bid on their own products using different personalities to inflate the product's price. Currently, it is possible to trace these types of criminals' online activities; however, the use of privacy software will allow criminals to remain behind the scene.

There are some major differences between the European Union (EU) and the United States regarding privacy over the Internet. The EU has enacted rigorous privacy legislation for data collected through the Web and has prohibited the transfer of data on EU citizens to countries whose privacy standards for Internet data do not equal those of the EU. The EU privacy standard places a great deal of emphasis on individual privacy. How much this might affect the development of e-commerce in Europe is difficult to foresee. Most likely, it will develop along different lines than in the United States. For example, in the EU, an e-commerce site such as Amazon.com could not personalize the site for each customer without first asking for the express permission of each customer [1].

Figure 10-3 The initial screen of Freedom.

Figure 10-4 The initial screen of PersonaValet.

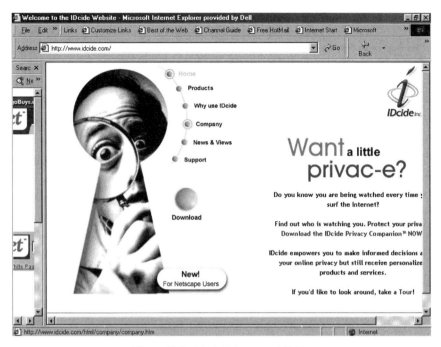

Figure 10-5 The initial screen of Idcide.

10-5 CRIME AND FRAUD

On August 25, 2000, a false press release distributed through the Web caused the market capitalization of Emulex Corporation to tumble by more than $2 billion in less than two hours. This issue has become so serious that U.S. government officials are seeking solutions to stop these cyber criminals. As will be discussed in Chapter 11, computer viruses and denial of service attacks are costing businesses billions of dollars every year.

Computer fraud is the unauthorized use of computer data for personal gain. This includes transferring money from one account to another or charging expenses to an account that did not use the service or product. Computer sabotage can involve destruction or disruption and disclosure of computer services. Computer criminals are those who modify, change, eliminate, hide, or use computer files for personal gain. They include insiders, extremists, and hackers. Hackers usually break into computer systems for personal satisfaction. Other computer criminals seek financial gain. Insiders commit more than 70% of computer crimes. This presents an even more difficult challenge when protecting e-commerce resources.

Table 10-2

Eight Facts about Computer Fraud

Computer fraud exists.

Computer fraud is difficult to discover in the conventional audit process.

Management is often reluctant to prosecute discovered computer frauds—or even to admit publicly that they have occurred.

Most auditors are not prepared by training and attitude to engage in computer fraud detection.

Most discovered computer frauds have persisted for some time and may be part of a group of concurrent frauds within the same organization.

Most discovered computer frauds reflect inadequate information system design.

The nature of computer fraud is not well understood by either data processors or auditors.

The public legislators and regulators all seem to believe that auditors can and will discover computer fraud in the normal course of their work.

Belden Menkus developed a list of eight facts about computer fraud and eight factors contributing to computer fraud. These factors bring the crime and fraud issues to the forefront of IT applications (summarized in Tables 10-2 and 10-3) [21].

Factors outlined in Tables 10-2 and 10-3 should assist the designers and users of e-commerce systems to guard against these serious problems. With careful planning and by following the guidelines introduced in Chapter 11, these problems should be minimized.

Table 10-3

Eight Factors Contributing to Computer Fraud

Aggregation of the information system's transaction-processing steps so that a review of what is taking place becomes impossible.

Detachment of the information system's ongoing operation from the physical or functional reality that it is supposed to reflect.

Inadequate design of the information system.

Insufficient discrimination as to the legitimacy of transactions processed by the information system.

Limits in the investigative tools for analyzing the knowledge that auditors may gain about the fraud.

Restricted ability to collect sufficient knowledge about the fraud itself—especially its scope and the extent of the loss that has occurred.

Toleration of errors by the information systems—either in data content or processing results.

Unrestrained, unmediated remote access to an information system that is subject to possible compromise or manipulation.

10-6 HEALTH ISSUES

Many health-related issues of computers, particularly video display terminals (VDTs), have been reported in recent years. There is, however, no conclusive study to indicate that VDTs have caused health problems, despite the many complaints about them. Work habits and how workers interact with VDTs do cause some physical problems, but health problems are not linked to the unit itself. More likely they are associated with the environment in which computers are located. Static electricity, inadequate ventilation, poor lighting, a dry atmosphere, inappropriate furniture, and too few rest breaks are all possible causes of problems.

Some of the health problems reported include eye and vision problems, such as fatigue, itching, and blurred vision; musculoskeletal problems, such as back strain and wrist pain; skin problems such as rashes; reproductive problems, such as miscarriage; and stress-related problems, such as headaches and depression. Properly designed computer rooms can resolve the majority of these problems.

The psychological problems associated with IT and e-commerce are primarily related to "resistance to change" attitudes—employees resist the new system in favor of the old. It has been a challenging task for many organizations to switch from regular mail to e-mail. This resistance is due to various reasons, among them economic concerns, uncertainty, and fear of losing a job. Experts in the field believe that a sound ergonomics program can resolve the majority of health issues of information systems. Ergonomics refers to the implementation of safe work practices between humans and machines. These machines can be parts of assembly lines, point-of-sale monitors, or, for the purposes of this book, a PC or a workstation that runs e-commerce applications.

Another health-related issue in recent years is the amount of time that some individuals spend on the Web. These individuals, known as "Internet junkies," spend almost all their free time on the Web. One single mother recently lost custody of her child because she was spending more time online than with her child. Too much time on the Web can create psychological, social, and health problems. This is especially important for young people. They should exercise rigorous discipline and use the Web only for noble applications and causes. At the same time, the Web and educational sites provide valuable learning opportunities on technology, science, and humanities. The time spent on these educational sites is a good investment. Also, the Web provides a powerful tool that can be used for conducting research on just about any subject. Using the Web could enhance the efficiency and effectiveness of a researcher by providing relevant and timely information.

10-7 DATA COLLECTION ON THE WEB

The number of customers doing online shopping is increasing at a rapid rate. Online shopping offers some advantages not found through traditional shopping.

This may include convenience, number of choices offered, and in many cases cheaper prices. By entering their credit card numbers, customers are able to quickly and conveniently make purchases over the Web. Many customers are reluctant to use their credit card number to make purchases because they fear that a computer hacker may get access to their number and charge purchases to their accounts. To make consumers feel more at ease, many credit card companies reimburse fraudulent charges. At the same time, other electronic payment systems are being developed (discussed in Chapter 6), such as e-wallets and smart cards that reduce customer exposure on the Web.

Some web sites on the Internet require users to enter their name, address, and employment information before they are allowed to use the site. Privacy concerns of customers include the thought that their personal information such as name, home address, phone number, and e-mail will be sold to telemarketing firms for a profit. Consumers do not want to be bombarded with junk e-mail. Also, consumers fear that while they are logged on the Web their entire computer could be searched without their knowledge. Users fear that their personal information store on computer files will be used without their consent for solicitation and other purposes.

Information that users provide while using the Web can be combined with other information and technology to produce new information. Two commonly used technologies are log files and cookies. Log files, which are generated by web server software, record a user's journey around a web site. Cookies use software that is embedded in the web browser. They provide information about the user's location and equipment. Naturally the site and information gathered and visited in a site can be recorded and used for unauthorized purposes. Cookies can be disabled; however, many users do not disable them. A user can disable cookies by installing a cookie manager. A cookie manager is a software program that enables the user to eliminate the cookies that a web site tries to attach to the user computer and/or the cookies that have already been placed on the user computer. Table 10-4 lists several cookie managers on the Web [18].

Table 10-4

Selected Examples of Cookie Managers

Anti-Cookie

Buzof

Cookie Cruncher

Cookie Master

Cookie Pal

Cookie Server

On the positive side, log files and cookies give companies the ability to assist the prospective customer in his or her next purchase. By identifying users, cookies can prepare and deliver customized web pages. However, many individuals see them as an invasion of their privacy. Some people believe that web sites should be designed with a feature to keep the user's information from being collected, and furthermore they believe any information should be collected only with the user's consent.

10-8 ELECTRONIC MAIL

Due to increased speed, ease of use, affordability and convenience, e-mails have astounding popularity. E-mails are routinely used in the e-commerce environment for customer notifications and confirmations, product announcements, and other marketing purposes. However, e-mail presents some serious privacy issues. Electronic lurking, and the abundance of junk e-mail have become a serious privacy concern. Junk e-mails are usually unsolicited commercial e-mails, such as an unwanted advertisement. Usually junk e-mails are sent in bulk to a large number of addresses using automated mailing software. Because many junk e-mailers use automated mailing software and sell their e-mail address lists, the volume of junk e-mail can quickly rise to an unmanageable level, clogging the recipient's in-box and preventing access to legitimate e-mails. Sending an e-mail message costs the sender virtually nothing. A junk e-mailer can send e-mail to thousands of addresses as cheaply as one. Because of this inexpensive process, even a fraction of a positive response can generate a great return on investment for the junk e-mailer.

Many individuals and employees are concerned about the security of their e-mail messages. Whether an e-mail is distributed through the Internet or other networks, individuals should assume that someone else potentially has access to their messages. Some experts believe that an e-mail is similar to sending an open postcard to somebody else through the post office. Therefore, others that come in contact with the card can see the contents of the postcard. As far as corporate e-mail is concerned, employees should assume that if they are using a computer that belongs to their employers, the content of their e-mail also belongs to the employer. At present, there is a lot of controversy surrounding the e-mail privacy, and several lawsuits have resulted. All indications point to the conclusion that e-mails are not fully secured [25]. However, legislation is being introduced in some countries (e.g., the United Kingdom) to clarify this situation.

Spam e-mail is unsolicited e-mail received in one's electronic mailbox. Spamming has created privacy and decency concerns. Some of these e-mails contain explicit language or nudity. Children open their e-mails not realizing what has been sent to them. Another area of concern is when a child tries to conduct a search on the Web. If search parameters include key words such as "toys," "pets," "boys," or "girls," the search engine brings up a list of sites that include links to pornography. Another concern for parents is mistaken or mistyped URLs. Marketers have learned that if their address is similar to the one that children will try, there is a high probability of web site visits. For example, http://www. whitehouse.gov will bring pictures of White House, whereas http://www. whitehouse.com will bring pornographic pictures. Some of these problems can be addressed using trademark legislation to protect and prevent misuse of domain names.

10-9 CENSORSHIP

Who will decide what should and what should not appear on the Web? Since the Web is not being controlled and run by a single government or a single organization, it is not feasible to censor offensive information. There are two types of information available on the Web: public and private. Public information could be censored for public policy reasons; however, information addressed to an individual should not be subject to censorship. Another important censorship problem occurs when items that are acceptable to the majority of society are offensive to a minority group, such as a political, religious, or cultural minority.

Some countries have tried to restrict or constrain Web access to their citizens. In the United States, citizens are against government intervention. Some governments forbid direct access to the Web. The governments of Burma and Singapore have attempted to censor the information provided on the Web. They feel threatened by the information their citizens could receive on the Web. Several countries only allow individuals who work for multinational corporations to have direct access to the Web. Some Asian countries have been successful at limiting their citizen's access to the Web. The Web contains racism, pornography, and extreme political views that some countries believe may destabilize their national security.

Although U.S. citizens do not want the government to intervene with the Web, many parents are concerned about what their children are exposed to while using the Web. How can parents control their children's access to the Web? Parents should be alerted to the potential hazards of the information superhighway. Several guidelines for the Web use have been published to inform parents of the benefits as well as the hazards of the new technology. Software programs listed in Table 10-5 prevent children's access to certain information.

Parents should counsel and teach their children to be aware of the potential danger and to use good judgment while using the Web. Pornography is not the only concern here; violence and adult language on the Web pose still another serious problem. Specific web browsers are entering the market that can further im-

Table 10-5

Software for Limiting Internet Access

Cyber Patrol
CyberSitter
CyberSnoop
Net Shepherd
NetNanny
NetRated
Safe Surf
SurfWatch

prove the children's security. For example, some of these web browsers accept e-mail only from another site that is using the same Web browser. This ensures that only a child can send e-mail to another child.

Another possibility would be to create different levels of user access similar to the current rating of motion pictures. Children would be prevented from accessing controversial or pornographic information. A method for the implementation of this system would be through the password or biometrics (discussed in Chapter 11) such as retinas of the eyes, hand geometry, or fingerprints.

10-10 ELECTRONIC PUBLISHING

How will the Web influence the publishing business? In recent years the Web has been competing with printed media and has attracted some attention in this space. Already several major newspapers and TV channels have gone online. Table 10-6 provides some examples.

An electronic medium compared with the traditional printed medium offers several advantages. Speed, cost, convenience, and flexibility are some of the prime advantages of electronic media. Electronic media can be presented through multimedia with an interactive capability offering various search features. An electronic publication is available to readers as soon as it is entered to the network, but printed publications must be printed, assembled, and distributed to the reader. In most cases, electronic publications will be easier to use than printed text. The reader can easily save articles on disks and then search their disks for a certain topic. Electronic media are not limited to text. They can include animation, video clips, as well as audio. For example, when a person views an electronic article about a particular bird, they might be exposed to video and audio

Table 10-6

Sample of Online Newspapers and TV Channels

ABC	<www.abc.com>
Chicago Tribune	<www.chicagotribune.com>
CNBC	<www.cnbc.com>
CNN	<www.cnn.com>
NBS	<www.nbc.com>
The New York Times	<www.nytimes.com>
The Washington Post	<www.washingtonpost.com>
Time	<www.time.com>

clips that illustrate the kind of sound the bird makes and the exact color and size of the bird.

On the negative side, experts believe that electronic publications may increase plagiarism and the amount of publications without peer review. One suggestion is to use the same quality controls that govern printed media for electronic publication. As far as plagiarism is concerned, one must rely on professional ethics and the fact that electronic media will detect plagiarized material more quickly due to the availability of advanced searches and a great number of readers who read the material on the Web.

10-11 SOCIAL DIVISION

Although, the price of computers has been decreasing at a steady rate, they are still not affordable by a significant part of the society. If more and more education and entertainment programs were offered through the Web, those who are not connected to the Web may be left out. As a result, the information superhighway and e-commerce may create a society of the "haves" and "have-nots" [22]. People from lower income communities are concerned that companies installing the cables that will be used for the Web in the future may subject some residential areas to the equivalent of economic red-lining. These citizens argue that companies will focus on installing cables in communities where a greater percentage of homes are expected to use the Web and where greater profits are expected. As a result, lower income areas that may not have the necessary equipment to access the Web will be neglected and kept from the benefits of Web access [22].

The information superhighway creates two groups in society: the information-rich and the information poor. Students without access will get further and further behind. Children may be given unequal opportunities to learn about computers and ITs. Those who have PCs at home have an advantage over those who do not have computers. Children with computers at home have readily available access to the vast array of resources on the Web. Naturally, these students will be able to write more comprehensive papers and learn about various subject matters in more depth. Interactive and virtual reality educational games offered through the Web may further increase the gap. Schools should start giving more computer access to all students. Also, the government should make computers more available in public places such as libraries, post offices, and other public places. Some schools have started loaner programs where students can borrow a portable PC for use after school hours. The results have been very positive so far. A partnership between schools, local governments, and local businesses is another solution for increasing student access to the Web.

10-12 COPYRIGHTS, PATENTS, AND PIRACY

According to "whatiscopyright.org,"

> Copyright is a protection that covers published and unpublished literary, scientific and artistic works, whatever the forms of expression, provided such works are fixed in a tangible or material form. This means that if you can see it, hear it and/or touch it— it may be protected. If it is an essay, HTML codes or a computer graphic that can be set on paper, recorded on tape or saved to a hard drive, it may be protected. Copyright laws grant the creator the exclusive right to reproduce, prepare derivative works, distribute, perform and display the work publicly. Exclusive means only the creator of such work, not anybody who has access to it and decides to grab it [2].

Although rapid technological changes have expanded most firms' information needs from internally derived and managed data to a broad spectrum of information and choices, laws relating to information use have struggled to keep up. Management, however, is still responsible for the misuse and abuse of its information, and litigation in this area is on the rise.

There are three main areas of concern for management [26]:

1. Provision of functionality without impinging on the intellectual property rights of external program creators (piracy)
2. Acquisition and utilization of external information without violation of copyright or licensing agreements (proprietary databases)
3. Utilization of information about individuals without violation of persons' rights (privacy)

There has been, and will continue to be, much industry infighting over intellectual property rights and the Internet, and e-commerce applications are adding to the problem. Intellectual property is a legal umbrella that covers protections involving copyrights, trademarks, trade secrets, and patents. These are intangible properties that individuals or corporations have developed. Although there has been a trend toward legal protectionism, very few cases have actually been settled. This issue is widespread throughout the world. World leaders have made several unsuccessful attempts to resolve it [10]. It should be noted that laws that are specific to a particular jurisdiction govern all trademarks, patents, and copyrights. Thus a patent granted in the United States does not apply in European countries, for example.

Eliot offers cautions due to the widespread variation in definitions and legal interpretations [10]. Trademarks protect product names and identifying marks. Smaller and newer companies have tended to pick a cute name that sometimes mimics that of a larger competitor or product. The courts have taken a dim view of this. Much confusion exists in the area of software copyright; the protection is supposed to be limited to an author's expression of ideas—not to the ideas themselves. As an example, there is no agreement in neither the courts nor the industry as to whether icons are ideas or expressions of ideas. The same principle applies to pull-down menus, keystroke sequences, and dialog boxes. Lawsuits are being used in the industry to simply scare off competitors, because of their length and expense. The benefits of obtaining a copyright, however, are substantial. A corporate copyright lasts 75 years in the United States, and then it must be renewed again. Other countries have different durations for copyright.

It is likely that patents are a better way to go for the software industry. A patent protects new and useful processes, but is extremely difficult to obtain. It generally takes several years to obtain a patent, with only a fifty-fifty chance that the courts will uphold it. The rewards are worth it, however, as patents grant a virtual monopoly for 17 years. Eliot advises that firms involve attorneys at each step of product development and assume both offensive and defensive positions [10]. According to Pavento [13], patents offer at least four critical advantages to businesses engaged in e-commerce:

- A patent may serve as an offensive weapon for battling competitors and protecting market share.
- A patent may serve as a defensive shield for protecting research and development, business, and marketing investments.
- A patent may create corporate value, resulting in the attraction of capital investment.
- A patent may create licensing opportunities.

Samuelson [24] details industry arguments for and against patenting program algorithms. In a survey with 667 respondents, there was overwhelming support for source and object code protection; strong objection to "look-and-feel" protection, and some support for algorithm patenting. The Supreme Court has generally said that algorithms are comparable to a law of nature or a scientific principle, and, since they do not involve transformations of matter, they do qualify for patent protection. Most insiders feel that these rulings are based on outmoded technology and should be reversed.

In discussing the subject of legal issues in these areas in general, Krass [16] states that although software developers are now firmly enforcing trade secrets, copyrights, and patents—and utilizing "legions of lawyers" to do so—these protections also stifle innovation and should be eliminated or, at least, controlled.

A number of important considerations relate to patents and copyrights: the limits are not yet established; litigation is an effective competitive weapon; judges and attorneys have limited technical knowledge; the length and expense of litigation; the specter of loss can devastate a small company; and these protections can limit innovation and stifle competition [16].

Laws concerning software piracy appear to be the most straightforward. The 1980 revisions to the Copyright Act of 1976 explicitly include computer programs. Both the individual and the organization can be held liable for unauthorized duplication and use of copyrighted programs. Contracts have been used to supplement copyrights in specific cases. These contracts are tailored to a particular program and provide additional protection for the originator. Trade secret laws—covering ideas, information, and innovations—are also being utilized as supplemental protection.

Straub and Collins [26] also refer to potential liabilities involved in downloading information from proprietary databases, combining such data with internal information, and reusing such recombined data. In some cases this information can be uploaded back to the Web under a new author. The law and precedent are still particularly unclear in this area, but several recent rulings suggest copyright infringement has resulted from such actions. Specific contracts between database vendors and subscribers appear to be the solution in current use. This is an area covered by the European Union (EU) Directive on database compilations.

Privacy is another important issue. The threat of the misuse of stored information about an individual in various databases is perhaps the general public's greatest fear in the information revolution. The computers ability to match records from different databases and make statistical inferences increases this perceived threat.

Some of this "information paranoia" is valid, since virtually every aspect of our lives is now routinely stored on various databases, and the potential for misuse is very high. Misuse of extremely sensitive information—such as health-related information—could serve to deny an individual employment, health insurance, and housing. There is legal recourse available, but it is, of course, both costly and, usually, too late—the damage has already been done.

It is incumbent upon management to develop specific policies and procedures to protect the collected data from abuse and misuse. Information liability and responsibility should be designated to a specific person—preferably one with

Figure 10-6 The initial screen of the Copyright web site <http://www.benedict.com>.

strong connections to functional managers. Security controls, ongoing steward-ship of personal data, and careful and limited dissemination of such information are paramount. As will be discussed in Chapter 11, organizations must establish comprehensive security measures in order to protect sensitive information.

The Copyright web site offers comprehensive information regarding various copyright issues. The initial screen is presented in Figure 10-6.

10-13 OTHER LEGAL ISSUES

Most of the legal issues related to the Web and e-commerce in the United States pertain to the Telecommunications Act of 1996, the Communications De-cency Act (CDA), and use of spamming. I will provide a summary of these im-portant issues below.

On February 1,1996, the Telecommunications Reform bill was passed by the United States Senate and the House of Representatives. The CDA was only a small part of the Telecommunications Act. According to Neil Randal [23, p. 274] an interpretation of this act is as follows:

Nobody could transmit obscene, lewd, lascivious, insulting, indecent materials or comments to anyone under the age of 18, or to anyone of any age if the intent was to harass, annoy, abuse, or threaten the recipient. Furthermore, an individual could not use an interactive computer service (such as Microsoft Network, America Online, Prodigy, and so forth) to make materials available that might under any circumstances, be seen or heard by people under the age of 18.

This bill resulted in various legal issues and raised some serious issues as follows:

1. Individuals can interpret the words in the bill differently.

2. What should individuals do to control the access of their personal and organizational web sites and be able to avoid liability issues?

3. It would be a challenging task to screen out those under 18 years old from adults when providing services that can be seen and heard in a broad geographical area.

4. Any restriction imposed on Web content would compromise its openness principle and the First Amendment.

5. Who's responsibility is it to prohibit young people from viewing obscene materials? Local, state, or federal government?

6. What is the role and responsibility of parents and schools in this process?

Some experts have recommended the V-chip as it will be used in new television sets to be used in PCs for blocking certain Internet offerings. The V-chip (*V* stands for violence) prescribes the insertion of a microprocessor chip in a TV set that can be programmed by responsible adults to prevent underage children from watching violent and objectionable programs. V-chips could automatically block selected programs, whereas current technology forces you to block an

Table 10-7
Pending Legislation

Censorship

Copyright

Crimes

Defamation

E-mail

Encryption

Privacy

Software licensing

Telecommunications

Trademarks

Table 10-8

Three Important Risks Regarding the Web, E-Mail, and Software Distribution

Risk #1	Employees may download pornographic materials to their office PCs using the corporate network. As a result, the corporation may be liable to legal challenges, harassment, free speech, privacy, and even copyright infringement.
Risk #2	Indecent e-mail exchanges among employees can leave their corporation open to discrimination and sexual-harassment charges.
Risk #3	Using the corporate network, employees may download and distribute unlicensed software. This again may leave the corporation with serious copyright and legal challenges.

entire channel. The Electronic Industries Association has been working on a V-chip technical standard for several years.

The American Civil Liberties Union (ACLU) immediately took legal action against various issues regarding this bill, but more specifically concentrated on what constitutes the definition of the term *indecent*. It may mean different things to different people. At present, there is comprehensive legislation pending on the issues outlined in Table 10-7.

To guard against legal issues and to avoid the three important risks outlined in Table 10-8, organizations must have a Web policy and advise their employees to follow the policy carefully [27]. For example, an organization must explicitly disclose its e-mail policy. Employees should know about the security and privacy of their e-mail. The employee should know about the company's Web policy. They should know that certain sites must not be accessed through the company's network.

10-14 TAX ISSUES

Generally speaking, "brick-and-mortar" businesses and e-businesses are subject to the same taxes. Until now, this has not been the case, since e-businesses are only required to file taxes on a voluntary basis. This tax relief has given e-businesses a strong competitive advantage over their "brick-and-mortar" counterparts.

A state's government has the power to tax businesses on the transactions held within its jurisdiction. For example, if you establish a business in California, this state has jurisdiction over your business, and you are subject to California taxes. The relationship between the government and the business is called nexus. As a company expands its business to other jurisdictions, the nexus becomes more involved. For example, if the above-mentioned business opens a branch in Washington, this state has jurisdiction over the portion of the income generated in

Washington, and the e-business is required to pay taxes on this portion of the revenue to Washington tax authorities.

Usually, e-businesses only accrue income and sales taxes. Any e-business established in the United States that generates income accrues federal income taxes regardless of the income's geographic source. United States tax law provides a credit for taxes paid to foreign countries by the e-business to avoid double taxation.

Sales taxes arise when a business creates a nexus with a state. The business collects taxes from its customers and pays them to the local government. On the other hand, when a company does business within a state where no nexus yet exists, the entity does not have to collect tax from its customers. Yet the customer has to pay the amount of tax that the business would have collected as if the transaction had been local. However, states usually do not enforce this tax law. This has been true in mail order purchases where the customer is supposed to pay the tax to his or her local state if the merchant has not collected the tax.

To deal with the current tax controversy, the U.S. government established the Internet Tax Freedom Act (ITFA). This Act proclaims "no state or political subdivision thereof shall impose any of the following taxes during the period beginning on October 1, 1998, and ending 3 years after the date of the enactment of this Act [6]:

1. Taxes on Internet access, unless such tax was generally imposed and actually enforced prior to October 1, 1998
2. Multiple or discriminatory taxes on e-commerce

The ITFA established the Advisory Commission on Electronic Commerce to put together appropriate recommendations on e-commerce and tax policy. Government representatives and private groups constantly lobbied the commission on the issue.

On the government side, proposals offered by people such as the Utah Governor Mike Leavit strongly opposed the tax exemptions currently enjoyed by e-businesses. In the private sector, two main groups pressured the Advisory Commission on Electronic Commerce on opposite points of view related to e-commerce taxation: e-fairness and e-freedom.

E-fairness was founded in 1998 to support taxing e-commerce transactions. This group sees three main problems of excluding e-businesses from taxation [4]:

1. Discriminatory tax policy. It is unfair for brick-and-mortar businesses to carry tax burdens, whereas e-businesses can make tax-exempt transactions of the same products.
2. Eroding state and local revenues. Sales taxes make 40% of state revenues that fund governmental services such as police, fire departments, health care, sanitation, and so forth.

3. Widening the digital divide. Shoppers that have the means to buy online will benefit from tax-free purchases, whereas less privileged consumers will carry the entire tax burden. This is another dimension of digital divide introduced in section 10-11.

E-freedom supports the idea of excluding e-commerce transactions from taxation. E-freedom claims that local governments should not be allowed to "use the Web as an excuse to impose their tax collection schemes on companies without a physical presence in their jurisdiction." The group's recommendations are the following [4]:

1. Permanently ban taxes on Internet access.
2. Amend the Internet Tax Freedom Act to make permanent the moratorium on discriminatory sales and use taxes.
3. Repeal the federal 3% excise tax on telecommunications.
4. Prohibit the discriminatory taxation of interstate telecommunications.
5. Prohibit government from erecting Internet tolls in the form of above-cost fees for the installation of telecommunications cable along right-of-ways.
6. Simplify state and local telecommunications taxes, filing, and auditing procedures.
7. Establish a clear nexus standard and definitions to determine when companies have sufficient physical presence that they can be required by a state to collect sales taxes.
8. Protect consumer privacy by prohibiting government from collecting data on individual consumer transactions and allow consumers and companies to arrange information sharing.

Tax on e-commerce transactions are viewed differently outside of the United States. Already (1999) the European Commission has proposed changes to the European VAT (value-added tax) system that would require non-EU companies to collect VAT on sales of electronically delivered products and services to EU customers. To enforce these new rules, a close cooperation among the participating countries is needed. Also, a system must be in place to avoid double taxations and any possible cheating. These rules and regulations are still evolving. An e-business with international operations must examine the tax law of each country that is going to sell products and services [11].

The following is my analysis and prediction of taxes on e-commerce operations:

1. Since e-commerce companies operate in many states and countries, eventually these companies will be subject to the tax laws of all these geographic areas.
2. An e-business eventually will be subject to several types of taxes, including income taxes, transaction taxes, and property taxes.

3. Income taxes are devised by federal, state, and local governments.

4. Transaction taxes include sales taxes, customs duties, and use taxes and are for those products and services that the e-business sells or uses.

5. Property taxes are devised by state and local governments for personal properties and the real estate owned by the e-business.

6. In any event, since the tax laws are changing constantly, the advice of a tax professional is recommended.

As mentioned earlier, e-commerce tax regulations are still changing and evolving. Policy makers should study example questions, such as those raised by Governor Mike Leavit of Utah:

1. Does it count if a customer places an order over the Internet and picks it up at a store?
2. Does granting a blanket tax exemption for online purchases motivate retailers and customers to try all kinds of creative maneuvers to avoid paying that extra 7% or so?
3. What if Wal-Mart hooks up its cash registers to the Internet?

These questions are crucial and will be debated in the days ahead by various e-businesses and tax authorities.

10-15 INTERNATIONAL ISSUES

It has been demonstrated that e-commerce has a lot to gain from global operations. Access to new markets, raw materials, and many new talents are all advantages of a global e-business. Some of the most common challenges in developing global e-commerce are currency conversions, international trade restrictions, tariffs, different business customs and foreign laws, language, taxation, culture, and infrastructures.

Properly designed e-commerce sites could reach a great number of customers outside of domestic boundaries. However, like any other information systems, implementing and maintaining global e-commerce has its own problems. Factors that impede the advancement of e-commerce internationally are outlined in Table 10-9.

Standardization can impact the development of global e-commerce on two fronts. First, the lack of international standards impedes the development of a cohesive system that is capable of sharing the information commodity across borders. Different electronic data interchange (EDI), e-mail, and telecommunications standards exist throughout the world. Consideration of all of them becomes impractical. Although open systems are increasingly popular, and the technology required to link diverse systems is present, few organizations have the working

Table 10-9

**Factors That Impede the Advancement
of Global E-Commerce**

Lack of standardization

Poor telecommunications infrastructures

Lack of skilled analysts and programmers

Diverse regulatory practices

Lack of empowerment

Differences in cultures, work practices, and politics

---

capital to absorb the expenditures necessary to integrate the various platforms. Consequently, the lack of appropriate international system development standards prevents many organizations from implementing global e-commerce.

Second, too much standardization can limit the flexibility needed to respond to local tastes and preferences, as well as time differences. For example, an operations system implemented in the United States may use the standard measuring system and the metric system in European facilities. For integration to be successful, additional development is necessary to provide conversion for comparative purposes. Additionally, information systems personnel who manage centralized e-commerce under international standards that share information commodities across time zones may encounter difficulties finding the appropriate time to bring the system off-line for backup and maintenance [14].

A balance must be realized between international systems development standards. These standards must allow ease of integration and modularization and enable custom tailoring of systems and applications to local needs.

The sharing of software becomes difficult and impractical when these factors are considered. It has been estimated that between only 5 and 15% of a company's applications are truly global in nature. Most applications are local and cannot be integrated into a global e-commerce infrastructure. Even if the software can be fully integrated globally, support and maintenance problems may be created. If the network goes down, who is responsible for bringing the system back online? Moreover, if an employee who speaks only Greek calls a user support line for the shared software, it lends an entirely new meaning to the concept of "help desk." Coordination and planning for variations in local needs impede the adoption of a truly integrated global e-commerce [6].

As mentioned earlier, an organization that implements global e-commerce must take into consideration the telecommunication infrastructures of the countries in which their subsidiaries reside. The organization may have the capital, the talent, and the motivation to implement a worldwide-integrated system, but it cannot bring some locations into the loop because the telecommunications infrastructure at that location cannot support the organization's requirements. Furthermore, the differences in telecommunications systems around the world make these systems difficult to consolidate. For example, implementing global e-commerce that encompasses 25 different countries becomes expensive and cumbersome when each country may have different service offerings, price schedules, and policies.

Diverse regulatory practices also impede the integration process. This does not necessarily apply to regulation on transboarder data flows (TDFs), but rather applies to policy regarding business practices and technological use. TDF regulation is not as large a problem as was once thought, because of the enforcers' unfamiliarity with the technologies. As a result, many organizations dictate to the appropriate authorities what their technology will be, totally disregarding formal regulation. Many countries also restrict the type of hardware and software that can be imported or utilized within that country. Additionally, some countries may not be serviced by the distributor or vendor with whom the organization normally deals [14]. The adoption of open systems technology may eliminate a large portion of this problem. However, as mentioned earlier, very few organizations are capable of adopting such systems.

Access to skilled analysts and consultants with the technical and conceptual knowledge to implement global e-commerce is one of the more critical factors that can impede successful development. Particularly, with the severe shortage of qualified information systems professionals in the United States and in Western Europe, this problem may further hinder the development of global e-commerce. When forming the integrated teams mentioned earlier, one must consider the nature of each culture. There are distinct differences in skill sets across national boundaries [14]. For example, experts from Singapore and Korea have been regarded as the best consultants in Asia, due to their work ethic and their broad skill base. Germans are recognized for their project management skills, whereas Japanese are known for their quality process controls and total quality management. Ideally, an organization would link various skill sets to form a sort of "dream team." However, cultural conflicts, politics, regionalism, and nationalism can hinder the cooperative environment necessary to achieve global integration.

A more subtle, American-based shortcoming to global e-commerce development is the unwillingness to release control and distribute authority. To achieve true information systems integration on an international scale, corporate information systems executives must empower key geographically dispersed personnel and rely on feedback and information-sharing technologies to maintain their global perspective [5].

10-16 INDUSTRY CONNECTION: SYMANTEC CORPORATION

Symantec Corporation
10201 Torre Avenue
Cupertino, California 95014-2132
Telephone: (408) 253-9600
Fax: (408) 253-3968
Web site address: <http://www.symantec.com>

Symantec and its major subsidiary, Norton, offer a range of utilities and software programs that complements and enhances operating systems, virus protection, data recovery, disk analysis and repair, and file monitoring and management. Symantec's visual Java development and debugging tools facilitate Web development and publishing by allowing programmers to create applications that add interactivity to their web pages. Symantec Corporation offers a broad range of products and services divided into three major categories:

- The Norton product lines of antivirus and PC-assistance software.
- The pcAnywhere, WinFax, and ACT! product lines that cater to remote user productivity.
- The Café product lines, which serve as Internet development tools.

Symantec offers LiveUpdate, which provides instant access to online updates, enhancements, support tips, and other useful information for selected products. Symantec offers fast updates and bug fixes, beta versions, and limited free trials of full-featured applications on its web site. Selected products include the following:

Norton AntiVirus There are several versions of this antivirus software for Lotus Notes, Novell NetWare, Windows NT, Windows 2000, NT Server, and so forth. Norton AntiVirus has been responsible for the detection and elimination of numerous types of computer viruses, including the Michelangelo virus of 1992.

Norton Your Eyes Only This is a security-protection product that provides automatic encryption using RSA Data Security, Inc.'s public key encryption technology. (Public key encryption technology was briefly mentioned in Chapter 6 and will be further discussed in Chapter 11.) It includes optional access control during boot-up to prevent any unauthorized access to information resources.

Café and Visual Café This is an Internet tool that helps build Java programs. It is useful for developing web pages, and its visual nature allows developers to see what they are developing as they develop applications.[1]

10-17 SUMMARY

This chapter provided a detailed discussion on the social, personal, organizational, legal ethical, international, and tax impacts of IT in general and e-commerce in particular. The presentation examined impacts on the workplace, privacy, crime, and health issues. The chapter explored data collection on the Web, censorship, electronic publishing, social division, copyrights, patents, piracy, and other legal issues of IT and e-commerce. The chapter concluded with a discussion on tax issues, examined some of the pending proposals, and reviewed international issues related to global e-commerce design and implementation, highlighting Symantec Corporation as the industry connection. A careful examination of these issues should increase the chances of success for any e-commerce application's introduction to an organization and reduce the legal, social, organizational, and personal issues of this growing technology.

10-18 REVIEW QUESTIONS

1. What are some of the potential negative impacts of IT in general and e-commerce in particular?
2. What are some of the impacts of IT and e-commerce on the workplace?
3. IT and e-commerce may improve the quality of certain jobs. What are some examples of these types of jobs?
4. What are some of the privacy issues and how could e-commerce invade our privacy?
5. What are some examples of e-commerce crimes?
6. How can e-commerce crimes be controlled?
7. What is telecommuting? How may telecommuting be used in the e-commerce environment?
8. What are some of the concerns regarding data collection on the Web? How might some of these concerns be resolved?
9. What are some of the legal and social issues of e-mail? What is spamming? How can it be avoided?
10. What is censorship? Is it a good idea to censor certain materials on the Web? Discuss.

---

[1]This information was gathered from the company web site and other promotional materials. For detailed information and any update contact the company.

11. What are some advantages of electronic publishing? Why might electronic publishing replace or reduce printed media? Discuss.
12. The Web may create social division or a subclass in the society. How is this possible? How can it be avoided or minimized?
13. What are some of the laws for copyrights? Patents?
14. How can we stop or reduce piracy?
15. In your opinion, will the legal issues related to e-commerce and the Web increase or decrease in the near future? Discuss.
16. What can organizations do to eliminate or at least reduce the legal issues of the Web? Discuss.
17. What are some of the tax issues of e-commerce?
18. In your opinion, should e-businesses pay taxes? Discuss.
19. How may e-commerce tax exemptions widen the digital divide? Discuss.
20. How can Web access be limited? What are some of available tools?
21. What are some of the drawbacks to using the Web anonymously? What are some of the possible social consequences? Discuss.
22. What are some of the international issues of e-commerce? How could they be resolved?
23. What are some of the differences in e-commerce privacy issues in Europe compared to the United States? What are some of the impacts of these differences on e-commerce growth? Discuss.

10-19 PROJECTS AND HANDS-ON EXERCISES

1. Log onto the web site of the Symantec Corporation at the following URL:

    <http://www.symantec.com>

    What are some of the e-commerce-related products and services offered by this company? Symantec Corporation is a major player in security products and Web publishing software. Investigate these claims.
2. Throughout the management information systems and computer literature there are numerous cases of computer crimes and fraud. In many of these cases, e-commerce has directly or indirectly been involved. Investigate one of these cases and come up with a possible solution that might have stopped the crime or fraud before it occurred. (Hint: the denial-of-access attack in February 2000 in several e-commerce sites is an example.)
3. A newly established catalog company needs your advice to put together a policy regarding the acquisitions and utilization of the Internet. They are new with online communications, and they have heard all sorts of horror stories regarding the social, organizational, and legal issues.

What would be your advice to this organization? Prepare a document that includes at least six pieces of advice in order of priority.

4. A midsized employment agency needs your advice regarding e-mail policy. They want you to help them to put together a one-page document to be distributed among all the employees throughout the organization. List ten items that you would include in this document. In your opinion, who should be involved in this process? Can this document serve as a universal document and be applicable to other organizations? Discuss.

5. Research the Internet service providers (ISPs) in your area and find out about the screening software offered by these providers. How effective are these software packages? What are some of their limitations? What are some of their strengths? Discuss.

6. Research the available legislation regarding computer crimes. What are some of the laws regarding pornographic materials on the Web? What are some of the laws related to junk e-mail and spamming? Discuss.

7. Research the legislation available on privacy. Do ISPs have the right to disclose personal information about subscribers? What are some of the laws regarding federal agencies? Do they differ from private organizations? Discuss.

8. It is a general belief that the Web and e-commerce may create a subclass in our society. What is your opinion? How can some of the equity issues of these technologies be resolved? Who should be involved in this process? Federal, state, or local government? Discuss.

9. Cyber Patrol and SurfWatch are two popular filtering software applications on the market. Investigate the effectiveness of these software programs. Can this software put the minds of parents at ease? Are these software applications able to block all the undesirable sites from viewing by people under 18? Discuss. What is your opinion on a rating system for the Internet? What do you think about the V-chip application for the Internet? Discuss.

10. By consulting the following sites, research one of the topics introduced in the chapter (crime, fraud, or organizational issues) and prepare a two-page report with a recommendation related to elimination or reduction of these social, organizational, legal, or personal issues:

Business Communications Review	<http://www.bcr.com>
Business Week	<http://www.businessweek.com>
Data Communications	<http://www.data.com>
Network Magazine	<http://www.networkmagazine.com>
Network World	<http://www.nwfusion.com>
Network Computing	<http://www.networkcomputing.co.uk/default.htm>
Telecommunications	<http://www.telecoms-mag.com/tcs.html>

11. The following sites provide comprehensive information on e-commerce privacy issues:

    <http://www.wired.com/news/politics/0,1283,37173,00.html>
    <http://grc.com/downloaders.htm>

    By examining the materials presented in these sites and other sources, put together five recommendations for protecting privacy in an e-commerce environment.

12. The following sites provide comprehensive information on anti-cookie:

    <http://www.cookiecentral.com/ccstory/cc5.htm>
    <http://www.cookiecentral.com/board/messages/4055.html>
    <http://www.softseek.com/Internet/Web_Browsers_and_Utilities/Privacy_and_Access_Control/Review_12631_index.html>

    By examining the materials presented in these sites, prepare a one-page document describing the applications, strengths, and shortcomings of these products.

13. The following sites provide comprehensive information on limiting Internet access:

    <http://www.netnanny.com>
    <http://www.safesurf.com>

    By examining the materials presented in these sites, prepare a one-page document describing the applications, strengths, and shortcomings of these products.

14. Pcworld.com <http://pcworld.com/pcwtoday> includes many current cases of e-commerce fraud, privacy, and other related issues. Log onto the site and research one of these cases. In your opinion, how could this particular crime have been stopped?

15. The following site provides current information on tax issues in the e-commerce world:

    <http://www.ecommercetax.com/faq.htm>

    By examining the materials presented in this site and other sources, prepare a one-page document describing the pros and cons of e-commerce taxation. In your opinion, should e-commerce transactions be taxed? If yes why? If no, why not? Discuss.

16. The following sites provide current information on ethical issues of e-commerce:

    <http://www.ethics.org>
    <http://www.ethix.org>

By examining the materials presented in these sites and other sources, describe ethical issues of e-commerce. How can these ethical issues be avoided?

17. The Global Internet Project provides information on the Internet's impact on society, globalization, and law. Log onto the site and examine its contents.

<www.gip.org>

18. Zero Junk Mail provides software products that are designed to block Spam. Log onto the site and examine its contents.

<www.zerojunkmail.com>

19. The following site provides comprehensive information related to copyright issues. Log onto the site and examine its contents.

<http://www.benedict.com>

20. The following site provides legal tools and information on personal, consumer, and business law, including a legal encyclopedia. Log onto the site and examine its contents:

<http://www.nolo.com>

21. The following site provides information on international legal aspects of e-commerce:

<http://www.lawstreet.com>

By examining the materials presented in this site and other sources, prepare a one-page document regarding the international legal issues of e-commerce. How are they different than domestic legal issues? Discuss.

22. The following sites can help you to investigate and receive assistance with online frauds. Log onto these sites and examine its contents.

   - Internet Fraud Complaint Center <http://www.ifccfbi.gov>
   - The Federal Trade Commission
     <http://www.ftc.gov/ftc/complaint.htm>

23. The following sites provide e-business globalization services. By examining the contents of these sites, prepare a report outlining 10 different services, with these sites offer.

   - Global CommerceZone Inc.   <www.gczone.com>
   - GoShip, Inc.   <www.goship.com>
   MyCustoms   <www.mycustoms.com>

10-20 KEY TERMS

Censorship, 340–341
Computer crime, 335–336
Computer fraud, 335–336
Cookies, 338
Copyrights, 343–346
Electronic mail, 339–340
Electronic publishing, 341–342
Health issues, 337
International issues, 351–353
Legal issues, 346–348
Log files, 338

Patents, 343–346
Piracy, 343–346
Privacy issues, 328–335
Pyramid-shaped structure, 327
Social division, 342–343
Spamming, 339
Star-shaped diamond structure, 327
Tax issues, 348–351
Telecommuting, 326
Virtual organization, 327–328

REFERENCES

[1] <http://www.eco.utexas.edu/Homepages/Faculty/Norman/long.extra/information/US-Eu.html>. Example: US versus EU internet privacy policy. (Date of access May 2, 2001).

[2] <http://www.whatiscopyright.org>. What is copyright protection? Copyright © 1998–2001 R. Delgado-Martinez. (Date of access May 2, 2001).

[3] <http://www.ecommercecommission.org/ITFA.htm>. Advisory Commission on Electronic Commerce, The Internet Tax Freedom Act (Date of access May 2, 2001).

[4] <http://www.e-fairness.org>. E-fairness: A level playing field for the new economy. (Date of access May 2, 2001).

[5] A Framework for Global Electronic Commerce." The White House <http://www.ecommerce.gov/framewrk.htm>. (Date of access May 2, 2001).

[6] Ambrosio, Johhanna (1993, August 2). "Global Software: When Does it Make Sense Share Software with Offshore Units?" *Computerworld,* pp. 74–77.

[7] Anonymous (1989, September 4), "Is Nothing Private?" *Business Week,* pp. 74–82.

[8] Bidgoli, Hossein (2000). "Handbook of Business Data Communications: A Managerial Perspective." Academic Press, Inc., San Diego, CA.

[9] Brousell, D. R. (1993, April 15). "The Virtual Data Center." *Datamation,* p. 104.

[10] Elliot, Lance B. (1989, September). "Patent Pending and Other Legal Threats." *AI Expert,* p. 13.

[11] Hardesty, David (2000, June 18). "Europe Proposes New Taxes on Non-EU Sellers." <http://www.ecommercetax.com/doc/061800.htm>

[12] Harvey, David A. (1991, October). "Health and Safety First." *Byte,* pp. 119–128.

[13] Jones & Askew, LLP, and Michael S. Pavento (1999). <http://www.versaggi.net/ecommerce/articles/e-business-models/patnets-for-models.pdf>. Copyright 1995–1999, Jones & Askew, LLP, All rights reserved. (Date of access May 2, 2001).

[14] Huff, Sid (1991, Autumn), "Managing Global Information Technology." *Business Quarterly,* v56, pp. 71–75.

[15] Klein, Mark M. (1994, October). "The Virtue of Being a Virtual Corporation." *Best Review,* pp. 88–94.

[16] Krass, Peter (1991, June 3). "Why So Many Lawsuits?" *Information Week,* p. 40.

[17] Labar, Gregg (1997, October). "Ergonomics for the Virtual Office." *Managing Office Technology,* pp. 22–24.

[18] Lin, Daniel, and Michael C. Loui (1998, June). "Taking the Byte Out of Cookies: Privacy, Consent, and the Web." *Computers and Society*, pp. 39–51.

[19] Martin, James A., Mark Gibbs, and Mark Grossman (1997, November). "Are you being watched?" *PC WORLD*, pp. 245–258.

[20] McQuick, Walker (1984, March 19). "Easing Tensions between Man and Machine." *Fortune Magazine*, pp. 58–66.

[21] Menkus, Belden (1990, June). "Eight Unfortunate Facts about Computer Fraud." *Internal Auditor*, pp. 70–73.

[22] Milone, Jr., Michael N., and Judy Salpeter (1996, January). "Technology and Equity Issues." *Technology & Learning*, pp. 39–47.

[23] Randal, Neil (1997). "The Soul of the Internet." International Thomson Computer Press, Boston, MA.

[24] Samuelson, Pamela (1990, August). "Should Program Algorithms Be Patented?" *Communications of the ACM*, p. 23.

[25] Sipior, Janice C., Burke T. Ward, and Sebastian M. Rainone (Winter, 1998). "Ethical Management of Employee E-mail Privacy." *Information Systems Management*, pp. 41–47.

[26] Straub Jr., Detmar W., and Rosann Webb Collins (1990, June). "Key Information Liability Issues Facing Managers: Software Piracy, Proprietary Databases, and Individual Rights to Privacy." *MIS Quarterly*, pp. 143–155.

[27] Tetzeli, Rick (1996, March 18). "Getting Your Company's Internet Strategy Right." *Fortune*, pp. 72–78.

ADDITIONAL SOURCES

Arnold, David (2000, November-December). "Seven Rules of International Distribution." *Harvard Business Review*, pp. 131–137.

Edberg, Dana, Fritz H. Grupe, and William Kuechler (Winter 2001). "Practical Issues in Global IT Management: Many Problems, a Few Solutions." *Information Systems Management*, pp. 34–46.

Chapter 11

Security Issues and Measures: Protecting Electronic Commerce Resources

Learning Objectives

After studying this chapter you should be able to do the following:

- Define e-commerce security and its important aspects.
- Understand fault-tolerance systems and identify e-commerce threats (natural and others).
- Describe security measures.
- Explain biometric and nonbiometric security measures.
- Understand the role of firewalls and encryption in protecting e-commerce data resources.
- Discuss a comprehensive e-commerce security policy.
- Explain measures that should be taken if disaster strikes.

INFORMATION BOX 11-1

Security Concerns In the E-Commerce World

According to IDC, an IT media and research company, the worldwide market for Internet security software increased from $3 billion in 1998 to $3.98 billion in 1999.

The data gathered from Defense Information Systems Agency (DISA) indicates that the Department of Defense (DOD) experienced over 250,000 attacks in 1997 alone! Also, data indicate that these attacks are over 65% successful.

More than 60% of the organizations using e-commerce throughout the world do not have a disaster-recovery plan.

Many organizations do not fully recover after a disaster.

Computer crime amounts to more than $10 billion lost every year.

Corporate America spent more than $6 billion on network security in 1997 alone.

Disgruntled employees and competitors are two major security concerns.

Hackers, crackers, computer thieves, computer criminals, and cyberpunks are becoming common terms.

Large organizations such as Microsoft, NASA, Netscape, Citibank, Intel, Chemical Bank, and America Online have had security problems.

Insiders commit more than 70% of security breaches.

More than 19,000 computer viruses have been reported.

More than 90% of all thefts are targeted at proprietary information, including manufacturing processes, sales information, research and development, customer lists, and pricing schedules.

Many computer attacks are not reported because of negative publicity.

Numerous organizations do not have a written policy on how to deal with network intrusions.

Tools that hackers use to commit break-ins, such as sniffers, crack, and Rootkit, are easily found free of charge on the Web. Also, journals like *Phrack and 2600: The Hacker Quarterly* provide hackers with informative tips.

Unauthorized alteration of data at a web site presents serious threats to the integrity of e-commerce.

Secure Courier offered by Netscape is based on secure sockets layer (SSL) protocol and allows users to create a secure digital envelope for the Internet transactions.

Loss of data integrity, privacy, service, and control are key security concerns in the e-commerce world.

INFORMATION BOX 11-2

Security Measures and E-Commerce at United Parcel Service (UPS)

Besides delivering packages, UPS also delivers documents electronically using the Internet. UPS Document Exchange was developed through a strategic alliance with Net Dox, Inc., and TumbleWeed Software. It uses two Internet delivery services, each with distinct features and comprehensive security systems. The UPS Online Dossier is for confidential and very critical documents. It utilizes the identity validation via digital certificates and a two-key encryption method. It provides document delivery confirmation, user insurance, and tracking as well as a third-party validation by Deloitte & Touche LLP. The UPS Online Courier is for customers requiring universal solutions for exchanging documents over the Web. It is built on an open environment allowing customers to send and receive documents regardless of the e-mail software, hardware, or operating system used by either sender or receiver. Security options include encryption, password protection, as well as tracking and receipt confirmation. To provide effective Internet services, UPS strikes exclusive deals with Infoseek, Lycos, and Yahoo!, the three leading Internet search and directory companies. Their strategic marketing approach is to drive traffic to their site.

SOURCE: This information was gathered from the E-commerce at UPS web site <http://www.ec.ups.com>. Copyright © 2000–2001 United Parcel Service of America, Inc. All rights reserved. (Date of access: April 24, 2001).

11-1 INTRODUCTION

This chapter discusses security issues and measures in the e-commerce environment. Many of these issues apply to both traditional business and e-businesses; however, this chapter focuses on the e-business and e-commerce sites that are particularly vulnerable to security threats. A comprehensive security system can protect data resources, the second most important resource (after human resources) in an organization. Important e-commerce threats, including natural, humanmade, intentional, and unintentional, are identified. Security measures including biometric, nonbiometric, physical, software, and electronic transactions securities are explained. The chapter reviews Computer Emergency Response Team (CERT) and other organizations that monitor security threats and vulnerabilities. Firewalls are explained as a prominent nonbiometric security measure, as is data encryption, a major software security system in the e-commerce environment. Guidelines for establishing a comprehensive security plan are provided, including recommended preparations to make before and after a disaster. The chapter highlights McAfee Associates as the industry connection.

11-2 E-COMMERCE SECURITY: THE BASIC SAFEGUARDS

Computer hackers and criminals are making national and international news. It's no wonder that executives in private and public organizations are taking computer and e-commerce security seriously. A comprehensive e-commerce security system protects customers, buildings, terminals, printers, CPUs, cables, and other hardware and software in an organization. Moreover, an e-commerce security plan protects data resources, the second most important resource (after human resources) in an organization. The data resources can be an e-mail message from a division supervisor to the CEO, an invoice transferred using electronic data interchange (EDI), the blueprint for a new product design, the outline of a new advertising strategy, or financial statements. Security threats exceed merely stealing data; they include such actions as sharing passwords with a co-worker, leaving a system unattended while logged onto the network, or spilling coffee on a keyboard. A comprehensive e-commerce security system protects hardware, software, procedures, customers, personnel, and e-commerce resources to keep intruders and hackers at bay. E-commerce security is broken into three important aspects: secrecy, accuracy, and availability [14]:

1. A **secret** system must not allow information to be disclosed to anyone who is not authorized to access it. In highly secure government agencies (the Department of Defense, Central Intelligence Agency, and the Internal Revenue Service), secrecy ensures that only authorized users are granted access. In business organizations, confidentiality ensures the protection of private information (payroll, personnel, and corporate data). In the e-commerce world, confidentiality ensures that customers' data are protected and will be used only for the intended purpose.

2. **Accuracy** ensures the integrity of data resources within the organization. This means that the security system must not allow the data to be corrupted or allow any unauthorized changes to the corporate database. Database administrators and web masters must establish comprehensive security systems for corporate databases. Authorized users must be identified and they must be given proper access privileges. Just imagine that the addition or elimination of a zero would be the difference between $100,000 and $10,000. In e-commerce transactions, accuracy is probably the most important aspect of a security system.

3. **Availability** ensures the efficient and effective operation of an e-commerce site and a computer system. In the e-commerce environment, availability ensures that the virtual storefront is always accessible to authorized users. It should also ensure quick recovery of the system to its normal operation after a disaster. In many cases, availability is the baseline security need for all authorized users; otherwise the secrecy and accuracy objectives of the system cannot be properly assessed.

A comprehensive security system in the e-commerce world must provide three levels of security (see Figure 11-1):

- Front-end servers must be protected against unauthorized access. (Level 1)
- Back-end systems must be protected to ensure privacy, confidentiality, accuracy, and integrity of data. (Level 2)
- The corporate network must be protected against intrusion and unauthorized accesses. (Level 3)

The goal in designing a comprehensive e-commerce security system is to first design a fault-tolerance system and then take all the possible measures for protecting the e-commerce data resources. A **fault-tolerance system** is a combination of hardware and software techniques that improves the reliability of an e-commerce site. There are several techniques and tools that can improve the fault tolerance of an e-commerce site. The following are among the popular techniques:

1. **Uninterruptible power supply (UPS)** is a backup power unit that continues to provide power to the network system during the failure of the normal power supply. Its most common application is to protect servers from power failures. A UPS unit performs two crucial tasks in case of power failure:

    a. It serves as a power source to run the server for a short time period.

    b. It provides a safe shutdown management service.

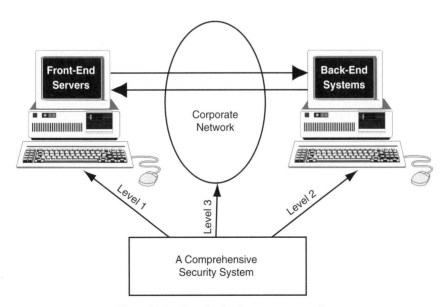

Figure 11-1 Three levels of e-commerce security.

A sophisticated UPS unit prevents additional users from accessing the server and sends an alert to the network administrator that the power has failed.

2. **A redundant array of independent disks (RAID)** is a fault-tolerance disk storage technique that spreads one file plus the file's checksum information over several disk drives. If any single disk drive fails, the data stored there can be reconstructed from data stored on the remaining drives. There are several levels of RAID solutions available that offer various combinations of cost, performance, and reliability.

3. **Mirror disks** are a fault-tolerance technique in which two disks containing the same data are provided so that if one fails, the other is available, allowing the system to continue operations.

11-3 E-COMMERCE SECURITY THREATS: AN OVERVIEW

E-commerce security is an important managerial and technical issue, and all e-businesses must be aware of the underlying factors. E-commerce security is concerned with unauthorized access to important data resources. Some e-commerce threats are controllable, some are partially controllable, and some are completely uncontrollable. Some are intentional, while others are made unintentionally. Table 11-1 summarizes several potential e-commerce threats.

Insiders or outsiders intentionally create some security threats, for example, the spreading of a computer virus by a hacker or disgruntled web master. Some security threats are unintentional. For example, an employee may erase a com-

Table 11-1

Potential E-Commerce Threats

Natural disasters	Other disasters
Cold weather	Blackouts
Earthquakes	Fires
Floods	Gas leaks
Hot weather	Neighborhood hazards
Hurricanes	Nuclear attacks
Ice storms	Oil leaks
Ocean waves	Power failure
Severe dust	Power fluctuations
Snow	Radioactive fallout
Tornadoes	Structural failure

Table 11-2

Internal E-Commerce Threats and Vulnerability

Type of threat	Sources of threats					
	Input–output operator	Supervisor	Programmer/ web master	Systems engineer/ technician	User	Competitor
Changing codes	x		x			
Copying files	x		x			
Destroying files	x	x	x		x	x
Embezzlement			x	x		x
Espionage	x	x	x			x
Installing bugs			x	x		x
Sabotage	x		x	x		x
Selling data	x	x	x		x	
Theft		x	x		x	x

puter file or format a data disk unintentionally. Some security threats (such as earthquakes) are natural and are not controllable (or are partially controllable). A comprehensive security system should allow only authorized employees to have access to e-commerce facilities. Table 11-2 summarizes the threats posed by insiders.

The damage from natural disasters is somewhat controllable. Buildings with special designs for earthquake protection are now available, and flood damage usually can be controlled. Frequently, computer rooms are designed separately from the rest of a structure to minimize potential hazards. Wiring, air conditioning, and fire protection should be of special concern. Locks and physical deterrents should prevent most computer thefts.

11-4 INTENTIONAL E-COMMERCE THREATS

Intentional computer and e-commerce threats usually fall into one of the following categories:

- Computer viruses
- Trojan horses
- Logic bombs
- Trap doors
- Denial-of-access attacks

11-4-1 Computer Viruses

The most highly publicized computer and e-commerce threat is the computer virus. A computer virus is a series of self-propagating program codes triggered by a specified time or event within the computer system. When the program or the operating system containing the virus is used again, the virus attaches itself to other files and the cycle continues. The seriousness of computer viruses varies, ranging from springing a joke on a user to completely destroying computer programs and data.

Computer viruses have made headlines worldwide. In 1988, one well-known virus attacked more than 6,000 computer installations. In December 1998 the Remote Explorer virus seriously challenged Microsoft NT workstations.

In late March 1999, two new computer viruses made the headlines: Melissa and Papa [11,13]. The **Melissa** virus is a Word 97 and Word 2000 virus spread via an attachment to e-mail. Most recipients opened the attached Word document because the e-mail appeared to be coming from a known friend, and the subject line read "important message." Once the document was opened, Melissa invaded the recipient's address book and mailed a list of pornographic web sites to the first fifty names. The **Papa** or **Papa.b** virus is distributed via an Excel spreadsheet file attached to e-mail. When recipients open the attached file, the Papa virus sent messages to the first sixty names in the recipient's address book.

In February 2000, computer hackers temporarily shut down several well-known sites, such as Yahoo!, ZD.net, and Ameritrade by bombarding them with bogus traffic. Later the same year, the "I Love You" virus infected millions of e-mail users throughout the world. Viruses have brought to the forefront the necessity of protecting computers from hackers, crackers, extremists, and computer criminals. Billions of dollars are stolen every year by computer criminals. Many organizations are reluctant to report their losses because they do not want to be recognized as vulnerable. With the popularity of e-commerce, this problem will only become worse.

Computer viruses can also be transmitted through a network. Probably the most dangerous type of virus comes from bulletin boards; this type of virus can infect any system that accesses the bulletin board. Bulletin boards are computer systems to which different individuals can post messages or computer programs that can be downloaded by others. Experts feel that the greatest national risks come from infecting large computers, such as those governing air-traffic control systems, those concerned with public safety, security, and defense, and those used by NASA. Computer viruses have been observed in many countries, including the United States, Germany, Switzerland, Italy, Great Britain, and Israel. Computer viruses can be installed or programmed into a disk controller, a hard disk, an operating system, or a floppy disk.

Computer viruses have been given various names. Table 11-3 lists some of the popular computer viruses.

Table 11-4 lists some indications that your computer may have been infected by a computer virus.

Table 11-5 lists some of the popular antivirus programs on the market [10].

11-4-2 COMPUTER WORMS

A worm is similar to a computer virus. It is called a worm because it travels like a worm from one computer in a network to another computer or site. A worm usually does not erase the data. It either corrupts the data or it copies itself to a full-blown version that eats up computing resources. Eventually it will bring the computer and/or network to a halt. An example of a computer worm is

Table 11-3
Popular Computer Viruses

ATOM

Azusa

Cascade

Dark Avenger

DMV

Flame

Frankenstein

Jerusalem

Junkie

Melissa

Michelangelo

NYB

Papa and Papa.b

Quandrum

Remote Explorer

Satan Bug

Stealth_Boot

Stoned

Tequila

Werewolf

Yankee Doodle

Table 11-4
Computer Virus Symptoms

Certain programs are bigger than normal.

Data disintegrates.

Data or programs are damaged.

Hard disk space diminishes significantly.

Keyboard locks.

Memory becomes constrained.

Screen freezes (no cursor movement).

Sluggish disk access.

Unexpected disk activity.

Unusual messages appear on the screen.

The computer takes too much time to boot.

the one that was unleashed by Robert Morris in November 2,1988, bringing more than 6,000 computers to a halt.

11-4-3 Trojan Horse

A Trojan horse program contains codes intended to disrupt a computer system and or an e-commerce site. Trojan horse programs are usually hidden inside a popular useful program. Historically, disgruntled programmers who are trying to get even with an organization have created Trojan horse programs. These pro-

Table 11-5
Popular Antivirus Programs
on the Market

Dr. Solomon's Antivirus Toolkit

F-PROT Professional

IBM Antivirus

Inoculan Antivirus

McAfee Virus Scan

Norton Antivirus

PC-cillin Antivirus

Thunder Byte Antivirus Utilities

grams may erase accounting, personnel, and financial data. Unlike computer viruses and worms, a Trojan horse program does not replicate itself. Although a Trojan horse program functions differently than viruses and worms, the end results are basically the same: damage and interruption of the computer and/or network system.

11-4-4 LOGIC BOMBS

A logic bomb is a type of Trojan horse used to release a virus, a worm, or some other destructive code. Logic bombs are triggered at a certain point in time or by an event or an action performed by a user. An action can be pressing certain keystrokes or running a specific program. An event may be loading a backup tape or the birthday of a famous person.

11-4-5 TRAP DOORS

A trap door (also called a back door) is a routine built into a system by its designer or programmer. This routine allows the designer or the programmer to sneak back into the system to access software or specific programs. A trap door is usually activated by the individual (or his or her agent) who designed the system. Usually the user is not aware of the problem; a keystroke combination or a specific login may set it off.

11-4-6 DENIAL-OF-ACCESS ATTACKS

A denial-of-service attack is a method hackers and crackers use to prevent or deny legitimate users' access to a computer or web server. Just imagine, 5,000 or more people surround a department store and block everybody who wants to enter the store. Although the store is open, it cannot provide service to its legitimate customers. These computer criminals use tools that send many requests to a targeted Internet server (usually the Web, file transfer protocol, or mail server), which floods the server's resources, making the system unusable. Any system connected to the Internet running Transmission Control Protocol services are subject to attack. Just imagine continuous phone calls to a traditional store. As soon as the store clerk picks up the phone, he or she finds out that this is a prank call. If this process continues, it prohibits the store's legitimate customers to get hold of the store operator and use the store's services or products. This is similar to denial-of-service attacks.

In February 2000, hackers launched denial-of-access attacks against a number of Internet sites, including eBay, Yahoo!, Amazon.com, CNN.com, and

E-Trade. Other sites affected included news provider CNN, technology news site ZDNet, and Buy.com. According to The Yankee Group, the sites experienced slowdowns in service that ranged from 2 hours and 45 minutes to 5 hours. The assaults are all of a type known as "distributed denial-of-service" attacks, in which a web site is bombarded with thousands of requests for information in a very short period of time, causing it to grind to a halt. The attacks usually come from several computers on the Web, and this makes it difficult to trace the attacks. A hacker secretly plants denial-of-access attack tools on several computers on the Web. These computers can be centrally controlled. The methods of how and what resources are flooded differ based on the tools used by the hackers. It is nearly impossible to trace the attack, particularly if the attacks come from several sites. Computers that unknowingly have denial-of-service attack tools installed are called Zombie agents or Drones. Several companies, including Symantec, offer tools that can reduce the risk of being attacked.

The research firm Yankee Group estimated that these attacks cost the industry approximately $1.2 billion (in 2000) by estimating revenue losses at the affected web sites, losses in market capitalization, and the amount that will be spent upgrading security infrastructures as a result of the attacks [1,12].

11-5 SECURITY MEASURES AND ENFORCEMENTS FOR E-COMMERCE: AN OVERVIEW

The first step toward securing a computer and e-commerce site is to generate a backup of each data resource. The backup files must be kept in a location away from the computer room. A comprehensive security system should include the following:

- Biometric securities
- Nonbiometric securities
- Physical securities
- Software securities
- Electronic transactions securities
- CERT

11-5-1 BIOMETRIC SECURITIES

Biometric security measures use elements from the human body to screen users. These security measures rely on the concept that a unique part or characteristic of an individual cannot be stolen, lost, copied, or passed on to others. Some of the drawbacks of biometrics are their relative high cost, acceptance by users, and the relative difficulty of installation. Biometric security measures are listed in Table 11-6.

1. **Fingerprint.** Whenever a user tries to access the system, his or her fingerprint is scanned and verified against the print stored in an electronic file. If there is a match, the access request is granted. If there is no match, access is rejected [6].

2. **Hand geometry.** Hand geometry measures the length of fingers on both hands, the translucence of the fingertips, and the webbing between the fingers.

3. **Palmprint.** The individual characteristics of the palm are used to identify the user. Palmprint is used by law-enforcement agencies to catch criminals.

4. **Retinal scanning.** Retinal scanning using a binocular eye camera is one of the most successful methods for security application. Identification of the user is verified by data stored in a computer file.

5. **Signature analysis.** Signature analysis uses the signature as well as the user's pattern, pressure deviation, acceleration, and the length of the time needed to sign one's name.

6. **Voice recognition.** Voice recognition translates words into digital patterns for transmission to the server. Voice patterns are recorded and examined by tone, pitch, and so forth. This technique is relatively new, and research is ongoing. Using voice to verify user identity has one characteristic that most other biometric technologies cannot offer. Voice recognition can work over long distances via ordinary telephones. A properly designed voice-based security system could provide major enhancements to the safety of financial transactions conducted over the telephone.

These different biometric techniques have been very effective in protecting the security of computer and e-commerce sites. They may not currently be justified financially for all organizations; however, with rapid cost reduction, improvements in quality, and further user acceptance, they present a viable alternative to traditional security systems.

Table 11-6

Biometric Security Measures

Fingerprint

Hand geometry

Palmprint

Retinal scanning

Signature analysis

Voice recognition

11-5-2 NONBIOMETRIC SECURITIES

In this group, callback modems, firewalls, and intrusion-detection systems (IDSs) are the three prominent security measures.

11-5-2-1 Callback Modems

Using a callback modem, the system validates access by logging the user off and calling the user back. By doing this the system separates authorized users from unauthorized users.

11-5-2-2 Firewalls: An Overview

A firewall is a combination of hardware and software that serves as a gateway between the private network and the Internet. Predefined access and scope of use are required, and all other requests are blocked. An effective firewall should protect both the export and import of data from and to the private network. Figure 11-2 shows a basic firewall configuration.

A firewall's protection is similar to a house with walls, windows, and doors. The walls and doors of the house prevent unauthorized people from getting in, while the windows still allow those in the house to see the outside. However, as we all know, houses with walls and doors can be entered by those who have both good and bad intentions.

If designed effectively, a firewall can look at every piece of data that passes into or out of a private network and decide whether to allow the passage based on the following:

- User identification
- Point of origin
- Point of destination
- The information contents

By careful examination of the packet that is trying to exit from or enter into the private network, a firewall can choose one of the following actions:

- Reject the incoming packet
- Send a warning to the network administrator

Figure 11-2   A basic firewall configuration.

- Send a message to the sender of the message that the attempt has failed
- Allow the message to enter the private network

11-5-2-2-1 Types of Firewalls

Based on their functions, firewalls have been broadly classified into two groups [7,9,15]: packet filter and application (proxy).

Packet filter firewalls control the data traffic (the export and import of data) based on datagrams. Datagrams are the basic units of communication in TCP/IP, the protocol of the Internet. A router usually performs packet filtering as data packets pass through the router's interfaces. A router's function is to direct datagrams of information from network to network, or from segment to segment within the organization's network. The filter examines fields in Internet Protocol (IP) packets such as source and destination IP addresses and source and destination ports. By checking these fields, the packet filter can allow or deny passage of packets. Factors that influence the rejection or acceptance of a datagram are based on the network application requested, protocol type, and the source and destination of the datagram. A packet filter firewall can be programmed to accept or reject a datagram based on the host that initiated the datagram. Programmable routers as firewalls can be purchased and have been compared to the Club car-antitheft device. These are sophisticated systems that include hardware, software, and consulting. All incoming connections are recorded, and an unsuccessful try might be a warning sign of an unauthorized attempt.

Packet filter firewalls may not be very efficient since they have to examine each packet individually, and they may be difficult to install. They may provide a false sense of security, and they usually cannot accurately record all of the actions taking place at the firewall. This makes it difficult for network administrators to find out how intruders are trying to break into the private network.

Application (proxy) firewalls are regarded as more secure and flexible and are therefore more expensive than packet filter firewalls. These firewalls are installed in the host computer. A dedicated PC or a workstation may perform this task. An application firewall controls the private network applications, such as e-mail, Telnet, and FTP at the individual or group level by focusing on the type of action and the time period in which the action is taking place. By concentrating on the time period, these firewalls can be very effective because many unauthorized attempts take place at night or after hours. Application firewalls are able to log actions that take place at the firewall. By using these data, network administrators are able to identify potential breaches to security that may be directed to the private network. Application firewalls can also filter viruses, a major security threat in the e-commerce environment. Because application firewalls perform a great deal of work to check for unauthorized activities in a network, they have a relatively slow processing speed. This in turn may bring down the performance of the whole network.

In large organizations, proxy servers are also used in addition to firewalls for protecting the security and integrity of a network. As discussed in Chapter 9, a proxy server is a server that acts as an intermediary between a workstation user and the Internet so that the organization can ensure security, administrative control, and caching services. Proxy servers separate the organization's network from the outside network, and a firewall server protects the organization's network from unauthorized outside access.

11-5-2-2-2 Choosing a Firewall

Firewalls do not provide complete security. Sophisticated hackers and computer criminals are able to threaten any security measure. Major break-ins have recently occurred at NASA, NATO, the Department of Defense, and General Electric. Some hackers use an "IP spoofing" technique, which makes private networks think that the hacker is a legitimate user. IP spoofing is the equivalent of forgery. Filtering software is available from major vendors of networking equipment. This filtering software will not allow access from an outside source to any internal data. Therefore, firewalls should be used with other security measures and policies (discussed later).

To improve the chances of success when choosing a firewall, an e-business should analyze the following points:

1. The e-business should first identify its objectives and the data that must be secured against intruders and computer criminals. A risk analysis should also be performed at this stage to assess the costs and benefits of a firewall.

2. The options and capabilities of the firewall candidates must be identified and analyzed in terms of the e-business needs. For example, if e-mail, Usenet, and FTP are some of the typical applications used by an e-business, then the firewall chosen must support at least these three activities.

3. The organization must decide between the two most commonly used types of firewalls: Packet filter and application (proxy), and then compare and contrast the features of each type against its security needs and goals.

4. The cost of firewalls with their features and capabilities must be identified and analyzed. The cost of a firewall varies significantly. E-business managers should also remember that the most expensive firewall is not necessarily the best. Some e-businesses (depending on their specific needs) may be able to obtain reasonable security by implementing a cheaper packet filter firewall.

5. The balance between security and user friendliness must be considered. Some firewalls place accuracy and security ahead of ease of use and functionality. Others put user friendliness before security, while trying to provide a good entry-level solution. An acceptable design requires trade-offs, and the best

policy is to design a system that best matches the organization's needs and objectives.

6. The vendor's reputation, support staff and maintenance, and update policies are important issues to identify and analyze before making the final decision. Because of the significant increase in demand for firewalls, the number of vendors is steadily increasing. Not all of these vendors offer quality products. The type of user support offered by these vendors is an essential criterion to consider before choosing a firewall.

7. To build a firewall from scratch is a viable option for some organizations. Although this option may be more expensive than choosing a readily available product, the tailor-made features and the flexibility offered by a firewall developed in-house may outweigh its costs. Table 11-7 lists some of the popular firewalls on the market.

11-5-2-3 Intrusion-Detection Systems

While firewalls protect external access, they leave the network unprotected from internal intrusions. An IDS can identify attack signatures, traces, or patterns, generate alarms to alert the network staff and e-commerce site manager, and cause the routers to terminate the connection with the suspicious sources. These systems can also prevent denial-of-service attacks. A denial-of-service attack (described earlier) occurs when an e-commerce site experiences multiple bogus attacks, and the site becomes so overwhelmed that it comes to a halt. The server cannot handle so many requests and displays a denial-of-service message

Table 11-7

Popular Firewalls on the Market

AltaVista Firewall (Digital Equipment Corp.)

Black Hole (Milkyway Networks, Inc.)

BorderWare (Secure Computing Corp.)

CrptoWall (Radguard Ltd.)

CyberGuard Firewall (CyberGuard Corp.)

FireWall-1 (CheckPoint Software Technologies, Inc.)

GFX Internet Firewall System (Global Technology Associates, Inc.)

Interceptor (Technologic, Inc.)

On Guard (On Technology Corp.)

PrivateNet (NEC Technologies, Inc.)

Secured Network Gateway (IBM)

TurnStyle Firewall System (Atlantic Systems Group)

to legitimate e-commerce site users. IDSs provide real-time monitoring of network traffic and implement the "prevent, detect, and react" approach to security. The e-commerce site managers should implement IDS in front of a firewall in every security domain. Although IDSs are necessary for security, their use has disadvantages that should be taken into account. IDSs require significant processing power and can affect the performance of the e-commerce site. They are relatively expensive and can sometimes mistake normal network traffic for a hacker attack and cause unnecessary alarms.

IDS development is in its infancy, and more sophisticated systems are expected in the near future. A number of third-party tools are available for intrusion detection. Table 11-8 lists five popular commercial products on the market.

11-5-3 PHYSICAL SECURITIES

Physical securities primarily control access to computers and networks and include devices that protect computers and peripherals from acts of theft. Physical security is achieved through measures such as those listed in Table 11-9.

Cable shielding is accomplished by braiding layers of the conductors to form a shield. This scheme protects the data from electromagnetic emanations. This is done by either shielding or by using a conduit. Shielding is more difficult with hardware devices than with cables.

Corner bolts and steel bolts are inexpensive methods of securing a microcomputer or workstation to a desktop or counter. These devices are a combination of locks and cables. Steel bolts are used to secure workstations to a heavy-duty locking plate, which is then bonded to an anchor pad that has adhesive on both sides. The pad is then adhered to a desk or counter.

Electronic trackers are secured to the computer at the AC power insert point. If the power cord is disconnected, a coded transmitter sends a message to

Table 11-8
Popular Commercial Intrusion-Detection Systems

Kane Security Analyst (Security Dynamics)
    <http://www.intrusion.com>

Cisco Secure IDS (formerly NetRanger) (Cisco Systems)
    <http://www.ieng.com/univercd/cc/td/doc/pcat/nerg.htm>

Network Flight Recorder (Network Flight Recorder)
    <http://www.nfr.com>

Omniguard Intruder Alert (AXENT Technologies)
    <http://houddini.com/axent/training/html/intruder_alert.html>

RealSecure (Internet Security Systems)
    <http://www.iss.net/securing_e-business/security_products/intrusion_detection/index.php>

Table 11-9

Physical Security Measures

Cable shielding

Corner bolts

Electronic trackers

Identification badges

Proximity release door openers

Room shielding

Steel encasements

Tokens

an alarm, which sounds, and/or a camera, which is activated to record the disturbance.

Identification badges are checked against a list of authorized personnel. Checks must be done on a regular basis so that any change in personnel is noted.

The proximity-release door opener is an effective way to control access to the computer room through the use of a small radio transmitter located in the authorized employees' identification badges. When the authorized person comes within a predetermined distance of the entry door, a radio signal sends a key number to the receiver, which unlocks the door for admittance.

Room shielding is spraying a nonconductive material in the computer room. This material reduces the number of signals transmitted or completely confines the signals to the computer rooms.

Steel encasements are designed to fit over the entire computer. The encasement is made of heavy-gauge welded steel. The encasement is kept locked, and the security administrator or another designated person has control of the key.

A **token** is a transmission device worn around the user's neck. The device activates the computer only when a user wearing a token is seated in front of the screen.

11-5-4 SOFTWARE SECURITIES

Software securities are designed to protect the system from loss of data integrity, unauthorized access, and to provide data security. Software securities are accomplished by one of the following:

- Access codes
- Data encryption
- Passwords

- Terminal resource security
- Electronic transactions securities

11-5-4-1 Access Codes

Access codes are the simplest form of access control, and the most basic security method is the missing-character code. Files and/or programs are listed in the directory incompletely. In order for the user to access the data, he or she must fill in the missing character(s). The challenge is that the authorized user must remember the missing characters.

11-5-4-2 Data Encryption

Data encryption transforms original information called plaintext or cleartext into transformed information, called ciphertext or cipher, which usually has the appearance of random, nonreadable data. The transformed information is called the cryptogram. The rules selected for encryption, known as the encryption algorithm, determine how simple or how complex the transformation process should be.

Simply put, data encryption means to scramble the original data to a form not understandable by the user and send it to its destination. At the receiving point the user will descramble the data to its original form by using a key. There are many different algorithms for encrypting data. Julius Caesar developed one of the oldest encryption techniques. He used a simple substitution algorithm in which each letter in the original message was replaced by the letter three positions further in the alphabet. For example, the word *top* will be transmitted as *wrs*. Figure 11-3 shows a simple example of this encryption technique. Endorsement of the Clipper chip by the Clinton administration sparked business interest in the development of encryption technology. A National Security Agency hardware security device, the Clipper chip would enable the government to decode computer or telephone communications, as they would hold the master key. Apparently, the purpose would be for use in FBI or other governmental investigations.

Encryption is basically the process of encoding and decoding data. It can also be used to provide digital signatures to authenticate sender identities and to verify that the message has not been altered. Encryption techniques use a key (password) to encrypt data. The size of the key varies from 32 bits to 168 bits. Naturally it takes much longer to break a larger key size than a smaller one. There are two main types of encryption:

- Asymmetric (also called public-key)
- Symmetric

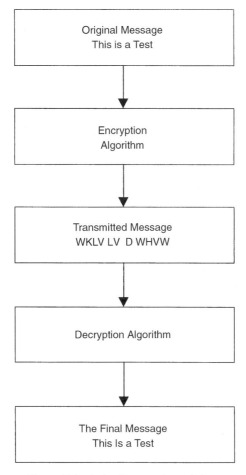

Figure 11-3 A simple encryption technique.

The **asymmetric** encryption technique uses two keys—a public key known to everyone and a private or secret key known only to the recipient of the message. The most successful implementation of public-key encryption is Rivest-Shamir-Adleman (RSA), one of the first public-key algorithms developed in 1977 by Ron Rivest, Adi Shamir, and Len Adleman at the Massachusetts Institute of Technology.

In **symmetric** encryption technique, the same key is used to encrypt and decrypt the message. A popular implementation of symmetric encryption is data encryption standard (DES). This official encryption technique of the U.S. government uses a 56-bit key. It was developed in 1975 and standardized by ANSI in 1981.

As mentioned in Chapter 6, digital signatures are vital to the success of on-line financial transactions [3]. Digital signatures use the RSA encryption algorithm in combination with another cryptographic technique known as message digests. A digest is created when an algorithm called a hash function is used to process the message, generating a numerical value unique to that message. Hash functions also make it computationally infeasible to re-create a message from its digest. These features virtually eliminate the possibility of modifying a message–message digest pair without detection. As explained above, message digests provide the assurance of message integrity. A message digest generated by the sender of the message is encrypted with the sender's unique private key. The message recipient can therefore verify the signature by first calculating his own digest of the received message, then decrypting the original digest with the sender's public key, and then comparing the two. If the two digests (one created by the sender, one by the receiver) are identical, the sender has simultaneously authenticated both the message sender and the message itself.

An alliance between Microsoft and Visa in November 1994 developed secure-transaction software to authenticate buyers and sellers in the Visanet payment system. This included everything from placement of bids to negotiation of deals [3].

Affordable hardware encryption is also being pursued by a number of companies; this is noted for being faster and more secure than software encryption.

A number of competitors (such as Visa and MasterCard) are working together to develop specifications for smart cards. Smart cards (explained in Chapter 6) are a hardware platform that contains miniature math coprocessors. They will be used for encryption of telephones, computers, and interactive TVs. To date, however, they have not been fully field-tested and remain expensive for the majority of consumers.

Cryptographic techniques of private and public keys rather than platform type are expected to be at the heart of the encryption debate. With private key encryption, both sender and receiver use the same key. This implies a one-to-one relationship and a unique set of private keys for each relationship, with each party holding a copy of the private key. Banks currently use DES, which incorporates a private key to conduct financial transactions on private networks. There are limitations because a prior relationship of trust must already have been established. Also, it would be cumbersome to send private keys to all parties with whom a user may want to communicate. Therefore, instantaneous communications or sending communications to more than one person, which both happen on the Internet, would not work with private key encryption.

Public key encryption probably works better for public networks (such as the Internet) where each business would receive a private key and a public key. This implies a one-to-many relationship, with a business holding the only copy of the private key. A business selling on a public network could publish its public keys as it would a telephone number. Customers would then have the capability to send their credit card numbers over the network using the public key. At the receiving end, a business would decrypt the message with its private key.

In addition to encryption and certification, three other areas of consideration are vital for e-commerce: authentication, confirmation, and nonrepudiation. The mere possession of a credit card number does not ensure that the user is legitimate. Two factors are crucial in authentication: what a receiver knows to be accurate and what a sender is providing to them. Passwords and personal information such as mother's maiden name, social security number, date of birth, and so on can be successfully used for authentication. Physical proof (such as fingerprints or retinal scans) works even better. Order confirmation and notice of receipt of goods must be incorporated into the e-commerce framework. Nonrepudiation is also necessary to bind trading partners to a deal [8]. Nonrepudiation is the process by which the sender of information is provided with proof of delivery, and the receiver is assured of the sender's identity. In this case neither party can deny either sending or receiving the information in question. This is essential for a secure e-commerce transaction.

11-5-4-3 Passwords

Passwords are sets of numbers, characters, words, or combinations of these that must be entered into the system for access. Passwords are the most basic access controls, and their composition determines their vulnerability to discovery by unauthorized users. The human element, which plays a major role in the success of password control, is one of the most notable weaknesses of the password security system. For example, the user may simply forget the password or intentionally or unintentionally give the password to an unauthorized user. Table 11-10 provides guidelines for improving the effectiveness of passwords as security measures.

Table 11-10

Guidelines for Improving the Effectiveness of Passwords as Security Measures

Change passwords frequently.

Passwords should be six characters or longer.

Passwords should not be written down.

Passwords should not be common names such as the first or last name of a user.

Passwords should not be increased or decreased sequentially.

Passwords should not follow any pattern.

Before an employee is discharged his or her password must be removed.

11-5-4-4 Terminal Resource Securities

Terminal resource security is a software capability that erases the screen automatically and signs the user off after a predetermined length of inactivity. There are also programs that allow users to access data only during certain times. Any attempts to access the system other than during the predetermined times results in the denial of access.

11-5-5 ELECTRONIC TRANSACTIONS SECURITIES

Electronic transactions security are concerned with the following five key issues:

1. **Confidentiality:** How can we ensure that *only* the sender and the intended recipient can read the message?
2. **Authentication:** How can the recipient know that the data are from the intended originator?
3. **Integrity:** How can the recipient know that the contents of the data have not been changed during the transmission?
4. **Nonrepudiation of origin:** The sender cannot deny having sent the data and the content of that data.
5. **Nonrepudiation of receipt:** The recipient cannot deny having received the data or the content of that data.

In addition to firewalls and encryption techniques that are often used to protect the security of data over the private and public networks, there are other security measures often used for providing comprehensive security over the Internet. These security measures include SSL, secure hypertext transfer protocol digital signatures, and public and private key secure electronic transmission (SET) (introduced in Chapter 6).

11-6 COMPUTER EMERGENCY RESPONSE TEAM

The Defense Advanced Research Projects Agency (DARPA) formed CERT (pronounced SUHRT) in response to a worm attack in November 1988 that halted more than 6,000 computers connected to the Internet. CERT is housed at Carnegie-Mellon University in Pittsburgh where it is part of the Networked Systems Survivability program in the Software Engineering Institute, a federally funded research and development center.

Currently, CERT focuses on security breach and denial-of-service incidents (episodes that happened several times in February 2000), providing alerts and incident-handling and avoidance guidelines. CERT also conducts an ongoing public awareness campaign and engages in research aimed at improving security systems. Network administrators and e-commerce site managers should always review the latest information provided by CERT. This information may assist in protecting vital e-commerce resources. Figure 11-4 shows the initial screen for CERT.

Other sources that provide comprehensive information and guidelines on various e-commerce security issues include the federal Computer Incident Response Capability (FedCIRC) and Computer Incident Advisory Capability (CIAC). FedCirc is the central coordination and analysis facility dealing with computer security issues affecting the civilian agencies and departments of the federal government. Figure 11-5 shows the initial screen for FedCIRC.

CIAC provides on-call technical assistance and information to Department of Energy (DOE) sites faced with computer security incidents. This central incident-handling capability is one component of the all-encompassing service provided to the DOE community. Other services CIAC provides include awareness, training, and education; trend, threat, vulnerability, data collection issues,

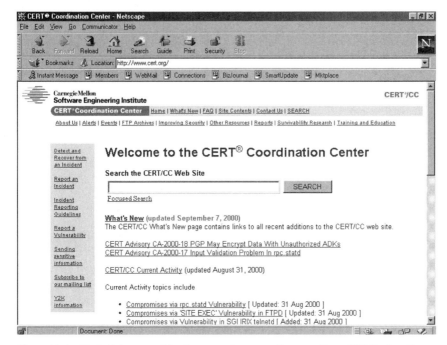

Figure 11-4 The initial screen of the Computer Emergency Response Team (CERT) <http://www.cert.org>.

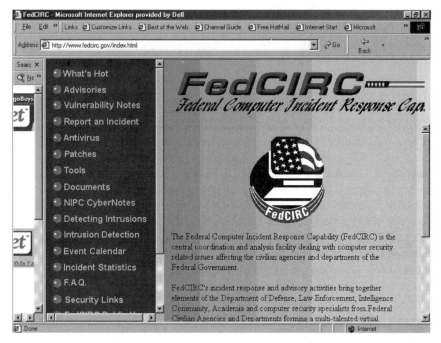

Figure 11-5   The initial screen for the Federal Computer Incident Response Capability (FedCIRC)
<http://www.fedcirc.gov/index.html>.

and analysis; and technology watch. CIAC is an element of the Computer Security Technology Center (CSTC) that supports the Lawrence Livermore National Laboratory [2].

11-7 GUIDELINES FOR A COMPREHENSIVE E-COMMERCE SECURITY SYSTEM

Some aspects of security measures can be improved with moderate expense. Other technical aspects need capital investment in software, hardware, infrastructure, and technical expertise. E-businesses should seriously consider the security threats and issues presented in this chapter, particularly those related to a specific e-business, and integrate them into their security plan. To establish a comprehensive e-commerce security plan, some or all of the following suggestions should be considered [4, 6, 16]:

1. Organize a security committee. The committee should include representatives from user groups (including finance, accounting, marketing, manufacturing, and personnel), top management, hardware groups, software groups, and the legal department. The committee will be responsible for the following:

    A. Setting security policies and procedures. A clear and precise e-commerce security policy plays a significant role in an organization. A lack of such policies and procedures may result in the failure of employees to understand what undesirable activities are and, consequently, the inability of the e-business to prosecute abusers.

    B. Assessing the effect of e-commerce security in the organization periodically.

    C. Distributing passwords and account numbers.

    D. Providing security training for key decision makers and computer users.

    E. Establishing the necessary protection plan for the e-commerce site.

    F. Developing a regular audit procedure for login and system use.

    G. Obtaining employee and top-management support for security policy enforcement.

    H. Evaluating and revising the security policies constantly.

    I. Labeling hardware and software with warning stickers.

    J. Overseeing the security policy enforcement.

    K. Advocating the use of paper shredders for computer waste papers.

    L. Designing an audit trail procedure for both incoming and outgoing data.

    M. Designing a computer operation log to record the log-on and log-off times for different users.

    N. Defining employee duties related to security enforcement.

    O. Documenting and labeling all hardware and software components.

2. Post the organization's security policies in a visible place and/or in front of any entry port (workstation or PC). The signs should state the organization's policies on security.

3. Encourage employees' sensitivity to security problems.

4. Revoke terminated employee's passwords and badges immediately so that a malicious ex-employee cannot be destructive.

5. Keep sensitive data, software, and printouts locked up to reduce the chance of accessing, stealing, or altering the information.

6. Exit from the programs and systems promptly. Log off and turn off the computer. This prohibits unauthorized access to sensitive data.

7. Limit employee access to files to reduce temptation.

8. Limit computer access to authorized personnel only. Curious personnel must be kept away from the system.

9. Consider unlisted telephone numbers. An unlisted number deters hackers and intruders to some degree.

10. Compare the communication log with communication billing periodically. The log should contain all of the outgoing calls with the users' name and call destinations and time in and out. Also, keep a log of calls in and out. Billing discrepancies should be investigated.

11. Be prepared for computer virus attacks by using antivirus utility programs and consider the following:

   A. Boot the computer with a known, write-protected operating system floppy disk.

   B. Install only licensed software purchased from reputable vendors. After installation, store the original copies in a secure off-site location.

   C. Do not use software that arrives with its packaging open.

   D. Do not install software brought to the office from a home computer.

   E. Install only the needed software on each computer.

   F. Whenever downloading or copying a file (from the Web or from other sources), check it first with antivirus software.

12. Observe the following against various computer threats:

   A. Install smoke detectors in the computer rooms.

   B. Keep fire extinguishers in and near computer rooms.

   C. Enforce "No Smoking" policies.

   D. Install alarm systems for fire and smoke.

   E. Maintain a steady temperature in the computer rooms.

   F. Maintain humidity levels between 20 and 80%.

   G. Equip the heating and cooling systems with air filters to protect against dust.

   H. Keep computers away from glass windows and high surfaces, particularly if you are in a high-risk earthquake region.

   I. Secure computer equipment against strong vibrations and make sure that other objects will not fall on them in case of strong vibrations.

13. Observe the following physical security measures:

   A. The simplest way to keep someone from walking out the door with your computer is to bolt it down.

   B. Use RADIS, mirror disks, and UPS in all cases.

   C. Use ID badges and a token in order to screen out unauthorized users.

14. Install firewall and intrusion detection software and consider other electronic transaction security measures discussed in Chapter 6.

These steps should be used as a guideline. Not every organization will need to implement every step; however, some may need to include even more steps to fit their needs.

11-8 PREPARING FOR A DISASTER

The sources of computer and e-commerce threats are numerous, controllable and uncontrollable, and can be done intentionally or unintentionally. In any event, an organization must be prepared to respond to a disaster if it occurs. One of the best security measures is to plan for disaster. The response process, known as the disaster-recovery planning system, can play a major role in putting the organization back on its feet.

A disaster-recovery plan is useful because it gives the organization a place to begin bringing the operation back to normal. It lists the tasks that must be performed and includes a map for recovery. Disaster may strike in one of the following forms:

- Environmental contamination
- Hardware and software failures
- Human errors
- Natural and other disasters (see Table 11-1)
- Power failure
- Sabotage
- Theft

It has been reported that over half of the traditional organizations throughout the world do not have a disaster-recovery plan in place. Many of these organizations would not be able to return to normal operations after a disaster. To guard against disaster, all businesses should take the following steps before disaster strikes:

- Back up all of computer files.
- Periodically review security and fire standards for your computer facilities.
- Periodically review the information released by CERT and other security agencies.
- Make sure the staff is properly trained and that they are aware of the consequences of possible disaster and what actions need to be taken to prevent such disasters.
- Regularly test your disaster-recovery plan with trial data.
- Identify all of the vendors and manufacturers of the software and hardware used in the organization. Record their most recent addresses, phone numbers, and web sites.
- Document all changes done to the initial hardware and software.
- Get a comprehensive insurance policy for your computer and e-commerce facilities.
- Use hot sites—separate computer facilities with all the needed equipment.

- Use cold sites—rooms with raised floors, air conditioning, and humidity control without the computer itself.
- Share ownership of backup facilities.
- Use decentralized computer facilities.
- Arrange a reciprocal agreement with another installation.
- Check and recheck the sprinkler systems, fire extinguishers, and halon gas systems.
- Review the insurance policy to make sure that the coverage is adequate.
- Keep backups in off-site storage, periodically check the backups by testing the recovery procedures, and keep a detailed record of machine-specific information, such as model, serial number, and so forth.
- Keep a copy of the disaster-recovery plan offsite.
- Go through a mock disaster.

11-9 STEPS TO TAKE WHEN DISASTER STRIKES

You have taken all the security measures and you have prepared for a disaster, and then disaster strikes. The following are some important steps that must be taken to return the operation to normal:

1. Contact the insurance company to confirm the agreement regarding the implementation of the recovery plan.
2. Restore the telephone lines and other communication systems.
3. Notify all the effected people, including customers, suppliers, and employees.
4. Implement a help desk for assisting the impacted people.
5. Put together a management crisis team to oversee the recovery plan.
6. Notify the effected people that the recovery is underway.
7. Document all the actions taken for getting back to normal.

11-10 INDUSTRY CONNECTION: McAFEE ASSOCIATES

McAfee Associates
2508 Bowers Avenue
Santa Clara, California 95051
Telephone: (408) 988-3832
Fax: (408) 970-9727
Web site address: **<http://www.mcafee.com>**

McAfee Associates, founded in 1989, is a leading supplier of antivirus software. McAfee uses the Web as a distribution medium, providing downloads of all McAfee products in their full functional forms. In addition to the Web, McAfee products can be purchased through distributors, corporate resellers, mail order, and retailers. In addition to antivirus software, McAfee offers network-management software that includes virus scanning, firewalls, authentication, and encryption capabilities. McAfee also has an online bug-tracking system that immediately notifies product development of the bugs and viruses that customers report and then informs customers as soon as the fixes are developed. The following are some of the products offered by McAfee:

VirusScan offers virus detection and removal features.

NetCrypto transparently encrypts all network sessions using industry-standard encryption algorithms.

PC Medic features a general protection fault (GPF) stopping alternative that saves the user's work. Most data lost due to crashes can be recovered with PC Medic. This product also offers automatic backup and fast restore.

The McAfee.com Clinic in addition to the antivirus service, this product cleans the user hard drive, speeds up the user system, and automatically finds software updates.

ZixMail is a secure document delivery, private e-mail, and message-tracking service that enables a user to send encrypted and digitally signed communications to any e-mail address in the world. This means that only the intended e-mail recipients will be able to open messages that have been sent.

McAfee Firewall software builds a protective barrier around the network and defends it from Internet hazards, such as a hacker trying to steal private information. It filters both incoming and outgoing communications between the network and the outside world.[1]

11-11 SUMMARY

This chapter discussed security issues and measures in the e-commerce environment. Different types of e-commerce threats were identified as natural, intentional, and unintentional. Security measures were discussed in terms of biometric, nonbiometric, physical, software, and electronic transactions. Firewalls, intrusion-detection systems, and data encryption—three popular security measures in the e-commerce environment—were discussed in some detail. CERT and other organizations that provide comprehensive information and guidelines

---

[1]This information was gathered from the company web site and other promotional materials. For detailed information and any update contact the company.

on various e-commerce security issues such as FedCIRC and CIAC were introduced. The chapter presented guidelines for establishing a comprehensive security system, and concluded with guidelines for disaster preparation, including steps to be taken if a disaster strikes. McAfee Associates was the industry connection.

11-12 REVIEW QUESTIONS

1. What is computer and e-commerce security?
2. Why must security issues be taken seriously?
3. What are the important aspects of an e-commerce security system?
4. What is a fault-tolerance e-commerce site? What are some of the techniques and tools used to improve the fault tolerance of an e-commerce site?
5. What are some examples of natural threats to an e-commerce site?
6. What are some examples of other threats to an e-commerce site?
7. What are some examples of intentional threats?
8. What are some examples of unintentional threats? How can an e-commerce site guard against intentional threats?
9. What is a computer virus?
10. How does a computer virus spread?
11. What are some of the sources of computer viruses?
12. How do you guard against a computer virus?
13. What are some of the popular antivirus programs on the market?
14. What is a Trojan horse?
15. What is a computer worm?
16. What are biometric security measures?
17. Compare and contrast biometric and nonbiometric security measures.
18. Why aren't more biometric security measures used to protect data resources? Discuss.
19. What are some examples of physical security measures?
20. What are some examples of software security measures?
21. What is a firewall?
22. What are two important types of firewalls?
23. Generally speaking, which type of firewall is more effective? Discuss.
24. What are some examples of the commercial firewalls on the market?
25. What is a denial-of-access attack? How does it start? How could it be controlled? Discuss.
26. How do you choose a firewall?
27. What are intrusion-detection systems? What are some commercial examples of this software?

28. How does the public and private key scheme work? Discuss.
29. What are some of the services offered by CERT? What are some other examples of organizations that offer security services and precautions? Discuss.
30. What is a disaster-recovery plan?
31. What are the components of a comprehensive disaster-recovery plan?

11-13 PROJECTS AND HANDS-ON EXERCISES

1. Log onto the web site of the McAfee Associates at the following URL:

   <http://www.mcafee.com>

   What are some of the software products offered by this company? What are some of the unique features of these products? What are some of the features of McAfee's firewalls? Who are some of McAfee's competitors?
2. Using quality of service, availability of knowledgeable staff, financial stability, and number of customers (user base) as four criteria for choosing an e-commerce security vendor, compare McAfee Associates, Symantec Corporation, and Check Point Software Technologies. Which vendor receives a higher score? What other criteria should be included in your evaluation? Discuss.
3. Cryptography plays a major role in e-commerce security. By reviewing the materials presented in the following site and other sources, prepare a two-page report on this important security measure. What are some of the shortcomings of this technique? Discuss.

   <http://world.std.com/~franl/crypto.html>

4. You have been asked to put together a security policy for an online gift shop. What will you include in this document? What are the major sources of computer threats for this e-business? How should this e-business guard against insider threats? What are some of the major outsider threats? Prepare a two-page report to be submitted to the CEO, accompanied with your recommendations.
5. How do you protect the security of your own PC? How do you deal with a computer virus? What are the steps that you should follow before you copy a file from a bulletin board? Among the guidelines introduced in section 11-7, which one(s) apply to you as a student? What should you do to protect your password?
6. What should the above-mentioned online gift shop (project #4) do to prepare for a disaster? What should be included in a disaster recovery

plan? Prepare a one-page document that outlines the recommendations that should be included in the disaster recovery plan.

7. By consulting the computer, e-commerce, and management information services (MIS) journals identify two of the effective antivirus software programs on the market. How do these software programs deal with unknown viruses? Discuss.

8. By consulting the computer, e-commerce, and MIS journals, compare and contrast a packet filter and an application (proxy) firewall. What are the major difference between these two classes of firewalls? Why is there such a price difference among these firewalls? Discuss.

9. The chapter listed a number of physical security devices. Visit the computer center of your school or an organization that you are familiar with and see which devices are being used. Why won't physical security alone provide comprehensive security for an e-business? Discuss.

10. The following web sites are used for virus identification:

    <http://www.nipc.gov> (this is the FBI National Infrastructure Protection Center and it has a LINKS page to several other virus and security sites that are GOV or ORG sites.)
    <http://www.avp.ch/avpve> (This is an AVP Virus Encyclopedia.)
    <http://www.symantec.com/avcenter> (This is the Symantec Anti-Virus Research Center.)

    Log on to these web sites and examine their offerings. They provide valuable information.

11. The following site provides comprehensive information and tools for guarding against denial-of-service attacks:

    <http://www.denialinfo.com>

    By reviewing the materials presented in this site and other sources, prepare a one-page document outlining your recommendations regarding dealing with this security threat. Why is it so difficult to completely guard against this security threat? Discuss.

12. The following site provides comprehensive information on extranet and intranet security:

    <http://www.extranet-strategist.com/archive/considerations.phtml>

    By reviewing the materials presented in this site and other sources, prepare a one-page document outlining your recommendations regarding protecting the security and privacy of intranets and extranets.

What are some of the major differences between securing of an intranet or extranet versus a local area network? Discuss.

13. The following sites provide comprehensive information on e-commerce security:

<http://ecommerce.internet.com/outlook/article/0,1467,7761_253601_2,00.html>
<http://www.microsoft.com/technet/ecommerce/ecomsec.asp#b>
<http://www.ecommercetimes.com/news/articles2000/000619-3.shtml>

By examining the materials presented in these sites, prepare a two-page paper regarding major issues in e-commerce security. Why can't security threats be eliminated completely? Discuss.

14. The following site provides valuable information on the vulnerabilities of web-based shopping cart applications:

<http://xforce.iss.net/alerts/advise42.php>

Log onto the site and examine its contents. Why is it important to secure a shopping cart in an e-commerce site? Discuss.

11-14 KEY TERMS

Accuracy, 366
Access codes, 382
Application (proxy) firewall, 377–378
Availability, 366
Cable shielding, 380
Callback modems, 376
CERT, 386–388
Computer security, 366–390
Computer virus, 370–371
Corner bolts, 380
Data encryption, 382–385
Denial-of-access attacks, 373–374
Disaster recovery planning, 391–392
Electronic trackers, 380–381
Fault-tolerance system, 367–368
Fingerprint, 375
Firewalls, 376–379
Hand geometry, 375
Identification badges, 381
Intrusion detection systems
   (IDS), 379–380

Logic bombs, 373
Mirror disks, 368
Palmprint, 375
Passwords, 385
Proximity release door openers, 381
Redundant arrays of independent disks
   (RAID), 368
Retinal scanning, 375
Room shielding, 381
Packet filter firewalls, 377
Secrecy, 366
Signature analysis, 375
Steel encasements, 381
Terminal resource security, 386
Token, 381
Trap doors, 373
Trojan horses, 372–373
Uninterruptible power supply
   (UPS), 367–368
Voice recognition, 375
Worms, 371–372

REFERENCES

[1] <http://ciac.ilnl.gov> Computer Incident Advisory Center. (Date of access: May 2, 2001).

[2] Appleby, Chuck (1995, January 2). "Making Security a Reality for All." *Information Week,* pp. 38–40.

[3] Bidgoli, Hossein, and Reza Azarmsa (1989, October). "Computer Security: New Managerial Concern for 80's and Beyond." *Journal of Systems Management,* pp. 21–27.

[4] Bidgoli, Hossein (2000). "Handbook of Business Data Communications: A Managerial Perspective." Academic Press, Inc., San Diego, CA.

[5] Forbes, Jim (1998, November 1). "Let Your Fingers Do the Log-on." *Network World,* p.12.

[6] Garfield, Monica J. (1997, Winter). "Planning for Internet Security." *Information Systems Management,* pp. 40–46.

[7] Marion, Larry (1995, February 15). "Who's Guarding the Till at the Cyber Mall?" *Datamation,* pp. 38–41.

[8] McCarthy, Vance (1996, May). "Building a Firewall." *Datamation,* pp. 74–76.

[9] Miastkowski, Stan (1998, March). "Virus Killers." *PC WORLD,* pp. 189–204.

[10] Nelson, Matthew, and Dan Briody (1999). "IT Managers Regroup After Melissas Hits." *INFOWORLD,* April 5, V. 21, Issue 14 cover.

[11] Niccolai, James (2000, February 10). IDG News Service. "Web Attacks Could Cost $1 Billion." PC World.com.

[12] Orubeondo, Ana, and Brooks Talley (1999). "Melissas—A New Twist to an Old Trick." *INFOWORLD,* April 5, V. 21, Issue 14, p.30.

[13] Sanders, Steven (1996, January). "Putting a Lock on Corporate Data." *Data Communications,* pp. 78–80.

[14] Seachrist, David, and Helen Holzbaur (1997, June). "Firewall Software for NT and Unix." *Byte,* pp. 130–134.

[15] Thayer, Rodney (1998, March 21). "Network Security: Locking in to Policy." *Security Policy,* p. 77.

Chapter 12

Building a Successful Electronic Commerce Site: A Life Cycle Approach

Learning Objectives

After studying this chapter you should be able to do the following:

- Explain four approaches to building an e-commerce site, including using online auctions, Internet shopping malls, web-hosting services, or building the site from scratch.
- Review the e-commerce development and management life cycle.
- Elaborate on various dimensions of a feasibility study.
- Discuss various implementation issues of an e-commerce site.
- Discuss important factors for choosing a software platform for an e-commerce site.
- Examine important issues for marketing and management of an e-commerce site.

INFORMATION BOX 12-1

E-Commerce in Action

ARNet, an Internet service provider (ISP), expanded its services to include e-commerce-hosting solutions for both small- and medium-sized businesses and now anticipates a growth rate of 100–200% per year.

Aureus, a provider of business process analysis and document management systems, created an online solution that helps companies put their existing document management installations on the Web, and they expect 50% of revenues to come from their new e-commerce solutions by year end.

Calberson, the French shipping company, created a web site that enables customers to track packages. They also developed remote administration, network services, and web hosting to retain their leadership position in the market.

CellNet, one of Australia's leading distributors of mobile phone accessories, linked 3,000 authorized dealers to a reliable supply-chain extranet, providing easy access to real-time product information and enabling prompt responses to customer inquiries.

Controx, a precision cutting-tool manufacturer, gained a technological advantage over its competitors by deploying a full-service business-to-business (B2B) extranet and customer relationship management solution that will yield an estimated 40% increase in sales and reduce service-call volumes by 50%.

Duck Head, an online apparel provider, doubled sales and profit margins with an online store.

eSeeds.com implemented a business-to-consumer (B2C) e-marketplace that gave Web-savvy gardeners immediate access to over 10,000 items from 30 vendors—and they experienced up to a 500% increase in monthly sales.

FirstEnergy deployed end-to-end electronic bill presentation and payment services to over 2.2 million customers, helping cut costs and improve customer service, promoting FirstEnergy's leadership position in the market.

Grupo Beeltah developed a B2C online sales channel that makes age-old Mexican crafts available over the Web, complete with customized catalog descriptions, inventory, back-end functionality, and billing solutions.

By going online, iGo, the nation's largest supplier of batteries and accessories for laptops, cellular phones, and camcorders, increased sales by 140%. They attribute this to customers finding what they need more easily and quickly.

Rediff.com, an India-based online retailer, yielded a 50% increase in sales and expects its traffic and online sales revenue to double within 2 years.

SC Sorensen, a Danish steel manufacturer, created a B2B online ordering facility to increase customer service.

INFORMATION BOX 12-2

E-Commerce in Action: StaplesLink.com at Staples

Staples, a multibillion dollar retailer that pioneered the office supply superstore industry, needed to bring a new purchasing channel to its medium- and large-size business customers. In addition to accommodating the business processes associated with corporate procurement, Staples needed to integrate the terms and conditions of the individual contracts through which it services its medium and large-size business customers. Staples asked IBM to design, develop, and implement its new Web-ordering system called StaplesLink.com. This scalable architecture is integrated with back-end ordering systems.

The online ordering system, based on IBM Net.Commerce PRO (now part of the IBM WebSphere Commerce Suite family), is customized for each contract customer. Items included in the contract are highlighted in the online catalog, and contract-specific prices appear on the online order form. "IBM's B2B e-commerce solution has enabled Staples to bring a new purchasing channel to its medium and large-size business customers," says Anne-Marie Keane, Vice President of B2B electronic commerce for Staples.com. "Needless to say, the web site has also reduced our cost of processing orders."

Because employees purchasing office products must obtain approval from various sources within their companies, StaplesLink.com also incorporates a purchase-authorization process. Approved orders are automatically routed by IBM MQSeries to Staples' back-end order processing and fulfillment systems, running on IBM AS/400 servers. Order status information is periodically fed back to the Net.Commerce system by MQSeries, allowing corporate buyers to see the status of their orders in near real time.

12-1 INTRODUCTION

This chapter discusses various issues for building and managing an e-commerce site. It highlights four popular approaches for building an e-commerce site, including online auctions, Internet shopping malls, web-hosting services, and building the site from scratch. Major phases for the e-commerce development and management life cycle (ECDMLC) are explored. These phases include problem definition and requirement analysis, feasibility study, formation of the task force, analysis, design, simulation prototyping, implementation, postimplementation audit and monitoring, site marketing, and management. The chapter explains various dimensions of a feasibility study for e-commerce site implementation and reviews important criteria for choosing e-commerce software platforms, highlighting Yahoo! as the industry connection. The materials presented in this chapter should provide succinct guidelines for organizations planning to establish an e-commerce presence.

12-2 FOUR APPROACHES TO BUILDING AN E-COMMERCE SITE

When a company decides to establish an e-commerce site and sell goods and services online, one of the following approaches are followed:

- Online auctions
- Internet shopping malls
- Web-hosting services
- Building the site from scratch

As will be discussed throughout this chapter, each approach has certain advantages and disadvantages, depending on the needs of a particular organization or business.

12-2-1 ONLINE AUCTIONS

As discussed in Chapter 3, many different online auction sites can be used to sell diverse groups of products and services. This option is a good choice for selling excessive inventories, memorabilia, or exotic cars. The following are among the popular auction sites:

- ebay.com
- ubid.com
- priceline.com

Figure 12-1 shows the initial screen of uBid.com.

Figure 12-1   The initial screen of uBid.com.

12-2-2 INTERNET SHOPPING MALLS

Internet shopping malls provide tools and capabilities to establish an online storefront. In addition to site-building capabilities, they also provide significant traffic, which can create potential customers for the online store. Popular examples include the following:

- merchandizer.com (This platform includes an interesting demonstration of how the system works.)
- store.yahoo.com (This platform provides all the instructions needed to build an Internet store.)

Figure 12-2 shows the initial screen of Yahoo! Store.

12-2-3 USING WEB-HOSTING SERVICES

With web-hosting services, a company outsources its Web resources. Most ISPs provide these services. Web hosting can provide an organization with an

Figure 12-2   The initial screen of Yahoo! Store.

instant Web environment that won't burden the corporate network with additional traffic. It reduces the need to recruit additional information technology (IT) and web staff, and in most cases lowers overall costs. Choosing which provider among so many competing providers needs careful analysis and evaluation. Cost, reliability, reputation of the provider, size of the customer base, years of experience, knowledgeable staff, technical support, training, news letters, and updates are among the important criteria to be carefully analyzed before choosing a web-hosting provider. The following are some of the large web-hosting providers:

- ANS Communications
- BBN Planet
- Epoch Networks
- InterNex Information Services
- WorldCom
- PSINet
- UUNET Technology

Figure 12-3 shows the initial screen of UUNET Technologies.

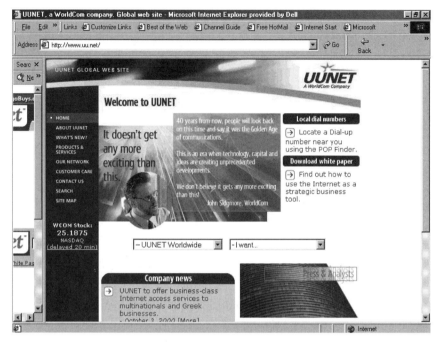

Figure 12-3 The initial screen of UUNET Technologies.

Some of the **advantages** of Web hosting include the following:

- It may be cheaper.
- It may be timelier.
- It may provide flexibility for the organization to concentrate on other projects.

Some of the **disadvantages** of web hosting include:

- Loss of control
- Dependency
- Vulnerability of strategic information

Some of the services offered by a typical web-hosting company include the following:

- Anonymous file transfer protocol (FTP) (discussed in Chapter 9)
- FTP access to your site
- Common gateway interface (CGI) capabilities (discussed in Chapter 9)
- Daily and weekly statistics related to the site performance
- Database access via structured query language (SQL) or open database connectivity (ODBC)

- Mail forwarding for your domain
- Disk space
- Registration of a domain name
- Secure sockets layering (SSL) and other security support (discussed in Chapters 6 and 11)

12-2-4 BUILDING THE SITE FROM SCRATCH

Most medium- and large-sized organizations build their sites from scratch using commercial site-building software. The organization usually follows a classic life cycle approach similar to construction of other information systems projects. I devote the rest of this chapter to this approach.

12-3 E-COMMERCE DEVELOPMENT AND MANAGEMENT LIFE CYCLE: AN OVERVIEW

The e-commerce development and management life cycle (ECDMLC) consists of a series of well-defined steps, including the following:

- Problem definition and requirement analysis
- Feasibility study
- Formation of the task force
- Analysis
- Design
- Simulation prototyping
- Implementation
- Postimplementation audit and monitoring
- Site marketing
- Management

12-4 PROBLEM DEFINITION AND REQUIREMENT ANALYSIS

In this initial phase, the organization sets goals and objectives for the e-commerce site and quantifies the outcome of the project. If the latter is done, the organization can then later measure the success and/or failure of the e-commerce project. In some cases the e-commerce projects are implemented to support and complement the existing operations of a business. In recent years this option has become very popular, especially among retailers, department stores, banks, brokerage firms, and home appliances. Examples include Wal-Mart, K-mart, Toys-R-Us, and Charles Schwab. In these cases, by establishing an online store these businesses complement their traditional business operations by capturing those customers that would not have made any transaction without the online store. In other cases, a brand new online store is created from scratch. Amazon.com is the most popular example of this type of online storefront.

When designing e-commerce sites, businesses must clearly identify strategic goals and objectives and carefully project the site's growth rate; otherwise these sites may become inefficient shortly after they are started. Traffic assessment is important to decide the required size and capacity of the circuit. During the problem definition and requirement analysis phase, the analyst or team of analysts must understand and analyze the current and future needs of the e-commerce site. The following questions must be carefully answered:

- Why is the e-commerce site built?
- What products and services will be offered through the site?
- What is the geographic scope of the system? Does it include international operations? If this is the case, then currency conversions, international trade restrictions, tariffs, language, and different business customs and international business laws must be considered.
- What are the hardware and software requirements of the site? Will it run on the existing infrastructure? Or does it need a new infrastructure?

The problem definition and requirement analysis phase is one of the most crucial phases of the ECDMLC. During this phase the design team tries to define and understand the scope of the site and its requirements. The advantages and disadvantages of the new business venture must be carefully analyzed, and they should also define the competition and other forces that have direct or indirect impact on the proposed e-commerce site. Major products and services that can be successfully sold through the site must be identified, as outlined in Table 12-1. Also, the materials presented in Chapter 3 should be studied to further determine the practicality and the future success of the e-commerce site.

During this phase of the ECDMLC, the following issues must be carefully examined:

- The strategic objectives of the organization
- The overall characteristics of the e-commerce site that can successfully support or achieve these objectives
- Critical success factors and their relationship to the e-commerce site
- Performance evaluation criteria for the proposed e-commerce site. The establishment of evaluation criteria ensures objectivity throughout the entire ECDMLC process.

Also during this phase the business model (discussed in Chapter 2) that the e-commerce site will use should be delineated. How will it make a profit? Once

Table 12-1

Popular Products and Services Purchased Online[a]

Airline tickets and travel
Apparel and footwear
Banking services
Books and music
Computer hardware and software and other electronics
Flowers and gifts
Stock brokerage services

[a]Reproduced from Chapter 2.

again, it should be noted that not all e-businesses are going to be successful. The fall of many e-businesses in 2000 and 2001 is a good indication that the winners are those who follow a sound business model.

12-5 FEASIBILITY STUDY

Feasibility is the measure of how beneficial or practical the development of an e-commerce site will be to an organization, and this study should be continuously performed throughout the ECDMLC. Senior executives are often frustrated by IT investments, including investments in e-commerce projects that are unrelated to the organization's strategic goals, where the payoff is inadequate or immeasurable, by poor relations between users and designers, and by designers' lack of consideration for customers' and users' preferences. A detailed feasibility study that focuses on all of the above categories can help to alleviate some of the frustrations that executive's experience regarding e-commerce investments [1,2].

A feasibility study determines the level of desirability of an e-commerce project, considering several factors. Before starting this phase, the objective of the system and the strategic goals of the organization must be carefully defined. During this phase of the life cycle, the analyst or team of analysts tries to investigate the feasibility of a proposed solution that may enhance the strategic position of the organization. The feasibility study includes four major dimensions:

- Economic
- Technical
- Operational
- Schedule

12-5-1 Economic

Economic feasibility is concerned with the costs and benefits of the e-commerce site. For example, if the gain from the implementation of an e-commerce site is $250,000 and the system would cost $300,000 to implement, implementation of this project is not economically feasible. To conduct an economic feasibility study, the analyst team must identify all the costs and benefits of the proposed system. For mission-critical applications, some organizations implement the project, regardless of the cost. The costs and benefits may be either tangible or intangible. The analyst must also be aware of the opportunity costs associated with the system as well. The real challenge for the analyst team is to portray an accurate assessment of the intangible costs and benefits. The analyst should attempt to estimate and attach a realistic monetary value to the intangible costs and benefits when conducting an economic feasibility study. The development and operating costs of an e-commerce project are tallied and used in an analysis that compares them with the financial benefits the system is expected to provide. Information on the benefits must be obtained before the cost-benefit analysis can be performed.

12-5-1-1 Costs of an E-Commerce Site

Tangible costs of an e-commerce site fall into two basic categories: development costs and operating costs, including the following:

- Carrier services costs
- Computer usage—computer time used for programming, testing, and simulation prototyping
- Cost of circuit (provided by common carriers or installing internally by the organization)
- Hardware costs
- Maintenance cost for monitoring equipment and software
- Operations costs for leased line or dial-up line usage
- Personnel costs—wages and salaries of consultants, systems analysts, network specialists, web managers, e-commerce specialists, programmers, data-entry clerks, computer operators, secretaries, and technicians
- Software costs
- Supply costs
- Training—the cost of training new and current employees who will use or be involved with the e-commerce project

Development costs are itemized and a budget established that includes the above cost categories. Many of the development costs, especially technical expertise (programmers, designers, and managers), are estimated with too much optimism, and this is one of the reasons that many e-commerce projects go over budget.

Operating costs recur throughout the life of the e-commerce project. Many types of operating costs are also determined through the use of estimates, and some operating cost figures can be obtained from vendors and suppliers. It is important to note that some operating costs are fixed and others are variable. Fixed costs occur regularly over time and at relatively fixed rates. Variable costs occur in proportion to usage.

The scope and complexity of an apparently feasible e-commerce project can change after the initial problems and opportunities are fully analyzed or after the system has been designed. Thus, an e-commerce project that is feasible at one point may become infeasible later. Feasibility checkpoints can be integrated into any ECDMLC. Thus, an explicit feasibility analysis phase in any life cycle should be considered to be only an initial feasibility assessment. A project can be canceled or revised at any checkpoint, despite whatever resources have been spent. If the organization does not cancel or modify such a project, it may miss windows of opportunity on more attractive projects later.

12-5-1-2 Benefits of E-Commerce Site

Similar to other information systems, e-commerce projects include both tangible and intangible benefits. **Tangible benefits** are the benefits that can easily be quantified and measured in terms of monthly or annual savings or of increased profit to the organization. For example, if the new e-commerce site enables an organization to carry out normal business operations with fewer employees to do the same amount of work, then it has savings or cost avoidance. For example, the amount of savings could be the salaries of three employees versus five. The e-commerce initiatives at Nestlé presented in Information Box 1-3 is a good example of these kinds of cost avoidance.

Intangible benefits are benefits that are difficult to measure and quantify. If these types of benefits are not at least identified, many e-commerce projects will not be justified. Some examples of intangible benefits include improved employee morale and customer satisfaction. Some of the benefits are in the form of cost avoidance or cost savings. Benefits normally both increase profits and decrease costs. Table 12-2 lists some of the benefits of an e-commerce site.

Additional intangible benefits of an e-commerce site may include the following:

- Improved inventory control
- More efficient use of human resources
- Improved communications
- Improved supply-chain efficiency
- Better realization of value chain

Table 12-2

Selected Possible Advantages of E-Commerce[a]

Doing business around the globe 7 days a week, 24 hours a day

Gaining additional knowledge about potential customers

Improved customer involvement

Improved customer service

Improved relationships with suppliers

Improved relationships with the financial community

Increased flexibility and ease of shopping

Increased number of customers

Increased return on capital and investment since no inventory is needed

Personalized service

Product customization

---

[a]Reproduced from Chapter 2.

An example will make the assessment of intangible benefits more clear. Say one of the intangible benefits of a new e-commerce project is improved customer service. How do you assign a monetary value to this? One way to look at this issue is by quantification of the intangible benefit. Customer service could lead to maintaining the present total sales and possibly increasing the total sales by a certain percentage in a business organization. If improved customer service means 10% growth, it means 10% of $15,000,000 for ABC Company. This means a $1,500,000 (15,000,000 × .10 = 1,500,000) increase in sales. If ABC Company has a 20% net margin, this translates to an additional $300,000 (.20 × 1,500,000 = 300,000) of net profit just by improving customer service.

12-5-1-3 Evaluation of Cost Effectiveness of an E-Commerce Site

The tools used to evaluate the cost effectiveness of an e-commerce site are partially based on the time value of money concept—a dollar today is worth more than a dollar one year from now. If the e-commerce site does not produce sufficient return or savings, then the money may be better spent elsewhere; however, a proper cost-benefit analysis can show that money spent on an e-commerce site (assuming a sound business model is followed) is a good investment relative to other investment possibilities. The time value of money concept are fundamental to cost-benefit analysis. The most popular analysis methods are payback, net present value (NPV), return-on-investment (ROI), and internal rate of return (IRR).

Once the cost-benefit analysis is completed and the supporting documentation tools utilized, details are compiled into a final form known as the cost-benefit analysis (CBA) report. The CBA report should sell the targeted opportunity to top management. Although there is no set format for the CBA Report, there are key sections that must be included in the presentation package. These sections are executive summary, introduction, scope and purpose, methodology of the study, recommendations, justifications, implementation plans, summary, and appendix items. The final section of the CBA report includes all the supporting documentation, such as charts, tables, graphs, and diagrams. Some examples of useful supporting documentation include organizational charts, workflow plans, floor plan layouts, statistical information, project sequence diagrams, and timelines or milestone charts. Once this section has been completed, the CBA report is ready for management review. Consider the following before you submit the CBA report to management [5]:

- Avoid using jargons.
- Be concise, objective, and factual.
- Don't overanalyze; know your target group background.
- Ensure all quantifiable aspects are included.
- Limit assumptions, be conservative rather than liberal in estimations.
- Set reasonable goals.
- Submit a schedule for the completion of the project.

12-5-2 Technical

Technical feasibility is concerned with the technical aspects of the e-commerce site. One way to investigate the technical feasibility would be to study the state of technology. A proposed solution may not be technically feasible for implementation; the technology simply may not exist for the implementation of the new system. For example, a full-featured voice-activated e-commerce site at this point is not technically feasible. However, given today's computer technology, this is not a major problem, and for many proposed solutions the technical support is available. Lack of technical feasibility may also stem from an organizational deficiency. A specific e-commerce project may not be feasible because the organization lacks the expertise, time, or personnel required to implement the new project. This is referred to as a lack of organizational readiness. If this is the case, the organization must first take the appropriate steps to prepare its employees and then consider the e-commerce project. Extensive training and ongoing education of key personnel may achieve this.

12-5-3 Operational

Operational feasibility is the measure of how well the proposed e-commerce project will work in the organization and how internal and external customers will feel about the proposed system. The major question is, Is the project worth implementing?

12-5-4 SCHEDULE

Finally, a feasibility study may be concerned with the schedule factor. Let's say an e-commerce project is feasible economically, technically, and operationally; however, it will not be ready within the time frame needed by an organization. For example, an organization may critically need mobile e-commerce to respond to a disaster that has paralyzed the existing network. However, if the new system cannot be delivered in time, the drain on the organization's resources created by the loss of customers may force the organization out of business. If this is the case, you may say the proposed e-commerce project is not feasible from the time-factor viewpoint. The issue of overtime and going over budget is a common problem in the information systems field. The designer(s) of e-commerce sites can minimize this issue by employing appropriate computer-assisted network engineering (CANE) tools and project management tools and techniques. Two commonly used project management and control tools are Gantt chart and PERT/CPM networks.

12-6 FORMATION OF THE TASK FORCE

As mentioned in Chapter 4, for the continued success of the e-commerce project and to provide a "buy-in" environment, different users must provide input about the system's design and implementation. Users' views must be highly regarded and nobody should feel left out. This issue has considerable significance, particularly *if* the e-commerce site will be used by more than one user group. Generally speaking, an e-commerce system has two groups of users: internal and external. **Internal users** are employees within the organization that will use or interact with the system on a regular basis. They are the best source of information simply because they use the system regularly and could provide important input regarding its strengths and weaknesses. **External users** are not the employees of the organization; they include customers, contractors, suppliers, and other business partners who use the system. In the case of e-commerce projects, customers play an important role. The e-commerce site must be easy to access, informative, and have answers to the all-important, typical customer questions. The task force should include representatives from the following areas:

- User groups
- Top management
- Hardware groups

- Software groups
- Legal department
- Graphics or art department

Including the representative from top management is very important. In a nontechnical fashion, the advantages of the e-commerce site should be explained to this group, including how the system will make the organization more competitive. The task force should work to precisely define the user's and customer's needs.

Using a task force for designing an e-commerce site is similar to joint application design (JAD) used by many system analysts. JAD is a joint venture between users, top management, e-commerce specialists, and data-processing professionals. It centers on a structured workshop (called a JAD session) where these users and e-commerce professionals come together to design an e-commerce site. It involves a detailed agenda, visual aids, a leader who moderates the session, and a scribe who records the agreed upon specifications. It culminates in a final document containing definitions for data elements, workflows, screens, reports, and general network specifications. A significant advantage of using JAD is that different functional areas of corporations have different agendas when it comes to creating an e-commerce site. Using JAD, an organization can be assured that all executives representing various departments are together in group interviews. This will help to avoid collecting narrow and one-dimensional information requirements [9].

12-7 ANALYSIS

The fourth step in the ECDMLC is the analysis phase. In this phase, the analyst or a team of analysts specifically defines the problem and generates alternatives for solving it. A variety of tools may be utilized during this phase. These may include the following:

- Interview
- Questionnaire
- Observation
- Statistical sampling
- Work measurement
- Form investigation and control
- Flow chart
- Data flow diagram (DFD)

The following are some of the issues and considerations that must be carefully analyzed:

- Make traffic analyses during the regular and peak periods.
- Circuit and configuration alternatives must be examined.
- Initiate capacity planning.
- Determine average circuit traffic versus peak circuit traffic. It is certainly beneficial to design an e-commerce site that handles peak traffic.

The output of this phase will be a clear problem definition, one or several alternatives, and some initial documentation relating to the operation of the e-commerce site.

12-8 DESIGN

As mentioned earlier, one of the major considerations for designing an e-commerce site is to define the geographical area to be covered by the system. To improve the e-commerce site efficiency and its security system, designers usually segment the network to a series of physical networks. During the design phase the team of analysts should also define a series of evaluation criteria. The following may be included among the evaluation criteria for an e-commerce site:

- High fault tolerance
- Very high mean time between failure (MTBF)
- Low mean time to repair (MTTR)
- Fast response time and an excellent security system

Fault tolerance is the combination of hardware and software technologies and procedures that improve the reliability of an e-commerce site. **MTBF** is a measure of the average time a given component is predicted to operate before it fails. **MTTR** is the average time it takes to repair a failed component. **Response time** is the time required for a user to receive a reply to a request. This is the elapsed time between the user's last keystroke or click of the mouse until the user sees the first character of the response. In the e-commerce environment, this is crucial. If it takes too long to download a page, the customer will leave and he or she may not ever return. The **security system** (discussed in Chapter 11) is a combination of hardware, software, and personnel that collectively protects the e-commerce resources from unauthorized access.

E-commerce site design is complex, and the e-commerce and network specialists may have to employ CANE tools. These tools facilitate the translation of technical solutions into physical network models. As a result, more often network and e-commerce professionals rely on network design and analysis tools to transform logical business models into physical models that address the interoperability functions of these complex network solutions. Network design and analysis tools are used throughout the e-commerce development life cycle, particularly during the design, simulation, and implementation phases. There are

Table 12-3

Network Design Tools

Caliper (Network Tools)

CANE (ImageNet, Inc.)

NetFormx (ImageNet, Inc.)

NetSuite Advanced Professional Design (NetSuite Development)

NetViz (Quyen Systems, Inc.)

Visio (Visio Corporation)

several of these tools available on the market with a varying price range. Table 12-3 lists some of these tools.

CANE tools usually provide a graphical user interface, pull-down menus, and toolbars to facilitate navigation throughout the software. They use mostly object-oriented applications that allow drag-and-drop of objects to speed up network model construction [3]. CANE tools offer significant advantages for designing complex network and e-commerce projects. Some of the advantages of CANE tools are summarized in Table 12-4 [6,8].

Table 12-4

Advantages of Computer-Assisted Network Engineering Tools

They increase the productivity of a network analyst by automatically discovering existing network components.

They increase the quality of network, analysis, and design efforts by reducing input and design errors.

Various diagramming and network-modeling tools facilitate the documentation process.

A network device library provides the necessary information to improve the quality of the design and documentation.

Network analysis and simulation tools ensure the interoperability and accuracy of the network design.

The IP Planner and Rapid Auto Discovery tools increase the network analyst's productivity by saving time in reentering data or making changes to the network.

The itemized shopping list or bill of material reduces the probability of omission errors and serves as an input to the request for proposal process (discussed in Section 12-10-1) in the procurement phase.

The object-oriented drag and drop capabilities speed up production of the network models.

Context-sensitive online help features allow the analyst to discover new capabilities.

Some of the disadvantages of CANE tools include high cost and extensive training needed to become proficient in using the advanced features.

The output produced by the team would be a document similar to a blueprint for implementation. This blueprint will include specifications for networking requirements and general network specifications for the e-commerce site.

12-9 SIMULATION PROTOTYPING

The prototyping methodology has been used for many years in the physical sciences. It is easier and cheaper to build a prototype of a system first than to build the entire system. By building and testing small models or prototypes, the problems and the solutions become more understandable. Building, using, and modifying a prototype enables the designers to better understand the problems, information related to the problems, alternative solutions, and perhaps to choose the best solution for a given situation. It is extremely important to include the users of the system and top management in the construction phase of the prototype because problems may arise that only the user and top management will be able to resolve. The construction phase increases the knowledge learned about the problem(s) that the system would resolve. Users and analysts will learn about the decision-making process of a given situation during the construction phase.

In the case of e-commerce projects, simulation prototyping allows systems analysts and e-commerce specialists to quickly and easily analyze and predict the performance of the system before its final implementation. The team of analysts first creates a model of the proposed system and tests the design for possible bottlenecks, problems, error rates, and the overall performance. Simulation modeling is an important technique for designing, monitoring, and assisting the implementation of an e-commerce site, and it should be used before the final implementation of the system.

As the e-commerce site expands in scope and diversity, the planning task for e-commerce managers becomes extensive. Some of the network-monitoring tools in wide use today collect traffic data, discover and display network topologies, and display alarms. They allow the e-commerce analyst to perform "what-if" scenarios. Using "what-if" scenarios, the analyst can determine network utilization; response times can determine if the routing capacity is sufficient. For example, questions such as the following can be answered during the simulation prototyping:

- What would be the impact on the throughput if a certain component were replaced with another component?
- In which part of the network will a bottleneck be created if traffic increases by 12%?

Simulation modeling allows new e-commerce sites or proposed changes to an existing site to be quickly evaluated before committing to a course of action. During simulation analysis, the computer outlines in detail the implications and consequences of a proposed network or change to an existing network. A typical simulation tool can answer the following questions:

- Link and node utilization, message delays, and congestion points in a network
- The performance of the current network topology based on historical or projected traffic loads
- Questions about the performance of a proposed network or new applications with historical network loads and projected loads
- E-commerce specialists can quickly predict network performance to avoid costly mistakes.

With historical network loads, managers have an important network technology-learning tool. Through establishing a network model and experimenting with alternatives, network analysts learn about networking technologies, especially the interactions between network components and applications. With projected loads it is easier to see whether the current network can handle expected traffic growth or how much time is needed before the network needs upgrading. One of the main advantages of simulation prototyping is reducing risk in design and implementation of an e-commerce site. The analyst can see the results and the outcomes of certain design features before committing a substantial capital investment. In addition, following every simulation run, network designers and e-commerce analysts are able to obtain individual performance reports on every component in the e-commerce site model, such as nodes, links, applications, and messages. Table 12-5 lists three popular network simulation tools.

Table 12-5

Popular Network Simulation Tools

COMENET III (CACI International, Inc.)

NetMaker XA (Make Systems)

OPNET (MIL 3)

12-10 IMPLEMENTATION

During this phase, configuration and procurement of the e-commerce site are completed, and the solution is transferred from paper to action. A variety of tasks will take place while the implementation phase is underway. These may include the following:

- Acquisition of new hardware
- Acquisition of new software
- Hiring new employees
- Training new and current employees
- Physical planning and layout design
- Coding
- Testing
- Security design
- Disaster-recovery specifications

12-10-1 REQUEST FOR PROPOSAL

An RFP is a written document with detailed specifications requesting bids for equipment, supplies, or services from vendors. RFPs assure that uniform and comparable documents will be received. A form for communicating business requirements from the customer to vendor, an RFP is usually prepared during the implementation phase of the ECDMLC. Proposals go into great detail in functional, technical, and business requirements of the proposed e-commerce system, making it a lengthy process lasting between 6 to 12 months. With the use of software programs, the Internet, and other online technologies, the cycle time can be reduced, productivity and quality improved, and processing cost reduced.

The main advantage of an RFP is that all vendors are fairly evaluated. Their replies are comparable because all vendors receive the same information and requirements. Furthermore, all vendors are given the same reply deadline, which avoids some vendors having more time to prepare their offers than the others.

One of the major disadvantages of an RFP is the lengthy process to write and evaluate the proposals. Technical staff has to spend many hours either writing the initial proposal or replying to the prospective vendors. An estimated time frame is approximately 6 to 12 months from beginning to end. With the rapid changes in e-commerce requirements and networking technologies, this lengthy time frame makes RFPs less desirable. Many companies cannot wait a year for a vendor decision, thus RFPs are only recommended for large, long-term e-commerce projects.

RFPs are needed to narrow a long list of prospective vendors to three or four. This process allows time for the best candidates to present their offers without wasting the vendors' or customers' time. As mentioned earlier, this activity takes place during the implementation phase after top management has approved the e-commerce site proposal requesting new hardware or software. Once that is approved, researching possible technical alternatives is necessary to focus on required hardware and software identified during the design phase. The complexity of the system-development process requires that many decisions are made prior to implementation of the system. An RFP provides comprehensive information for the vendor to supply a bid; it also gives the vendor an opportunity to decide whether or not to pursue the project. Before submitting an RFP to the prospective vendor, the organization must decide whether to submit one RFP to all vendors or one RFP for hardware, one for software, and one for services. Usually multivendors are cheaper. However, the maintenance of different components from different vendors becomes a more challenging task.

12-10-2 ACQUISITION OF NEW SOFTWARE

Choosing software for the e-commerce site is an involved and multifaceted task that needs careful analysis and considerations. As Table 12-6 shows, several

Table 12-6

Popular E-Commerce Site-Building Products

Bigstep.com (Bigstep.com Corp.)

FreeMerchant (freemerchant.com, a division of Network Commerce Inc.)

Cat@log Builder (The Vision Factory Inc.)

Electronic Commerce Suite (iCat Corp.)

ezMerchant (Binary Tree Software)

IBM Net.Commerce (IBM Corp.)

Intershop Online (Intershop Communications)

Lotus Domino.Merchant (Lotus Development Corp.)

Merchant Builder (The Internet Factory Inc.)

MerchantTrax (ICOMS)

Virtual Spin Internet Store (Virtual Spin LLC)

Microsoft Bcentral (bcentral.com)

Ecargo.com (ecargo.com)

Table 12-7

Important Features of E-Commerce Site-Building Tools

Back-end functionality (This includes all the activities conducted in the background by the e-commerce site, such as inventory management and order processing.)

Catalog services (ability to create online catalogs with pictures and product descriptions)

Cost (initial, maintenance, and upgrade costs)

Credit authorization (ability to authorize customer's credit online.)

Customer service features (ability to personalize the e-commerce site based on a registered customer's preferences, such as querying shipping orders)

Customizable features

Database support (Compatibility with the format of the existing customer and product databases and legacy systems in use)

Ease of use and administration

Marketing support (for banner advertising and other Web advertising discussed in Chapter 7)

Payment options and links to other online merchants and compatibility with popular electronic payment systems (discussed in Chapter 6).

Product pictures (This is similar to catalog capabilities and should be able to include the picture and description of a product or service.)

Product and service searches

Programmability (allowing modifications and changes to customize the e-commerce site to meet the specific needs and requirements of a specific organization)

Reporting features, including order, customer, and statistical reports

Scalability (to grow horizontally and vertically with the organization: how many products and how much traffic can it handle now and in the future?)

Shopping cart capabilities

Site-building templates

System requirements

Source: [7]

alternatives are available. These products differ in terms of functionality, ease of use, price, platform supported, and scalability, and it is important to understand the advantages and disadvantages of each with respect to the strategic goals and objectives of a given organization. Table 12-7 lists important criteria that must be carefully examined before choosing one of these software platforms.

Bigstep.com and **freemerchant.com** are two popular tools that provide step-by-step instructions for building e-commerce sites. Figure 12-4 shows the initial screen of FreeMerchant.com. Figure 12-5 shows the initial screen of Bigstep.com.

Figure 12-4   The initial screen of FreeMerchant.com.

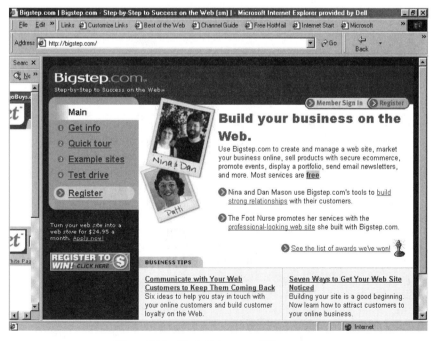

Figure 12-5   The initial screen of Bigstep.com.

12-11 POSTIMPLEMENTATION AUDIT AND MONITORING

During this phase the team of analysts attempts to verify the suitability of the e-commerce site after the implementation. The team tries to collect data and talk with the users, customers, and other people affected by the new e-commerce site to make sure that the system is doing what it was designed to do. If the objectives of the e-commerce site have not been met, then the analysts must take corrective actions. Providing online help, internal search engines, and aggressive marketing campaigns should encourage new customers to use the site. The site managers should constantly collect information from current users and try to improve site functionality based on these suggestions.

12-12 SITE MARKETING

Designing an e-commerce site even with full functionality and elegance does not guarantee its success. The site should be aggressively marketed. A combination of traditional and web marketing must be used to promote the site. A combination of tools and techniques (introduced in Chapter 7) and the guidelines outlined in Table 12-8 should be utilized.

12-13 MANAGEMENT

Once the e-commerce site is in place, site management begins. The management of an e-commerce site, as with any other information system, includes planning, staffing, organizing, directing, and controlling. In the planning phase, the e-commerce site manager's role includes predicting and preventing e-commerce site problems. A detailed master plan must highlight the goals and objectives of the e-commerce site for the next 3 to 5 years and the current and projected resources for the e-commerce projects.

E-commerce site management entails much more than just making sure the cables that connect various devices are intact and functioning properly; it means managing everything connected to the e-commerce site, such as servers, desktops, application programs, host computers, user groups, the Web, and many other resources.

Managing the site means ensuring efficient and reliable operation. E-commerce sites have become large and increasingly complex. Most large e-commerce sites are going global, and they need to maintain both domestic and

Table 12-8

Methods for Promoting the E-Commerce Site

Register the site under all popular search engines, directories, and web portals.

Market the site to existing customers; they will be the first to appreciate the added convenience of online business.

Join online discussion groups about the products and services and promote the site to people already interested in the company's offerings.

Exchange URL links with other web sites that offer companion goods or services. Many web sites provide free links to other sites as a service to their visitors.

Participate in free banner ad exchanges. Some services allow banners ad to be freely exchanged with comparable sites. The organization agrees to carry banner advertising in exchange for other sites carrying the organization's banner ads.

Use e-mail lists to send out notices or newsletters regarding the products and the online store.

Offer giveaways, contests, games, quizzes, and coupons.

Use message boards and special interest malls.

Use online classified advertisements.

Use splash screens.

Add the e-commerce site URL to all company letterheads, brochures, and business cards.

Offer a discount marketing effort for all people who buy the company products and services from the site.

Publish articles about the new e-commerce site and partner with other companies with a similar customer base.

Do a press release.

Use traditional media (TV, radio, magazines, and so forth).

international networks in order to stay competitive. These large e-commerce sites do not come cheap. Success requires a proper integration of people, policies, procedures, and technologies. With the current state of technological development, the e-commerce site manager's duties have expanded to include integrating voice, video, and data management as well as Internet, intranet, and extranet resources for conducting business nationally and internationally. By taking inventory of the hardware, software, human resources, and company policies and procedures, the e-commerce site manager can decide which aspect(s) of e-commerce site management he or she is capable of managing internally and which aspect(s) should be outsourced. The e-commerce site manager should solve sites problems reactively rather than proactively [4].

12-14 INDUSTRY CONNECTION: YAHOO!, INC.

> Yahoo! Inc.
> 3420 Central Expressway
> Santa Clara, CA 95051
> Phone: (408) 731-3300
> Fax: (408) 731-3301
> Web site address: <http://www.Yahoo.com>

Jerry Yang and Dave Filo founded Yahoo! in April 1994. Yahoo! began as a search engine for finding information on the Web. It was incorporated in 1995 and now provides a variety of products and services on the Web. What began as a hobby for two Stanford electrical engineering Ph.D. candidates turned into a comprehensive Internet company. Yahoo! offers Yahoo! Store, which is a site-building tool that allows you to build a fully functional and pleasant-looking storefront in a very short period. The only requirement for using this site-building tool is an ISP and a browser. With Yahoo! Store, making changes to the site is easy, and the excellent reporting tools tell the user where each visitor came from, what pages they visited, and what they placed in their shopping carts. However, this tool is more suitable for small to medium-sized storefronts, and existing database files must be converted to ASCII format before importing. Some of the other products and services offered by Yahoo! are summarized below:

Yahoo! Travel is an online service where you can check flight times, dates, and price, and book airline tickets, car rental, or hotel rooms.

Yahoo! Classifieds list jobs, cars, real estate, and so forth. In the editorial section you have the Daily What's New, Weekly Picks, What's Cool, and others. The Today's News includes classified ads, comics, current event coverage, finance and stock quotes, lottery results, TV listings, and more. In the reference there are city maps, yellow pages, white pages, and so forth. You can also get free service for the Yahoo! Pager, which notifies you when your friends are online so you can send them instant messages. A customized free service allows you to personalize such information as news, stock quotes, and Yahoo! Mail and to subscribe to the monthly Yahoo! Internet *Life Magazine.* In addition, World Yahoo links to other countries, such as Germany, Italy, Japan, and others. If you need information on the large cities in the United States, you enter the U.S. zip code for Yahoo! Get Local to receive information on a given city.

Other services include local weather, sports scores, maps, classifieds, message boards, chat, movie listings, and web sites. You can get connected with your own free e-mail address to use from home, at work, or from a hotel while traveling. Yahoo! works with several companies to provide these various products and services. WorldCom, Microsoft, Amazon.com, and Visa International are some of the current Yahoo! partners. Other popular services include Yahoo! Shopping, Arts and Humanities, Business and Economy, Education, Entertainment, Government, Health, News and Media, Recreation and Sports, Science, and much more. For more information on any of these categories, just click on the desired option.[1]

12-15 SUMMARY

This chapter discussed various issues and technologies for building and managing a successful e-commerce site. It highlighted four popular approaches for building an e-commerce site including online auctions, Internet shopping malls, web-hosting services, and building the site from scratch. Major phases of the ECDMLC were explored. These phases included problem definition and requirement analysis, feasibility study, formation of the task force, analysis, design, simulation prototyping, implementation, postimplementation audit and monitoring, site marketing, and management. The chapter explained various dimensions of a feasibility study for e-commerce site implementation, reviewed important criteria for e-commerce software platforms and RFP. The chapter concluded with a series of important guidelines for promoting an e-commerce site, highlighting Yahoo! Corporation as the industry connection. This chapter should provide a road map for organizations planning to establish an e-commerce presence.

12-16 REVIEW QUESTIONS

1. What are four approaches for building an e-commerce site?
2. What are some of the advantages of using online auctions? Of Internet shopping malls? Of web-hosting services?
3. What are the phases included in the ECDMLC?
4. What are some of the activities that must be performed during the requirement analysis phase of ECDMLC? What questions must be answered?
5. What are two types of e-commerce projects? Why is the problem definition phase of ECDMLC so important? Discuss.
6. What are the objectives of the feasibility study phase of ECDMLC?
7. What are the four major dimensions of a feasibility study?

---

[1]This information was gathered from the company web site and other promotional materials. For detailed information and any update, contact the company.

8. What are some of the intangible benefits of an e-commerce project? What are some of the tangible costs? How do you quantify the intangible costs and benefits?

9. What are some of the tangible costs and benefits of an e-commerce project?

10. What are the differences between operating and development costs of an e-commerce project?

11. What are some of the tools and techniques for the evaluation of cost-effectiveness of an e-commerce project?

12. What issues must be considered before the e-commerce specialist submits the cost-benefit analysis report?

13. What issues must be considered during the technical feasibility phase of an e-commerce project? During the schedule feasibility? During the operational feasibility?

14. What are some of advantages of a task force for designing an e-commerce site? Who should participate in the task force? Why is it important to include a representative from top management in the task force? Discuss.

15. What activities must be performed during the analysis phase of ECDMLC? What are some of the tools used by the e-commerce analyst during the analysis phase? Discuss.

16. What activities must be performed during the design phase of ECDMLC? What are some examples of evaluation criteria for developing an e-commerce site?

17. What are CANE tools? Why are they used? What are some examples of commercial CANE tools on the market?

18. What are some of the capabilities of CANE tools? What are their disadvantages? Discuss.

19. What are the advantages of simulation prototyping? What tasks can be monitored using network simulation tools?

20. What are project management tools? Why are they used? What activities or functions can be managed using a project management tool?

21. What is a request for proposal (RFP)? Why is it prepared? During which phase of the ECDMLC is an RFP prepared? Discuss.

22. In your opinion, should an organization prepare one RFP for hardware, software, and e-commerce services and submit it to a prospective vendor, or should it submit separate proposals for hardware, software, and services to different vendors? What are the advantages and disadvantages of each approach? Discuss.

23. What criteria must be considered before choosing a software platform for an e-commerce site?

24. What activities must take place during the postimplementation audit and monitoring phase of the ECDMLC?
25. What is e-commerce site management? What activities should an e-commerce site manager perform?
26. What are the responsibilities of an e-commerce site manager?
27. What are some of the guidelines for promoting an e-commerce site?

12-17 PROJECTS AND HANDS-ON EXERCISES

1. Log onto the web site of the Yahoo! Inc. at the following URL:

   <http://www.Yahoo.com>

   What e-commerce products and services are offered by this company? What is the e-commerce strategy of Yahoo!? Why has Yahoo! been so successful in the e-commerce world? Discuss.

2. BackWeb provides Push software for e-business solutions that solve the problem of timely, accurate, critical information delivery across corporate networks and the Internet. By examining the materials presented in this chapter and other sources, prepare a one-page report identifying the applications of push technology in e-commerce operations. In addition to web marketing, do you see any other applications of this technology in the e-commerce environment? Discuss.

   <http://www.backweb.com>

3. The List™ is the buyer's guide to Internet Service Providers—those companies that provide access to the Internet. By examining the materials presented in this site and other sources, identify 10 major criteria for choosing an ISP for business use.

   <http://thelist.internet.com>

4. The following site is an example of a regional Internet mall in south Florida:

   <http://www.sf-mall.com>

   Log onto the site and examine its offerings. What types of marketing services are offered through a mall such as this?

5. The following site is an example of a specialty Internet mall, Golf Mall:

   <http://www.thegolfmall.com>

   Log onto the site and examine its offerings. What types of marketing services are offered through a mall such as this?

6. The following site is an example of general-purpose Internet mall, Choice Mall:

<http://mall.choicemall.com>

Log onto the site and examine its offerings. What types of marketing services are offered through a mall such as this?

7. The following sites provide e-commerce solutions, issues and services:

<http://www.ilux.com/index.html>
<http://www.webmasterbase.com>
<http://sitepoint.com>
<http://www.ecommercetimes.com/news/viewpoint2000/view-000512-1.shtml>
<http://www.fabulousweb.com/e6.htm>

By examining the materials presented in these sites and other sources, identify 10 services and solutions offered by these sites. What are some of the differences among these competing sites? Discuss.

8. Direct Hit ranks sites based on the number of hits received. In which phase of e-commerce site design might such a service be useful?

<www.directhit.com>

9. Companies pay to be placed higher in GoTo's listings. In which phase of e-commerce site design might such a service be useful?

<www.goto.com>

10. The following sites allow you to register your domain name:

<http://register.com>
<http://namesecure.com>
<http://domainname.com>
<http://greatspot.cc>

In which phase of e-commerce site design might such a service be useful?

11. The following site allows you to register for shorter and simpler names for easier access:

<http://web.realnames.com>

What is the advantage of this type of registration?

12. The following sites provide comprehensive information on Web hosting services:

<http://www.networkcomputing.com/801/801cn2.html>
<http://www.webjump.com>
<http://www.affinity.net>

By examining the materials presented in these sites and other sources, prepare a two-page report outlining major Web housing companies, their services and the advantages of using such e-commerce services.

13. The following site provides comprehensive information on how to introduce e-commerce to your organization:

<http://www.ecomcity.com/budget.html>

By examining the material presented in this site and other sources, identify 6 recommendations to a prospective company for introducing e-commerce to its employees.

14. The following site provides comprehensive information on choosing an e-commerce suite:

<http://users.aol.com/aleong1631/ecommercesuite.html>

By examining the materials presented in this site and other sources, identify 10 criteria for choosing an e-commerce suite in order of priority.

15. The following site provides comprehensive information on international e-commerce:

<http://www.networkcomputing.com/1023/1023f2.html>

By examining the materials presented in this site and other sources, identify five key differences in designing e-commerce for global operations versus an e-commerce with domestic coverage.

12-18 KEY TERMS

REFERENCES

[1] Bensaou, M., and M. Earl (1998, September-October). "The Right Mind-Set for Managing Information Technology." *Harvard Business Review,* v. 76, no. 5, p. 119.

[2] Bidgoli, Hossein (2000). "Handbook of Business Data Communications: A Managerial Perspective." Academic Press, Inc., San Diego, CA.

[3] Borck, James R. (1997, October 13). "Networking product reviews." *InfoWorld,* p. 72.

[4] Duffy, Jim (1998, August 31). "Cisco to Make Web Management Splash." *Network World,* pp. 1–2.

[5] Dymtrenko, A. (1997, January). "Cost-benefit analysis." *Records Management Quarterly,* v. 31, no. 1, pp. 16–20.

[6] Harbaugh, Logan (1997, August 4). "Build the perfect LAN—products from network tools, ImageNet, and NetSuite help take the pain out of designing networks." *Information Week,* pp. 60–68.

[7] Leong, Anthony (1998). "Choosing an E-Commerce Suite." <http://users.aol.com/aleong1631/ecommercesuite.html>.

[8] Passmore, David (1998, April). "Modeling the Network." *Business Communications Review,* pp. 20–22.

[9] Wood, Jane, and Denise Silver (1989). "Joint Application Design." John Wiley and Sons, New York.

Part IV

Appendix and Glossary

Appendix A

Basic Web Literacy and Instructions for Creating Web Pages

Learning Objectives

After studying this appendix you should be able to do the following:

- Define hypertext markup language (HTML).
- Review important commands and instructions in the Web environment.
- Develop, modify, and publish simple web pages.
- Define Java, JavaScript, JavaBeans, VbScript, Dynamic HTML, and ActiveX.

A-1 INTRODUCTION

This appendix provides a general overview of Web development and simple hypertext markup language (HTML) syntax. After defining HTML, I then review important commands and tips in the Web environment. The process of creating an HTML document is reviewed, including step-by-step instructions for creating a simple web page using Netscape Composer. This example covers the Web development process as well as how to create links, modify an existing web page, and publish a web page on the Web. Microsoft FrontPage, a sophisticated authoring tool, is described, as well as the criteria for designing a sound web site. I conclude with definitions of some of the popular web programming languages and tools, including Java, JavaScript, JavaBeans, VBScript, dynamic HTML, and ActiveX. This presentation provides basic knowledge regarding simple web page development and the process of editing and modifying an existing web page. For more advanced discussion, consult the references.

A-2 WEB PRESENCE: AN OVERVIEW

The objective of this appendix is not to provide in-depth web development instructions; rather, providing a general introduction to Web development should prove useful when working in a hands-on session creating or modifying an existing page.

A web page or a home page is the starting point for an online store. Careful considerations must be given to this important aspect of a successful e-commerce program. Ease of use, appearance, and the type of information provided by the page play an important role in the overall success of e-commerce operations. Table A-1 lists important characteristics of a sound web page.

Table A-1
Important Characteristics of a Sound Web Page

Readability: It should not to be too crowded.

Soothing: Choice of color should be consistent throughout the site.

Easy to navigate: The right information should be easily accessible.

Right size: It should not be too big or too short.

Downloading speed: It should not take too much time to download (especially the first page).
  Moderate use of graphics: Graphics should be used only if they convey a message, because they significantly increase the file size.

Moderate use of multimedia: Too much multimedia materials put a heavy overhead on the page.

Recency of the page: The site should be updated frequently.

Availability of contact information: A site should include easy-to-find contact information, including telephone, e-mail, and fax numbers.

Display in different browsers: The page should display the same information in different browsers.

Figure A-1   The initial screen of the Home Depot.

Figure A-2   The initial screen of Toyota.

Figure A-3 The initial screen of Sears.

Figure A-4 The initial screen of CDnow.

If you decide to develop a web page, visit other web pages in the same or a similar business as yours. These pages will provide you with some initial ideas. The following are examples of four web pages from four different segments of the market. You have seen many other pages throughout this book. Take a few seconds to review these pages and analyze the message they are sending to their customers. Figure A-1 illustrates the initial screen of the Home Depot; Figure A-2 illustrates the initial screen of Toyota; Figure A-3 illustrates the initial screen of Sears.com; and Figure A-4 illustrates the initial screen of CDnow.

A-3 WHAT IS HYPERTEXT MARKUP LANGUAGE?

HTML is the authoring language used to create documents on the Web. HTML defines the structure and layout of a Web document by using a variety of tags and attributes. HTML codes are not case sensitive. Table A-2 lists several important HTML tags.

Table A-2

Important Hypertext Markup Tags[a]

<H1> Bidgoli web site </H1>
Displays the text as a size 1 heading.

<CENTER><H1> Bidgoli Web Site </H1></CENTER>
Centers the text as size 1 on the page.

<H1 ALIGN=CENTER>Bidgoli</H1>
Centers the text as size 1 on the page.

<A HREF="http://www.amazon.com">Amazon</A>
The URL must be in a pair of quotations. The text between the beginning link tag and the ending link tag becomes the underlined text on the web page.

<IMG SRC="mypicture.gif">
An online image ="mypicture.gif" is inserted. GIF and JPEG are two accepted formats for images on the Web. JPEG files have jpg extension and GIF files have gif extension.

<HR> enters a horizontal rule.

<P> starts a new paragraph.

<UL> and </UL> are used for unordered list.

<OL> and </OL> are used for ordered list.

<A HREF=mailto:hbidgoli@csubak.edu><I>Hossein Bidgoli</I></A>
This will open the default e-mail on your system. In this particular case, it will send an e-mail to the author.

---

[a]HREF, hypertext reference; GIF, graphics interchange format; JPEG, joint photographic experts group (also called JPG)

The usual structure for an HTML document is as follows:

<HTML>
<HEAD>
(You enter here the description of the page)
</HEAD>
<BODY>

And ends with:

</BODY>
</HTML>

All the information you'd like to include in your web page fits in between the **<BODY>** and **</BODY>** tags.

A-4 IMPORTANT COMMANDS AND TIPS IN THE WEB ENVIRONMENT

The following commands and tips make navigating the Web more manageable:

1. To view a web page (open it in Netscape Communicator), click on **File, Open Page,** and then enter the address of a page. Click on the **Open** again. You can also click on the **Choose File** option to choose among the available files.

2. To view the source document in Netscape Communicator do the following:
- Click on **View** on the menu bar.
- Click on **Page Source.**

To close it, click the **X** on the upper right corner.

In the Edit mode you can copy a section of the source document by click and drag (highlighting) and then using **CTRL+C.**

3. Notepad or WordPad from Microsoft Accessories or any other word processing program can be used to create an HTML file. However, when you save your work, you must give the file an **.htm** extension.

4. **Ctrl+Home**   To move to the beginning of a document or site
5. **Ctrl+End**   To move to the end of a document or site
6. **Ctrl+C**   To copy the highlighted text
7. **Ctrl+V**   To paste
8. **To register a web page with a directory such as Yahoo!, do the following:**
   1. Go to the end of the Yahoo! page.
   2. Click on How to Suggest a Site.
   3. Follow the step-by-step instructions.

Other directories and search engines have something like this.

9. The error message: **Unable to Locate Server** is caused by the following:

a. A wrong URL has been entered.

b. The server is down.

10. **MANAGING BOOKMARKS:** Click on Communicator then click on **Bookmarks.** The **Edit Bookmarks** option allows you to edit a bookmark.

11. **THE EDIT COMMAND IMPORTANT OPTIONS:**

The **Find in Page** and **Find Again** options under the **Edit** menu can be very helpful especially in long documents.

The **Edit, References** option allows you to change the default **Home** to your own desired page when you start Netscape. This page can be your starting e-commerce site.

12. **SEARCHING THE WEB:** Each search engine uses its own version of a program known as a **spider** to automatically search the Web periodically, finding new pages and adding them to its database. Therefore, it is a good idea to use multiple search engines to make sure that all the relevant information has been located.

13. **SAVING AN IMAGE FROM THE WEB**

1. Right-click on the image.

2. Click on the **Save As** option.

3. Specify a drive.

Remember to give the proper credit to the site.

A-5 CREATING HYPERTEXT MARKUP LANGUAGE DOCUMENTS

To create an HTML document you either write HTML codes directly in an editor such as Microsoft Notepad or you use one of the authoring tools, such as the following:

- Adobe PageMill
- Macromedia Backstage Designer
- Macromedia Dreamweaver
- Microsoft FrontPage
- Netscape Navigator Gold
- Netscape Composer
- SoftQuad HotMetal Pro

Most popular applications software, such as Microsoft Office, Corel, and Lotus, allow you to create HTML documents from within the application. You create your document as usual, except you save it by choosing the **web page** option or the HTML option. To save this paragraph in HTML format in Microsoft Word, do the following:

1. Create the paragraph first (if it has not been created yet).
2. Click on **File.**
3. Click on **Save As.**
4. In the **File name** text box enter a name.
5. Click the down arrow icon in the **Save as type** text box and choose **Web Page,** as shown in following screen.

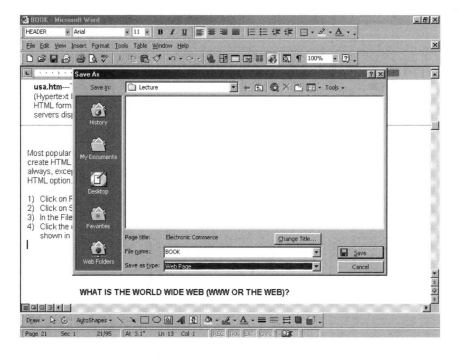

6. Click the **Save** icon.

If you view the source code of this document using a browser such as Netscape Navigator or Microsoft Internet Explorer, you will see that all the HTML tags have been entered.

A-6 AN EXAMPLE OF A WEB PAGE USING NETSCAPE COMPOSER

In the following pages I explain the step-by-step process of creating a web page using Netscape Composer. Although this web page is not designed for an online store, it shows you the basics of a web page design. The experience learned in this process should be applicable to other web page-development processes. The end result should be similar to the following screen.

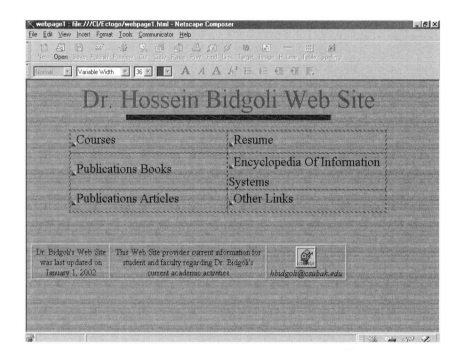

Before you start this assignment, you must have the following files in your default drive:

bkgrnd2, bullet, and email (gif files)

Naturally, you can replace these files with any gif file of your choice. There is clip art available free of charge on the Web. You can create your own gif file by taking a picture using a digital camera or by scanning an existing picture and saving it in gif format. We copied these files from the following two sites:

<http://www.barrysclipart.com>
<http://www.nzwwa.com/mirror/clipart>

To copy an image from the Web (assuming the image is not copyrighted), right-click on the image and then click on the **Save ImageAs** option or **Save Picture As,** and then specify a drive and a directory. You can change the name of the image while you are copying it if you so desire. However, if the image is copyrighted, you must have a written permission from the copyright holder.

The following four files, **courses, books, articles,** and **resume,** are HTML files. You can create these files in Microsoft Word or any other word processor and then save them in HTML format, as explained in section A-5. Under Other Links, you may include a link or links of your choice. In this example I leave it empty.

The **encyclopedia** is the URL of the *Encyclopedia of Information Systems* for which the author serves as editor-in-chief: <http://www.apnet.com/infosys>

1. Start Netscape Communicator.
2. Click on **File, New, Blank Page,** this puts you into Netscape Composer.
3. Click on **Format, Page Colors and Properties.**
4. Click on **Colors and Background** tab.
5. Click on **Choose File.**
6. Change to the directory that includes all your graphic files and double-click on **bkgrnd2.**
7. Click on **OK.**

At this point your desired background is tiled.

8. Click the upper-left corner of the page (if needed) and click the **Table** button (the second tool from the right on the composition toolbar).
9. Enter the parameters as they appear in the following figure:

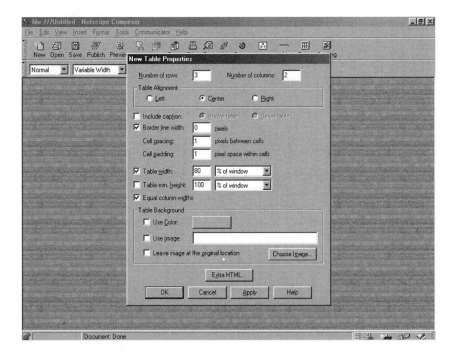

10. Click on **OK.** At this point your screen should be similar to the following figure.

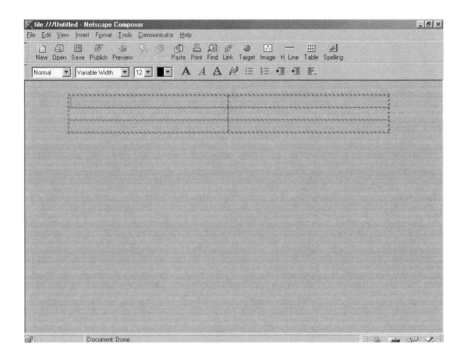

11. Click below the table and press the **Enter key twice.**
12. Click the **Table** button and enter the parameters specified in the following figure.

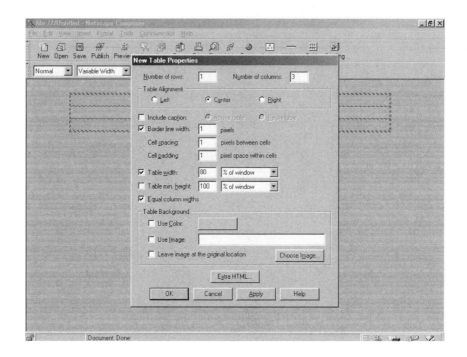

13. Click on **OK.**
14. Right-click inside the first cell in the second table from the left and then click the **Table Properties** in the pop-up menu.
15. Click the **Cell** tab and enter the parameters as they appear in the following figure and click on **OK.**

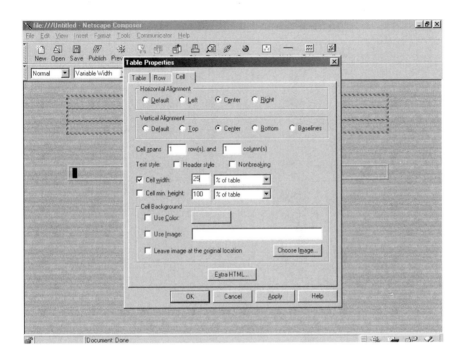

16. Right-click inside the second cell in the lower table, click **Table Properties,** and enter **50** for the cell width and everything else similar to the above figure, and then click on **OK.**

17. Right-click inside the third cell in the lower table, click **Table Properties,** and enter **25** for the cell width and everything else similar to the above figure, and then click on **OK.** At this point your screen should be similar to the following figure.

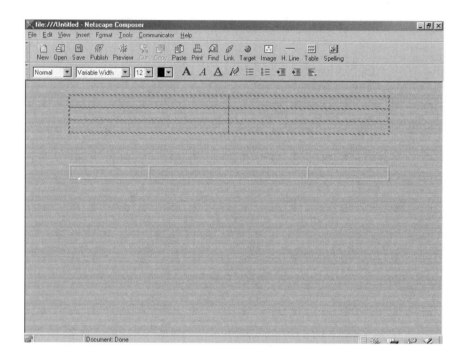

18. Click the top-left cell on the top table and then click the **Image** button. (The fourth button from the right on the composition toolbar.)
19. Click on the **Choose File** option. In your default drive double-click **bullet.**
20. Click the third alignment button from the left, enter **12** in the **Top and bottom** text box in the **Space around image** area, and click on **OK.** At this point your screen should be similar to the following figure.

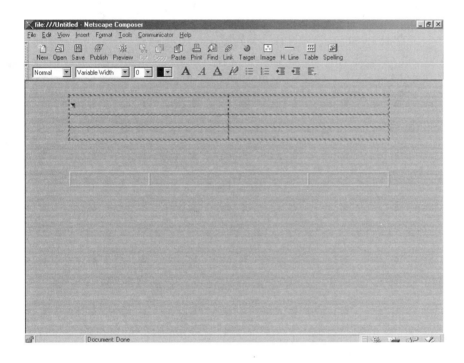

21. Right-click the **bullet** and then click on **Copy** from the pull-down menu. Right-click on the other five cells in the top table (one-by-one) and then click on **Paste.** At this point your screen should be similar to the following figure.

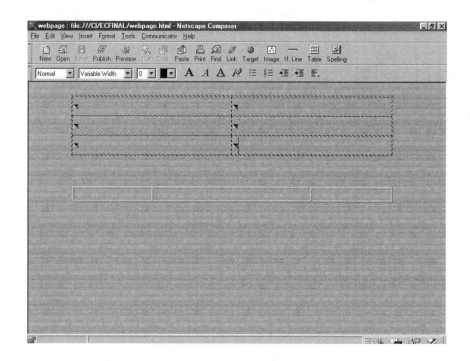

22. Point to the upper left corner of the screen and press the **Enter key once.** Press the **Up arrow once** and type **Dr. Hossein Bidgoli Web Site.**

23. Select the text that you just entered (using click and drag), right-click it and click the **Character Properties** option.

24. Click the rectangle in front of **Use Color** option, click row 3, column 2 (red color) enter **36** for the **Font Size,** click Paragraph tab, click **Center,** and then click on **OK.**

25. Next to each bullet enter the text shown in the following screen.

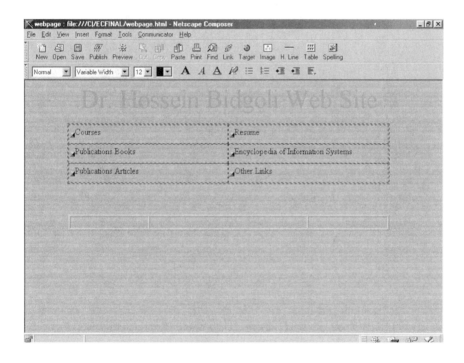

26. Enter the information in the first two cells in the lower table as shown in the following screen.

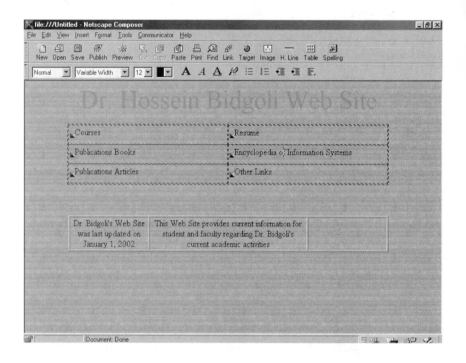

27. Move the mouse pointer to the third cell in the lower table. Click the **Image** button on the Composition toolbar.
28. Click the **Choose File** option.
29. Choose the correct directory and double-click the **email** image.
30. Click on **OK.** At this point your screen should be similar to the following figure.

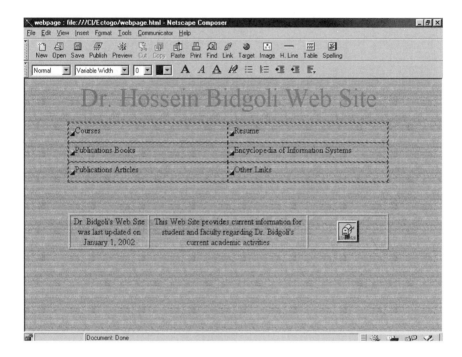

31. Press **Shift+Enter** keys in the third cell in the lower table. Type **hbidgoli@csubak.edu**

32. Select the e-mail address text that you just entered and click on the **italic (Ctrl+I)** button on the Formatting toolbar. At this point your screen should be similar to the following.

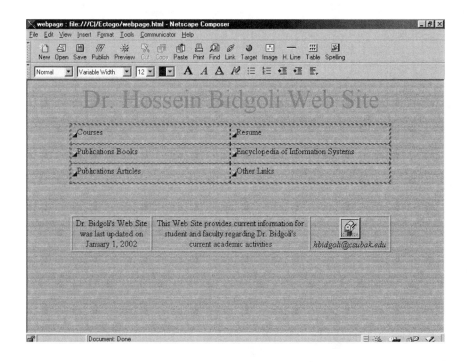

33. Select all the text in the upper table and change the font to **18.** Click on the Spelling button on the toolbar and check for any spelling errors. At this point your screen should be similar to the following screen.

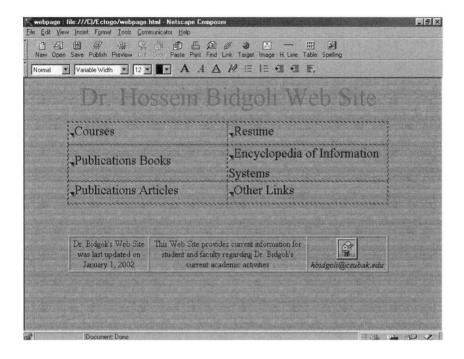

A-7 CREATING LINKS

34. Select **Courses,** right-click the selected text, and then click **Create Link Using Selected** on the pop-up menu. At this point your screen should be similar to the following.

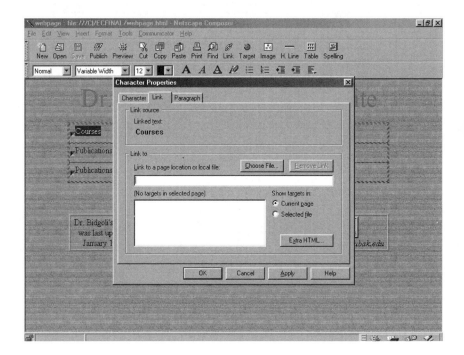

35. Enter the URL of the desired site into **Link to a page location or local file.** Please remember that the file you are linking to must be in HTML format. To finalize this click on **OK.**
36. Repeat steps 34–35 for the other five cells in the top table.
37. Right-click the e-mail image, click the **Create Link Using Selected,** and then enter **mailto:hbidgoli@csubak.edu** in the **Link to a page location or local file** text box and then click on **OK.**

A-8 DRAGGING AND DROPPING IMAGES

You can go to the following web site and right-click a rule and drag and drop it into your web site.

<http://home.netscape.com/browsers/createsites/rules.html>

We copied the first rule and dropped it under Dr. Bidgoli's name. At this point your screen should be similar to the following.

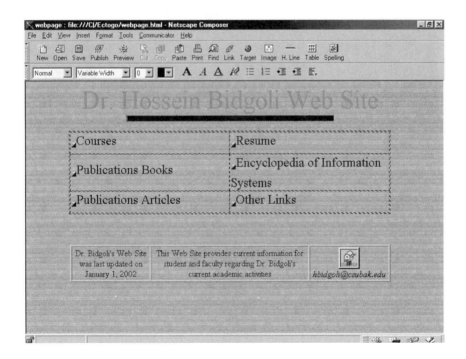

A-9 SETTING IMAGE PROPERTIES

After entering an image you can right-click it and then change its properties. As seen in the following screen, you can change the height, width, and spacing.

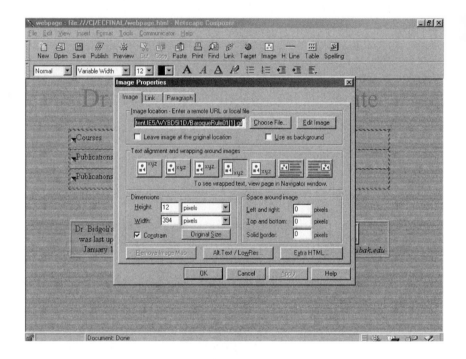

The alignment can be changed through the Paragraph tab (as seen in the following screen). For example left, center, or right.

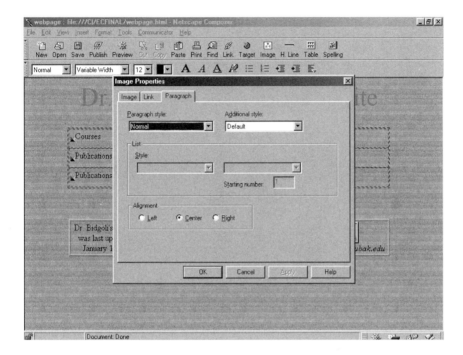

A-10 PUBLISHING A WEB PAGE

Publishing a web page means transferring the local file to a web server. As long as you have access to a web server, you will be able to publish your web page. Just about all ISPs, such as MSN and AOL, provide their customers with server access to publish their pages. As soon as your page is on a web server, the entire cyberspace world can see your web site. Netscape Composer provides a simple method to publish your work. This is how it is done.

1. While you are in Composer, click the **Publish** button (the fourth button from the left on the Composition toolbar). You will see a screen similar to the following.

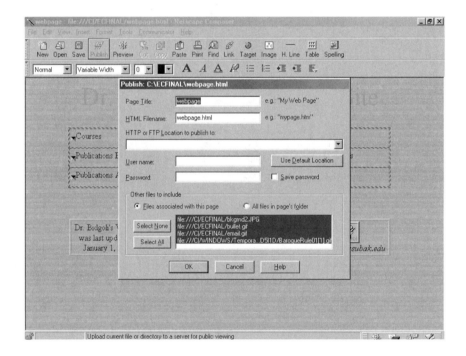

2. Enter the user name, password, and then enter the address of the web server.
3. Click the **OK** button, click on **Continue,** and click on **OK.**
4. All your files including the graphics will be transferred to the web server. Now, you or anybody else will be able to access your page by its URL from any place in the cyberworld!

After your web page is on a web server, you can register it through many of the search engines such as Yahoo! or AltaVista. Then your web site can be searched similar to any other web sites.

A-11 EDITING AN EXISTING WEB PAGE IN NETSCAPE COMPOSER

After creating your web page using Composer, its contents, elements, and properties can be modified. To modify the page, follow these steps:

1. Using **File, Open Page,** open your page in Composer.
2. Right-click the element that you would like to modify. For example, in the following figure we right-clicked the Courses. You can choose any of the options from the pop-up menu.
3. After modifications, save the web page under its current name.

You can also use the drag-and-drop technique to add more features to your web page or to delete some of the existing features.

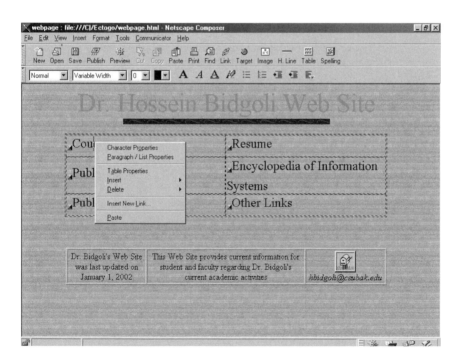

A-12 EDITING AN EXISTING WEB PAGE IN AN HYPERTEXT MARKUP LANGUAGE EDITOR

The page that we just created is saved under "webpage.html" in the default drive. Let's say you would like to change **Bidgoli** to **Johnson.** This is one way to do it:

1. Start Notepad from the Windows Accessories.
2. Click on **File, Open.** In the File name text box type the name of the HTML file (your Web Page). In our case it is webpage.html.

Click on **Open.** You will see the HTML listing of the web page as displayed in Table A-3.

Change the name and any other modifications and save it again. Go back to Netscape and open your web page. The change is already reflected.

Table A-3

Hypertext Markup Language Listing of webpage.html

```
<HTML>
<HEAD>
  <META HTTP-EQUIV="Content-Type" CONTENT="text/html; charset=iso-8859-1">
  <META NAME="Author" CONTENT="Hossein Bidgoli">
  <META NAME="GENERATOR" CONTENT="Mozilla/4.05 [en] (Win95; I) [Netscape]">
  <TITLE>webpage</TITLE>
</HEAD>
<BODY BACKGROUND="bkgrnd2.JPG">

<CENTER><FONT COLOR="#FF0000"><FONT SIZE=+4>Dr. Hossein Bidgoli Web
  Site</FONT></FONT></CENTER>

<CENTER><IMG SRC="../WINDOWS/Temporary Internet
  Files/Content.IE5/WYBD5I1D/BaroqueRule01[1].gif" HEIGHT=12 WIDTH=394></CENTER>
 
<CENTER><TABLE BORDER=0 COLS=2 WIDTH="80%" >
<TR>
<TD><IMG SRC="bullet.gif" VSPACE=12 HEIGHT=9 WIDTH=9
  ALIGN=CENTER>Courses</TD>

<TD><IMG SRC="bullet.gif" VSPACE=12 HEIGHT=9 WIDTH=9
  ALIGN=CENTER>Resume</TD>
```

(continues)

Table A-3 *(continued)*

```
</TR>
<TR>
<TD><IMG SRC="bullet.gif" VSPACE=12 HEIGHT=9 WIDTH=9
   ALIGN=CENTER>Publications
Books</TD>
<TD><IMG SRC="bullet.gif" VSPACE=12 HEIGHT=9 WIDTH=9
   ALIGN=CENTER>Encyclopedia
of Information Systems</TD>
</TR>
<TR>
<TD><IMG SRC="bullet.gif" VSPACE=12 HEIGHT=9 WIDTH=9
   ALIGN=CENTER>Publications
Articles</TD>
<TD><IMG SRC="bullet.gif" VSPACE=12 HEIGHT=9 WIDTH=9 ALIGN=CENTER>Other
Links</TD>
</TR>
</TABLE></CENTER>
 
<BR> 
<BR> 
<CENTER><TABLE BORDER COLS=3 WIDTH="80%" >
<TR>
<TD ALIGN=CENTER VALIGN=CENTER WIDTH="25%">Dr. Bidgoli's Web Site was last
updated on January 1, 2002.</TD>
<TD ALIGN=CENTER VALIGN=CENTER WIDTH="50%">This Web Site provides current
information for student and faculty regarding Dr. Bidgoli's current academic
activities.</TD>
<TD ALIGN=CENTER VALIGN=CENTER WIDTH="25%"><IMG SRC="email.gif"
   HEIGHT=40 WIDTH=40><BR>
<I>hbidgoli@csubak.edu</I></TD>
</TR>
</TABLE></CENTER>
 
</BODY>
</HTML>
```

A-13 MICROSOFT FRONTPAGE: AN OVERVIEW

A more sophisticated tool for developing a web page is Microsoft FrontPage. The FrontPage environment is similar to a word-processing environment. You can create HTML documents with different levels of complexity and import HTML files from other sources. You will still have the capability to integrate Office documents such as an Excel worksheet into your web page. FrontPage also

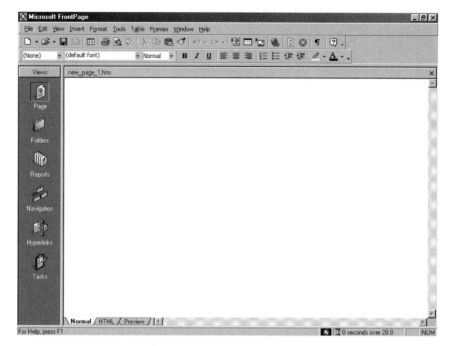

Figure A-5   The Initial Screen of Microsoft FrontPage.

offers extensive online help and a Wizard that assists in developing web pages. Figure A-5 shows the initial screen of FrontPage 2000. As an exercise, try to design the web page that we developed earlier in FrontPage.

A-14 WHAT IS JAVA?

Traditionally, applications have run on personal computers utilizing complex operating systems that require lots of memory and local storage. However, many tasks do not require high-powered PCs. This is where Java computing comes in. Developed by Sun Microsystems in 1995, Java is a user-friendly language that allows written software applications to run on many platforms. It was derived from C++, a popular object-oriented programming language. Java is sometimes called the Internet programming language. Software developers who write programs in other programming languages have to write a different version of each program for different operating systems. Not so with Java.

Java is an applications development platform that replaces PCs with simple network computers equipped with small memory and often no hard drive. Java applications normally reside on a server and are delivered to the client as needed, centralizing data storage on servers and easing client–computer administration. Java downloads nuggets of application code, known as applets, from server to client on demand, regardless of computer platform. Java accomplishes this by running on top of other platforms and by using generic codes, called bytecodes, that are not specific to any physical machine or platform. Bytecodes are instructions written for the Java Virtual Machine. Programs written in the Java language can run anywhere a Java Virtual Machine is present, regardless of the underlying operating system.

Java applets are different from ordinary applications in that they reside on centralized servers. Applets are delivered over the network to the user on request. The dancing cartoon character, a voice clip that starts giving you vocal instructions as soon as you click on it, and bouncing balls are all examples of applets developed using Java. Many of the impressive animation and sound elements of today's web sites would be impossible without Java.

At the beginning of the Internet development era, Internet designers and web masters started moving printed documents to the Web. Naturally these documents were not dynamic. These were plain text or graphics migrated from papers to the Web. Java changed all this in a very short period.

So how does Java accomplish this multiplatform status? The programs written in Java can be understood by a universal platform, called the Java platform. This platform resides atop a computer's regular platform. This universal platform is an extra layer of software that has been accepted as a standard by the majority of the major players of the computer industry. The Java platform translates Java instructions into instructions that the platform underneath can understand. This is the major difference between Java and all the other languages. There is no compiler here.

There are several reasons for Java's success. Cost of ownership is a major reason for the transition from traditional PC client machines to network computers. The total cost of owning a networked Windows-based PC exceeds the total cost of owning a networked computer utilizing Java. All network and application management in Java computing is accomplished at the server rather than at each individual desktop. Providing software updates and upgrades, configuration assistance, technical troubleshooting, and user support is easier in a Java environment. Another reason for Java's success is its simplification of the creation and deployment of applications. Applications created in Java can be run on any computing platform, thus saving the costs associated with developing software for multiple platforms. Also, because the applications are stored on centralized servers, there is no longer a need to have people insert disks or ship CDs to update a user's software. A third reason for Java's success is that it is based on the same protocol as the World Wide Web (TCP/IP). Java is widely accepted and has attracted attention for its ability to tap the full potential of the Internet. As more internal networks are deployed using TCP/IP, Java usage will increase. Java is extensively used in intranets and extranets development.

A-15 WHAT IS JAVASCRIPT?

JavaScript, another programming tool for the Web, was first initiated at Netscape Corporation. A JavaScript is a stored set of instructions included as part of a standard HTML document. JavaScript statements are contained in an HTML document within the **<script>** and **</script>** tags. Generally speaking, Java Script is easier to learn and use than Java; however, it lacks some of the portability of Java and the speed of bytecode. JavaScript is very useful for small applications that run on the web client or server. Since Java applets run on almost any platform (e.g., Windows, Unix, Mac OS, etc.) without requiring recompilation, it is generally regarded as the most commonly used programming tool for developing Web applications.

A-16 WHAT ARE JAVABEANS?

JavaBeans are object-oriented programming interfaces developed by Sun Microsystems that allow the user to build reusable applications or program building blocks called **components** that can be used in a network on any major operating system platform. Similar to Java applet, JavaBean components (or "Beans") can be used to provide a web page with interactive capabilities, such as computing interest rates, mortgage payments, or varying page content based on the user or browser characteristics. To build a component with JavaBeans, the user writes language statements using Sun's Java programming language and include JavaBeans statements that describe component properties, such as user interface characteristics and events that trigger a Bean to communicate with other Beans in the same program or elsewhere in the network.

A-17 WHAT IS VBSCRIPT?

Visual Basic Scripting Edition (VBScript) is a scripting language developed by Microsoft and supported by Microsoft's Internet Explorer web browser. VBScript is based on the Visual Basic programming language, but it is a lot easier. Similar to JavaScript, VBScript provides web developers with the abilities to include interactive features and controls, such as buttons and scrollbars, on their web pages.

A-18 WHAT IS DYNAMIC HYPERTEXT MARKUP LANGUAGE?

Dynamic HTML refers to web content that changes each time it is requested and loaded to the web browser. For example, the same URL could result in a different page depending on any number of factors, such as:

- Geographic location of the user
- Previous pages viewed by the user
- Profile of the user
- Time of day

There are many technologies and applications that allow the user to generate dynamic HTML, including CGI scripts, cookies, Java, JavaScript, and ActiveX.

A-19 WHAT IS ACTIVEX?

ActiveX is the name Microsoft has given to a set of object-oriented programming technologies and tools. The main technology is the **Component Object Model.** The main part that the user creates when writing a program to run in the ActiveX environment is a component. This self-sufficient and independent program can be run anywhere in the user ActiveX network. ActiveX is Microsoft's response to Sun Microsystems Java technology. An ActiveX control is nearly the equivalent of a Java applet.

A-20 SUMMARY

This appendix provided a general familiarity with web development and simple HTML syntax. It defined HTML and then reviewed some of the important commands and instructions in the Web environment. The appendix presented the step-by-step process of creating an HTML file and a simple web page. This example highlighted the web-development process, including creating links, modifying an existing web page, and publishing a web page on the Web. The appendix provided a quick review of Microsoft FrontPage and concluded with definitions of some of the popular Web programming languages and tools, including Java, JavaScript, JavaBeans, VBScript, dynamic HTML, and ActiveX. This presentation should provide you with a basic background regarding simple web page development and the process of editing and modifying an existing web page. For more advanced discussion, consult the references.

A-21 PROJECTS AND HANDS-ON EXERCISES

1. Using a word-processing program such as Microsoft Word, create a one-page résumé. Save it in HTML format. Try to open this file in Netscape Navigator or Microsoft Internet Explorer. How does it look?

2. Open this file in Notepad or another editor and try to understand some of the HTML tags. How many of them do you know? Add a paragraph, and save it under the same name, and reopen it in Netscape Navigator. Examine your changes.

3. Using the example introduced in section A-6, design a web site for the ABC Company that sells five products on the Web. The site should display product names, descriptions, and prices. Also include a section that tells the visitors about this company and contact information.

4. The following sites provide comprehensive tutorials on HTML:

   <http://lcweb.loc.gov/global/html.html>
   <http://dellnet.snap.com/directory/category/0,16,dellnet-13111,00.html?st.sn.sr.1.cat>
   <http://dellnet.snap.com/directory/category/0,16,dellnet-51505,00.html?st.sn.sr.1.cat>

   Log onto these sites and review the basics of HTML. What are some examples of new HTML tags introduced in these sites?

5. The following sites provide comprehensive information on Java:

   <http://java.sun.com/docs/books/tutorial>
   <http://www.apache.org/info/jdk-102.html>

   Log onto these sites and examine their contents. Based on the materials presented in these sites and other sources, prepare a four-page paper on the basics of Java. How do you compare Java with one of the computer languages that you know? Why has Java become so popular? Discuss.

6. The following sites provide comprehensive information on JavaScript:

   <http://javascript.internet.com>
   <http://www.javascript.com>
   <http://javascriptweenie.com>

   Based on the materials presented in these sites and other sources, prepare a three-page paper on the basics of JavaScript. How do you compare JavaScript with one of the computer languages that you know? Why has JavaScript become so popular? Discuss.

7. The following site includes free rules and bullets:

   <http://home.netscape.com/browsers/createsites/rules.html>

After logging onto the site, click on **Tool Chest.** Browse through the site and try to copy some of these rules and bullets and integrate them into your web site.

8. The following sites provide interesting clip art that can be integrated into your web page.

<http://www.nzwwa.com/mirror/clipart>
<http://www.clipartconnection.com>
<http://www.barrysclipart.com>

Log onto these sites and browse through them.

9. The following site provides all sorts of web-development materials:

<http://www.wdvl.com/WDVL/Stats/Top/100.html>

Log onto the site and examine its contents.

REFERENCES

[1] Eckel, Bruce (2000). "Thinking in Java." Prentice Hall Computer Books, Upper Saddle River, NJ.
[2] Flanagan, David (1998). "JavaScript: The Definitive Guide." 3rd edition. O'Reilly & Associates.
[3] Grant, Scott T. (2001). "Core Java E-Commerce." Prentice Hall, Upper Saddle River, NJ.
[4] Liang, Y. Daniel (2001). "Introduction to Java Programming." 3rd edition. Prentice Hall, Upper Saddle River, NJ.
[5] Shelly B. Gary, Thomas J. Cashman, and Denise M. Woods (2000). "HTML Complete Concepts and Technology." Course Technology, Cambridge MA.
[6] Sklar, Joel (2000). "Principles of Web Design." Course Technology, Cambridge MA.
[7] Winsor, Janice, Brian Freeman, and Bill Anderson (1999). "More Jumping JavaScript." Prentice Hall, Upper Saddle River, NJ.

Glossary

ActiveX: Is the name Microsoft has given to a set of object-oriented programming technologies and tools.

Ad impression: One surfer viewing one ad.

Application (proxy) firewall: A type of firewall installed in the host computer. A dedicated PC or a workstation may perform this task. It controls the private network applications such as e-mail, Telnet, and FTP at the individual or group level by focusing on the type of action and the time period in which the action is taking place.

Application server: A type of server that stores computer applications that users can access from their workstations.

ARPANET: Defense Department Advanced Research Projects Agency network that served from 1969 through 1990 as the basis for early networking research, and as a central backbone network during development of the Internet.

Authentication: The process of verification of the authenticity of a person and/or a transaction.

Backbone: High-capacity telephone links, coaxial cables, microwaves, fiber optics, and satellites used as information-carrying channels for the Internet.

Bandwidth: Information-carrying capacity of a network.

Banner ads: Typically 468×60 pixels in size, with simple animation, they commonly appear on popular web sites. By clicking on these banner ads a surfer either is transferred to another web site or a short marketing message is displayed.

Business process reengineering (BRP): Involves close scrutiny of the core business activities and effective design of those activities.

Business-to-business (B2B) auctions: As opposed to consumers, corporations use B2B auctions. One of the major applications of B2B auctions is to get rid of excess inventory used by many companies.

Business-to-consumer (B2C) e-commerce: Businesses sell directly to consumers.

Business-to-business (B2B) e-commerce: Involves electronic transactions among and between businesses.

Buyer-controlled marketplace: A buyer or a group of buyers opens an electronic market place and invites sellers to bid on the announced products or request for quotations (RFQs).

Cable shielding: A security measure by braiding layers of the conductors to form a braided shield.

Certificates authorities: Organizations and individuals who issue digital certificates and validate the holder's identity and authority.

Certificates: A mechanism for establishing confidence in the relationship between a public key and the entity that owns the corresponding private key.

Charge cards: Plastic cards similar to credit cards except they have no revolving credit line.

Circuit switching: An electrical connection between the sender and receiver nodes is established based on demand for exclusive use of the circuit until the connection is terminated.

Click ratio: Indicates the success of a banner ad in attracting surfers to click on the ad. For example, if a banner ad receives 2000 impressions and there are 400 clicks, the click ratio is 20%.

Click-through rate (CTR):   This is computed by dividing the number of clicks a given advertising program receives by the total impressions bought.

Click: The opportunity for a surfer to click on a URL or a banner ad to be transferred to another web site or to view a marketing message, as recorded by the web server.

Client/server model: Client software runs on the local computer and communicates with the remote server requesting information.

Commerce server: A type of server that allows users to "shop" on the Internet and is configured to allow secure electronic financial transactions.

Computer virus: A series of self-propagating program codes triggered by a specified time or event within the computer system.

Concentrator: Combines data on a communication line to improve the efficiency of a communications medium.

Consumer auctions: Buyers purchase products or services that are not easily available at a fair price.

Consumer-to-business (C2B) e-commerce: Individuals sell to businesses.

Consumer-to-consumer (C2C) e-commerce: Individuals using the Internet and Web technologies sell to each other.

Cookie: Information that a web site puts on the surfer hard disk so that it can remember something about the surfer at a later time and date. This information is used to record the surfer preferences when using a particular site, his or her surfing habits, and pattern of surfing.

Copyright: A legal protection for ideas, designs, and intellectual properties.

Corner bolts: A combination of locks and cables that secures workstations to a heavy-duty locking plate, which is then bonded to an anchor pad that has adhesive on both sides. The pad is then adhered to a desk or counter.

Cost per click (CPC):   The cost for every click on an advertisement.

Credit card: A plastic card used to charge against the customer's credit; by far the most popular method used in electronic payment systems.

Cyberspace: The knowledge and collective environments or places created by computer networks.

Data encryption: A security measure that transforms original information called plaintext or cleartext into transformed information, called ciphertext or cipher, which usually has the appearance of random, nonreadable data.

Database server: A type of server that is configured to store vast amounts of data for access from users' workstations.

Debit card: A plastic card that functions similar to a check in that the charges will be deducted from the customer's checking account.

Denial-of-access attacks: A method hackers and crackers use to prevent or deny legitimate users' access to a computer or web server.

Digital signatures: An electronic rather than a written signature that authenticates the identity of the sender of a message or the signer of a document.

Digital subscriber line (DSL): This common carrier service is promoted as one of the high-speed access capabilities to remote local area networks and the Internet, providing speeds of up to 51 Mbps (million bits per second).

Directories: Software platforms that index information based on keywords in a document. Yahoo! is one of the most popular directories on the Web.

Disk server: A server with large-capacity hard drives that enables users to store files and applications for later retrieval.

Distributed data processing (DDP): The processing power is distributed among several locations. Databases, processing units, or input–output devices may be distributed.

Double auctions: Both sellers and buyers submit bids, and they are then ranked from highest to lowest to generate demand and supply profiles. From the profiles, the maximum quantity exchanged can be determined by matching selling offers (starting with lowest price and moving up) with demand bids (starting with highest price and moving down).

Dutch auctions (descending-price auction): Usually more than one item is up for bid at a time, and the winning bidder pays the same price for all the items, which is the lowest winning bid.

Dynamic host configuration protocol (DHCP): This protocol automates and simplifies the assignment of TCP/IP addresses to workstations on the network.

Dynamic hypertext markup language (HTML): Web content changes each time it is requested and loaded to the web browser.

E-commerce business models: Different techniques and procedures used by e-businesses to generate revenue and to stay viable using the Web and Web technologies.

Economic feasibility: The costs and benefits of the e-commerce site.

Electronic business (e-business): Any electronic transaction (e.g., information exchange), which subsumes e-commerce. E-business encompasses all the activities a firm performs for selling and buying services and products using computers and communications technologies.

Electronic check (e-check): An electronic version of a paper check. It uses the same legal and business protocols associated with traditional paper checks.

Electronic commerce (e-commerce): Electronic buying and selling on the web.

Electronic data interchange (EDI): An application-to-application transfer of business documents between computers using industry-defined standards.

Electronic data interchange standards: Agreed upon rules and regulations that are followed by different organizations that make EDI applications among the participating businesses a possibility.

Electronic funds transfer (EFT): Electronic transfer of money by financial institutions.

Electronic gift: Sending electronic currency or a gift certificate from one individual to another. The receiver can spend this gift in his or her favorite online stores that accept this type of currency.

Electronic mail (e-mail): Creating and transferring documents (letters) over communications media.

Electronic money (e-money or e-cash): Standard currency converted into an electronic format and used to pay for online purchases.

Electronic payment systems (EPS): Paying for goods and services through electronic means as opposed to cash and checks.

Electronic tracker: Device secured to the computer at the AC power insert point. If the power cord is disconnected, a coded transmitter sends a message to an alarm, which sounds, and/or a camera, which is activated to record the disturbance.

Electronic wallets (e-wallets): Are similar to smart cards, these include stored financial value for online payments.

English auction (ascending price, open-outcry, or open auction): A bidder openly offers a price and the maximum bid wins. In this type of auction, there usually is a minimum bid. If nobody offers a price larger than the minimum bid, the item is usually pulled and not sold.

E-procurement: Conducting procurement functions (buying goods and services) over the Web.

Extranet: A secure network that uses Internet and Web technology to connect two or more intranets of business partners, enabling business-to-business communications.

FAQs (frequently asked questions): A document that contains questions and answers regarding a specific topic, application, or Internet service. Before asking questions or posting a message, it is a good idea to read the FAQ of a given site. This can be very helpful to answer commonly asked questions raised by the customers and visitors.

Fat client: A desktop computer that offers more processing power at the desktop compared to a thin client.

Fax server: A server with software and hardware components that allow users to send and receive faxes from their workstations.

File server: A server with large-capacity hard drives that enables users to store data files for later retrieval.

File transfer protocol (FTP): Used for file transfers between a local hard drive and an FTP server.

Fingerprint: A biometric security measure that scans a user's fingerprint and checks it against the print stored in an electronic file.

Firewall: A combination of hardware and software that serves as a gateway between the private network and the Internet. Predefined access and scope of use are required, and all other requests are blocked.

Flame: Insult—a slang term used on the Web to mean an emotional or inflammatory note, usually written in response to another message.

Hand geometry: A biometric security measure that uses the length of the five fingers on each hand as well as the translucence of the fingertips and the webbing between the fingers.

Hit: Every element of a requested page (including text, graphics, and interactive items) is counted as a hit to a server. Hits are not the preferred unit of site traffic's measurement because the number of hits per page varies widely depending on the number of graphics, the type of browser in use, and the size of the page.

Home page: Starting point for each WWW server that contains information about the location including textual, graphical, and audio and visual formats. This is the starting point of an e-commerce site.

HTML (hypertext markup language): The authoring language used to create documents on the Web.

HTTP (hypertext transfer protocol): A set of standards used to govern the way data are transmitted across the Web.

Hypermedia: An information-storage system in which each page of information can include embedded references to images, texts, sounds, or video clips.

Hypertext: Using this feature, the user can search in any direction—between files, applications, and computers.

Instant messenger: A communications service that enables a user to create a private chat room with another user.

Intelligent agent: Combination of hardware and software that is capable of rule-based reasoning.

Internet 2 (I2): A collaborative effort by several major universities in the United States and a group of corporations. Started in 1987, I2 has been envisioned as a decentralized network where participating universities in the same geographic region will form an alliance to create and found a local-connection point-of-presence called Gigapop.

Internet phone: Use of the Internet rather than the traditional telephone company infrastructure and rate structure to exchange spoken or other telephone information.

Internet shopping malls: These sites provide tools and capabilities to establish an online storefront. They also provide significant traffic that can create potential customers for the online store.

Internet: A collection of millions of computers and network systems of all sizes. The Internet is the "network of networks." The information superhighway, the net, or the Web are also known as the Internet.

Internet-based electronic data interchange (open EDI): Transmitting EDI transactions via the Internet instead of other communications networks.

Intranet site marketing: All the activities for promoting the acceptance and utilization of an intranet site, such as user and top management involvement and ongoing education.

Intranet: A network within the organization that uses Web technologies (TCP/IP, HTTP, FTP, SMPT, HTML and XML) for collecting, storing, and disseminating useful information throughout the organization. This information supports e-commerce activities such as sales, customer service, marketing, and so forth.

Intrusion detection systems (IDS): A software program that could identify attack signatures, traces, or patterns, generate alarms to alert the network staff, and cause the router to terminate the connection with a suspicious source.

IRC (Internet relay chat): A user can conduct written, interactive communication via the Internet with other users worldwide.

ISDN (integrated services digital networks): Allows the networking of telephones, PCs, mainframes, printers, and fax machines using ordinary twisted-pair telephone line and digital transmission technology to send voice, data, and images over the same line.

Java: Developed by Sun Microsystems in 1995, this user-friendly language allows written software applications to be run on many platforms. Java downloads nuggets of application code (known as applets) from server to client on demand, regardless of computer platform.

JavaBeans: These object-oriented programming interfaces developed by Sun Microsystems allow the user to build reuseable applications or program building blocks called components that can be used in a network on any major operating system platform.

JavaScript: A stored set of instructions included as a part of a standard HTML document. JavaScript statements are contained in an HTML document within the <script> and </script> tags.

Local area network (LAN): Two or more computers and other peripheral equipment in close proximity connected together.

Log files: Generated by the web server software, these files record a user's journey around a web site.

Logic bombs: A type of Trojan horse used to release a virus, a worm, or some other destructive codes. Logic bombs are triggered at a certain point in time, by an event, or by an action performed by a user.

Lurk: To read, without posting, messages to a newsgroup or an e-mail discussion list. Lurking is recommended behavior for individuals new to a list or group.

Mail agent: A type of intelligent agent that performs many activities related to an e-mail program, such as generating autoresponse messages and selectively forwarding incoming messages.

Mail server: A type of server configured to allow users to send, receive, and store e-mails.

Marketing mix: Product, price, promotion, and place data.

Meta tag: A special HTML tag that provides information about a web page.

Metropolitan area network (MAN): A type of network designed to deliver data, video, and digital voice to all organizations within a metropolitan area.

Micropayment systems: Similar to e-Wallets, these include stored financial value for online payments; however, they are used for small payments such as pennies and fractions of pennies.

Mirror disks: A fault-tolerance technique in which two disks containing the same data are provided so that if one fails, the other is available, allowing the system to continue operations.

Multiplexer (mux): A hardware device that allows several devices to share one communication channel.

Navigational tools: Allow the user to surf the Web. Microsoft Internet Explorer and Netscape Navigator are two popular examples.

Net: Internet, the Web.

Netiquette: Etiquette appropriate for the Internet use; a list of suggestions for how to behave when using the Internet.

Nonbusiness and government e-commerce: Using e-commerce functions and technologies for improving productivity by government agencies and by nonprofit organizations.

Online auctions: Buying and selling goods and services in an auction format using the Web.

Operational feasibility: The measure of how well the proposed e-commerce project will work in the organization and how internal and external customers will feel about the proposed e-commerce project.

Organizational (intrabusiness) e-commerce: Using e-commerce functions and technologies for improving productivity within an organization.

Packet filter firewall: A type of firewall that controls data traffic (the export and import of data) based on packets passing through the network.

Packet switching: Using packet switching, a message is transmitted by dividing it into fixed-length packets and then sending the individual packets to their destination. Connections don't need to be established before data transmission begins; in other words, no virtual circuit is needed.

Page view (PV): One surfer viewing one web site page.

Palmprint: A biometric security measure that uses the individual characteristics of the palm to identify the user.

Patent: Protection for new and useful processes and ideas that is extremely difficult to obtain compared to copyright (in the U.S.). It generally takes several years to obtain a patent.

Payment by utilities: Uses the monthly utility bills, Internet, or phone bills for online payment.

Payment cards: Plastic cards that include stored financial value that can be transferred from the customer's computer to the merchant's computer.

Peer-to-peer local area network (LAN): Peer-to-peer networks allow computers to access files on each other's hard drives, share peripherals such as printers and modems, and share access to applications such as e-mail, all while each PC remains usable as a workstation.

Point-to-point connection in an electronic data interchange environment: EDI partners establish a direct computer-to-computer link through a private network.

Point-to-point protocol (PPP): One of the TCP/IP services that performs error checking and recovery functions, it can handle synchronous as well as asynchronous communications.

Point-to-point tunneling protocol: One of the TCP/IP services that creates secure connections between private networks over public networks.

Print server: A type of server configured to allow users to print to network printers.

Product-brokering agent: A type of intelligent agent that collects relevant information about customers, such as items purchased, customer profile, address, age, gender, purchase history, expressed preferences, and implicit preferences to be used for marketing purposes.

Proximity-release door opener: A security device to control access to the computer room. Access to the computer area is gained through the use of a small radio transmitter located in the authorized employees' identification badges. When the authorized person comes to within a predetermined distance of the entry door, a radio signal sends a key number to the receiver, which unlocks the door for admittance.

Proxy bidding: Placing a maximum bid that is held in confidence by the online auction site. The system will use only as much of the maximum bid as is necessary to maintain the bidder's high-bid position.

Proxy server: A type of server used to store previously accessed web pages, making later retrieval much quicker.

Public key cryptography: Encryption that uses a pair of keys, one private and one public. In comparison, private key cryptography uses only one key for encryption.

Public networks: Wide area telecommunications facilities owned by common carriers and resold to users by subscription.

Push technology: Relevant marketing information is pushed to the user based on his or her prior inquiries, interests, or specifications.

Pyramid-shaped structure: In this organizational structure, three distinct layers of management exist: lower (operational), middle (tactical), and upper (strategic).

Redundant arrays of independent disks (RAID): A fault-tolerance disk storage technique that spreads one file plus the file's checksum information over several disk drives. If any single disk drive fails, the data stored thereon can be reconstructed from data stored on the remaining drives.

Remote access server (RAS): A type of server that allows remote users to connect to network resources, such as network file storage, printers, and databases.

Request for proposal (RFP): A written document with detailed specifications requesting bids for equipment, supplies, or services from vendors. Use of an RFP assures that uniform and comparable documents will be received.

Retinal scanning: A biometric security measure that scans with a binocular eye camera. Identification of the user is verified by the data stored in a computer file.

Room shielding: Spraying a nonconductive material in the computer room for security. This material reduces the number of signals being transmitted, or completely confines the signals to the computer room.

Router: A network interconnection device and related software that connect two network systems that control the traffic flow between networks.

RTFAQ (Read the frequently asked questions): Instructions to read the FAQ document before posting messages containing questions that have already been answered within the FAQ.

Schedule feasibility: Determining whether the e-commerce project will be ready within the time frame needed by an organization.

Sealed-bid auction: The bidder submits only one bid and the bid is kept secret from other bidders. The bidder with the highest bid wins and pays his or her bid.

Search engine: Provides access to various resources available on the Web, such as library searches for writing a term paper or making a reservation for an airline ticket. Google and AltaVista are two popular examples of search engines.

Secure sockets layer (SSL): Introduced by Netscape Corporation, a relatively secure method to encrypt data transmitted over a public network such as the Internet.

Seller-controlled marketplace: Businesses and consumers use the seller's products catalog and order products and services online.

Serial line Internet protocol (SLIP): One of the TCP/IP services that provides a reasonably fast, low overhead service that is typically used to connect to UNIX hosts and Internet service providers.

Server-based LAN: A LAN with a central computer that provides application, file, security, and communications services.

Shopping agent: A type of intelligent agent similar to a World Wide Web Navigational agent that is capable of doing comparison shopping and finding the best price for a specific item.

Signature analysis: A biometric security measure of the user's pattern, pressure deviation, acceleration, and the length of the time needed to sign his or her name.

Simulation prototyping: Allows e-commerce specialists to quickly analyze and predict the performance of the e-commerce site before its final implementation.

Site marketing: A combination of traditional and Web marketing tools used to promote the e-commerce site.

Smart cards: Stored financial value and other important personal and financial information used for online payments.

Splash screen: An initial web site page used to capture the surfer's attention for a short period, and which usually directs the surfer to the web site.

Spot leasing: Search engines and directories such as Yahoo! offer a space (spot) on their web sites that can be leased by any business for advertising purposes.

Star-shaped structure: An organizational structure consisting of only decision makers and unskilled labor. It eliminates middle-management personnel.

Steel encasement: A heavy-gauge, welded steel security device designed to fit over the entire computer. Only the security administrator or another designated person has access to the key.

Supply chain: The integrated network of suppliers, transportation companies, and brokers that provide materials and services to the customers (businesses and consumers).

Supply-chain management: The active participation and cooperation of supply-chain suppliers and other companies to improve products, services, procedures, and processes using information systems and e-commerce technologies.

Surf: To browse the Internet without any particular destination in mind.

SYSOP: System Operator.

Task force: A group of representatives that directly or indirectly use and have impact on the success or failure of an e-commerce application, such as developing an intranet, extranet, or other e-commerce applications.

TCP/IP (Transmission Control Protocol/Internet Protocol): The standard and software that divide data into packets and forward the packets to the IP protocol layer in the TCP/IP stack.

Technical feasibility: The technical aspects of the e-commerce site.

Thin client: A desktop computer that offers less processing power at the desktop compared with fat clients.

Third-party controlled marketplace: This B2B model is controlled neither by sellers nor buyers, but rather by a third party. The marketplace generates its revenue from the fees generated by matching buyers and sellers.

Three-tier and n-tier architectures: A type of client server architecture, a three-tier (multi-tier) architecture removes the application processing from both the client and the back-end server and places it on the middle-tier server by itself, while leaving the presentation on the client and the data management on the back-end server.

Token: A transmission device used as a security measure worn around the user's neck. The device activates the computer only when a user wearing a token is seated in front of the screen.

Total quality management: A management philosophy aimed at creating an organization committed to continuous process improvement and customer satisfaction.

Trading partner agreements: A B2B e-commerce model that tries to automate the processes for negotiating and enforcing contracts between participating businesses.

Traditional commerce: Selling products and services to generate profits using traditional infrastructures.

Trap door (also called a **back door**): A routine built into a system by its designer or programmer that allows them to sneak back into the system to access software or specific programs.

Trojan horse: A Trojan horse program contains codes intended to disrupt a computer system and or an e-commerce site. Trojan horse programs are usually hidden inside a popular useful program.

Two-tier architecture: A type of client server architecture, the client is often provided with the capability to handle both presentation and application processing.

Uninterruptible power supply (UPS): A backup power unit that continues to provide power to the network system during the failure of the normal power supply.

URL (universal resource locator): A naming convention that identifies an e-commerce site or a web site. For example, the URL of Amazon.com is: <http://www.amazon.com>.

Usenet and newsgroup agents: With features that are specific to newsgroups, these agents provide sorting and filtering functions and can access specific groups to send and receive information.

User groups (newsgroups or discussions): Groups of individuals that share opinions and ideas using the Internet to communicate and share these ideas with others.

Value-added network (VAN): An alternative for transferring EDI transactions offered by major EDI providers, such as Sterling Commerce.

Value chain: A series of activities designed to satisfy a business need by adding value (or cost) in each phase of the process.

VBScript (Visual Basic Scripting Edition): A scripting language developed by Microsoft and supported by Microsoft's Internet Explorer Web browser, VBScript is based on the Visual Basic programming language, but it is a lot easier to use.

Vickrey second-price auction: Similar to sealed-bid auction, the bid is sealed, and each bidder is unaware of other bids. The item is awarded to highest bidder at a price equal to the second highest bid (or highest losing bid).

Virtual private network (VPN): A new value-added network that runs on the Internet and appears to the user as a private network.

Voice recognition: A biometric security measure that translates words into digital patterns for transmission to the server. Voice patterns are recorded and examined by tone and pitch.

Voice-based e-commerce: Conducting e-commerce activities using voice (natural language).

Web-hosting services: Third-party companies who offer complete e-commerce services including design and implementation of an e-commerce site.

Web portal: A portal or gateway for the WWW that serves as an information search organizer. Portals provide single-point integration and navigation through the Web. Portals create an information community that can be customized for an individual or a corporation.

Web server: A type of server configured to store HTML pages for access over the Internet.

Wide area network (WAN): A network that is not limited to a certain geographical area. It may span several cities, states, or even countries. Usually several different parties own it. The geographical scope of a WAN can be from intercity to across international borders.

Wireless e-commerce: Conducting e-commerce activities using mobile and wireless networks.

World Wide Web navigational agents: These agents allow the user to navigate the vast resources available on the Web, providing better results in finding information.

Worm: Similar to a computer virus, a worm usually does not erase data, but either corrupts or copies itself to a full-blown version that eats up computing resources.

XML (extensible markup language): A subset of the standard generalized markup language (SGML), XML is a recent and flexible technology for creating common information formats and shares both the format and the information on the e-commerce infrastructure.

Yankee auction: A type of English auction where multiple quantities are offered. The highest bidder gets all the items requested, and the remaining items are sold at successively lower prices.

Index